THE
HARVARD LAW SCHOOL

A MEMENTO OF THE OBSERVANCES HELD
ON THE ONE HUNDRED AND FIFTIETH ANNIVERSARY
OF THE SCHOOL'S FOUNDING

———————

THE PAST HAS EARNED OUR GRATITUDE.
THE FUTURE HOLDS OUR HOPE.

———————

September the Twenty-Third

1967

THE LAW
AT HARVARD

A History of Ideas and Men, 1817–1967

THE LAW
AT
HARVARD

A History of Ideas and Men, 1817–1967

ARTHUR E. SUTHERLAND

THE BELKNAP PRESS OF
HARVARD UNIVERSITY PRESS
CAMBRIDGE, MASSACHUSETTS 1967

Remembering my friends and teachers
between 1922 and 1925

Foreword by
Austin Wakeman Scott

DANE PROFESSOR OF LAW EMERITUS

It has been my good fortune to be associated with the Harvard Law School for sixty years, or about two-fifths of the period of its existence. I entered the School as a student in 1906. After my graduation in 1909 I was for six months simply an alumnus. But when Dean Ames became fatally ill in December of that year I was asked to give his courses on equity and pleading for the rest of the academic year. In May 1910 I gladly accepted an appointment as Assistant Professor, and was elected on the same day that Roscoe Pound was elected Story Professor. I remained on the faculty for fifty-one years, retiring in 1961. As Professor Emeritus I have come daily to the Law School ever since.

Shortly before I entered the Law School, President Eliot in an address to the alumni said that the Law School was the most successful of the university's professional schools. He then said, "And if there be a more successful school in our country or in the world for any profession, I can only say that I do not know where it is. The School seems to have reached the climax of success in professional education." These were strong words, but the law students of my time were fully convinced that they were true.

When I entered the School there were seven professors and two assistant professors. They constituted the whole of the faculty during my three years as a student, the two assistant professors becoming full professors in my last year. The professors were James Barr Ames, John Chipman Gray, Jeremiah Smith, Samuel Williston, Joseph H. Beale, Eugene Wambaugh, and Joseph D.

Brannan. The assistant professors were Edward W. Warren and Bruce Wyman.

The professors were not at all alike, except that they were all graduates of Harvard College and of the Harvard Law School. Dean Ames had come to the Law School as an assistant professor just after his graduation and never engaged in the practice of the law. On the other hand, Gray was the head of a great Boston law firm all his life. But this never interfered with his teaching. I do not think that he ever missed a class, and he spent a good deal of time in an alcove of the reading room in Austin Hall which we used to call the House of Lords, where he was ever ready to give aid to inquiring students. Smith not only had practiced law but had been a judge of the highest court of New Hampshire. I remember that when a question arose whether the judges make law or discover law, he said, "They make law. I've done it myself." Williston and Beale had both engaged in the practice of the law to some extent, but their interests were primarily in the teaching of law. Williston and Ames were supreme teachers, complete masters of the Socratic method. Beale also was a great teacher, but in a different way. He, like Dr. Samuel Johnson, talked for victory. His precise and logical mind sometimes led to conclusions which seemed to many of the students to be wrong. The result, however, was that he caused more heated discussions among the students than did any of his colleagues. Edward Warren was a task master and as such was very effective in drilling the students in the intricacies of the law of real property. Wambaugh introduced us to constitutional law; Brannan, to bills and notes.

There was not then, and the earlier records show that there never had been, a typical Harvard Law School professor. Each had something of his own to contribute and in his own way.

But it was not only the professors who made the Law School great. The students did their part. I remember that when I graduated from the School I happened to run across Dean Ames in the street. I told him how much I appreciated the privilege of being taught by the members of the faculty. He said to me, "It is not the faculty of the School which makes it what it is, but the students." We have always had, as we now have, a remarkable student body. The greatness of the School is not, however, due to the individual students who make up the student body. It is something more than this. It is the spirit which prevails among them which I think makes it stand out among educational institutions. I do not know how or when that spirit was created. Perhaps it came from the atmosphere which Story seems to have had the power to create. When Eliot became President he deplored the condition of the Divinity School and the Medical School, but of the Law School he said that "The common life of sympathetic association of the body of students, all in eager pursuit of the same end, is a very valuable part of the training which the school supplies. The incessant discussions and contests which go on among them, and in fact the whole tone and atmosphere of the place are most stimulating and wholesome." I can attest that this was true at the time when I was one of the seven hundred students at the School.

Although President Eliot said sixty years ago that the School seemed to have reached the climax of success in professional education, there is no doubt that if it had not changed during the ensuing years there would have been an anticlimax. But the School has changed profoundly, as Professor Sutherland has shown in this history. I think, although I am perhaps a prejudiced observer, that the Law School is giving to the students of this day a preparation in the field of the law, whether for the practice of the law or for service on the bench or for other public service or for teaching, even better than that which it gave when I was young.

I hope that the students and alumni of the School, and all those who are interested in it, will share with me the pleasure I have had in reading Professor Sutherland's account of the progress of the School through the last century and a half.

Preface

The Harvard Law School, one hundred and fifty years old in 1967, has now attained a respectable middle age among institutions cultivating the law "as a science." This seems a good time to write this book, a time to pause for a backward glance over the road we have traveled.

Fortunately predecessors have left such complete chronicles that an entirely fresh start is unnecessary. Charles Warren in 1908 searched the archives with his accustomed thoroughness to turn up the materials for his *History of the Harvard Law School.* Faculty and graduates worked together to produce the *Centennial History* in 1918. Today one might very sensibly be content to write a sort of coda for those two books, telling only what happened in the last third of the School's life.

Instead it seemed more attractive to write a new account from the beginning, an account of ideas of law, and of the men who held these ideas. What prompted the founding of the School? What were the founders' conceptions of law "as a science," to use a phrase then much in use? What was the source of their concepts? How have those ideas developed at our School through the last century and a half; what have our teachers written and taught about them? How have our students received them and thought about them? To set out any part of this reasonably well, the book must tell of many people and events outside our School; of changes in men's thoughts about justice in America and elsewhere; of the writings in which scholars left their thoughts for those who came after.

Everything has antecedents. The law at Harvard had beginnings long before 1817. The library from its original foundation in 1638 has contained works on the law. Among the 329 books John Harvard left to the college were *The whole volume of statutes at large . . . since Magna Carta untill the 29th yeere of Ladie Elizabeth,* printed in London in 1587, and William Lambarde's *Eirenarcha, or Of the Office of the Justice of Peace,* published in 1588. In that beginning Puritan time the college library mainly served to prepare men for the ministry, but a seventeenth century New England minister was a man of full learning, concerned alike with temporal and spiritual rule. In 1638 when the Massachusetts General Court wished to compile a code of laws for the colony, it turned over this task to an Ipswich parson. In 1647 Henry Dunster, president of Harvard, presented a petition to the Commissioners of the United Colonies of New England concerning various college problems, of which the greatest (as usual with colleges) was its financial support. He wrote "seinge the publicke library in the Colledg is yet defective in all manner of bookes, especially in law, Philosophy and mathematicks, the furnishinge whereof would be both honourable and proffitable to the Country in generall and in speciall to the schollars, whose various inclinations to all professions might thereby be incouraged and furthered, we therefore humbly entreate you to use such meanes as your wisdomes shall thincke meete for supply of the same."

The "publicke library in the Colledg" did not greatly increase its common-law collection during the next seventy-six years. The Harvard library catalogue of 1723 does list a number of works of history and political theory, and a surprising collection of books on Roman and civil law. Although John Leverett, then president of the college, had practiced law, had been a judge, and been speaker of the Massachusetts House, the library's common-law collection was still small. Besides the Statutes at Large from Magna Carta to 29 Elizabeth which had been one of John Harvard's books, there was a subsequent volume containing the Statutes at Large from 35 Elizabeth to 4 Charles — probably Charles I. There was a 1606 volume entitled *Kalendar of the Statutes of England.* The library's most recent collection of English legislation was John Keeble's 1684 Statutes at Large. There was a volume listed as *Massachusetts – Law – Book* published in Boston in 1714. There were two volumes of Coke's *Institutes* and a work called *Elementa Jurisprudentiae,* with no author stated, published at Oxford in 1627. There were no volumes of reported English cases. In 1723 the law at Harvard was certainly not up-to-date, but the men who regulated the life of the college gave its scholars access to the fundamentals.

Thirty years later, in England, Dr. William Blackstone of All Souls, Oxford, began a course of lectures which in time had a profound influence across the Atlantic at Harvard. Blackstone undertook to educate well-to-do young gentlemen in the common law as a preparation for their voluntary public duties in that station in life to which it had pleased God to call them. He told his undergraduates, "I think it an undeniable position that a competent knowledge of the laws of that society, in which we live, is the proper accomplishment of every gentleman and scholar; an highly useful, I had almost said essential, part of liberal and polite education." Trying thus to serve a need for general education, Blackstone made the common law respectable for study by the undergraduates of England's two ancient universities, and so almost inadvertently accomplished history's greatest single improvement in professional training for common lawyers. Three years later, in 1756, Charles Viner supported Blackstone's innovation by a generous bequest which founded an Oxford chair for common-law studies; Blackstone was elected as the first Vinerian Professor. His lectures, revised and published in the 1760's as *Commentaries on the Laws of England,* became the most widely read of all Anglo-American law texts, before or since Blackstone.

In 1773 a discriminating Harvard librarian prepared a *Select Catalogue of Books in the Cambridge Library Frequently Used at Harvard by Those Not Yet Advanced to the Grade of Bachelor of Arts.* A foreword, written in the Latin then still conventional for decorous scholarship, explained that the full library catalogue was extremely long and that it included books on all the sciences and the arts, written in almost all languages, most of them beyond the grasp of young students. So, the cataloguer explains, he has in his abridged catalogue listed for the most part books written in the vernacular tongue, omitting those in foreign languages or those which treat of "specialized disciplines, such as Medicine or Jurisprudence," but including books directed to the general culture of the mind. And in this select company he includes "Blackstone (Judge) all his Works."

Isaac Royall, once a landed gentleman of Medford, Massachusetts, a loyalist refugee during the American Revolution, made his will in 1788 at Kensington, England, endowing at Harvard a "Professor of Laws in said College or a Professor of Physick and Anatomy which ever the said Overseers and Corporation shall judge to be best for the benefit of said College." No one can demonstrate, by explicit words in Royall's will or in his surviving letters, that Viner's endowment of a chair at Oxford prompted Royall's gift to Harvard, but the resemblances are too close for mere random coincidence. If Viner's gift did not bestir Royall, still the same currents of opinion must have moved both givers. So a man who undertakes to write a history of the law at Harvard must contemplate the ideas that gave rise to the Vinerian Chair; when Viner made his will those ideas had been developing for centuries. This book has thus had to transcend some temporal limitations of its subtitle. Principally purporting to tell of ideas and men between 1817 and 1967, it necessarily seeks origins far back of the first of those years.

And then, too, temptation to a little prophecy has been hard to resist. The past has more than antiquarian interest. Like men rowing in a boat, we can steer by our wake; we can gauge the forward course of our school by watching the course we have traveled. This alternate looking back and glancing ahead is a grateful exercise. The long journey we have made has been a good one. We can take pleasure imagining the way of our successors.

To helpful friends and colleagues in the Law School and outside its precincts I owe a great debt for open-handed aid given through the years while this book was in preparation. Dean Griswold in 1964–65 released me from a large part of my teaching duties at the School, when this history was approaching completion. Without this rather rare increase of leisure, I could never have brought these chronicles to an end. Earl Borgeson, the School's Librarian, was cooperative to the fullest extent. I am more than grateful to Philip Putnam, the Assistant Librarian, a valued friend since 1922, whose encyclopedic knowledge of the library is only equaled by his alert scholarly cultivation. Dr. Edith Henderson regards research as a joy, not a task; for her, custody of the School's rare books and manuscripts is not a watchman's duty, but an opportunity for the advancement of learning. I owe and give her much gratitude. Faculty brethren who as students or as teachers have known the School longer than I, have been endlessly generous with time and with material. But for these and many other well-deserving friends, this book could never have come to be.

The greatest debt of all I owe to the senior among us, Austin Wakeman Scott. Forty-five years ago he began to show me and my classmates what our School could mean, and this demonstration has continued ever since. When I returned to the School in 1950, I found, to my great pleasure, that I had been given a room in Langdell next to his. He gave me much-needed help in the calling we both follow. When the writing of this book began, he contributed hour after hour of his time, through month after month, to counsel, to talk of the School's past which for me was a luxury. He read the chapters as they were prepared. He turned over to me extracts from his letters to his father, written in his student days; he gave me papers accumulated through a lifetime at the School. He showed me in the gentlest and least dogmatic ways how this history ought to be written. In any just sense he is more its author than I am. Only his modest insistence has kept me from putting his name on the title page above mine, and in much larger letters.

Arthur E. Sutherland

Cambridge, Massachusetts
January 1967

Contents

Illustrations

THE LAW
AT HARVARD

A History of Ideas and Men, 1817–1967

I

The Beginning

Blackstone's lectures at Oxford in 1753 inaugurated university instruction in the common law. Of course Englishmen had studied the common, the civil, and the canon law for centuries before Blackstone; but until his time Oxford and Cambridge, then the only two English universities, had ignored their country's indigenous legal system. Granted, by the 1400's and perhaps even earlier, the Inns of Court and Chancery Inns in London had come to be something comparable to a university of the common law — with each Inn a component college, requiring regular exercises by its students.[1] The apprentices led collegiate lives, listened to learned lectures delivered by their seniors, educated one another in the common law by saturation in talk and in thought about it. But though at the Inns young fifteenth century Englishmen were given some general education along with their law, as time went on the Inns limited their instruction to professional subjects. The apprentices did not find there the stimulus to general thought that derives from scholarly coexistence of several systematic dis-

---

[1] The Inns of Court were and are four in number: Lincoln's Inn, Gray's Inn, the Inner Temple and the Middle Temple. Revivified during the past century, they perform a major function in English legal education. The Chancery Inns, originally ten or more preparatory schools for the Inns of Court, gradually abandoned their instructional functions. The last one was sold in 1903. The story of the Inns, like other parts of English legal history, is most easily accessible in Sir William Holdsworth's monumental *History of English Law*, hereafter cited as Holdsworth. See II, 493 (4th ed., London, 1936). See also Robert R. Pearce, *A History of The Inns of Court and Chancery* (London, 1848). Sir John Fortescue, who became a member of Lincoln's Inn early in the fifteenth century, during the 1460's wrote his *De Laudibus Legum Angliae*, in dialogue form, in Latin, for the instruction of a young Lancastrian prince in exile during the Wars of the Roses. In the forty-ninth chapter he writes the earliest known account of the Inns of Court and Chancery Inns. A modern account of the Chancery Inns and their final liquidation can be found in Sir Cecil Carr's *Pension Book of Clement's Inn* (Selden Society, London, 1960).

ciplines at a university; the collective Inns never constituted a
studium generale. By 1700 life in an Inn was something like residence in an ancient, tradition-laden club, combined wtih apprenticeship to an exasperatingly complex and archaic profession.
If a young man sought a coherent theory of justice and the
state, he found at the Inns of Court no institutional guide. Meantime while Tudors succeeded Lancastrians and Stuarts succeeded
Tudors, while ingenious men began to devise the beginnings of
a mechanical age, while England was developing her modern
constitution, Oxford and Cambridge, though they took pride in
teaching the law based on Roman doctrine, somewhat supercil-
iously continued to turn their backs on their own country's native
legal system.[2]

Roman law, of course, has always been entirely respectable
for a university scholar. Continental universities taught the classical Roman and the later civil [3] law systems in order to train
young men for professional careers to which that learning was
relevant. Petrarch's father, an ambitious notary who wished for
his son Francesco the nobler status of a Doctor of Civil Law, in
1316 sent the boy to the University of Montpellier, and four years
later transferred him to the even more distinguished University
of Bologna. The father was probably saddened, as fathers are apt
to be, when the son abandoned law before he took his degree,
and turned to poetry instead.[4]

At Italian, French, and Dutch universities medieval scholars,
brought up on Justinian's *Institutes,* wrote treatises on the civil
law that lawyers came to cite as authority, much as American
lawyers now cite their Law Institute's *Restatements.* Perhaps these
medieval treatises carried even more weight than our *Restatements* now do, for the books of the learned doctors had no com-

[2] Fortescue gave his young prince an obviously convincing reason for this:
"*Prince.* But, my good Chancellor . . . I beg you to inform me why the Laws
of England, which are so useful, so beneficial and desirable, are not taught in our
Universities." *Chancellor.* "In the Universities of England the sciences are taught
only in the Latin tongue whereas the Laws of England are writ in, and made up
of, three several languages, English, French and Latin."

[3] "Roman law" came gradually to be "civil law," a term used by common-law
scholars to describe the law of continental Europe when today's institutions had
assumed something like their present form. The two adjectives "Roman" and
"civil" have imprecise edges when used to describe law.

[4] See Morris Bishop's *Petrarch and His World* (Bloomington: University of
Indiana Press, 1963). *E converso,* two aspiring young poets were lost to the law
in Blackstone and Story. But perhaps neither one quite promised to become a
Petrarch.

petition from great accumulations of decisional precedent. And this law of the continental nations made a contribution to medieval England. In the Middle Ages England was intellectually and dynastically allied to the Continent. The Church, common element of all western civilization, took to England her canon law with its medieval legal scholarship and its Roman antecedents. Some higher clergy in England, steeped in the Roman tradition, became judges in English lay courts. As the twelfth century was coming to its close and the thirteenth was beginning, England stood at a fork in her legal road, saw two ways of her law: the Roman, strengthened by the long tradition of the august Catholic Church and of the great civilian writers; and on the other hand, the indigenous legal tradition of insular England, vigorous, growing, attached to the English land.

In this medieval moment appeared two of the five law books, written in England during six centuries, which deserve to be called Institutional Treatises.[5] The first of the two was a book written perhaps in 1189, ascribed to Henry II's Justiciar Ranulf de Glanvill. The second was Henry de Bracton's *De Legibus*, which appeared about sixty years later.[6] A man who was forty-five years old when John signed the Magna Carta in 1215, and who lived to be eighty or so, could have heard of the appearance of both these books during his own lifetime.

An unknown author wrote the treatise we now call "Glanvill" about 1189. What title the author chose for his handwritten book, indeed whether he gave it any, we do not know. A subsequent editor or copyist headed it with magnificent amplitude "Incipit Tractatus de legibus et consuetudinibus regni Anglie tempore

[5] "Institutional" is an adjective now most often applied to certain noted Scots writers of the seventeenth century. The term suggests acceptance so widespread, authority so august, that an "institutional" book has an authority like that of an established line of decisions. Professor Eugene Wambaugh of Harvard Law School left us his judgment (and very good it was) as to what English legal authors attained a comparable rank. In 1903 he wrote in the preface to his edition of Littleton's *Tenures*, "Glanville, Bracton, Littleton, Coke, Blackstone: these are the five masters." Professor Holdsworth endorses Wambaugh's judgment; see his *History of English Law*, II, 573 (3rd ed., 1923). See generally Joseph Henry Beale, *A Bibliography of Early English Law Books* (Cambridge: Harvard University Press, 1926).

[6] The other three of these great writings were Littleton's *Tenures*, published in London in 1482 or 1483; Coke's *Institutes*, which appeared in the first half of the seventeenth century; and Blackstone's *Commentaries*, published in the 1760's. John Adams, studying law under the guidance of Massachusetts practitioners in the late 1750's, felt obliged to gain some familiarity with all of these authors except Blackstone, whose commentaries had not yet appeared.

Regis Henrici Secundi compositus, iusticie gubernacula tenente illustri uiro Rannulfo de Glannuilla, iuris regni et antiquarum consuetudinum eo tempore peritissimo." Sir William Holdsworth thought that Bishop Hubert Walter, himself a distinguished judge, may have actually written the book, perhaps with Glanvill's advice and counsel. No one really knows. About 1265 an author who revised the book called it "Summa que vocatur Glaunvile." [7]

Glanvill is the earliest treatise on the common law. It was written in medieval law Latin, a language even then strange to the ears of most men, and ill-suited to describe English government and law as it had come to be seven hundred years after the legions had left Britain. The author of Glanvill, cramped by the archaic Roman-law conventions of arrangement of legal writing, was somewhat hard-put to expound English law under Roman headings and terms. For centuries this same difficulty was to bother successor writers on law in England, who had been taught the Roman law in universities, where Justinian was respectable but where academics ignored as merely practical their own common law and the contemporary government of England. Medieval scholars were as suspicious of innovation as their successors have remained to this day.

Though the author of Glanvill tried to give his treatise a Roman-law form, its substance was native English. The twelfth-century book shows the English lawyer's characteristic concern for the procedure in the interstices of which substantive law was being secreted. Writs in all their diversity drew much of Glanvill's attention. He expounded the infinite variety of medieval land law, its tenures lay and ecclesiastical, its wills, dowers, heirships, wardships, marriage rights, escheats, advowsons. Here appeared all the apparatus by which England regulated the right to use land, her economic substance. In a life of husbandry land law outranked

[7] "The Summa Called Glanvill." For an excellent short account of Glanvill see Holdsworth, I, 188f (3rd ed., 1923). In 1965, under the editorship of G. D. G. Hall of Exeter College, Oxford, Thomas Nelson and Sons, Ltd., and the Selden Society brought out a distinguished edition of Glanvill, with the Latin text and an English translation on facing pages. Here we follow Hall's rendering "Glanvill;" various books offer a pleasing diversity of spelling. Professor Joseph H. Beale of the Harvard Law School wrote an excellent short account of Glanvill's life and of the book which bears his name, as an introduction to a reprint of John Beame's 1812 translation, published by Byrne and Company, in 1900. For *Summa que Vocatur Glaunvile* see F. W. Maitland, "Glanvill Revised," *Harvard Law Review,* 6:1 (1892); Hall cites a rendering as "glaunuyle" in the same phrase; see Hall's Introduction, xxxi, n. 7.

contract law. The commercial bargain was much less prominent in Glanvill's legal system than in ours. Dealing with indebtedness in his tenth book, Glanvill had to brrow Roman law terms: "is qui petit, pluribus ex causis debitum petere potest. Aut enim debetur quid ex causa mutui, aut ex causa venditionis, aut ex commodato, aut ex locato, aut ex deposito, aut ex alia justa debendi causa." [8] He ends with a description of criminal law and procedure; he clearly explains the difference between presentment by jury, and appeal by a private accuser. In medieval England as in eighteenth century America, men were bewildered by a multiplicity of discrete rules and wanted comprehensible texts on the whole law. The author of Glanvill sought with much success to supply this need.

Sixty years after Glanvill, a churchman-judge was working at another book now better remembered than Glanvill's. Henry de Bratton, or Bretton, or Bracton, was a Devonshire parson; his works show that he had studied Roman law somewhere. He rose to be Chancellor of Exeter Cathedral, a judge of the court *coram rege*, a justice in eyre,[9] and a judge of assize. About 1250 he wrote in Latin a large part of his treatise on English law, which he never finished. He must have been much influenced by Glanvill; his book bears a similar title, *De Legibus et Consuetudinibus Angliae*. Bracton's diligence was prodigious. In preparation for his treatise he compiled from the rolls of the Common Bench, from rolls of pleas heard before Henry III himself, and from certain eyre rolls, a notebook of about 2000 cases decided in the first twenty-four years of the reign of Henry III.[10] His *De Legibus*, composed and multiplied by pen and ink before printing began, comes to us through a confusing collection of medieval manuscript copies, somewhat imperfectly edited by a man named Tottell in 1569. Sir Travers Twiss between 1878 and 1883 pub-

---

[8] X, c. 3. The Latin text is that of George E. Woodbine's 1932 edition, but I have rashly inserted a comma after "petit." John Beame in his English translation of 1812 renders this passage: "the plaintiff may found his demand on a variety of causes. His debt may arise either upon a lending, or a sale, or a borrowing, or a letting out, or a deposit, or from some other just cause inducing a debt." Again I insert a comma, here after "lending."

[9] That is, *in itinere*, on a journey; a justice traveling around the country to try cases. Holdsworth, I, 264f (6th ed., 1938).

[10] Holdsworth, II, 235 (3rd ed., 1923). Professor Maitland brought out an edition of Bracton's notebook in 1887. "Rolls" are records of courts or other public agencies written on sheepskin. Many different series survive. Holdsworth, II, 18of (3rd ed., 1923).

lished a re-edited translation of Bracton's treatise. Holdsworth wryly commented that Twiss's edition was "based for the most part upon that of Tottell, to the errors of whom he has added." [11] Pained by various anomalies — for example, Twiss's translation of the Roman "actio negotiorum gestorum" as "action on the case" — Holdsworth perhaps overlooked useful aspects of Twiss's work. Twiss made Bracton accessible to generations of readers more concerned with the broad sweep of law in medieval England than with blunders of translation which, while they properly irk scrupulous scholars, do not seriously distort Bracton's general scope. Bracton himself, at the end of his first chapter, begged "the reader, if he should find anything superfluous or erroneously stated in this work, to correct and amend it, or to pass it over with eyes half-closed, since to retain everything in memory, and to make no mistakes, is an attribute of God rather than of man." Every critic tempted to condemn another's work might well think on this touching request, made by one of the most truly learned of writers on English law. To find errors in another man's book is far easier than to write one's own book containing none.

Bracton's introduction demonstrates his civil law training. He proposed the conventional division of the law into persons, things, and actions; but like English writers after him he found new British wine ill-suited to old Roman jars. *De Legibus* is a long work; an attempt at more than a sketch of the arrangement of its contents would here serve no good purpose. The author divided his treatise into five books. The first begins with political theory and jurisprudence; with the nature of royal sovereignty, predicated both on force and on law; with the nature of law, of justice, and of rights. Next Bracton turns to persons: to serfs and freemen, to royalty and lords, to fathers and sons. The first book ends with the classification of "things."

The second book concerns the manner of acquiring "dominium" of things. One is touched to see that Bracton's first example is capture of a wild animal, a standard instance for teaching, from Roman writers to this day.[12] Things in Bracton's classification include not only what we now call personalty, but also, lands. The

---

[11] Holdsworth, II, 241 (3rd ed., 1923). The unfortunate Twiss did make some howlers. T. E. Scrutton has listed some outstanding ones in "Roman Law in Bracton," *Law Quarterly Review*, 1:425 (1885).

[12] See *Pierson v. Post*, 3 Caines (N.Y.) 175 (1805), the first case in A. James Casner and W. Barton Leach, *Cases and Text on Property* (Boston, 1951).

second book thus includes a considerable discussion of medieval land law.

The third book concerns actions, as we still call them, lawsuits, civil and criminal. The arrangement so far is that of Justinian's *Institutes*, though the substance described is the law of medieval England, and much of the law in the third book we should now call substantive, rather than procedural. The early Englishman's penchant for multiple forms of action then overmasters the author: the fourth and fifth books, like the third, treat of actions and writs, in which appear the rights of possessors and owners. Bracton, like Holmes nearly seven centuries later, found it difficult to think about rights without remedies.[13]

Today's student finds in Bracton little or no information directly relevant to law in the twentieth century. The forms of action to which Bracton devoted so much of his treatise have gone forever. The society governed by his laws and customs has disappeared long since; his serfs were long ago freed; his knights are dust, their good swords rust, the status of their souls is debatable. But Bracton demonstrated that a wise and scholarly man could arrange the complex law of his time in a logical, understandable way, so that a diligent reader could see a picture of the whole. This achievement is still matter for our wonder and for our emulation.

There was no reason in the nature of things why England should not have produced a procession of institutional writers following after Glanvill and Bracton, expounding the whole of English law as it developed, shaping it into a systematic corpus, restating it century after century to suit the society and government of the authors' times. There was no compelling reason why professors at the two English universities should not have gradually merged their Roman-law tradition with the indigenous body of English common-law doctrine, made it one coherent whole as Bracton had begun to do, and as the Scots did for their own law.[14] There

[13] "Legal obligations that exist but cannot be enforced are ghosts that are seen in the law, but that are elusive to the grasp." *The Western Maid*, 257 U.S. 419 (1922) at page 433.

[14] In the later Middle Ages Scotland began to "receive" the civil law, blending it with her indigenous system. Young Scotsmen went to continental universities to study law under "the foreign doctors," and then came home to practice. Scottish judges wrote *Institutes* in the seventeenth century, continuing the civil-law tradition and developing a modern Scots law in combination with it. This evolution deserves much more space here than the limits of the book permit. For the

might have been fourteenth century Blackstones. For historical reasons this did not come about — "historical reasons" being a way of saying that something happened the way it happened but nobody knows why. Medieval secular civil law withered on the English vine; outside a university a secular civilian had few places to go. Classical Roman law continued at Oxford and Cambridge as an elegant antiquity.

Canon law, the law of the Church, did survive as an important part of the curricula of those universities until the time of Henry VIII. From the fourth and fifth centuries onward the continental canon law had developed into a system coexisting with secular Roman jurisprudence, separate from but parallel to the secular civil law, like it ultimately based on the classical law of the Romans. Ecclesiastical courts controlled a large part of the whole field of law. The status of the great numbers of persons in some sort of holy orders; the law as to wills of personal property; lands given as alms; tithes and other spiritual dues; marriage, divorce, and legitimacy; some of the criminal law which had a religious link — all were in the jurisdiction of courts-Christian, and canonical jurisprudence was a profitable area for lawyers. Ambitious young men had practical motives to study canon law and learned scholars had reason to teach it in universities.[15]

The ultimate appellate head of this supranational canon law system was the Pope with his Curia. His jurisdiction, conflicting in so many ways with the asserted powers of lay rulers, from time to time aroused their angry retaliation, easily understandable by a modern American lawyer who sees the wrath of state authorities when the far-off Supreme Court declares their action

---

development of university instruction in the law in Scotland, see Dean T. B. Smith's study of his country's tradition in volume I of *The British Commonwealth: the United Kingdom* (London, 1955), pages 688–691. On civil-law form in Sir James Stair's 1681 *Institutions of the Law of Scotland* see Archibald Hunter Campbell's *Structure of Stair's Institutions* (Glasgow, 1954). In the last four decades of the eighteenth century, John Millar, Regius Professor of Civil Law at Glasgow University, developed a sociologically oriented attitude toward the law which remarkably suggests twentieth century ideas in the United States. See William C. Lehmann, *John Millar of Glasgow* (Cambridge: Cambridge University Press, 1960).

[15] For canon law in English history, see generally Sir Frederick Pollock and Frederic W. Maitland, *History of English Law before the Time of Edward I* (Cambridge: Cambridge University Press, 1895), chap. IV, "Roman and Canon Law;" Frederic W. Maitland, *Roman Canon Law in the Church of England* (London, 1898); Plucknett, "Roman Law and English Common Law," *University of Toronto Law Journal*, 3:24 (1939).

invalid on grounds which some critics denounce as "natural law." The Constitutions of Clarendon, issued by Henry II in 1164 in an effort to limit canonical jurisdiction, and the violent death six years later of Thomas à Becket, Archbishop of Canterbury, were episodes in this centuries-long dispute. The horrified reaction produced in Englishmen's minds by Becket's murder in the cathedral increased the power of Church courts for generations.

The great contest between Henry VIII and Rome over the King's Spanish divorce brought about the end of instruction in canon law at Oxford and Cambridge. Among even more dramatic actions, Henry put a stop to this teaching. By establishing instead, at Oxford and Cambridge, Regius chairs of the civil law — chairs, that is, of the Roman law not concerning church matters — he "threw a sop to disappointed students but seasoned it with a Roman, not an English, sauce." [16] Roman law was more respectable for an elite than profitable for ordinary practitioners. Pollock and Maitland state the situation somewhat emphatically: "As to Roman law, it led to nothing. For a while in their enthusiasm men might be content to study for its own sake this great mass of human wisdom, of almost superhuman wisdom, so it must have seemed to them. But it soon became plain that in England there would be no court administering Roman law, unless it were the court of a learned university." [17]

Perhaps this sweeping statement by two eminent legal historians needs explanatory qualification. Civil law, the evolved Roman law of continental Europe, still had an importance in England despite Henry's Spanish divorce and its sequelae. Relations with continental nations required that English diplomats have some resources of civil law expertise. A maritime nation would inevitably need lawyers skilled in admiralty, for which the civil law offered a uniform system. And the end of canon law as an English university study did not end all English ecclesiastical courts; church law continued in England despite independence from Rome, and civilian professors at the universities trained civilians for the duties which canonists had earlier performed. In 1565 an "Association of Doctors of law and advocates of the Church of Christ at Canterbury" leased London premises from St. Paul's,

---

[16] Harold Greville Hanbury, *The Vinerian Chair and Legal Education* (Oxford, 1958), p. 5.

[17] Pollock and Maitland, *History of English Law* (1895), I, 102.

which came to be called Doctors' Commons. The doctors earned
their title by proceeding to the doctorate of civil law at Oxford
or Cambridge. In a way the Commons were analogous to one of
the Inns of Court. Doctors' Commons remained a highly select
society of specialists in admiralty, probate, and divorce business
until they were dissolved in 1858.[18] The existence of the Doctors'
Commons for more than three centuries after Henry's Spanish
divorce demonstrates that at least some useful instruction for
qualification in one or another branch of the legal profession has
continued at English universities ever since they have existed.
But the doctors of Doctors' Commons were not doctors of the
common law.

Roman law continues in the curricula of English and some
American universities to this day,[19] studied and admired as a
respected branch of traditional classical learning; preserved in
the clarity of its Latin like some ancient creature still fixed in
translucent amber, perfect though long dead.

After the thirteenth century most of the secular law in England
was genuinely English common law, but for hundreds of years
after Bracton it grew in disconnected bits and pieces. To master
it was difficult. During nearly five centuries various English authors wrote books on various aspects of their indigenous law,
which was developing in a mass of judicial decisions interspersed
with occasional statutes. Their treatises were topical, not inclusive. Until Blackstone produced his *Commentaries* in the 1760's
no writer gave a panoramic view of English legal theory as a
whole. No English book between Bracton and Blackstone did
what Justinian's *Institutes* of Roman law had done for the continent of Europe, what Glanvill and Bracton had tried to do for

[18] David Copperfield, considering a profession for himself about 1830, questioned his more sophisticated friend Steerforth about the Doctors' Commons.
Steerforth replied: "Doctor's Commons — a lazy old nook near St. Paul's Church-
yard . . . It's a little out-of-the-way place, where they administer what is called
ecclesiastical law, and play all kinds of tricks with obsolete old monsters of acts of
Parliament, which three-fourths of the world know nothing about, and the other
fourth supposes to have been dug up, in a fossil state, in the days of the Edwards.
It's a place that has an ancient monopoly in suits about people's wills and people's
marriages, and disputes about ships and boats . . . the advocates are civilians —
men who have taken a doctor's degree at college — which is the first reason of my
knowing anything about it." See *David Copperfield* (Fireside Edition, London,
1850), pp. 396–397.
[19] After a quarter-century's lapse at the Harvard Law School, Professor Charles
Fried reinstituted instruction there in Roman law in 1964.

England, or what seventeenth and eighteenth century "institutional" writers succeeded in doing for Scotland.

About 1480, halfway between the Norman Conquest and the present generation, Judge Thomas Littleton wrote a book on the English law of real property which a century and a half later inspired Coke to write his first *Institute*, "Coke upon Littleton." Littleton's *Tenures* was, as Holdsworth notes, "the first great book upon English law not written in Latin and wholly uninfluenced by Roman law." [20]

Thomas Littleton was born about 1407, studied law at the Temple, rose through the usual steps of a successful English lawyer, and in 1466 became a judge of the Common Pleas. He died in 1481. Probably he wrote the *Tenures* shortly before the end of his life. The book was printed in London in 1481 or 1482, the first work on English law ever produced on a printing press. A second edition appeared in 1483; by 1628 when Coke brought out his *First Institute, or a Commentary upon Littleton*, the *Tenures* had run through more than seventy editions. [21]

Toward the close of the fifteenth century while Littleton was practicing law, deciding cases as a judge, and writing his treatise, land was still the principal form of wealth in England. How it was held, conveyed, devoted to "uses," devised, and inherited — these were matters of daily concern to the English people, and to the lawyers who understood the intricate set of substantive rules, enforced by an obscure procedural maze, which governed the English land law. Then, as now, lawyers mainly earned a livelihood by understanding and applying the legal regulations affecting the economy, and Littleton in his *Tenures* provided a usable guide to economic law for English students and practitioners.

Littleton's book served for hundreds of years. In the third quarter of the eighteenth century in British America, lawyer-preceptors of young aspirants to the law still set their apprentices to reading Littleton's *Tenures*, with Coke's *Commentary* on them, though Littleton had written his book before Englishmen knew of the American continent and though Coke's England of the 1620's had little resemblance to New England in 1750. Important as Littleton's book was in its day, it never was a systematic de-

---

[20] Holdsworth (3rd ed., 1923), II, 573.
[21] Professor Wambaugh's 1903 edition contains a biographical sketch of Littleton and a bibliography of the previous editions of the *Tenures*.

scription of the whole English law, and it grew less and less adequate as the two centuries after the 1480's radically changed the world Littleton knew.

In 1628 Coke reincarnated Littleton's work by his *First Institute*. Coke's admiration for Littleton was unbounded. In his preface he wrote of the *Tenures*, "this book is the ornament of the common law, and the most perfect and absolute work that ever was written in any humane science." Coke's *First Institute* is a somewhat rambling commentary on Littleton's *Tenures*, an *omnium gatherum* from Coke's lifetime of reading, stored in his astonishing memory, and then displayed helter-skelter in his book. Indeed all four of Coke's *Institutes* have this character. The reader feels as if he were walking through the halls of an ill-ordered town museum, for which the curator had accepted all gifts offered, a few charming, some informative, some only battered curios not attractive to a casual visitor. Coke's intellectual acquisitiveness was superb; without him and his exposition of Magna Carta in the *Second Institute* we might not today still cherish the Charter as a rallying point of freedom. John signed the Charter in 1215; Coke's *Second Institute*, published in 1642, brought it back to life after the founding of Harvard College.

But still Coke was not the clear systematizer the common law needed. Perhaps he was too professional; perhaps, despite his wit and learning, he had spent too many years in the patient drudgery of the law, piling precedent on precedent in his accumulative mind. Joseph Story, just out of Harvard College in 1798, undertook to read what he called "the intricate, crabbed, and obsolete learning of *Coke on Littleton* . . . where nothing was presented but dry and technical principles, the dark and mysterious elements of the feudal system, the subtle refinements and intricacies of the middle ages of the common law, and the repulsive and almost unintelligible forms of processes and pleadings . . . I took it up, and after trying it day after day with very little success I set myself down and wept bitterly." [22] Story finally conquered *Coke upon Litteton* and felt better for the effort, but his satisfaction may have stemmed more from a virtuous sense that he had demonstrated resolute endurance, than from any great enlightenment about real property law in Massachusetts at the close of the eighteenth century.

[22] See Story's Autobiography in his *Miscellaneous Writings*, W. W. Story, ed. (Boston, 1852), pp. 19, 20.

The Beginning

Coke's politics may have had something to do with the continued popularity of his *Institutes* in the early United States. He was, after all, a great opponent of an English king. And the Americans had a war with another English king a century and a half after Coke. In 1826 Thomas Jefferson wrote to James Madison about the choice of a professor at the University of Virginia:

In the selection of our Law Professor, we must be rigorously attentive to his political principles. You will recollect that before the revolution, Coke Littleton was the universal elementary book of law students, and a sounder whig never wrote, nor of profounder learning in the orthodox doctrines of the British constitution, or in what were called English liberties. You remember that our lawyers were then all whigs. But when his black-letter text, and uncouth but cunning learning got out of fashion, and the honied Mansfieldism of Blackstone became the student's hornbook, from that moment, that profession (the nursery of our Congress), began to slide into toryism, and nearly all the young brood of lawyers now are of that hue. They suppose themselves, indeed, to be whigs, because they no longer know what whigism or republicanism means. It is in our seminary that that vestal flame is to be kept alive.[23]

Perhaps in Coke's day, and perhaps later, to write wise Institutes of the common law required a certain dashing amateurism, a willingness to make inclusive statements without being reduced to embarrassed silence by the consciousness that nothing is simple and that all statements require qualification. Perhaps Francis Bacon should have been the institutional author of the 1620's; he had exactly the needed adventurousness. He was willing to try anything. He did try almost everything. Scientist, historian, essayist, he wrote of all things with a disdainful elegance. While he was Attorney General, in 1616 or early 1617, he proposed to King James "the compiling and amendment of the lawes of England." He set out an ambitious plan for preparation of a legal history; for drafting a sort of "restatement" of decisional law (he called it the "reducing or perfecting of the course or corps of the common laws"); and for composing "certain introductive and auxiliary books touching the study of the laws." He also proposed an edited set of decisions, year by year, with the irrelevancies and the merely repetitious cases left out. Finally he proposed "reforming and recompiling of the statute law," repealing what

[23] *Works* (P. L. Ford, ed., New York, 1905), XII, 455, 456. Was Jefferson perhaps thinking not of Coke upon Littleton but of his *Second Institute*, which includes his commentary on Magna Carta?

was obsolete, mitigating excessive penalties, and "reducing of concurrent statutes heaped one upon another to one clear and uniform law."

He had great ideas. In his "Proposition to His Majesty Touching the Compiling and Amendment of the Laws of England" he wrote:

> For the auxiliary books that conduce to the study and science of the law, they are three; Institutions; a treatise *De regulis juris*; and a better book *De verborum significationibus*, or terms of the law. For the Institutions, I know well there be books of introductions (wherewith students begin) of good worth, especially Littleton and Fritzherbert's *Natura brevium*; but they are no ways of the nature of an institution; the office whereof is to be a key and general preparation to the reading of the course. And principally it ought to have two properties: the one a perspicuous and clear order or method; and the other, an universal latitude or comprehension, that the students may have a little pre-notion of everything, like a model towards a great building. For the treatise *De regulis juris*, I hold it, of all other things, the most important to the health (as I may term it) and good institutions of any laws: it is indeed like the ballast of a ship, to keep all upright and stable; but I have seen little in this kind, either in our law, or other laws, that satisfieth me. The naked rule or maxim doth not the effect: It must be made useful by good differences, amplifications, and limitations, warranted by good authorities; and this not by raising up of quotations and references, but by discourse and deducement in a just tractate.[24]

Francis Bacon never accomplished any substantial part of what he proposed, but even so he was known and read in eighteenth century Massachusetts. Bacon's *Elements of the Common Laws of England*, only 150 pages long, is a sample of what he could have done if he had not been so diverse, so involved in ambition, politics, extravagance, and natural science; but perhaps the defects of his qualities made a greater accomplishment impossible. His intellectual daring was inconsistent with long, steady toil on a single theme. Preparation of Institutes of the English law called for the combined qualities of a genius and a drudge. Francis Bacon was a genius; he was hardly a drudge. Until Blackstone wrote his *Commentaries* in the 1760's, no one published a book for the study of the common law which accomplished anything like Bacon's unwritten Institutions.

[24] Bacon's "Proposition" is the first paper in his *Law Tracts*. Internal evidence shows that the essay was written in 1616 or 1617.

The Beginning

The foundation of systematic legal study at Harvard owes much to the example of Blackstone's work at Oxford. To evaluate his influence, one must understand what his ideas supplanted. What was an enlightened student's preparation for the bar in America, just before Blackstone published his *Commentaries?* John Adams left such an account in his diary and autobiography. We know what books were available to him, and what books he was advised to read. We can assume that he had excellent advice for its day, and had access to the best existing doctrinal texts. We know that he had the intellectual curiosity to study what his preceptors advised. That is to say, he probably had the best professional legal education available in English America in the years 1756–1758. He read law for two years under the direction of James Putnam in Worcester, and beginning in October 1758 did additional reading advised by Jeremiah Gridley, a leader of the Boston bar who owned one of the finest collections of law books in British America.[25]

Adams' reading was remarkable both for what it included, and for what it necessarily lacked. He read standard works of political history and political philosophy. He read some solid civil law material: Justinian's *Institutes* annotated by Arnoldus Vinnius, which Adams drew from the Harvard library; and Van Muyden's *Compendiosa Institutionum Justiniani Tractatio in Usum Collegiorum.* On October 5, 1758, Adams noted in his diary, with a touching vanity not unknown in later centuries, "Few of my Contemporary Beginners, in the Study of the Law, have the Resolution, to aim at much Knowledge in the Civil Law. Let me therefore distinguish myself from them, by the Study of the Civil Law in its native languages, those of Greece and Rome." [26]

But for the study of the common law, the basic law of Massachusetts where he intended to practice at the bar, he had neither a comprehensive systematic text such as ten years later he would have had in Blackstone's *Commentaries*, nor a systematic curriculum, a reading list prepared by a thoughtful preceptor which

---

[25] Jeremiah Gridley, 1701–1767, A.B. Harvard 1725, was a learned and courageous man. He was counsel for the Crown in the Writs of Assistance case in 1761, but this advocacy did not diminish his general popularity.

[26] A sort of classic momentum must have prompted Adams to include Greeks among writers on the civil law. One wonders what Greek authors he might have had in mind. On October 25 he asked Gridley's advice on studying Greek. Gridley said that it was "a matter of meer Curiosity."

pieced together discrete texts to make up a logical whole. His study must have been exactly what he later described it: a "dreary ramble." He read Christopher Saint Germain's *Doctor and Student.* He read Hawkins' abridgment of *Coke upon Littleton,* and then Coke's own four *Institutes.* He read Hawkins' *Pleas of the Crown,* Hale's *History of the Common Law,* and Wood's *Institute of the Laws of England.* He mentions study of two sets of reports, Salkeld's and Lord Raymond's. He attempted some knowledge of Glanvill, Bracton, Britton, and Fleta.[27]

Of the common-law books John Adams read in preparation for admission to the bar, Thomas Wood's *Institute of the Laws of England* of 1720 came the closest to the book Bacon had suggested and to the books Blackstone published seven years after Adams was admitted to the bar. Even so, any resemblance was decidedly remote. Wood had published his book in London in 1720, but Adams could have used the eighth edition, which updated Wood's text to 1754. A demand for law books which in thirty-four years called forth eight editions of Wood's somewhat pedestrian work, is eloquent of the undernourished state of legal literature. Yet the learned Wood, barrister and Doctor of Laws, had had worthy aspirations. In the preface of his *Institute* he described his early discouragement with the available materials of legal study (a common theme in lawyers' memoirs for years), and told how he nevertheless took heart. Seeing "That many Parts of our Common and Statute Laws were Disused or Abrogated; That the Niceties in Pleadings and Practice were lessen'd by Statutes or by New Inventions; I Entertain'd Hopes, that Now it might not be Impossible, to Sort, or to put in some Order, this Heap of Good Learning; and that a General and Methodical Distribution, Preparatory to a more Large and Accurate Study of Our Laws, might now be made."

Wood's preface sounds as if he intended to write a book like Blackstone's *Commentaries,* but he actually produced a work more like a modern digest, or an abridgment, as men called such a book in that day. To carp at Wood is easy; but for his time he was not doing badly. He drew up a compendium of items, a statement of rules, citing statutes and cases with equal facility.

[27] Adams describes his reading in his diary for October 1758, *Diary and Autobiography* (Lyman Butterfield, ed., Cambridge, Mass., 1961) I, 44f, and in his autobiography, III, 270f.

He sought to restate the law of his era as it was, in a series of categorical propositions, with little or no effort to explain it, without any sociological balance of interests, of which perhaps he had not thought or which he may have deemed irrelevant. So despite his commendable effort Wood still left students to plod along on their dreary ramble. His *Institute* did little to make of the law a "scientific" whole.[28]

Though Wood's *Institute* fell short of what his preface proposed, his ideas of instruction in the law were ahead of his time. In 1708 he had suggested that the English universities offer the common-law system in their curricula. Wood made this proposal in a pamphlet, purporting to be a letter from Wood to the unnamed head of an unnamed college at Oxford. He entitled it *Some Thoughts Concerning the Study of the Laws of England in the Two Universities*. He wrote:

In the Universities there are publick Professors of the Roman Law, and Lectures read in the Schools upon some general Titles of it. And young Men think themselves obliged to read an Institute of the Imperial Law, and a Comment upon the Title De Regulis Juris; and then to study Grotius and Puffendorf. Every one who pretends to be a Scholar, ought to read thus far in the Civil Law, and to know the best Books in that Profession. These two last Authors have drain'd out of many Volumes of the Civil Law, the greatest part of the Rational Learning concerning the Natural Rights of Mankind, which our English Lawyers do not disallow of. But if you go farther in this Study have a care lest you take a Fancy (as too many have done) of bringing our Laws to the Standard of the Civil Law in *every Point*, and without enquiry what is in use or not; because it sets the Understanding of an Englishman upon a wrong Biass, and makes him less capable of serving at home in many publick Stations . . .

But to persuade young Scholars to the Study of the Common Law, after three or four Years spent in other Arts and Sciences, let them be inform'd, that if they qualify themselves to read some Reports or Arguments in our Law, they may learn from thence Plainness of

[28] Henry Fielding, barrister and London police magistrate, considered Wood's *Institute* a sort of *Everyman's Handy Guide to the Law*. In 1742 Fielding wrote of an evening's argument between a surgeon and a parson at a country inn: "as this parish was so unfortunate as to have no lawyer in it, there had been a constant contention between the two doctors, spiritual and physical, concerning their abilities in a science, in which as neither of them professed it, they had equal pretensions to dispute each other's opinions . . . The surgeon drew his knowledge from those inestimable fountains called *The Attorney's Pocket Companion* and Mr. Jacob's *Law Tables*; Mr. Barnabas trusted entirely to Wood's *Institutes*." This learned disputation is recorded in the fourteenth chapter of *The History of the Adventures of Joseph Andrews*.

Expression without Affectation; Perspicuity of Method; solid Reasoning without scholastic Niceties: And what better End can thay propose by their *other* Studies? I may say of the Common Law, as an ingenious Gentleman has said of the Mathematicks, That it will accustom the Mind to Attention, give it a Habit of Close Reasoning, and free it from Prejudice and Credulity.

Wood's pamphlet shows that in 1708, forty-five years before Blackstone began lecturing, at least one thoughtful Englishman saw the need for new and more systematic means to study the common law, and saw that it should be studied in universities. If John Adams had begun his 1756 studies at Oxford, he would have found admirable guidance from Blackstone, already lecturing there, though his first *Commentaries* were not published for nearly another decade. If Harvard had followed Wood's advice and had set up its own professorship of common law by 1756, Adams' way would have been still simpler.

"Scientific" instruction in the common law began at Oxford in 1753 because an English politician refused to appoint a talented scholar to a Regius professorship of civil law. The politician wanted to turn the academic patronage to a more regular party man. Political influence in university affairs has rarely had more benign results. Its misuse in 1753 set Blackstone to lecturing on the common law instead of the civil law,[29] and in time contributed to the establishment of the Harvard Law School.

In that year young William Blackstone of All Souls, Doctor of Civil Law, hoped for Oxford's Regius chair. This ancient chair went by royal appointment; it was actually in the gift of Henry Pelham, then Prime Minister. Pelham's older brother, the Duke of Newcastle, destined to become Prime Minister the next year, handled the professorship as a bit of petty patronage. Blackstone went to see the Duke; the Duke asked the Doctor whether if made professor he would support the party in power. The unhappy scholar could only say, a little stiffly, that he would perform his lecturing duties to the best of his poor abilities. A more compliant civilian, Herbert Jenner, got the appointment; his

---

[29] An admirable recent account of Sir William Blackstone and Viner's foundation of a common-law chair at Oxford is given by Harold Greville Hanbury of All Souls College, in his 1958 volume *The Vinerian Chair and Legal Education.* I undertook a much more summary narration, with a short bibliography, in "Blackstone after Two Centuries," one of the essays in *Perspectives of Law* (Boston: Little, Brown, 1964), a festschrift in honor of Professor Austin Wakeman Scott.

name is now known only to curious antiquaries. Blackstone, thus rejected, turned for advice to his friend William Murray, the Solicitor General. Murray advised him to start lecturing anyhow, without a professorship. The Oxford of the mid-eighteenth century permitted such spontaneous discourse by its scholars, for the benefit of any students who might choose to listen. The scholar whom Newcastle had rejected chose for his subject the common law, and became the most successful systematizer of that science the world has ever seen. He began his course of lectures on November 6, 1753, and at once became phenomenally popular. He put rational order in a legal system which had conspicuously lacked such exposition. Students came from as far away as America to hear Blackstone explain and clarify English common law logically and completely. Pirated sets of his students' lecture notes found a ready market. Blackstone demonstrated both the need for and the possibility of university instruction in a corpus of learning which before his day had only been taught by hit-or-miss apprenticeship.

Meantime, in 1752, the notably prosperous English author of a monumental digest of case law conceived the idea of bequeathing to Oxford his published work and some of his accumulated earnings to endow a professorship and some scholarships of English law. Charles Viner was for his time a one-man editor of something like the present West Publishing Company's *Decennial Digest*. Appallingly industrious, Viner had toiled for fifty years compiling a twenty-four volume *Abridgment of Law and Equity, Alphabetically Digested under Proper Titles with Notes and References.* The eighteenth century was litigious (like other centuries); most English law was case law; lawyers could look up relevant precedents in Viner's *Abridgment.* It was a valuable property. When Viner died in 1756 he left to Oxford his copyright, the unsold copies, and £12,000 in other personalty to endow a professorship of the common law of England with as many fellowships and scholarships in the same branch of learning as the bequest might support. Viner's gift may well have been one of the impulses that ultimately induced the founding of a similar chair at Harvard.

Viner had first drafted his will a year before Blackstone unsuccessfully sought Oxford's Regius chair of civil law, hoping for a career quite different from that which he finally followed. One may hesitate to ascribe Viner's original idea to an Oxford scholar twenty-nine years old, in 1752 still comparatively obscure. But Viner had himself studied at Oxford many years earlier and so may well have kept in mind affairs at the university. In 1749 Blackstone had been appointed Recorder of Wallingford, a quiet Thames-side Berks village twenty-odd miles north of Viner's home in Aldershot. Both men were legal antiquarians. Both may well have known Wood's pamphlet on English law in the universities. It is pleasant to imagine Blackstone, after he had discharged some minor duty of his part-time judicial post at Wallingford, riding on to dine with the older scholar at Aldershot, and over a little wine talking about Wood's proposal for study of the common law at Oxford and Cambridge. And when Viner finally executed his will in 1755, Blackstone was becoming famous for the brilliant lectures that he later published as *Commentaries*. Perhaps Viner had Dr. Blackstone in mind.[30]

Viner's will gave the selection of the new professor to a board of five; one was to be the Chief Justice, one was to be named by All Souls College, of which Blackstone was a fellow and of which he had been the diligent and successful treasurer and librarian. By 1758, when the time had come for the first appointment to the Vinerian Chair, Blackstone's friend and adviser Murray had become Chief Justice of England. Blackstone was then the only scholar lecturing on the common law in any university. His selection for the Vinerian Chair was not surprising.

In his inaugural lecture the new professor urged that if universities would attend to the common law as well as the civil, substantial advantages "might result to the science of the law itself." "Science of the law" is a phrase with overtones of the times.[31] In 1758 any up-to-date comprehensive treatise on the common law would have to be "scientific." Scientific progress had deeply affected the climate of opinion among intellectuals in England, France, and the United States, though this spirit had not yet appeared in the literature of the common law. The seventeenth century had seen a steady rise in the understanding

[30] Hanbury, a distinguished successor of Blackstone in the Vinerian Chair, doubted that Blackstone had inspired Viner's gift. See his *Vinerian Chair*, p. 12.

[31] The "science" of law, using the term with its modern meaning, was a concept dear to Dean Langdell at Harvard in the 1870's; it was still highly influential there in the 1920's, and the idea is much alive in "social science" today. See below, Chap. VI and VIII.

of learned men about the universe in which they lived. Neither dynastic wars that tore Europe apart, nor a revolution in England which, in one phase or another, brought battle, murder, and sudden death to many men in most parts of the British Isles, had stopped the international growth of scientific studies. Galileo, Kepler, and Newton looked at the stars with telescopes, reduced what they saw to mathematical formulas, and stated in Latin that the cosmic system operated according to discernible laws. They saw a universe as regular as the clocks which were the mechanical marvels of the time. Men looked through primitive microscopes and began biological studies which in time would arouse speculation whether living creatures, too, were ruled by systems of law as orderly as the spacious firmament. Learned scholars talked and wrote letters to one another about their natural philosophies; they formed societies to bring their discoveries to one another's attention. Then, as now, the cynically wise sometimes jeered at the theoretical scientists. Charles Stuart, hearing that his Royal Society was studying atmospheric pressure, tossed off for his Restoration friends a *mot* about these impractical people who were "spending time only in the weighing of ayre." [32] The King could not have known that underneath their studies lay principles which in time would displace his tall ships with far faster navies, borne on the air that sustained Charles' joke.

As the eighteenth century succeeded the seventeenth, science became the thing among fashionable people. A Neapolitan forerunner of today's popularizers wrote "Il Newtonianismo per le Dame." [33] In France, Diderot and his fellow encyclopedists reduced all human knowledge to segments convenient for easy reading, accessible to any man who could get at the volumes and could understand them. Montesquieu, looking across the Channel, discovered in England a systematic ordering of government even better than the English themselves thought they had, perhaps because Montesquieu's England was even better than England really was. Precisely because Montesquieu gave his idealized England a constitution more attractive, more optimistic about

[32] See Sir George Norman Clark, *The Later Stuarts* (Oxford, 2nd ed., 1950), p. 42.
[33] See Carl L. Becker, *The Heavenly City of the Eighteenth-Century Philosophers* (New Haven: Yale University Press, 1923), lecture II, "The Laws of Nature and of Nature's God," esp. pp. 6of.

rational human government than the actualities of Hanoverian politics, the *Esprit des Lois* helped to persuade thoughtful men in Philadelphia and New York in 1787 and 1788 that they could by reflection and choice construct a more perfect constitution for themselves and their posterity.[34]

Today one must read Blackstone's word "science" without its overtones of the mid-twentieth century. For us it connotes observation of natural phenomena which can be tested under controlled conditions; it means careful measurement and recording of observations, followed by wise generalization from these particulars. In Blackstone's day, the third quarter of the eighteenth century, "science" was a much more inclusive term. The faith of the Enlightenment was still possible for men. The cosmos was an explicable, rational whole. As the unwearied sun from day to day did his Creator's powers display and publishèd to every land the work of an almighty hand, just so there were constant and universal principles of human nature, to discover which was the chief use of history; the system of those principles was as much science as the system of Addison's spacious firmament. The common law, in the eighteenth century, could be part of a scientific synthesis of all human learning.

So Professor Blackstone, publishing his Vinerian Lectures as *Commentaries*, wrote "Of the Nature of Law in General":

Law, in its most general and comprehensive sense, signifies a rule of action; and is applied indiscriminately to all kinds of action, whether animate or inanimate, rational or irrational. Thus we say, the laws of motion, or gravitation, of optics, or mechanics, as well as the laws of nature and of nations. And it is that rule of action, which is prescribed by some superior, and which the inferior is bound to obey.

Thus when the supreme being formed the universe, and created matter out of nothing, he impressed certain principles upon that matter, from which it can never depart, and without which it would cease to be. When he put that matter into motion, he established certain laws of motion, to which all moveable bodies must conform. And, to descend from the greatest operations to the smallest, when a workman forms a clock, or other piece of mechanism, he establishes at his own pleasure certain arbitrary laws for its direction; as that the hand shall describe a given space in a given time; to which law as long as the work conforms, so long it continues in perfection, and answers the end of its formation . . .

Man, considered as a creature, must necessarily be subject to the

[34] The Federalist Papers cite Montesquieu repeatedly. See Numbers 9, 43, 47, 78.

laws of his creator, for he is entirely a dependent being . . . And consequently, as man depends absolutely upon his maker for every thing, it is necessary that he should in all points conform to his maker's will.

This will of his maker is called the law of nature . . .

This law of nature, being co-eval with mankind and dictated by God himself, is of course superior in obligation to any other. It is binding over all the globe, in all countries, and at all times: no human laws are of any validity, if contrary to this; and such of them as are valid derive all their force, and all their authority, mediately or immediately, from this original.

But in order to apply this to the particular exigencies of each individual, it is still necessary to have recourse to reason; whose office it is to discover, as was before observed, what the law of nature directs in every circumstance of life; by considering, what method will tend the most effectually to our own substantial happiness.[35]

Between 1765 and 1768 Blackstone, in his four volumes of *Commentaries*, had recourse to reason to consider what rules of law would tend to the most substantial happiness of the English people respecting the rights of persons and the rights to things, respecting private wrongs and public wrongs. His classifications are not easily understandable today. In them are overtones echoing Justinian's *Institutes*. One feels, a little, that the manqué Regius Professor of Civil Law is showing, somewhat defensively, that the common law is susceptible of arrangement as systematic, as rational, as the jurisprudence of Rome, which he had not been chosen to teach. Blackstone's social justifications for the rules he expounds are not always convincing. In many respects he was retrospective rather than foresighted; he did not perceive that his England was entering on the industrial revolution which was to change the whole structure of property, of classes, of society. But with all this neglect of things to come, so easy to see at Harvard after two centuries, so much less easy at Oxford in 1760, Blackstone was probably the most influential writer on the common law as a whole the world has ever known. For he undertook to demonstrate that England's legal system was not a hodge-podge of rules, justified if at all only by their age; he tried to show that Englishmen had rationally, by trial and error through the centuries, worked out a system of social regulation which produced the greatest satisfaction for themselves, the justest rule for their common existence.

[35] Introduction, section the second.

Blackstone's book at once ran through a series of editions. The *Commentaries* succeeded not because Blackstone gave sound sociological explanations of the reason of the law, but because, remarkably, he made any such explanation at all. Before any other writer on the common-law system, he undertook to account for the legal order by demonstration that it had developed as a reasoned system intended to promote the welfare of the people who lived within it. His exposition was far more than a device to help men remember a multitude of rules; rational order suddenly made the whole system intellectually respectable. The common law became part of the orderly universe of the eighteenth century philosophers; it moved as part of the cosmic clockwork. No longer seeming a farrago of unrelated regulations, it was now a philosophy, a legal "order," with effects demonstrably deriving from purposes. It was thenceforth acceptable for study in a university, just as the systematic Roman law, with its Latin texts hallowed by the learned doctors of a dozen centuries, had so long been accepted. After Blackstone, the common law was a science.

He gained an American audience almost as fast as he won readers in England. In 1760 John Adams wished he had "Mr Blackstones Analysis." [36] His *Commentaries* revolutionized the study of law in America. Lawyers cited Blackstone in American courts as today they cite opinions of their state's highest court. Young James Iredell wrote to his father in London, in July 1771, asking him to

be so obliging as to procure Dr. Blackstone's Commentaries on the Laws of England for me and send them by the first opportunity? I have indeed read them through by the favor of Mr. Johnston who lent them to me; but it is proper I should read them frequently and with great attention. They are books admirably calculated for a young student, and indeed may interest the most learned. The law there is not merely considered as a profession but as a science. The principles are deduced from their source, and we are not only taught in the clearest manner the general rules of law, but the reasons upon which they are founded. By this means we can more satisfactorily study, and more easily remember them, than when they are only laid down in a dictatorial, often an obscure manner. Pleasure and instruction go hand in hand.[37]

[36] Adams, *Diary and Autobiography*, I, 169. The "Analysis" was a 1756 preview of the *Commentaries*.

[37] Griffith John McRee, *Life and Correspondence of James Iredell* (New York, 1858), p. 91. Iredell became a judge of the North Carolina Supreme Court in

Iredell need not have sent to England for a set of the *Commentaries*. Prior to 1771 at least 1000 sets were imported to America for sale at £10 each. A Philadelphia publisher brought out an American edition in 1771–72. Booksellers and individuals subscribed in advance for 1400 sets at $8 each. "John Adams, Barrister at law, Boston" appears in the subscription list. New York booksellers took 239 of the sets; Boston bookstores, 60; those of Philadelphia, 84; of Norfolk, Williamsburgh, and Winchester, Virginia, 97.[38] Edmund Burke, speaking on reconciliation with America in the House of Commons in 1775, told that body that almost as many copies of the *Commentaries* had been sold in America as in England. Americans were, Burke pointed out, a litigious people. Young men, seeing the law as a career leading to prosperity and political preferment, sought better sources for its study.

Professorships of law at American colleges were proposed even while the War of Independence was continuing. In 1777 a committee of the Connecticut Assembly proposed that the state endow three chairs at Yale, one of law, one of medicine, and one of oratory. The plan never came to fruition, for the Yale Corporation feared that public support connoted partially secular control, which "would be not an addition & Enlargement but Abolition of the original Constitution of the College." However, while the discussions were under way, Dr. Stiles, at the request of the Yale Corporation, drafted a curriculum for the professorship of law which might be laid before the General Assembly of the state.[39] His plan, like Blackstone's, was remarkable for its recognition that the study of law was a useful discipline for men not intending to practice, but wishing to fit themselves for public service. President Stiles proposed four series of lectures. The first would start with Roman law, pass over without detailed attention the modern continental civil law, then "go directly to England and consider how much of the jus civile entered into the juris-

---

1777. Washington appointed him to the Supreme Court of the United States in 1790.

[38] See the preface to Hammond's *Blackstone* (San Francisco, 1890).

[39] *Literary Diary of Ezra Stiles*, F. B. Dexter, ed. (New York, 1901), Sept. 27 and Dec. 3, 1777; Feb. 12 and Feb. 27, 1778 — II, 214, 233, 254, 260. The diary does not set forth the plan, but a footnote to the entry of December 3, 1777, states "A copy of the plan is preserved among Dr. Stiles' papers"; Warren obtained a copy from the Yale library and reproduced it. The plan proposes the earliest law professorship ever suggested in the United States (Warren I, 166–168).

prudence of England, for the greatest part of the Jurisprudence of America has been adopted from England." The second series was to concern the English common law, with particular attention to the portion "received" in the United States. The third series of lectures would concern the "codes" of the thirteen states, with the "spirit and governing principles of each code. Connected with this will be a particular representation of the jurisprudence of Connecticut, the Courts and their jurisdictions, and as much of the course of practice as is founded in principle, and not merely official, for this is best learned at the Bar and by living with a lawyer." Last was to be a series on what would now be called comparative government, political theory, and international law.

President Stiles saw far. In his proposed curriculum appear features characteristic of American law school regimes in the late twentieth century, with their introduction to the development of legal institutions in England, and the later reception and growth of these institutions in the American common-law and statutory systems. Stiles proposed the study of much that we now include in constitutional and international law. In all these studies the Yale student of Stiles's day was to concentrate on legal theory, not attempting to learn to practice law. Stiles wisely found, as young lawyers and their elders find today, that the practical application of the law can only be learned by what is actually apprenticeship, no matter how it be described. Unhappily the proposed Yale professorship of law was not then founded, though the President himself later gave some lectures and held recitations following part of his admirable plan. He used "Vattel's *Laws of Nature & Nations*" and Montesquieu's *Esprit des Lois,* noting that Montesquieu's book had been "recited in Jersey College perhaps three or four years."[40]

The first American professorship of law came into existence in 1779 in Virginia's William and Mary College. Jefferson tells in his autobiography that when he became governor in that year, he also became a Visitor of William and Mary. He thereupon set up a chair of "law and police," and to the duties of the moral philosophy professor added instruction in the law of nature and nations. Judge George Wythe, later chancellor of Virginia and

[40] *Literary Diary of Ezra Stiles* for March 12, 1789, and June 22, 26, 1793, III, 345, 497.

one of the most influential teachers of law in the history of this country, received the first appointment to the new chair of law. For a few months in 1779–80 Captain John Marshall, still an officer in the Virginia Line but relieved from active duty as the War of Independence had quieted somewhat, studied law under Wythe at William and Mary. In June 1784 Thomas Jefferson, then Governor of Virginia, paid a visit to President Stiles of Yale; they talked about the instruction in law at William and Mary. Stiles noted in his diary "Blacston the Basis of Law Lect. in Wm & Mary Coll., Philosophy, Medicine and Law seem to be their object." [41] Chancellor Wythe held the chair of law and police until 1800, when at 74 he resigned to be succeeded by St. George Tucker, one of the judges of the Virginia General Court. Judge Tucker brought out an edition of Blackstone in 1803; his preface, dated July 1802, is an admirable analysis of the subject matter of a well-rounded legal education in that day. In 1817 the laws of William and Mary College provided: "For the degree of Batchelor of Law, the Student must have the requisites for Batchelor of Arts; he must moreover be well acquainted with civil History, both Ancient and Modern, and particularly with municipal Law and Police." Appropriately, the 1817 pamphlet "Officers, Statutes and Charter of the College of William and Mary" states that "Tucker's Blackstone is the textbook for the Law class."

Proposals for a Harvard chair of law began as early as 1778 when former Provincial Governor Thomas Pownall wrote James Bowdoin that he intended to add to the endowment of the Hollisian Chair of Mathematics and Natural Philosophy, or found a chair of "Political Law." He did give Harvard some Kennebec land, but a tax sale clouded the title and what little Harvard realized never founded a chair. Other proposals in the 1780's were equally unproductive.[42]

Judge Tapping Reeve of Litchfield, Connecticut, made the most notable forward step in legal education during the 1780's when he founded his private law school in that charming village in 1784. To the clapboard former law office where his school met, students came from every state in the Union. Judge Reeve

[41] *Ibid.*, June 8, 1784, III, 124, 125.
[42] For these early proposals see Albert West, "Thomas Pownall," *Massachusetts Law Quarterly*, 38 (1953): 23, and Warren, *Harvard Law School*, I, 284.

taught the law "as a science, and not merely nor principally as a mechanical business; nor as a collection of loose independent fragments, but as a regular well-compacted system."[43] During the career of the Litchfield school, from 1784 to 1833, it educated sixteen United States senators, fifty congressmen, forty justices of higher state courts including eight chief justices, two justices of the United States Supreme Court, ten governors, five cabinet members. In its forty-nine years of life it had about 1015 students in all; of these perhaps 300 or so came during the years before 1800.

The success of the Litchfield Law School had several causes. Judge Reeve and his associates James Gould and Jabez Huntington were evidently able and attractive teachers. The school offered systematic instruction, with carefully prepared lectures and moot courts for practical instruction. The Harvard Law School library has a number of sets of student notes taken at the Litchfield school, including those of Lonson Nash, who attended Litchfield in 1803. Nash's notes show that Judge Reeve explained the reasons for rules of law, and supported them by citations to cases — mostly English — and by frequent references to Blackstone's *Commentaries*. Nash compiled 1514 pages of notes in three volumes. He evidently considered them a compendium of permanent value, for he prepared a detailed alphabetical index. Apparently students usually took preliminary notes from lectures, and prepared from these a revised, legible version. Nash transcribed his completed notes in substantial calf-bound books or else prized them enough to have his notebooks so bound later. Preparation of such compendia, revising them from first drafts, reading the authorities cited in the lectures, discussing the material with other students, all were planned parts of the instruction. Students were "examined" every Saturday, probably orally. A catalogue of the school explained:

The examinations . . . consist of a thorough investigation of the

[43] This comment on the Litchfield School is in the second of Dwight's "Letters" on "Learning, Morals &c. of New England." See p. 295 of vol. IV of the 1823 edition of Timothy Dwight's *Travels in New England and New York* (New Haven, 1821–22; London, 1823). The Litchfield Law School has always impressed Harvard teachers. See Joel Parker, *The Law School of Harvard College* (New York, 1871), and Dean James Barr Ames's address "The Vocation of the Law Professor," delivered at the University of Pennsylvania in 1901, in his *Lectures on Legal History* (Cambridge: Harvard University Press, 1913), p. 354. My description of the Litchfield School is largely drawn from these two books.

principles of each rule, and not merely of such questions as can be answered from memory without any exercise of the judgment. These examinations are held by Jabez W. Huntington, Esq., a distinguished gentleman of the bar, whose practice enables him to introduce frequent and familiar illustrations, which create an interest, and serve to impress more strongly upon the mind the knowledge acquired during the week.[44]

Compared to the amiable neglect characteristic of much law-office apprenticeship the superiority of this systematic education is evident. When Tapping Reeve opened his Litchfield school he offered probably the best professional instruction available in the United States. His success was not surprising.

In August 1790 the College of Philadelphia appointed James Wilson, Associate Justice of the Supreme Court, as professor of law. Justice Wilson projected an ambitious set of lectures which were quite different in conception from Tapping Reeve's training. He planned to cover constitutional law, international law, the origin and rules of the common law, civil law, law merchant, and maritime law. This modest offering was designed "to furnish a rational and useful entertainment to gentlemen of all professions, and in particular to assist in forming the Legislator, the Merchant, and the Lawyer." Justice Wilson's first discourse was a distinguished occasion. President Washington and his cabinet were there; so were the Governor of Pennsylvania, members of the Congress and of the state's legislature. The presence of Mrs. Washington and other ladies added a social note. Wilson originally meant to continue the lectures through a period of three years, covering the vast panorama he originally proposed. He completed the first year's stint, and part of the second, but he grew discouraged by a lack of general interest. Perhaps he fell between two stools; perhaps he was too general for the law student and too professional for the general hearer. In 1792 the College of Philadelphia merged with University of Pennsylvania; the university gave Wilson an appointment similar to that he had had in the college, but he delivered no further lectures. Those he had given were published in 1804.[45]

His discourses are elegant, learned, and significant for their ideas on the Constitution. Wilson had been educated at St.

---

[44] Warren, *Harvard Law School*, I, 185. One sees signs of the "case method."
[45] *Works*, ed. Bird Wilson (Philadelphia, 1804), vols. I, II, III.

Andrews, Glasgow, and Edinburgh universities, had signed the Declaration of Independence, had been in the Continental Congress, had been a member of the Constitutional Convention of 1787 and of the Pennsylvania ratifying convention. He had been a part of the Republic's constitutional inception; but he was not a professional law teacher nor a teacher of law for professionals, and indeed never claimed to be. He was one of several men who in the late eighteenth and early nineteenth centuries briefly lectured at American colleges, seeking to demonstrate that law, in the wide meaning of the term, is a suitable element in the education of any cultured man.[46]

The most ultimately fruitful of these impermanent lectureships was James Kent's at Columbia between 1793 and 1798. At first his lectures were well attended; then his hearers dwindled and gradually disappeared; he resigned his professorship in 1798, and in the same year Governor John Jay appointed him a justice of the New York Supreme Court. In 1824, having become in turn chief justice, then chancellor and a reviser of his state's constitution, Kent returned to his lecturing. The fruits of his early and later lectures were his *Commentaries on American Law*. On Kent's *Commentaries*, with Blackstone's, generations of American law students were nourished. Young Oliver Wendell Holmes prepared a twelfth edition of Kent's *Commentaries* in 1870-1873. As late as the first years of the twentieth century young men who contemplated "reading law" in an office could still assume, in some parts of the United States, that Blackstone and Kent would be the staples of their diet.

College professorships of law were fairly frequent in early nineteenth century America. Timothy Dwight, President of Yale, in a tableau of the college and university professorships in New England in 1811 and 1812,[47] wrote that in 1812 Yale had "A president; five professorships academical; and three medical. The academical professorships are — of theology; of law, natural and political; of mathematics and natural philosophy; of chemistry and mineralogy; and of languages and ecclesiastical history."

[46] This is a concept which then, for a while, may have fallen into some disuse. But Oliver Wendell Holmes was University Lecturer in Constitutional Law at Harvard College in 1870. Public law began to revive in the Department of Government of Harvard in the time of Abbott Lawrence Lowell, and seems increasingly to thrive there in our own time.

[47] See Dwight, IV, 295f.

Brown, Dwight wrote, had an "academical" professorship of law in 1811; Middlebury had a similar professorship in 1812.

How much all the eighteenth and early nineteenth century American professorships owe directly to the Vinerian bequest and to Blackstone, one cannot say with assurance. Similar intellectual movements were simultaneously stirring on both sides of the Atlantic. The spirit of the times that prompted Viner and Blackstone was animating America in the 1700's. Men in America, like men in Europe, were looking for "science" in the law as in everything else. Franklin was "scientific"; Cadwallader Colden, a Doctor of Medicine from Scotland who became colonial lieutenant-governor of New York, was a botanist and medical author more American than Scot. Blackstone's lectures and books seized the imagination of thousands of men in America. The new study of law "as a science" in England and the new study in America had antecedents in common. The law at Harvard probably has some collateral as well as some direct kinship with the law at Blackstone's Oxford.

II

Isaac Royall

Many men contributed in many ways to the establishment of the Harvard Law School; many more have helped to continue and to advance it. But beginnings are always dramatic moments; one man here deserves special mention: Isaac Royall, an eighteenth century Massachusetts magnate, a loyalist refugee during the Revolution. He died in England in 1781, regretting his Medford home. By his will he endowed at Harvard "a Professor of Laws in said College or a Professor of Physick and Anatomy."

Massachusetts of the early 1770's had many different social and economic groups. In the hilly western counties there were upland farmers and lumbermen; nearer the sea lived their perhaps more sophisticated farming brethren, like the Adamses of Braintree. In white-clapboarded churches in the towns Congregational ministers preached, successors of the old Puritan theocracy, whose certainties were becoming a bit unsettled by the early stirrings of the Unitarian movement. Sailors and tradesmen clustered around the ports. Boston was the greatest and busiest harbor but, in the aggregate, the smaller Salem, Marblehead, Gloucester, and New Bedford and the ports on the Cape and the islands rivaled Boston's trade. In these towns merchants lived and traded, some of them stately and secure like Charles Apthorp and John Hancock of Boston, patrons of fine craftsmen like the silversmith Paul Revere. In Boston and some other ports commercial magnates built great houses from the profit of their ships' voyages. There were a few noted lawyers like Jeremiah Gridley and John Adams. A small group of men who had made or inherited fortunes in the sugar plantations of the West Indies chose to come and live in the more tolerable climate of Massachusetts.

Isaac Royall

The great folk lived with a spacious leisure quite unlike the urgent industry of Puritan immigrants a century earlier. They took pride in beautiful possessions, dined with one another in some state, and, one hopes, felt no bitter foresight that much of this would soon end in the tragedy of war between neighbors. Many were characteristically English in their attitudes, Anglican rather than Puritan in their religion. Some of them were founders and mainstays of Christ Church in Cambridge, built facing the Common in 1760 to minister to the local Anglicans and whatever students at Harvard adhered to the Thirty-Nine Articles and reacted against Congregational strictness. The families who held pews in 1770 were staunch supporters of the Crown: Royalls, Vassalls, Olivers, Lees, Phipses, Lechmeres, Borlands, and Apthorps. Isaac Royall of Medford was a member of the first Vestry. The first rector, the Reverend Mr. East Apthorp, son of the eminent Boston merchant, came in 1761 with his young wife to live in the handsome rectory he had built in Cambridge, with its wide, many-paned windows looking down to the Charles across a gentle slope of meadow and a stretch of tidal marsh. But colonial resentment was rising against whatever seemed to symbolize English patronizing superiority. Three years later the Apthorps left for what they then thought a temporary stay in England, their departure shadowed by ill-tempered whispers that George the Third was about to appoint Apthorp a Massachusetts bishop. Dr. Jonathan Mayhew, sharp-spoken pastor of the West Church in Boston, had written of Apthorp House in 1763 with the italics then conventional: "It is supposed by many that a certain *superb edifice* in a neighboring town, was even from the foundation designed for the *Palace* of one of the *humble successors* of the Apostles." [1]

The Vassalls of Cambridge were one of the great Tory families with fortunes founded on West Indian sugar. Two Vassall houses still stand kitty-corner across Brattle Street from one another, the larger now shown to busloads of daily visitors as the Longfellow house. Still other houses of the established gentry stood in pleasant grounds facing the Charles, farther out along the "road to Watertown." The Royalls of Medford, allied by mar-

[1] The quotation occurs in Mayhew's *Observations on the Charter and Conduct of the Society for the Propagation of the Gospel in Foreign Parts* (Boston, 1763), p. 107. See Wendell Garrett, *Apthorp House* (Cambridge, Mass., 1960). The house, now owned by Harvard, is the Master's Residence at Adams House.

riage with the Cambridge Vassalls, like them were West Indian sugar planters who had come to live in Massachusetts. Something of the Royall state appears in the picture of Isaac Royall and his family, painted in 1741 by the fashionable society portraitist Robert Feke, when Royall was 22.[2] The picture, now owned by Harvard, hangs in the Langdell entrance hall, facing portraits of early professors of the Law School, across the great circular desk designed for Dean Pound. As students, teachers, and visitors come and go all day, some few may pause to think of the will, executed by an exile during the War of Independence, which provided for Harvard's first professorship of law.

Feke painted young Royall as he was a third of a century before Lexington and Concord. He is standing, dressed in a scarlet coat and a white neckcloth. His attitude suggests the patronizing magnificence of self-confident, aristocratic youth. Beside him sits his wife Elizabeth, holding their small daughter Elizabeth. Mary Palmer, Mrs. Royall's step-sister, and Penelope Royall, Isaac's sister who later married Henry Vassall, sit with Mrs. Royall. The twenty-two-year-old Royall heir surveys the ladies with benign elegance.

The Royalls' house and grounds in Medford suited the family's distinguished state. Governor John Winthrop had acquired the land — five hundred acres — in 1631, and six years later had built the original house. Isaac Royall's father, also named Isaac, paid £10,350 for the property in 1732. In the course of five years he rebuilt the house on the design of a titled Englishman's house in Antigua, and in 1738 moved to Medford with his family and Negro "servants." The younger Isaac Royall was married in King's Chapel to Elizabeth McIntosh of Boston on March 27, 1738. On his father's death in the following year the twenty-year-old son inherited the estate. He was fond of the Medford place, and proud of it. He wished, as he long after wrote in his will, that "My Mansion House and the lands and all the rest of my entailed Estate in Medford . . . go by the name of Royallville a name by which I have for some years past called it & which I desire always to have it go by."[3]

[2] For a description of Feke's painting of the Royall family and biographical sketches of the persons in the picture, see Henry Wilder Foote, *Robert Feke, Colonial Portrait Painter*, (Cambridge: Harvard University Press, 1930), pp. 179f.

[3] Part of the twenty-first paragraph of Isaac Royall's will of 1778. His house, restored and refurnished, is now owned by the Royall House Association.

Isaac Royall was an eighteenth century Massachusetts magnate, a loyalist refugee during the Revolution. He died in England in 1781, regretting his Medford home. By his will he endowed at Harvard "a professor of Laws in said College." This portrait of Royall and his family was painted by Robert Feke in 1741 when Royall was 22.

Isaac Royall

As years went on Isaac Royall became chairman of the Medford Selectmen, a member of the General Court, one of the Governor's Council, and Brigadier-General of the provincial forces — thereby for the rest of his life entitling him to allow people to call him General Royall. He not only was a vestryman of the Anglican Christ Church in Cambridge but had a pew in Boston's King's Chapel, that outpost of Anglicanism in a congregational city. He was not a college man, and in the highly literate atmosphere of Massachusetts this may have caused him some wistfulness. He had lived with his parents in Antigua far from any university, until the family moved to Medford when he was eighteen. Perhaps in the 1730's sugar-planting gentry moving to Massachusetts from the British West Indies thought college needless or even unsuitable for a family heir then in his nineteenth year. Furthermore young Royall married shortly after his father brought his family to the grandly rebuilt house in Medford, and when the father died the next year Isaac Royall was left responsible for managing the family affairs. He had no opportunity to study at a college. Still it was appropriate for a man of property and a leading gentleman of the province to be a patron of learning. When the college lost most of its library in the Harvard Hall fire of 1764, Royall contributed to its restoration.

In the 1770's he must have been an unusually substantial property owner, as such matters went in America. He owned sugar plantations in Antigua [4] which, his will suggests, Royall thought would be a chief source of family revenue. He owned "Royall-ville" in Medford. After the custom of progressive men of that day he had acquired rather large uncleared tracts in the west, that is to say, in the hilly parts of Hampshire and Worcester counties in Massachusetts, in the towns of Granby and Royalston. Undoubtedly he counted on the increase in the value of the uplands as the country attracted more settlers. For his daughters he made suitable marriages to young men of substance: Mary became the wife of George Erving, a Boston merchant; Elizabeth [5] married Sir William Pepperell, a baronet, grandson of Lieutenant-General Sir William Pepperell of Kittery, who in 1745 had commanded

---

[4] In a 1779 letter he wrote with a certain modest grandeur of his "little estate" there.

[5] The second Royall child who was named Elizabeth. Little Elizabeth of the Feke portrait died in 1747, when she was seven years old.

the British forces at the capture of Louisbourg on Cape Breton Island.

Thus by family background and connections, by experience serving the Crown in the province, by habit of life, Isaac Royall was a loyalist. American loyalists faced an unhappy choice in 1775 when civil war became inevitable. Ordinary foresight must have suggested that a separatist party in the American colonies might ultimately succeed, and that those who had shown loyalist sympathies would in that event suffer from the rough intolerance of the victors. Even if the Royal Navy and the King's disciplined, scarlet-coated regular regiments should eventually disperse the rebels and restore British provincial order, a kindly person would feel little pleasure in seeing the armed reconquest of his American neighbors.

On the other hand, for General Isaac Royall to join the rebellious colonists was impossible. When a man is fifty-six years old, as Royall was in 1775, change of a lifetime's political attitude is difficult. By April of that year the militia soldiers who might otherwise have served under his orders had become revolutionary minutemen, alerted to fight Gage's redcoats if they sortied from Boston. Royall's sons-in-law were partisans of the Crown. His wife had been dead for five years. Three days before the fighting broke out at Lexington and Concord, Royall left his great house in Medford and went to Boston, intending to go thence to Salem, and sail for his Antigua plantations. Unfortunately for these plans the military situation moved Gage to put a stop, for a while, to civilian journeys in or out of Boston.

By and by Royall found it possible to sail for Halifax, firmly held by the British navy; he still intended to sail from that port to his estates in Antigua. Again events spoiled his journey. Smallpox was sickening Halifax. General Royall lived for a year in the township of Windsor, thirty miles north of Halifax on an inlet of the Bay of Fundy. When General Howe, with the fleet of his brother the Admiral, evacuated Boston in March 1776, Howe took some civilian loyalists with him to Halifax; to Royall's surprise these newcomers included his daughter Mary Erving and her husband. Royall's other son-in-law Sir William Pepperell and the now motherless Pepperell children had left Boston for England in February 1776. Isaac Royall was unwell. The Ervings, he later wrote, "over persuaded me to give over my voyage to

Antigua and to come with them to England as it was easy to get from London to Antigua . . . as I did not know whether I should ever live to see my Grandchildren again if I did not." [6]

So the family came together again in England. Isaac Royall settled in Kensington, and as occasion served wrote back to American friends of his wish to return to Medford, of his thought of marrying again, of his regret at the "troubles," as he called the Revolution, of his annoyance when the Massachusetts authorities, despite his public service, started proceedings to confiscate his property. Royall's letters complained of continued poor health. He wrote of his occasional aid to less prosperous displaced loyalists. He wrote, a bit pathetically, of the inaccessibility of the King's ministers, Lord Dartmouth, Lord North, and Lord George Germaine, when he tried to see them. He found it difficult to remember that a great man in Massachusetts was not necessarily a great man in England, and that visits from loyalists who were doubtless deserving and certainly inconvenient could be unwelcome to a Ministry trying to conduct a war with France and with thirteen rebellious colonies. [7]

At Kensington, on May 26, 1778, Royall made an elaborate will; on November 31, 1779, he executed a codicil. [8] The will made numerous small bequests to his friends and relatives. His Medford properties — his "entailed estate" — he devised in trust for his descendants, as if he thought that all the "troubles" would finally be straightened out. For this history of the Harvard Law School the important paragraph of Isaac Royall's 1778 will is "item 12." In it Royall made gifts to Medford for its school, and to Harvard College for a professorship.

I give devise and bequeath unto the town of Medford in the County of Middlesex in the Province of Massachusetts Bay but now by information since called the State of Massachusetts Bay for the use and better Support of the School of said Town one hundred acres more or less of that part of my land in the Township of Granby formerly known by the name of South Hadley in the County of Hampshire in the Province or State aforesaid which hundred Acres is leased to

---

[6] In a letter written by Isaac Royall in 1779 from Kensington, England, to Edmund Quincy, executor of the will of Isaac Royall, senior. The Massachusetts Historical Society kindly supplied a photocopy, now in the Law School archives. Quoted by permission of the Massachusetts Historical Society.

[7] Kenneth Roberts' novel *Oliver Wiswell* gives a vivid picture of loyalists in London in 1777.

[8] Copies of the will and codicil are in the Harvard Law School library.

Ebenezer Darvin all the remainder of said tract of land in said Granby containing eight or nine hundred acres more or less also all my right in a tract of land in the County of Worcester containing in the whole Nine hundred and twenty eight acres which I bought of the Province of Massachusetts Bay on the twenty Eighth day of December one thousand seven hundred and fifty two in Company with the Hon'ble James Otis Esquire, John Chandler Esquire and Capt. Caleb Dancy I give devise and bequeath to the Overseers and Corporation of Harvard College in Cambridge in the County of Middlesex aforesaid to be appropriated towards the Endowing a Professor of Laws in said College or a Professor of Physick and Anatomy which ever the said Overseers and Corporation shall judge to be best for the benefit of said College and they hereby shall have full power to sell said Lands and to put the money out to Interest the income whereof shall be for the aforesaid purpose.

In case of default of issue he gave half of any lapsed share of his "entailed estate" to build and support a hospital for the poor, half to Harvard for the professorship. By his 1779 codicil he gave to Harvard for the professorship a two-hundred-acre lot in Royalston, Worcester County, and the residue of his undivided interest in any other land in Royalston. He died in England in 1781.

Even after nearly two centuries, the pathos of the war and its bitterness of neighbor against neighbor is highlighted by Royall's gifts to Harvard. All the life he and his family had known was over. They were at home nowhere now. Still he clung to his Massachusetts past. He was a generous man. He may well have wished to leave a pleasant memory in America for his children and grandchildren in case they should return there after the war ended, regardless of which side might prevail. One can only guess at his reason for prescribing law or "Physick and Anatomy" as the subject of his professorship. He may have seen, or owned in his Medford library,[9] a set of Blackstone's *Commentaries;* he could well have heard of Viner's bequest to Oxford. Law was becoming a "science"; medicine was another. Royall's choice of subjects was up-to-date.

One should neither undervalue nor overemphasize the effect of Royall's devise to Harvard. Before long the common law would in any event have appeared in its curriculum. William and Mary College in Virginia had already in 1779, followed Oxford's ex-

---

[9] Royall considered his personal library important enough to divide it, by items 5 and 6 of his will, between his daughter Mrs. Erving and his granddaughter Elizabeth Royall Pepperell.

ample by establishing a chair of law, and had installed George Wythe as its first professor. In the last third of the eighteenth century the Harvard College library received a series of gifts of law books. Men were discussing a Harvard chair of law in the mid-1780's, before anyone knew what could be salvaged from Royall's lands in Granby and Royalston. Still, as it turned out, his gift may well have applied a final impulse. Trustees neither like to, nor legally can, let income go unused indefinitely. As we see in the late twentieth century when foundations make "matching gifts," a comparatively small endowment for a useful purpose may be a stimulus to finding more finances. Royall's gift did set Chief Justice Parker to delivering Harvard's first lectures on law, and led him to report that an organized school was necessary.

Today, recollection of Isaac Royall serves another purpose. Americans are sometimes historically myopic, not perceiving the crises through which our predecessors lived, not remembering their endurance, their generous impulses which could survive even ingratitude, disappointment, and disillusion. Royall's portrait in Langdell is a wholesome reminder in other difficult days.

Harvard came near losing her Royall lands by confiscation during the war. The outbreak of the Revolution was not a playful business. Men were getting killed on both sides. Those who decided for the American cause, risking everything they had, felt that Loyalists who took refuge in Boston with Gage and the redcoats or, worse yet, left Massachusetts for Halifax or England had abandoned to the better cause whatever they left behind. Massachusetts took over the Vassall houses in Cambridge for the use of the military in 1775; the Medford Selectmen, less bitter toward Royall, for several years let Royallville stay in the hands of Dr. Simon Tufts, a good friend of Royall's who at his request had undertaken to act as custodian. Finally, on May 25, 1778, three years after Royall departed, the Selectmen certified to the judge of probate their belief that "the said Isaac Royall voluntarily went to our enemies and is still absent from his habitation and without the State." But perhaps this proceeding was still a friendly one, begun for Royall's protection; the probate judge granted official "agency" of Royall's estate to the same Dr. Tufts.

As the war grew older, men became tired and vindictive. On April 30, 1779, the Massachusetts legislature passed "An Act to confiscate the Estates of certain notorious Conspirators against the Government and Liberties of the Inhabitants of the late Province, now State, of Massachusetts-Bay." That statute named as two such "notorious conspirators" Isaac Royall's sons-in-law George Erving and Sir William Pepperell, with a number of other Mandamus Councillors,[10] and various other dignitaries under the late provincial government, and stripped them of their properties. Though Royall was not listed in the Conspirators Act, he fell within the general terms of another less drastic statute passed the same day, "An Act for confiscating the Estates of certain Persons commonly called Absentees." This Absentee Act was not automatic, as the Conspirators Act was; it prescribed various judicial procedures before a man would lose his property because he had sought Gage's protection and not returned. If the forfeiture proceedings could be dragged out long enough for the war to end and for tempers to cool, Royall and his successors in interest might still escape the proscription. On May 26, 1780, Royall's friend Dr. Simon Tufts wrote a rather cryptic letter to Edmund Quincy apparently about Royall's property: "the Court say very kind words but have only received the petition of Mr. Hall and mine and as we say, *Hung it up*, and by what I can Learn from them, will remain in that Situation for a time . . . Rhode Island Government have confiscated his Estate . . . This State by their Attorney General have filed a bill here for the same purpose — But I am informed by a gentleman that the Court will stop it." [11]

Royall died in 1781. Two years later the treaty which ended the War of Independence granted to the loyalists a somewhat ambiguous guaranty that they could recover their American assets. Harvard was, of course, not a loyalist absentee, but she claimed through one, and Harvard's position became stronger as the Loyalist position improved. Article III of the federal Constitution of 1789 opened the Supreme Court to loyalist suits against confiscating states. In 1793 one of the Vassalls procured such a

[10] The Mandamus Councillors were prominent loyalists designated by Crown writ to replace the former provincial Council. The advocates of independence bitterly resented them. Isaac Royall had been designated a Mandamus Councillor but had never accepted the office.

[11] The letter is in the collection of the Massachusetts Historical Society, and a photocopy is in the Harvard Law School library. Isaac Royall's will gives his Mount Hope Farm, in Bristol, Rhode Island, to his granddaughter Elizabeth Royall Pepperell. The letter is quoted by permission of the Massachusetts Historical Society.

writ against Massachusetts and had it served on Governor Hancock, who immediately called the General Court in session to deal with this legal crisis. The *Massachusetts Mercury* fulminated: "The precept now served on the Governor and Attorney General is for moneys arising from the sequestered property of a refugee . . . If he should obtain what he has sued for, what a wide extended door will it open for every dirty Tory traitor to his country's liberties to enter." [12] Such suits gave rise to the Eleventh Amendment of 1798, which barred access to the federal courts in suits against a state by a foreign national or by a citizen of a state other than that of suit. Although state courts were still open to loyalists, they, and perhaps their successors in interest, were evidently going to have a hard time collecting American assets. On the other hand, Jay's Treaty of 1794 strengthened the position of loyalists seeking their assets, and so, derivatively, strengthened Harvard's claim to Royall's devise.

Still, realization of investable funds from the Royall lands took Harvard a long time. The will only came to probate in Massachusetts in 1786, five years after Royall's death. Upland Massachusetts was a troubled area in the later 1780's. Most of the fighting in Shay's Rebellion took place in Worcester and Hampshire counties during the winter of 1786–87. In the hills ill-feeling against absentee loyalists and their well-to-do friends must have persisted after that date. In 1795 the college employed a lawyer to locate the lands Royall had devised to Harvard. He found some sold for unpaid taxes, some stripped of timber, some occupied by settlers who refused to vacate. But the Massachusetts courts had never escheated the Royall lands under the Absentee Act of 1779, and in 1796 Harvard sold the Granby acres for $2,000. The treasurer invested the proceeds at 6 percent and began to reinvest the interest as it came in. This $2,000 was the largest sum Harvard realized from Royal's devise, the most substantial financial impulse toward the original founding of the Law School. In 1805 the General Court by Resolve [13] facilitated the disposition, for the benefit of Royall's devisees, of the lands he had left to his loyalist descendants. Though this measure was perhaps not nec-

[12] Issue of July 16, 1793. Charles Warren describes the Vassall case and other better known similar litigation in *The Supreme Court in United States History* (Boston: Little, Brown, 1924) I, 93f. *Chisholm v. Georgia*, 2 Dallas 413 (1793), is the most famous instance.

[13] Chap. 77, Resolves 1804, Jan. 31, 1805.

essary to perfect Harvard's title, still the university [14] and prospective purchasers of its Royall lands must have felt more secure. In 1808 Harvard sold 133 Royall acres in Winchendon for $837.90; in 1809 the sale of another 250 acres in Westminster brought the university $100. By 1815 the proceeds of these sales, with reinvested interest, amounted to a capital fund of $7,592.50; the treasurer also had on hand $432.27, the preceding year's interest not yet reinvested. All things considered, this was competent salvage. It was enough to provide Harvard's first course of lectures on law.

[14] The Massachusetts constitution of 1780, drafted by John Adams, referred to Harvard College as "this university."

III

Parker and Stearns: 1817–1829

Harvard waited until 1815 to appoint her first professor of law under Royall's devise. She waited ninety-five years after she had established the Hollis chair of divinity, thirty-three years after she had created her first professorship of medicine, thirty-four years after Isaac Royall's death, eleven years after the university received the first $2,000 under his will. The main reason for this tardy inception was simple lack of enough money. Accumulation at compound interest had been necessary even to make a start. Charles Warren suggests also that the latter part of the delay resulted from renewed troubles with England, the Embargo Act, and consequent years of financial depression which correspondingly depressed the business of lawyers and so discouraged the Corporation from starting instruction in the law.[1]

But notable legal careers were developing around 1800. Joseph Story began to study law in 1798; by 1811 he had made a conspicuous success in practice and in politics, had built himself one of the great houses of Salem,[2] and had become a justice of the Supreme Court of the United States. In 1801 Daniel Webster began to read law in Thomas W. Thompson's office in Salisbury, New Hampshire; in 1804 he moved to Boston, finished his studies in the office of Christopher Gore, later governor of Massachusetts, and was admitted to the bar in Boston in 1805. Webster refused appointment as clerk of the Court of Common Pleas in Hillsborough County, New Hampshire, an office worth $1,500 a year

[1] *Harvard Law School*, I, 285.
[2] Story has left an account of his professional beginnings and his prompt success in the autobiographical sketch written for his son in 1831. See his *Miscellaneous Writings*, pp. 19–21. His Salem house is now owned by John Ward of that city. The National Park Service has proposed it as a National Historic Site.

43

in fees, then a substantial income. He correctly foresaw a better career at the bar. He began practice in New Hampshire in 1806; by 1812 when he was elected to Congress he had become one of the most noted lawyers in his state. John Lowell graduated from Harvard in 1786 and was admitted to the Massachusetts bar in 1789. In 1803 he retired from active practice, exhausted by overwork and concern over the unsuccessful defense of a client charged with murder. A lawyer does not exhaust himself by lack of business. Lowell in fourteen years had accumulated a competence sufficient to let him travel and rest in Europe for three years, and on his return to devote the remainder of his life to eminent unpaid public service. New England in the early 1800's was not a bad place for an able man to practice law.

To be sure, a lawyer's business in 1800 could involve niggling little matters, as it did in the days of the Year Books, and as it does today. The reports of cases decided by the Massachusetts Supreme Judicial Court, compiled by its first reporter, Ephraim Williams, begin with the Berkshire September term in 1804. Williams' reports start with a suit on a note for £100; the next case involves a covenant of title to a parcel of land sold for the same sum; the third reports a trial before the full bench on an indictment for breaking and entering a shop and stealing goods in the night.[3] Nobody grew rich on fees earned at such judgment days in the Massachusetts hills. But careers of lawyers who prospered between 1790 and 1815 demonstrate that New England businessmen in the larger harbor cities waged more financially important litigation. At the Essex term in November 1804 the court decided *Livermore v. The Newburyport Marine Insurance Company*,[4] which involved a suit on a policy covering the schooner *Five Sisters* and her cargo on a voyage from Newburyport to Europe and back. At the Suffolk 1805 term the court heard *Lewis v. Gray*,[5] an action on a note for $4122.68, which involved a balance on accounts of more than $21,000. And these were appellate matters; other substantial litigation began and ended in the trial courts.

One should judge the sums involved remembering the value of the dollar; under the Judiciary Act of 1789 the United States

[3] See 1 Mass. Rep. 1 *et seq.* (1804).
[4] 1 Mass. 264.
[5] 1 Mass. 297.

44

district judges for the district of Maine, New Hampshire, and Connecticut were paid $1000 a year; for the district of Massachusetts $1200; associate justices of the Supreme Court of the United States received $3500 annually; the salary of the Attorney General of the United States was $1500. The short-lived Circuit Court Act of 1801 gave most circuit judges $2000 annually, but provided $1500 for those in less populous Circuits.[6] An industrious New England lawyer in the early years of the eighteenth century could expect comparative prosperity.

But was a career at the bar one for which a university should offer training? Scholars may have felt disturbed at the idea. One is reminded of the uneasiness that beset many academics nearly a century later at the prospect of a School of Business at Harvard. Training for the practice of law may have seemed to many men in 1815 something like training in merchandising methods. If education was to be practical, it would not be academically respectable; if it was to be respectably academic it must be professionally unprofitable. Professors and lawyers are highly conventional folk. The Governing Boards of Harvard might have chosen to use Royall's gift for a medical professorship. But in 1815 four of the seven Fellows of the Corporation were lawyers: John Lowell, John Phillips (later Mayor of Boston), Christopher Gore (former governor who had been elected to the United States Senate in 1814), and the Treasurer, Judge John Davis. Many of the Overseers were Lawyers, among them Josiah Quincy, who in 1829 was to succeed John Kirkland as President of Harvard.

The Governing Boards decided to apply the Royall fund "towards the Endowing a Professor of Laws" instead of a "Professor of Physick and Anatomy." The Corporation first offered Isaac Royall's professorship to one of their own Fellows, John Lowell. In our time a phenomenon not entirely uncommon is the lawyer with energy and wisdom who practices vigorously and successfully for a number of years, and is then able and inclined to spend the rest of his life in useful service to philanthropy and public affairs. This was John Lowell's career. In 1810 the Harvard Corporation elected him a Fellow, as a generation earlier that body had elected his father, whom President Washington had appointed a United States district judge. By 1815 John

---

[6] 1 Stat. at L.72; 2 Stat. at L.89. See also Story's "Report on the Salaries of the Judiciary," in his *Miscellaneous Writings*, p. 58.

Lowell had had experience both with the law in action and with the business of the university. He had available time to give to Harvard, which made him a natural leader in finally putting Isaac Royall's gift to effective use. Josiah Quincy later described John Lowell as yielding to none in zeal and affection for Harvard, a man of great learning and influence who "felt the power and possessed the spirit to attempt to lift the College upwards and to bestow upon it more of the character, as it already had the name, of a University." [7] In early 1815 Judge Davis, Harvard's Treasurer, told Justice Story that the Corporation was contemplating a professorship of law; [8] but selection of the professor was a critical question. On August 18, 1815, at a meeting of the Corporation attended by only four of the seven members, President Kirkland, Judge Phillips, Dr. Lathrop, and Treasurer Davis, that body

> *Voted*: That the corporation are desirous of taking measures to have delivered annually at the University for the benefit of the more advanced students a competent number of lectures on jurisprudence and that $400 of the income of the legacy of the late Isaac Royall, Esq., be appropriated each year towards a compensation for such lectures.
> *Voted*: To choose a gentleman to perform this service under such title and regulation as may hereafter be determined. John Lowell, Esq., was chosen.[9]

Kirkland thereupon wrote to Lowell that it was "thought necessary to have in view a proper lecturer before taking steps to complete the institution" and that the Corporation thought Lowell eminently fitted. Lowell refused the chair.

The temptation to write history as it might have happened is almost irresistible. Had Lowell accepted the new professorship, he could have dedicated to it all the time necessary to make the study of law at Harvard a significant part of the university's life. Harvard came to lean years in the late 1820's, and the Law School

---

[7] Josiah Quincy, *History of Harvard University* (1840), II, 354. President Quincy here speaks both of Chief Justice Parsons and of Lowell.
[8] Story so wrote his close friend Charles Pinckney Sumner (Senator Sumner's father) on June 31, 1815; William W. Story, *Life and Letters of Joseph Story* (Boston, 1851) I, 273.
[9] This version of the votes appears in two drafts of Kirkland's letter to Lowell, dated August 19 and 21, 1815. Harvard College Papers, VII and VIII. The records of the Corporation give a shorter version of the resolutions. This and subsequent quotations from Harvard records are printed by permission of the President and Fellows of Harvard College.

went into a near fatal decline; John Lowell might have kept matters going better, might have used his close friendship with leaders of the New England bars to attract able students, might have raised endowment, might have written books on the law as vigorous as his Federalist pamphlets. His administrative talents might so have cultivated an earlier growth of the Law School. On the other hand, John Lowell probably lacked the patient tolerance essential to any educating. He demonstrated the opinionated abruptness which was part of his decisive and confident character when he resigned from the Harvard Corporation in 1821 in a tiff with some other Fellows. Lowell was deeply conservative; he would not have been an innovator in legal education. His refusal of the Royall Chair may have been a good thing, for the 1828 crisis in the Law School's affairs ended with Story's appointment in 1829. Nothing could have turned out better. Retrospective reconstruction is a futile exercise after all.

At any rate, John Lowell, refusing the new professorship in 1815, urged instead the appointment of his Harvard classmate Isaac Parker, who the year before had become chief justice of Massachusetts and a Harvard Doctor of Laws. On September 4, 1815, the Corporation chose Chief Justice Parker as the new professor. They designated Messrs. Gore and Lowell a committee "to devise the rules and statutes for the professorship above named, and report." On September 14 the Corporation formally voted to name the new professorship for Isaac Royall.

The committee recommended statutes for the Chair:

Statute 1st. For the present, and so long as the principal support of the Professor shall be derived from the fund bequeathed by the late Hon. Isaac Royall, Esquire, the Professor shall be entitled "Royall Professor of Law"; but the Corporation reserved to themselves the right, with the assent of the Overseers, to change the title of said Professor, whenever and as soon as any such additions shall be made to the aforesaid fund as to render the sum bequeathed by the aforesaid Royall the smaller part of the whole foundation, or for any other good and sufficient reason not repugnant to the will of the said Royall.

Statute 2nd. The said Professor of Law shall be elected in the same manner in which other officers of the College are chosen, and shall hold the office during good behavior, but the Corporation, with the assent of the Overseers, may at any time remove him for any cause, which they may deem just and sufficient.

Statute 3rd. The said professor shall enjoy the privileges and rank which appertains of right to the other Professors in the College; but he shall not be obliged to reside in the town of Cambridge, nor shall he be called upon to take any part in the immediate government of the College, unless required so to do by the Corporation and Overseers; he shall, however, when requested by the Corporation, give his opinion on any questions of law immediately affecting the College, provided the delivery of such opinion shall not interfere with the said Professor's other duties.

Statute 4th. The said Professor shall enjoy all the authority while delivering his lectures to the students, as to the preservation of order and decorum and the regulation of the deportment of the students which other professors are entitled to exercise; and for any indecorum during his exercises or insult offered to him, the students shall be subject to such penalties as are provided in like case as to the other officers of the College; which penalties it shall be the duty of the immediate government, after examination, to apply.

Statute 5th. The said Professor shall before he enters on the duties of his office, subscribe these statutes, as well as the usual declaration prescribed in such cases to the other Professors.

Statute 6th. The course of lectures shall be delivered in some of the College Publick Rooms and shall consist of not less than fifteen; and until further order, the same shall be attended only by the Senior class among the Undergraduates; but the officers of the College including the Overseers and Corporation together with all the Resident Graduates shall have a right to attend the said Lectures gratis.

It shall be lawful for the said Professor to admit any other persons, not resident at the College on such terms and conditions as shall to the said Professor seem proper; provided that such arrangements be made as to numbers and seats at the lectures, as may consist with the suitable accommodation of the members of the College who attend.

Statute 7th. It shall be the duty of the said Professor to exhibit in a course of lectures, the theory of law in its most comprehensive sense; the principles and practical operation of the Constitution and Government of the United States and this Commonwealth; a history of the jurisprudence of this State under the Colonial and Provincial as well as under the present government; an explanation of the principles of the Common Law of England, the mode of its introduction into this country, and the sources and reasons of its obligation therein; also the various modifications by usage, judicial decision, and Statute; and, generally those topics connected with law as a science which will best lead the minds of students to such inquiries and researches as will qualify them to become useful and distinguished supporters of our free system of government, as well as able and honorable advocates on the rights of the citizen.[10]

On October 11, 1815, the Corporation adopted these statutes; on

[10] Harvard College Records, V, 208–209, quoted in Warren, *Harvard Law School*, I, 296–297.

the next day the Overseers concurred in the designation of Chief Justice Parker as the Royall Professor.

2

Parker was amiable, cheerful, endowed with common sense. Story wrote of Parker, when he died in 1830, that his mind was

cautious but liberal . . . a mind which with sufficient knowledge of the old law was yet not a slave to its forms; which was bold enough to invigorate it with new principles, not from the desire of innovation, but of love of improvement . . . [he had] sobriety of judgment; but at the same time, a free spirit . . . He may have had less juridical learning than some men; but no man more thoroughly mastered all that was before him.[11]

This balanced but kindly estimate of a brother judge bears internal evidence of its praiseworthy purpose, a public tribute to a departed friend. Story had fewer inhibitions when he was talking informally. He remarked to some students in November 1843:

Judge Parker was a good-natured, lazy boy when at college, became a good-natured, lazy lawyer, and made afterward a good-natured, lazy judge. He was universally beloved, always decided right, but gave miserable reasons for his opinions. While in the profession he used always to decide according to his own common sense, steering by the light of the Ten Commandments, and to advise his clients that that was the law.[12]

In 1834 William Sullivan wrote:

Chief Justice Parker was not supposed to be a learned lawyer when he first took his seat on the bench; but he proved to be one of the ablest judges that ever sat in this court. He was naturally disinclined to labor; but he had a clear and powerful mind . . . Whether his labors, or those of Chief Justice Parsons, in the same seat, were most useful to the Commonwealth, is a point, on which there may be difference of opinion. They were both eminently useful, but were, in many respects, very different men. They died at the same age, and

[11] "Sketch of the Character of Isaac Parker," in Story's *Miscellaneous Writings*, p. 813.
[12] Rutherford B. Hayes noted these remarks of Story's in Hayes's diary for November 27, 1843; Hayes was then a student at Harvard Law School, and often abstracted lectures in his diary; Charles Richard Williams in his *Life of Rutherford Birchard Hayes* (Columbus, Ohio, 1914), I, 36, quotes the statement, but does not disclose whether Story made it in a lecture or in offhand conversation. This and subsequent quotations from the Hayes papers are printed by permission of the Rutherford B. Hayes Library, Fremont, Ohio.

probably Parker could not remember as many hours of study, in his whole life, as Parsons could remember days.

The good-natured Judge Parker's portrait hangs in the Law School, in the Langdell entrance hall. So far as painted canvas can, it confirms Sullivan's contemporary description:

Parker was a man of middle stature, of full person and face, light or red complextion, blue eyes, and very high forehead, and remarkably bald. His manners were simple and without pretension to polish. He was very affable, amiable, and unpretending; and a most companionable, and agreeable associate, in private life. Perhaps no man excelled him in kind and friendly feelings. He used snuff immoderately; it affected his voice in his latter years, and may have had some agency in producing his sudden and lamented death.[13]

In our degenerate times installation of a professor of law is an informal matter. The dean (or perhaps one of his aides, a functionary the Latin orators at Commencement love to call a *Decanullus*) shows him his new office, complete with the new professor's name on the door, a telephone, empty bookshelves, and a half interest in a secretary. He receives by mail an impressive certificate of his appointment by the Governing Boards. Without more ceremony he assumes his place in our community of memory and hope.

A century and a half ago these matters were ordered with becoming pomp. Chief Justice Parker, Royall Professor-designate, was holding court on circuit until March, which delayed until April 17, 1816, the festival rites of his inaugural. When the day finally came the Overseers met in the Philosophy Chamber in Harvard Hall. The governor and lieutenant-governor were there. A procession formed of undergraduates, resident graduates, officers, Overseers, visitors, noted guests; they marched out of the Yard through the north gate, went 'round and re-entered the Yard by the gate fronting University Hall. There some of the junior participants formed two ranks between which the greater dignitaries passed and entered the chapel in University Hall.

[13] William Sullivan, *Familiar Letters on Public Characters and Public Events from the Peace of 1783 to the Peace of 1815* (Boston, 1834), letter LXXIII, p. 388. Sullivan was an interesting man who lived from 1774 to 1839. He was a Harvard A.B. of 1792 and practiced law successfully in Boston until his wife inherited enough money to relieve him from the need of day labor. He then took to writing. His *Familiar Letters*, his best known book, was republished in 1847 with notes and a sketch of the author written by his son, under the title *Public Men of the Revolution.*

President Kirkland offered prayer, delivered a Latin address on the importance of the profession of the law, and directed that the statutes of the new professorship be read. When that was done Kirkland declared Isaac Parker the Royall Professor of Law, bade him welcome, and invited him to deliver his inaugural address.

Perhaps Parker's words on that day were the greatest service of his life. His perception of the part a university should play in the formation of the legal profession was so wise, so prophetic, that he deserves quotation. Of the law he said:

A science like this is worthy to be taught for it cannot be understood without instruction; it should be admitted into fellowship with its fellow sciences, for like them, its ends are noble. Its fundamental and general principles should be a branch of liberal education in every country, but especially in those where freedom prevails and where every citizen has an equal interest in its preservation and improvement. Justice ought therefore to be done to the memory of *Royall* whose prospective wisdom and judicious liberality provided the means of introducing into the university the study of the law . . .

It is obvious that in the short course of lectures of which the present state of the institution will admit, nothing like a law education can be attempted; and, indeed, I am satisfied, after reflection upon the subject, that such an attempt, if practicable, would not be useful for undergraduates, who cannot devote the time necessary for any tolerable proficiency, without too great an abstraction from other studies, most of which are essential prerequisites to the study of the law . . .

At some future time, perhaps, a school for the instruction of resident graduates in jurisprudence may be usefully ingrafted in this professorship.

The Chief Justice, obviously and wisely, did not suppose that, in the seminary he envisaged, young resident graduates who might there study law would so become equipped at once to begin its public practice. He went on to explain that the university study he had in mind would be "preparatory to that acquisition of practical knowledge of business which may always be better learnt in the office of a distinguished counsellor." [14] So it is to this day. A modern law school does not purport to qualify its graduates for immediate independent practice. They are ready to serve useful apprenticeships in which they assume great responsibility for aiding their seniors. But training lawyers still

[14] Parker's inaugural address appears in full in *North American Review*, May 1816.

takes not only thorough training in classroom law, but some further years of practical experience under sound professional guidance.

The proposal to establish a "school for the instruction of resident graduates in jurisprudence" which Isaac Parker made at his inauguration and thereafter may have been his one great insight. His lectures as Royall Professor have not survived as Blackstone's did; Parker delivered the first discourse on June 5, 1816, and, as he somewhat vaguely reported, gave "seventeen or eighteen" lectures that summer rather than limiting himself to the statutory fifteen. The amount of material he undertook to discuss was amazing; the breadth of the stream suggests shallow waters. His first report stated:

> The subscribed, Royall Professor of Law at the University of Cambridge, reports that he delivered a course of lectures to the Senior Class in June and July last, consisting of an introductory lecture recommending the subjects of his course to their attention, four lectures comprising the Juridical History of the Colony, Province and Commonwealth with its various changes — one lecture on the organization of the judicial power of the State, one on the organization and powers of the courts of the United States — one on the Constitution of the Commonwealth and the various historical events which led to its adoption — one on the Constitution of the United States and the several antecedent confederacies — a lecture on Natural Law, one on the history of the common law, one on the civil law, one on ecclesiastical law — a history of the titles to real estate in this Commonwealth — on personal contracts and property — on the domestic relations — with two or three lectures on some of the subjects intended as explanations and illustrations, and a concluding lecture of a monitory nature in relation to the studies, deportment and general principles by which their success in life and usefulness to the public would be covered — On the whole, 17 or 18 lectures.
>
> The young gentlemen were, as far as I could discern, attentive, and their behavior unexceptionable; some of them took minutes and in conversation with them I was satisfied they had comprehended the subjects.
>
> I do not know the number that attended but think from the appearance there were not less than three fourths of the class present at every lecture.[15]

Parker's lectures hardly constituted a course of study. So far as we know he assigned no readings in preparation for his lec-

[15] Warren quotes Parker's report (*Harvard Law School*, I, 202, 303) but does not say where he found it. The Harvard College Papers for 1816 and 1817 do not contain it.

tures, and he gave no examinations to stiffen the attention of his hearers, not even the weekly oral quizzes called examinations in the academic regimes of that day. The students were passive recipients of whatever the Royall Professor offered them; his report that some took "minutes" suggests that the rest merely listened. Education occurs only when the student labors to educate himself; by this measurement Judge Parker's students assimilated only mild doses of law.

But one should not underrate Parker's work in 1816–17. His lectures probably accomplished what he hoped. Necessarily they were experimental popular discussions of matters then novel in Harvard's program; they had to hold the attention of their hearers by their general attractiveness. Sixty years later an undergraduate of the 1820's wrote:

Judge Parker's course comprised such facts and features of the common and statute law as a well educated man ought to know, together with an analysis and exposition of the Constitution of the United States. His lectures were clear, strong, and impressive; were listened to with great satisfaction, and were full of materials of practical interest and value. He bore a reputation worthy of his place in the line of Massachusetts chief justices; and the students, I think, fully appreciated the privilege of having for one of their teachers a man who had no recognized superior at the bar or on the bench.[16]

The Harvard Law School owes a great deal to Isaac Parker. Despite the limitations of his academic equipment Harvard needed the sound qualities he could give. Hard common sense, long experience with practicing lawyers seen from both sides of the bench, afforded him insights which a typical professor might have lacked. Probably early in 1817 he renewed with the Corporation his suggestion of an organized school of law within the uni-

[16] This estimate is that of the Reverend Dr. Andrew Preston Peabody, in his 1888 *Harvard Reminiscences* (Boston), p. 8. Dr. Peabody's book suggests the grace and charm of its author, a kindly and religious man but very far from a benign simpleton. He was many things at Harvard, from a prodigy who, in 1824, at the age of thirteen entered college as a junior, to an A.B. in 1826, a student in the Divinity School, a proctor in a residential hall, a tutor in mathematics, preacher to the university, Plummer Professor, and, in 1868–69, acting president. He knew nineteenth century Harvard, its men and its spirit, as few can have known it. His *Harvard Reminiscences* at times sound a note of amused and sophisticated tolerance for the frailties of mankind, for example, in his description of "certain ancient resident graduates who had become water-logged on their life voyage" (p. 211). Their charity suggests the feeling which led the Harvard chapter of Phi Beta Kappa to compose the touching inscription on the plaque erected to Dr. Peabody's memory in Memorial Church.

versity, the theme he had advanced in his inaugural address. He submitted this recommendation in a paper written in his own hand; later some one noted on it in pencil "May 14, 1817," the day on which the Corporation considered Parker's proposal. He reviews the disadvantage of "reading law" in the office of a practitioner who is too busy to tutor his students; he makes a half-apology for the limitations under which he himself suffered as a professor, limitations imposed by the urgency of his duties as chief justice which, for him, made teaching an avocation. A year's experience as Royall Professor had shown Parker that if Harvard were to found a law school to serve for professional formation, some qualified professor would have to undertake teaching and administration as his principal concern, not as an activity ancillary to another calling. Judge Parker wrote for the Corporation's considerations

The present mode of education is necessarily deficient, as it is obtained principally in the offices of eminent practitioners, who are unable from their constant application to business, to act the part of instructors. It is believed that a school at Cambridge, under the immediate care of a learned lawyer, whose attention would be principally directed to the instruction of his pupils, would afford opportunities for laying a solid foundation of professional knowledge, which would be cheerfully embraced, and would be found highly beneficial. The undersigned proposes that there should be a vote of the Government, establishing such a school, and constituting a department connected with the University.

He would, he wrote, give to the School as much time as his judicial duty permitted.[17]

Parker proposed a tuition of $100 a year, which he described as "the average price of education in the country." What he meant is not clear; Harvard's annual tuition for undergraduates was $20 in 1807; it did not reach $55 until 1825. The student also required shelter, food, clothing, and books; the total annual cost of maintaining an undergraduate in Harvard in 1816 ran somewhere between $300 and $600. Perhaps Parker meant that $100 was the average annual fee then charged by a first-rate lawyer for accepting a pupil in his office. If so the cost seems a bit high, considering the diffuse and random instruction such a master usually gave his apprentice, and the amount of copying office papers and similar donkey work the apprentice usually did for his master.

[17] Harvard College Papers, vol. VIII; Warren, *Harvard Law School*, I, 305.

In 1816 better methods of studying law were under consideration at other American universities. David Hoffman, newly appointed professor of law in the University of Maryland, in that year wrote *A Course of Legal Study; Respectfully Addressed to the Students of Law in the United States*. Hoffman, an extraordinarily perceptive scholar, deserves credit for clear and early exposition of many ideas that later bore fruit at Harvard. He was at home in the civil law as well as in English legal literature. Eminent success at the Maryland bar had given him a hardheaded understanding of the value, to the practitioner, of a comprehensive theoretical foundation on which to build a knowledge of practical detail. His exposition of the idea that the law is consciously devised for the good of the society in which it exists is surely not surprising; politicians and philosophers have emphasized this theme for centuries beyond remembering. Nevertheless, rediscovery and clear restatement of an obvious theme is a service for which the world rightly looks to successive generations of scholars; and Hoffman, in his *Course of Legal Study* lucidly stated this aspiration to sociological shaping of law more than sixty years before Holmes published his *Common Law*, nearly a century before Pound began his exposition of sociological jurisprudence at Harvard, and well over a century before Jerome Frank in *Law and the Modern Mind* sounded a keynote for writers on legal realism in 1930.[18]

Hoffman wrote with a disciplined, sophisticated style. "If law be a science and really deserve so sublime a name, it must be founded on principle, and claim an exalted rank in the empire of reason; but if it be merely an unconnected series of decrees and ordinances, its use may remain, though its dignity be lessened, and he will become the greatest lawyer who has the strongest habitual or artificial memory. Jurists should strive toward that object, for which all laws are framed, and all societies instituted, the Good of Mankind." [19] Legislators, judges and law writers may well draw their material from books not conventionally "legal." Hoffman quotes Sir James Mackintosh [20] for approval of such

---

[18] See Dean Eugene V. Rostow's discussion of the legal realism movement in the first chapter of his *Sovereign Prerogative* (New Haven: Yale University Press, 1962).

[19] *A Course of Legal Study* (Baltimore, 1817), p. xi.

[20] Sir James Mackintosh, born in Invernesshire in 1765, studied medicine at Edinburgh, then moved to London, and first attracted attention by his *Vindiciae Gallicae*, an answer to Burke's *Reflections on the French Revolution*. Mackintosh left medicine for the bar, became a judge in India, and subsequently entered

nonlegal sources, still discussed with blame and with praise, a century and a half later.

No system of moral philosophy can surely disregard the general feelings of human nature, and the according judgment of all ages and nations. But where are these feelings and that judgment recorded? . . . The usages and laws of nations, the events of history, the opinions of philosophers, the sentiments of orators and poets, as well as the observations of common life, are, in truth, the materials out of which the science of morality is formed; and those who neglect them are justly chargeable with a vain attempt to philosophize without regard to fact and experience, the sole foundation of all philosophy.

Books of theory alone are of course not enough, writes Hoffman. The student must go to the reported cases; but he must have a theoretical foundation. The Maryland professor provides a detailed bibliography as the main part of his book; he explains the inclusion of the various works he prescribes, and suggests the method of their study.

Hoffman's work was well known at Harvard. In 1817 Mr. Justice Story wrote for the *North American Review* a long and favorable discussion of Hoffman's regime, calling it "by far the most perfect system for the study of the law which has ever been offered to the public." It would "demonstrate to the understanding of every discerning man the importance, nay, the necessity, of the law-school, which the Government of Harvard College have, so honorably to themselves, established at Cambridge." Story's article demonstrated his own scholarship, and his alert interest in the most advanced contemporary thought about university education in the law, a cause to which he gave effective help all the rest of his life.

As Story's words indicated, Harvard's Governing Boards, earlier in 1817, had accepted Parker's proposal for a School of Law.

At a meeting of the Corporation of May 14, 1817, present, 1, The President; 2, Mr. Gore; 3, Judge Davis (Treas.); 4, Mr. Lowell; 5, Judge Phillips.

The Royall Professor of Law, having represented to this Board, that, in his opinion and in that of many friends of the University, and of the improvement of our youth, the establishment of a school for the instruction of students at law, at Cambridge, under the patronage of

---

Parliament. He is now best remembered for his writings on history and moral philosophy. The quotation here is drawn from Mackintosh's *Introductory Discourse* (London, 1799), p. 15; it occurs in Hoffman's *Course of Legal Study*, p. 74.

the University, will tend much to the better education of young men destined to that profession, and will increase the reputation and use-fullness of this Seminary; and the Corporation concurring in these views, it was voted, as follows:

1. That some Counsellor, learned in the law, be elected, to be denominated University Professor of Law, who shall reside in Cambridge, and open and keep a school for the instruction of graduates of this or any other university, and of such others as, according to the rules of admission, as attorneys, may be admitted after five years study in the office of some Counsellor.

2. That it shall be the duty of this officer, with the advice of the Royall Professor of Law, to prescribe a course of study, to examine and confer with the students upon the subjects of their studies, and to read lectures to them appropriate to the course of their studies, and their advancement in the science, and generally, to act the part of a tutor to them, in such manner as will improve their minds and assist their acquisitions.

3. The compensation for this instruction is to be derived from the students; and a sum not exceeding one hundred dollars a year shall be paid by each one attaching himself to this school; but this sum shall be subject to be reduced hereafter by the Corporation, if, in their judgment the emoluments of the school shall make such reduction reasonable, and consistent with the interests of the establishment.

4. The students shall have access to the college library on such terms as the Government of the University shall prescribe, and a complete Law Library be obtained for their use as soon as means for that purpose may be found.

5. The students shall be permitted to board in commons on the same terms as the other members of the college; and such accommodation shall be afforded them in respect to lodging rooms, as may consist with the urgent claims of the existing establishment.

6. As an excitement to diligence and good conduct, a degree of bachelor of laws shall be instituted at the University, to be conferred on such students as shall have remained at least eighteen months at the University School, and passed the residue of their noviciate in the office of some counsellor of the Supreme Court of the Commonwealth, or who shall have remained three years in the school, or if not a graduate of any college, five years, provided the Professor having charge of the same shall continue to be a practitioner in the Supreme Judicial Court.

7. The Students shall have the privilege of attending the lectures of the Royall Professor of Law, free of expense, and shall have access to the other Lectures of the University usually allowed to be attended by resident graduates, without charge, or for such reasonable compensation, as the Corporation, with the assent of the Overseers, shall determine.

8. The law students shall give bonds for the payment of the college

dues, including the charge of the Professor for instruction, which shall be inserted in the quarter bills and collected by the college officer; and the sums received for instruction, shall, when received be paid over by said officer to the Professor.

9. The Law Students shall be on the same footing generally, in respect to privileges, duties and observances of College regulations, as by the laws pertain to resident graduates.

Voted That the foregoing votes constituting a new department at the University be laid before the Overseers that they may approve the same if they see fit.

Agreeably to the statutes relative to a Law School at the University, Ballots being brought in the Hon. Asahel Stearns was chosen.[21]

The Law School was thus to be a mingled graduate and non-graduate institution, open to Harvard graduates or those of any other university, and "such others as . . . may be admitted after five years study in the office of some Counsellor." The plan provided for a new University Professor of Law,[22] resident in Cambridge, who was to "open and keep" the School, and give continuous administrative and educational attention to its students. The Statutes of the School put on the University Professor the main burdens of planning and conducting its program. With the advice of the Royall Professor, he was to prescribe a course of study for candidates in law, "examine [23] and confer with" them, "generally, to act the part of a tutor to them," and "to read lectures to them appropriate to the course of their studies."

On June 12, 1817, the Overseers concurred in the Corporation's plan for a Law School, and on June 26, they concurred in the choice of Asahel Stearns as the University Professor of Law. He had graduated from Harvard College in 1797, and had got his first learning in the law by studying in the office of Timothy Bigelow at Groton. He had formerly practiced law in two Massachusetts towns, Lunenburg and Charlestown. When he assumed his pro-

[21] See Warren, *Harvard Law School*, I, 305, who dates the birth of Harvard Law School May 14, the day of these votes. Would not the date of approval by the Overseers be more appropriate?

[22] In 1817 a "university professor" was one who derived his sustenance from general university funds rather than from a "name" endowment. The term now describes the occupant of one of the new chairs created under a 1936 plan for scholars of distinction not attached to any department, working "in such a way as to cross the conventional boundaries of the specialists."

[23] "Examine" as there used means to question orally about current studies. When the first students were candidates for degrees the Corporation devised a more formal inquest into the state of their learning, as a criterion of their qualification.

fessorship at the age of forty-three he had recently ended a term in Congress, and he was district attorney for Middlesex County, whose Court House stood where the Harvard Cooperative Society building now stands, facing the present-day Harvard Square. His duties as prosecutor were probably not very time-consuming, and he continued in that public office along with his university professorship.

3

When did the Law School come into being? In any real sense there was no single instant of birth; the School developed through months and years. But June 12, 1817, the day on which the Overseers agreed to "the establishment of a school for the instruction of students at law, at Cambridge, under the patronage of the University" is as good a day as any to mark the origin of the Harvard Law School.

Corporate personality has always mystified people. For a century and a half men have quite rightly been ascribing an identity to the Law School within its parent Harvard University. The School has accumulated deep loyalties, great traditions, warm affections, sometimes dislikes more or less violent. Walter Bagehot, a century ago, reminded political scientists that the British Constitution in long-established practice differed widely from the description of Britain's fundamental structure prescribed in a few institutional documents like the Great Charter and the Bill of Rights. To the Briton "the Constitution" means some of his habits of government so established by long usage that they constitute a prescription as difficult to change as parts of the Constitution of the United States. The Harvard Law School has never had a separate charter like the charter of Dartmouth College. In the legalities of its life, its students, its officers of instruction and administration, its magnificent collection of writings, its buildings, and its funds, all are ascribable to the President and Fellows of Harvard College. Yet the School has its Constitution. No sensible man would suggest that it has no identity. Its flavor, its habits of study, the qualities of its students and its teachers, its customs, its pride, all for better or for worse are distinguishable from other parts of the university. The School is very much a part of Harvard, but it needs no parchment and pressed wax to give it a personality of its own.

Harvard's offer of the degree of Bachelor of Laws as "an excitement to diligence and good conduct" of its students instituted a degree new at that university. Candidates at Harvard could earn this distinction by successfully completing whatever academic achievements might be prescribed, and by remaining in residence for eighteen months, for three years, or for five years. Eighteen months of residence sufficed for those who "passed the residue of their noviciate in the office of some counsellor of the Supreme Court of the Commonwealth." As at the present day, those who already held a first degree from some college or university could earn a Bachelor of Laws by successfully completing three years of study in residence. Candidates with no previous degree could become Bachelors of Laws by five successful years of resident study of law at Harvard.

A truly excellent university school of law must have four essentials. Fundamental is an honorable, brilliant, mature, energetic, and imaginative group of students, large enough to produce among themselves that interaction which is the most effective means, perhaps the only effective means, of a vigorous intellectual life. They must have a deep conviction that the law is an essential element of civilization; they must bring to their study a developed consciousness that man cannot decently exist in a society without effective norms to make social coexistence tolerable.

The school must also have teacher-scholars, sufficient in number to maintain the same intellectual interaction among themselves, and to stimulate it among the students with whom they live and study. They must have the same urges and convictions essential for the students, but these traits must have been matured and deepened by experience and thought, and by their own exposition of ideas, spoken and written, which will stimulate and guide students. These teachers must have acquired some wise foresight from their experience and thought, to the end that their study and writing and intellectual guidance may relate not only to the past but may look to the movement of society in the years ahead when the older men will have left the scene, and when their students will in their turn play leading parts in the wise guidance of developing civilization.

The school must have an apparatus of books. Decent social existence of mankind requires resolution of an endless series of conflicts between inconsistent aspirations of one man and another, and between aspirations of groups of men inconsistent with aspirations of other groups. To resolve every such conflict of interest as if it were brand new would be as wasteful of irretrievable energy and time as solving each morning, by original intellectual effort, the mechanics of buttoning a shirt. Some human needs can be served reasonably well by doing what has been habitual. The experience of the race in resolving social conflicts is collected in books; a university school of law needs all the books it can get, conveniently accessible. Many books requisite for study of philosophy, of government, of history, of other established academic mysteries are also necessary or desirable for any scholarship related to the law. The catalogues of the Harvard College library, beginning nearly a century before the Law School came into being, show that the university's governors understood this from the beginning. But if a school of law is to flourish, its library must be close at hand, where its students, of all ages and ranks, can live with books as they live with one another. Scholars in the law must come to use their apparatus of books as familiarly, as easily and instinctively, as a trained soldier uses his rifle. "Legal" books or other, they must be ready to hand.

A school must have a house for its scholars and its library. The intellectual reaction of collegial existence only occurs when older and younger scholars can live together, eat together, talk easily together, write and read in consultation with one another, excite one another by their explorations and their discoveries. Those who founded the Colleges at medieval English universities knew this; so did the lawyers who founded the Inns of Court. Term dinners in halls, dwelling quarters on staircases off old courtyards, excited argument of an evening about the reasons for things as they are and as they should be, a chance for privacy in study when privacy is needed, and a timely chance for community existence with fellows in the mystery, — these ancient amenities and their modern analogues have always been far more than pleasant luxuries. One can do without them, as one can do without much else and still do well enough. But all are essentials for living the best scholarly life.

The growth of these four elements — students, scholar-teachers, a library, and a house — during the Harvard Law School's life, cannot be recounted in neatly separated essays. Each element depends on the others: students seek great teachers; talented men will give up much to teach able students; great books well housed draw both. To some extent all four prerequisites depend on factors extraneous to the school itself. Wars, financial depressions, sometimes even fashion, can affect the resort of students to any academy. No man, no matter what his resources, can create at one stroke a school in which all four requisites are vigorously reacting. A company of scholars must grow.

4

The Corporation quartered its newborn Law School in two or three ground-floor rooms of a onetime dwelling, formerly the house of President Webber, sometimes called "Farrar House" for another former occupant, often in 1817 called "College House Number 2." It was a gambrel-roofed structure standing on the west side of what is now Harvard Square, a little north of the present building of the Harvard Trust Company. At 1430 Massachusetts Avenue today's passer-by sees the modern refurbished entrance to a nineteenth century brick mansarded former dormitory. An inscription on the glass doorway denominates this office building "College House." It stands on the spot where the Harvard Law School began its life.

In the fall of 1817 Charles Moody Dustin of Gardiner, Maine, appeared at the School for enrollment. His name is the earliest in the pen-and-ink alphabetical record book showing student registration in the years 1817 to 1840. Dustin had no previous degree, and left before 1817 ended. He was fated to live only until 1824; he died at Thorndike, Ohio. Of Charles Dustin this is all we know; he was the first of about forty thousand students who in the last century and a half have spent some time at the School.

Six students came in the first year. During the entire Parker-Stearns tenure, from 1817 to 1829,[24] one hundred and four men spent shorter or longer periods in residence. More than half, fifty-five, had already taken Harvard A.B.'s. Nineteen held that degree from other colleges or universities; six from Dartmouth, three from Brown, two each from Hampden-Sidney and Williams, and one each from Bowdoin, Columbia, North Carolina, Princeton, Union, and Yale. Although the School was already predominently a grad-

---

[24] Chief Justice Parker resigned in November 1827. Stearns stayed until April 1829. Here it seems wise to treat the tenure of the two as a single unit.

uate institution, thirty of its first one hundred and four students held no previous degree. The year 1820 saw the largest enrollment in any one year of the Parker-Stearns era; twenty-four men spent at least part of 1820 at the School. Probably there were never more than about twelve men in residence at any one time; to be precise is difficult, for students could and did come or go at almost any moment of the year, and the record book omits the date of arrival during the early years. Orderly arrangement of classes was impossible; there was no "class" of a given year in the modern sense.

During those twelve years, 1817 to 1829, only twenty-five men, less than one in four of those enrolled, became Bachelors of Laws; six took the degree in 1820; two in 1822; two in 1823; nine in 1825; one in 1826; four in 1827; and one in 1828. Three of these men, William Howard Freeman, LL.B. 1825, Luther Stearns Cushing, LL.B. 1826, and Robert Birchett, LL.B. 1827, had taken no previous degree. Almost a third of the graduate students, twenty-two of the seventy-four, took LL.B.'s; but only three nongraduates of thirty proceeded to Bachelors of Laws.

One should not attach too much significance to degrees in the 1820's. Emory Washburn entered the Law School in 1820, never took his LL.B., became governor of the Commonwealth, was first holder of the Bussey Professorship of law, and wrote the basic text on real property which cut the pattern for instruction in that subject to this day. And indeed Roscoe Pound, who came to the School in 1889, who stayed only one year and never took an "earned" law degree, became dean of the School, and in his time was the most eminent legal scholar in the world. In the 1820's legal education was a practical matter. A man read law in an office or studied in a school not primarily for academic rank, but to enable him to qualify for a license to practice law and to cope with professional duties thereafter. He came to Harvard when he felt a need for organized study of law and left when he thought he had had enough.

After a century and a half no one can say what law students of the 1820's thought about their stay at the School. Compared to three hundred undergraduates they were very few. The four or five Harvard A.B.'s in residence at the Law School at any one time undoubtedly felt at home, though perhaps they were a little wistful with their college classmates gone away. Dartmouth and Hampden-Sidney men and their brethren from other colleges, and *a fortiori* the graduates of no college at all, must have felt like cats in a strange garret. Law students were eligible for rooms only after Harvard College undergraduates had had first choice; they probably got sorry enough lodgings. But they worked under Professor Stearns in what amounted to a tutorial system, kept exemplary notes of lectures, and carried on a vigorous moot-court program with regular meetings. Some of them became great men in their calling. Caleb Cushing came in 1818 and stayed one year; Rufus Choate entered in 1820 and spent only a few months at the School. Neither took a degree; both, like the great majority of their fellows, finished their studies of law elsewhere. Both had eminent careers in professional and public life. How much credit the School can claim for such men, no one can say. Indeed any teacher in somber moments can wonder what his part has been in the formation of his students, and can only comfort himself with the reflection that every teacher feels the same doubts.

Harvard, in those days as now, was a pleasant community. The entire university's population was smaller than that in one of the present undergraduate houses; every member could know every other. A college whose president was the gentle and urbane Kirkland, whose faculty included George Ticknor in Romance Languages, Edward Tyrrel Channing as Boylston Professor of Rhetoric and Oratory, Edward Everett in Greek, and Joseph Green Cogswell in science, must have been a stimulating place. And Cambridge in the 1820's was a charming village. James Russell Lowell [25] wrote of it thirty years later:

Boston was not yet a city, and Cambridge was still a country village, with its own habits and traditions, not yet feeling too strongly the force of suburban gravitation. Approaching it from the west by what was then called the New Road (so called no longer, for we change our names as readily as thieves, to the great detriment of all historical association), you would pause on the brow of Symonds' Hill to enjoy a view singularly soothing and placid. In front of you lay the town, tufted with elms, lindens, and horse-chestnuts, which had seen Massachusetts a colony, and were fortunately unable to emigrate with the Tories, by whom, or by whose fathers, they were planted. Over it rose the noisy belfry of the College, the square, brown tower of the church, and the slim, yellow spire of the parish meeting-house, by no means ungraceful, and then an invariable characteristic of New England religious architecture. On your right, the Charles slipped

[25] LL.B. 1840. The quotation comes from his *Cambridge Thirty Years Ago* (1854); he must have been five years old at the time he describes.

smoothly through green and purple salt-meadows, darkened, here and there, with the blossoming black-grass as with a stranded cloud-shadow. Over these marshes, level as water, but without its glare, and with softer and more soothing gradations of perspective, the eye was carried to a horizon of softly rounded hills. To your left hand, upon the Old Road, you saw some half dozen dignified old houses of the colonial time, all comfortably fronting southward. If it were early June, the rows of horse-chestnuts along the fronts of these houses showed, through every crevice of their dark heap of foliage, and on the end of every drooping limb, a cone of pearly flowers, while the hill behind was white or rosy with the crowding blooms of various fruit-trees . . .

We called it "the Village" then (I speak of Old Cambridge), and it was essentially an English village, quiet, unspeculative, without enterprise, sufficing to itself, and only showing such differences from the original type as the public school and the system of town government might superinduce. A few houses, chiefly old, stood around the bare Common, with ample elbow-room, and old women, capped and spectacled, still peered through the same windows from which they had watched Lord Percy's artillery rumble by to Lexington, or caught a glimpse of the handsome Virginia General who had come to wield our homespun Saxon chivalry. People were still living who regretted the late unhappy separation from the mother island, who had seen no gentry since the Vassalls went, and who thought that Boston had ill kept the day of her patron saint, Botolph, on the 17th day of June, 1775. The hooks were to be seen in Massachusetts Hall from which had been swung the hammocks of Burgoyne's captive redcoats.

Parker and Stearns did their best to build the Law School. The Chief Justice undoubtedly carried out his promise of 1817 "to bestow as much of his time upon the school as can be spared from his other public duties, and . . . in the intervals of his judicial labours, visit the school as often as possible, converse with the students on the subjects they may be engaged in, examine them occasionally, and as often as possible read to them a prepared lecture upon such subjects as shall be found most conducive to their improvement." [26] But his judicial duties were exacting and

[26] See his letter to the Corporation written early in 1817, page 54 above. Occasionally some one wonders whether Parker was part of the Law School faculty, or whether the Royall professorship was solely ascribable to Harvard College. One answer may be that a century and a half ago the two functions were less distinct than they have since become. On May 14, 1817, the Corporation directed Professor Stearns to devise a curriculum for the Law School and supervise the studies of its members "with the advice of the Royall Professor of Law" (page 57 above). Of course Stearns could advise with Parker even if Parker were on another faculty. On August 28, 1820, an examining committee of Fellows

imperative. In September 1825 the Supreme Judicial Court held a Berkshire County term in Lenox, and a term for the counties of Hampshire, Franklin, and Hampden at Northampton. In October the Court held a Worcester County term at Worcester, a Middlesex term at Cambridge, a term at Plymouth for the counties of Plymouth, Barnstable, Bristol, and Dukes County, and a term at Dedham for Norfolk County. In November the Court held an Essex term at Salem. It then recessed until March 1826, when it held a term for Suffolk and Nantucket counties in Boston. Beside these stated duties, in June 1826 the Court rendered an advisory opinion to the House of Representatives of the Commonwealth, at that body's request. Days on the bench obviously require many days of work in chambers. Undoubtedly the Royall Professor worked with much effort and good will earning the $400 salary appropriated for his Harvard lectures, but most of the time he must have directed his thoughts elsewhere.

Asahel Stearns has never been given the credit he deserves for his energetic day-in-day-out planning, teaching, and administration of the School. Andrew Preston Peabody, who knew him in the 1820's, afterward wrote of him: [27]

Professor Stearns was regarded as second in legal learning to no man of his time. He published a work on "Real Actions", which gave him reputation; and he was one of the commissioners for revising the Statute Law of Massachusetts. He was warmly interested in the public charities of his day, exercised a generous hospitality, and was equally respected and beloved. He was a man of grave and serious aspect and demeanor, but by no means devoid of humor, and was a favorite in society. His wife was a lovely woman, full of good works; and there was never a sick student in college whom she did not take under special charge, even watching with him by night, superintending all that was done for his relief and comfort, and, in his convalescence, feeding him from or at her own table till he could return without loathing to the coarse fare of Commons' Hall.

He was well read. Dr. Peabody tells of a journey to the White Mountains in a stagecoach, when Stearns, Peabody, and some students were fellow passengers with a decidedly dour clergyman. At the sight of Mount Washington the severe cleric observed that

reported to the rest of the Corporation and the Overseers that "at a meeting of the Faculty of Law at the College" they had examined six candidates. A "meeting of the Faculty of Law" sounds like more than one person.

[27] *Harvard Reminiscences,* p. 52.

A NORTH EAST View
or
THE HOUSE of SAMUEL WEBBER A.M., and of The COURT HOUSE

By an actual survey

In 1817 Harvard quartered its new Law School in two or three ground-floor rooms of "College House Number 2," once President Webber's. This drawing, perhaps made about 1800 by a student as an exercise in surveying, now hangs in Langdell Hall.

the magnificent scene must be mean and paltry in God's eyes. Stearns calmly quoted Pope:

> To Him no high, no low, no great, no small:
> He fills, he bounds, connects and equals all.

Professor Stearns had all the qualities of a great teacher of law except forward-looking imagination. He was experienced and learned in the law, was completely devoted to duty, took endless pains with the program of the School, planned the instruction with intelligent care, worked literally day and night with and for his students. He dedicated his *Law and Practice of Real Actions* to the Harvard law students "as testimony of his earnest desire to aid them in the honorable and laborious study of American Jurisprudence."

He deserves no ungenerous blame for not foreseeing the future; but allotment of blame and estimate of optimum qualification for planning a curriculum useful for the year after next are quite different matters. When Asahel Stearns became a university professor in 1817 the steamboat was revolutionizing American travel. Business corporations organized to manufacture textiles were springing up in Massachusetts. John Marshall's Supreme Court was foretelling the dominance of the federal government over the states. The Winning of the West, as a future president was to call it, was already well under way; westward continental occupation was to affect the American Constitution and law in many new ways. Meantime Stearns was writing a text on a variety of law suits soon to disappear when badly needed reforms of procedure made them unnecessary. Stearns was no crusader for law reform. He was the first really systematic teacher of law at Harvard; he began many teaching procedures which have persisted at the Law School to the present day; for this he has had scant justice. But Stearns did not write or teach for the future, and foresight is one essential of greatness. Yet any man can well ask himself, a little sadly, how much of his own work has really been done with due regard to the changes tomorrow will bring. If the questioner is honest with himself, he probably hangs his head.

Appointed University Professor of Law on June 26, 1817, Stearns went to work at once. From the first he saw the necessity of a separate law library, immediately accessible to students of the School. On July 11 he sent to President Kirkland a draft for a public announcement of the School's establishment, and on the following day the Boston *Daily Advertiser* carried a notice of the School's beginning, listing the privileges which it would give to its students. They were to have "access to the College library, and a complete Law Library, to be obtained for their use." Another announcement on July 28 somewhat elaborated this statement: "The Law Students are to have access to the University Library (consisting of 20,000 volumes), upon the same terms as other resident graduates, as well as to the Law Library which shall be established."

Harvard College had from the beginning included in its library a few books concerning the common law, a collection of Roman law and civil law material, and books on what would now be considered political theory or political science. The fire of 1764 destroyed Harvard's collection of about 5000 books save for a few volumes which were out on loan. Like some other disasters this may have had good results, may have stimulated gifts of even better works. After the fire Thomas Hollis, whom Warren calls "father of the Law Library," gave the college a number of rare and valuable books on legal subjects, including some classical common-law treatises, Bracton, Glanvill, Horne's *Mirror*, Barrington's *Observations on the Statutes*, and Bacon's *Historical Discourses*. Hollis must have considered the common law important for prerevoluntionary Harvard. He also included in his gift a substantial number of books on civil law, on ecclesiastical law, and Prynne's "Soveraigne Power of Parliaments and Kingdomes," which the 1790 catalogue lists under *Jus Naturale et Politicum*.

In 1779 Chief Justice Theodore Atkinson of New Hampshire bequeathed to the college £100 to buy "such books as may be thought useful in the study of civil, statute and common law of England. The books so purchased to be placed in that part of the College library assigned for the donations made by the Province of New Hampshire, the gilded letter T. A. to be impressed upon one of the covers of each volume." In 1787 John Gardiner, a native of Massachusetts who had been educated at the Inns of Court, gave the college a number of desirable legal treatises. In 1814 the Corporation authorized the purchase of $300 worth of books at the sale of the library of the late Chief Justice Parsons. On September 5, 1817, the Corporation authorized the Treasurer and the "Professor of Law" to spend $500 to buy law books. As enthusiastic book buyers will, Stearns spent the whole $500, spent another

$100 given by Mr. John Howe of Boston, and spent $81.74 more out of his own pocket. The Corporation on November 17, 1819, approved this largesse and, remarkably enough, authorized the University Professor of Law to take into his custody from the college library such books as "the Committee of the Corporation" might think proper. Stearns assembled books from all these sources in the quarters allotted to the new Law School in College House Number 2.

In library management as in society generally, liberty and authority tend to conflict. In 1819 a committee of Overseers appointed to visit the library made a report deploring this "parcelling out the Library into private houses, beyond the care of the College Librarian." Still the separate law library grew. Between 1817 and 1826 Christopher Gore, late governor of the Commonwealth, gave to the college for the use of law students the greater part of his own library including rare old books which had belonged to Robert Auchmuty, James Otis, Jeremiah Gridley, and Samuel Sewall.[28]

In 1826 the Overseers' library committee, commenting on the continued removal of law books from the main library to the office of the "Professor of Law," suggested "the propriety of having a catalogue of what is now called the Law Library." Later in that year two students, John B. Hill and William B. Stearns (son of Professor Stearns), at the request of the School's other students, prepared the first law library catalogue. The pamphlet, printed by "University Press — Hilliard and Metcalf," is twenty-five pages long. The present Law School library copy contains ink notes in an unknown hand on the flyleaf, explaining odd pen-and-ink symbols inserted opposite the several titles. These indicate the sources of the books in the law library. They identify Governor Gore's contributions; books withdrawn from the general college library; books listed in the law library, but still shelved in the college library. Some books belonged to the University Professor individually; some he had had purchased for the School "to be paid for

[28] Robert Auchmuty was a prominent lawyer in Boston, in prerevolutionary times. He was a friend of Otis, Quincy, John Adams, and other men well known in Massachusetts of the 1770's. But Auchmuty, an ardent loyalist, removed to England in 1776. His property was confiscated and in 1784 his library was sold by order of the authorities. Samuel Sewall, 1757–1814, Harvard A.B. 1776, practiced in Marblehead, went to Congress, was an associate justice of the Massachusetts Supreme Judicial Court from 1801 to 1813, and chief justice, 1813–1814. For John Adams' older friend and adviser Jeremiah Gridley see above, Chap. I, note 25. James Otis does not need a footnote.

out of the Makepeace debt." Some he had bought in 1817 and 1819 with funds furnished by the college, and with the donation of $100 from John Howe of Boston; some were given by a resolve of the legislature obtained by the professor in 1818. The cataloguers used the zero symbol for a sorrowful category: "Books missing."

The Makepeace notation deserves a comment. Professor Stearns not only taught law but, in addition to his other duties, from time to time acted as counsel to the university. In 1823 Stearns was trying to collect $4293 which one Royal Makepeace owed to Harvard. Stearns effected a settlement by taking Makepeace's note for $4310; Makepeace then, for a credit of $3200 on the note, conveyed a one-fifth interest in four lots, and three acres of marsh, all near Lechmere Point. In 1825 Stearns had spent $700 of his own money for the Law School's books, and was hoping to make it up out of the Makepeace proceeds.

The 1826 catalogue includes 1752 volumes in all. Aside from books which had been withdrawn from the college library, and from Professor Stearns's own books, there were about 280 titles ascribable to the law library proper.[29]

From 1817 to 1832 the Corporation continued to house its Law School in two or three rooms on the ground floor of College House Number 2. The handful of students lived wherever they could find quarters, and if they chose could eat rather dreary meals for $1.75 a week at the college Commons in University Hall. They had permission to live in such university lodgings as might "consist with the urgent claims of the existing establishment," an offer which probably gave law students no great choice. Dr. Peabody wrote of College House Number 2, and its next-door structure College House Number 1:

The upper stories of these buildings were occupied, in part, by undergraduates who could not get rooms within the college-yard; in great part, by certain ancient resident graduates who had become water-logged on their life-voyage, by preachers who could not find willing hearers, by men lingering on the threshold of professions for which they had neither the courage nor the capacity . . . in fine, by such waifs of literary purlieus as in these faster days would be speedily blown away.[30]

[29] See J. H. Arnold, "The Harvard Law Library," *Harvard Graduates' Magazine* 16:230 (1907); and the *Centennial History of the Harvard Law School* (Cambridge, 1918), Chap. III. One title often includes several volumes.

[30] *Harvard Reminiscences*, pp. 210–211. In 1825 Professor George Ticknor had

In the spring of 1825 Stearns earnestly urged the Corporation to provide more suitable quarters for the School. A memorandum of the steward, Stephen Higginson, dated July 18, 1825, recites Stearns's aspiration to a new brick house, where twenty students could live at an annual rental of $30 each, where the professor could have an office, and where students could work in a library thirty feet square. Professor Stearns, the steward, and the "college mason" (evidently in 1825 mention of this functionary was comprehensible without explanation) estimated that the building would cost $7500. The rooms thus vacated in College House Number 2 would not be unprofitable; they could accommodate "mechanicks" and their families who had "requested to be admitted tenants of College." For the proposed new Law School building there was available "College land near the Court house." [31] On August 15, 1825, the President laid Stearns's proposal before the Corporation, which appointed President Kirkland, Judge Jackson, and Mr. Prescott a committee to look into the terms of construction and the means of raising funds, and "to take into consideration such measures as may be proper for enlarging the means of instruction in the Law School." Unfortunately these proposals came when the finances of the university were declining, and the School struggled along in College House Number 2 until September 1832, when it moved to the new Dane Law College in the Yard.[32]

From the day of his appointment Stearns energetically worked at the system of instruction in the new School, and the subject matter he intended to cover. One can follow his methods by reading his term reports to the President, required by university statute beginning with 1825; but perhaps a diligent student's lecture notes, now in the Law School archives, give even better insight.[33] Primary guidance of study at the School came from formal lectures delivered throughout the year by Professor Stearns, and by Judge Parker after the adjournment of Court in the spring. Some at least

---

procured a new Harvard statute allowing alumni of any college to become resident graduates for a fee of five dollars. They were entitled to "engage a college chamber and remain members of the academic society indefinitely, and a considerable number did so while waiting for jobs. Some of them were difficult to get rid of." S. E. Morison, *Three Centuries of Harvard* (Cambridge, Mass., 1936), 107.

[31] College Records, XI, 67.

[32] In the usage of the time "college" could mean a structure as well as an institution of learning.

[33] The student was Asahel Stearns's nephew Luther Stearns Cushing, LL.B. 1826. He served as a lecturer at the Law School, 1848–1851.

of Stearns's students, like Tapping Reeve's students at Litchfield, reduced their lecture notes to orderly and well-phrased form, carefully written in bound books evidently meant for permanent use.

In his first lecture in the fall term of 1825 Stearns told his hearers the purposes of a system of public justice, and why its study was suitable for a man of learning in a university. His second lecture described more particularly the subject matter of the curriculum. As one might expect from the author of *Law and Practice of Real Actions*, Stearns put the study of real property at the head of his regimen. It was, he told his students, "the foundation of our whole system of jurisprudence." For its study, and for study of the law generally, he stressed the importance of a knowledge of English history, especially in relation to feudal law. He recommended the works of Reeves, Gilbert, Littleton, Coke on Littleton, and Cruise,[34] but had the realistic wisdom to tell his students that in the United States of the 1820's much of the classic tenurial law had small relation to modern conveyancing.

Stearns's second grand division concerned personal rights and personal property. To what we now call the law of tort he gave brief mention, saying nothing about the embryonic law of negligence, then only vaguely adumbrated in other writers' discussions of reasonable care in bailments. He treated of the law of contract, using it to introduce some comparison with the civil-law system, pointing out that what we now call the law of commercial transactions, the law of admiralty, and the "law of nations" have links with systems outside that of the common law. Practice, pleading, evidence, and equity procedure, he told the students, would have attention during the year. The treatment of criminal law would necessarily be brief. Stearns proposed a reasonably planned course of study, but one finds it a bit curious that he scarcely hinted at constitutional law, when *Marbury v. Madison, Fletcher v. Peck, Martin v. Hunter's Lessee, McCulloch v. Mary-*

[34] John Reeves, *A History of the English Law from the Time of the Saxons to the End of the Reign of Elizabeth* (1783–7) — in 1826 the School's library had a 1787 edition; Lord Chief Baron Sir Geoffrey Gilbert, *The Law of Tenures* (1730) — in 1826 the School had the fourth edition of 1796; William Cruise, *Digest of the Law of Real Property* (1804–7) — in 1826 the School had two copies of the American edition of 1808. Littleton and Coke need no introduction here.

land, the *Dartmouth College Case,* and *Gibbons v. Ogden*[35] all were in the immediate past.

Coordinate with the lectures were readings in texts. Blackstone, of course, was conspicuous; the *Commentaries* were fortified by other works then standard. Stearns required recitations on this literature; he "examined" students dialectically about the required readings, and explained misconceptions and obscurities. Well conducted, such dialogues are admirable teaching and learning procedures, alike useful for the direct participants and for those who for the moment are only listeners, provided the listeners have read the material in advance and critically follow the dialogue. Stearns's term reports to President Kirkland show that these recitations and examinations were the most frequent teaching procedures in the School's curriculum.

The study of law, or anything else, goes forward prosperously only when the student explores and acquires learning for himself. From medieval times in Europe to the present day in all American faculties of law, an essential part of education has been disputation — some procedure by which the student is required to prepare himself by advance study and then to sustain or attack a "thesis," a proposition, in the face of opposition equally well prepared. Stearns established at Harvard from the first a system of moot courts; for their sessions he posed in advance carefully constructed human situations which, supposedly, had provoked litigious controversy turning on one or several points of law. The students, like law students from time immemorial, prepared themselves by study of the authorities. On the appointed evening (Monday nights seem to have been preferred) those designated as counsel argued the case before a court, sometimes with Stearns as chief justice, sometimes with a student. Students for the moment not participating took notes, a useful art to acquire, as young lawyers soon find out when they go to court with their seniors. In due course the chief justice delivered his judgment on the law, and then doubtless commented on the quality of the young men's advocacy, as his successors in the same School do to this day.

The Law School archives have records of these moots as early

[35] Reported respectively 1 Cranch 137 (1803); 6 Cranch 87 (1810); 1 Wheaton 304 (1816); 4 Wheaton 316 (1819); 4 Wheaton 518 (1819); and 9 Wheaton 1 (1824).

as February 1820, kept by the students who took part. Their successors, reading these accounts a century and a half later, find themselves entirely at home. One has to evaluate the process remembering the small numbers of students in residence, and the consequent frequency of opportunities for everyone to participate. Most of the time in the School's first decade its student population fluctuated between half-a-dozen to a dozen men. Some had had law office experience before coming to the School, which gave them a head start. In 1825–26 students argued thirty-seven moots lasting two to three hours each; in 1826–27 there were thirty-five moot courts.

On Monday evening, February 21, 1820, Professor Stearns submitted a case for discussion at the next moot:

> An administrator of an estate supposing it abundantly solvent paid the full claims of several creditors to a considerable amount. Two years from the time of his taking out letters, claims to such an amount against the estate as to render it insolvent unexpectedly appeared. He represented it as such, commissioners were appointed and after examining the claims of all the creditors those paid as well as those unpaid, reported that the estate could pay but 75% on the original demands. The question is (that is to be decided) can the administrator recover back from the creditors whose demands he fully paid, the excess above 75% which he has paid them.

Counsel upholding the affirmative in this matter were Charles William Cutter, A.B. Harvard 1818, and Wyllys Lyman, A.B. Yale 1817. Opposed to them were Grenville Mellen, A.B. Harvard 1818, and Emory Washburn, A.B. Williams 1817. The case was duly heard on Monday, March 6, and as no student's name appears as chief justice, one gathers that Professor Stearns presided. Whoever the judge was, he decided against the administrator's claim.

As the years added experience, the proposed cases were more elaborately stated. On Monday evening, June 14, 1824, the following case was proposed for argument at the session after next.

Prince vs. *Patten.*

This is an action of trespass for breaking and entering the plaintiff's close, and taking and carrying away his cherries.

Upon the trial on the general issue with leave to give special matter in evidence, it was proved that the plaintiff's cherry-tree overhung the highway the soil of which belonged to the plff. — and the dft. in passing along rode under it, and pulled off a bunch of cherries.

It was objected on the part of the dft., that as he had a right to travel on any part of the highway, the plff. could not maintain this action for *breaking his close*; but should have brought an action of trespass on the case, or trover.

The judge instructed the jury, that tho the dft., and the public, had an easement upon the plff.'s land, to travel and use it as a highway: still the plff. was entitled to maintain an action of this sort against any one, who meddled with the soil, or took any thing growing upon it. And he directed the jury to find a verdict for such damage as the plff. had sustained. The jury returned a verdict for the plff. with two mills damage.

After verdict the dft. moved in arrest of judgment, upon the ground that the damages were less than any denomination of current coin, and therefore could not be satisfied without his paying half a cent, which would be more than twice the amount due: And dft. contended that any judgment, which cannot be satisfied without paying double the amount, must be erroneous.

He also moved (if judgment should not be arrested) that the verdict should be set aside, and a nonsuit entered, because the judge misdirected the jury, by instructing them that the action of trespass *quare clausum fregit* can be maintained in this case.[36]

On July 2, 1824, Edward Jackson Lowell, A.B. Harvard 1822, argued the case for the defendant Patten, and Daniel Weld, A.B. Harvard 1823, argued for Prince. On Thursday evening July 22, 1824, the chief justice, again Stearns, one supposes, decided in favor of the plaintiff.

Evidently the moots were successful. The regularity with which students kept records, the participation of many different students as counsel, the ingenuity of the questions set for argument, all bespeak a good program for the study of cases. Sometimes counsel were required to prepare pleadings [37] as well as arguments. As anyone well knows who has tried to conduct instruction of this sort, the teacher's work is onerous. Stearns reported in August 1826:

A large portion of the Professor's time is employed in selecting and preparing suitable questions and cases for argument at the moot court, and in assisting the students to put them into this form of judicious action, examining their declarations, pleas, replications,

[36] Stearns, or perhaps the student justices, suggested cases to start the researches of counsel, here 6 Mass. 456 and 5 Mass. 370. Quotations from the archives are by permission.

[37] "Pleadings," one reminds the lay reader, are not emotional supplicatory speeches on behalf of a client. The term is a technical one; pleadings are formal written statements defining the conflicting contentions of the opposed parties in litigation.

demurrers, bills of exceptions, motions, etc. and directing them in the course of their investigations and researches. But of the amount of time thus employed, and of that also which is devoted to answering the numerous questions and solving the doubts which occur to the students, (and which they are encouraged and desired to suggest with freedom when they occur), it is impossible to make any correct estimate.[38]

By the mid-1820's the School's whole teaching program was well developed. Chief Justice Parker and Professor Stearns delivered their scheduled lectures — Parker, eighteen; Stearns thirty-eight. In January 1826 Stearns reported to the Overseers that in 1826–27 he held sixty-nine "reviews and examinations by classes," exercises in which twenty to thirty questions were put to each student on the subjects of the lectures and assigned texts. Students were also required to write twenty-nine "dissertations" in that year, and besides the moots, engaged in thirty-four "disputations," which seem to have been debates less formal than the arguments before the moot court.

Search has not turned up any copies of student "dissertations" preserved for modern scrutiny, as we now keep the best third-year papers. Work on dissertations could have been excellent training. The number of students was so small in the Parker-Stearns era that Professor Stearns could give his own critical attention to each such piece of work, reviewing each student's writing, criticising his authorities, his reasoning, his language. Then, as now, an important part of any lawyer's work is the study of questions of law and preparation of documented opinions. The dissertations were directly useful professional training.

A diligent student thus had available at Harvard in Stearns's day a systematically planned legal education, carefully supervised, employing many of the techniques of the best law schools today, with a far larger proportion of the teacher's time devoted to each student than is possible in almost any modern school. Stearns's curriculum, sensible if not brilliant, could be surveyed in eighteen months of intensive work. Had he been given the art of foresight he might have seen that by the time his students were in their forties they would be concerned less with the classic land law and more with new forms of business organization, with business regulation, with questions of public law concerning relations be-

[38] See Warren, *Harvard Law School*, I, 357.

tween the growing central government and the diminishing states. But within the confines of the material he undertook to cover, his teaching was excellent. Distinguished lawyers came from his seminary.

Some critics have suggested that Parker and Stearns did no more than set up a simulated law office in the lower floor of College House Number 2, giving their students only what they could have got by reading with a practitioner. Perhaps there were in Massachusetts of that day practicing lawyers who had the time, imagination, and experience required to give their apprentices planned instruction like that in the School, but if so, one wonders how they found time to practice law. We have an account of study in Daniel Webster's Boston office when Charles Francis Adams and Robert C. Winthrop were reading there at the end of the 1820's. Senator Webster was much in Washington. "His local business was attended to by his junior partners. Even when at home he was generally too busy to give much attention to his students, whose duties were to copy papers, look up cases and prepare briefs . . . At very long intervals he discoursed a little on the great principles of jurisprudence and more often favored them with a passing insight into contemporary politics." [39] Looking up law and preparing briefs can be most instructive; but such casual work in a law office, varying hit or miss with whatever business came in, was not the equivalent of the carefully planned and supervised School under Stearns's administration.

In the earlier years the Corporation did not award degrees relying only on the certificate of Professor Stearns; the President and the Fellows provided examiners external to the Faculty of Law to determine the fitness of candidates. On November 16, 1819, the Corporation voted "that Mr. Lowell, Judge Jackson, and Judge Story be a Committee to examine in such way as they may think most suitable, the candidates for the Degree of Bachelor of Laws at the next Commencement and report upon their qualifications to this Board." The three Examiners decided to assign to candidates subjects for dissertations which the candidates would then prepare and on which they would undergo oral examination by

[39] Charles Francis Adams (1807–1886), son of John Quincy Adams, studied in Webster's office for a few weeks in 1829. Robert C. Winthrop (1809–1894) studied in Webster's office some time between his Harvard A.B. in 1828 and his admission to the Massachusetts bar in 1831. The account of study under Webster comes from Robert Winthrop, Jr., *Memoir of Robert C. Winthrop* (Boston, 1897).

the committee. In the summer of 1820 six young men were ready for this ordeal. The examiners assigned as subjects for dissertations:

1. The Rules of Descent and Distribution of Real and Personal Property by the Civil Law, the Law of England and the Law of Massachusetts.

2. The several injuries to which the Heir is liable in relation to his right of succession to Real Property, and the several remedies by Entry or Action which are furnished by the Laws of England and of Massachusetts.

On August 28, 1820, at "a meeting of the Faculty of Law at the College," the committee examined the six candidates, who "read Dissertations on questions previously proposed to them by the Board, in which they evinced their diligence, learning and accuracy." The committee recommended them to the Corporation and Overseers as duly qualified.[40] With the committee's report went Professor Stearns's certificate that the six candidates had all been members of the University Law School one year and a half or more, during all of which time each of them had pursued his legal studies with diligence and success, and that each had produced satisfactory evidence of having completed the "period of his noviciate." On Commencement Day, August 30, 1820, Charles F. Gove, a Dartmouth graduate, a graduate of Yale named Wyllys Lyman, and four Harvard A.B.'s, John W. Proctor, Samuel E. Sewall, William R. P. Washburn, and Joseph Willard, became Harvard's first Bachelors of Laws. It is worth noting that Proctor, Washburn, and Willard had already been members of their bars more than six months.

Stearns worked hard. In addition to preparation and delivery of lectures, preparation of suitable questions for argument at moot courts, and help to students in preparation for their arguments, he was much engaged in conferences with individual students on other aspects of their study; he encouraged them to consult with him about any difficulties. Any teacher knows the endless time and energy this can consume. Stearns worried about the cost of academic legal education. Reading law in an office provided less

[40] The "Faculty of Law" consisted, one assumes, of Judge Parker and Professor Stearns. The term "Faculty of Law," which suggests a sense of establishment, is that used in the report made to the Corporation by John Lowell, chairman of the examining committee. See Harvard College Papers, IX, 47, and Warren, *Harvard Law School*, I, 339.

systematic learning, but the courts of all states recognized it as an acceptable means of qualifying for the bar, and a young man could live at home and work his way copying papers and doing necessary drudgery for his lawyer-tutor. Thus he could save much of the very considerable expense of study at a university. Stearns understood the threat that this competition presented to the Law School, and in his reports reminded the President of it.

Academic ritual at Harvard in the 1820's was not unrelievedly solemn. Chancellor Kent, just retired, visited Harvard at Commencement time in August 1823. On August 28 Story presided at the annual Phi Beta Kappa banquet, and Kent, of course, was there. This was the era of toasts. After a series of lesser dignitaries had pledged the Chancellor, Story gave: "Our distinguished guest, who so administered the law of the land as to make New York the Land of the Law." Kent rose while the applause was continuing, and proposed in return: "Massachusetts, the land of Story as well as of song." [41]

The Corporation rightly valued the University Professor's merits. On Commencement Day in 1825, when Harvard gave honorary Doctorates of Laws to Henry Clay and other distinguished men, it included Asahel Stearns among its new Doctors. That day nine young men received Harvard's LL.B.

The year 1825 was the peak of the Parker-Stearns era. The Law School did not grow as the 1820's went on. Instead, numbers began to dwindle; by the spring of 1829 only a couple of forlorn students of law continued in residence. Probably many causes combined to bring about this change for the worse. The Law School was not the only part of Harvard to go into a decline in the middle and late 1820's, but the School was new and small. Old-fashioned parents and some of their sons still questioned its usefulness. It was the most vulnerable department of the university.

5

Curiously enough from today's point of view, one popular discontent with the university was its religious radicalism. The Unitarian movement, growing for a generation or more, had deeply

[41] John T. Horton, *James Kent: A Study in Conservatism* (New York, 1939), pp. 264–266.

influenced the Harvard faculty, and by the early 1820's had come to be a cause of bitter criticism. The widespread feeling that Harvard was a hotbed of religious infidelity or utter atheism may have brought some parents to withdraw their sons or not send them to Harvard in the first place. Money troubles arose. In 1825 the General Court discontinued an annual appropriation of $10,000 for the university which it had been making for the past decade; in 1824–25 Harvard's expenses were $5000 more than its income.

Academic disputes produced rifts. Young George Ticknor was an educational radical. Newly returned from Europe to take up his professorship of the French and Spanish languages and of belle-lettres, he was urging that Harvard abandon its somewhat schoolboyish methods of instruction by frequent recitations and adopt freer procedures resembling those of the German universities. Ticknor won some disciples but offended others on the faculty; most professors were more conventional than he. Then, too, there broke out at Harvard one of the rows, perennial in American colleges, about faculty aspiration to membership on the Governing Boards. The faculty was defeated. Schisms have a way of getting noised abroad and are not always wholesome for college well-being.

At such times of tight money and academic wrangles, governing boards are apt to call for the help of hardheaded men who have met payrolls, and have no nonsense about them. In 1826 the Corporation elected to its membership Nathaniel Bowditch, author of *The Practical Navigator*, A.M. *honoris causa*, 1802, a strong-minded, highly intelligent businessman, experienced in the shipping industry which had long made New England's living.[42] He forthwith began an investigation of the university's finances. The Harvard Treasurer, a member of the Corporation, Judge Davis of the United States District Court, was honorable and scholarly, but was perhaps not qualified, either by taste or experience, to trim financial sail in a storm as closely as the Practical Navigator found necessary. Stephen Higginson, who had long served Harvard as steward, was another fiscal officer, another obvious target. No one has ever suggested that either of these men was in any way corrupt, but perhaps both were a little inept.

---

[42] For an account of the financial difficulties of the 1820's see Morison, *Three Centuries of Harvard*, pp. 219f. The full title of Bowditch's book was *The New American Practical Navigator*; it was published in Newburyport, Massachusetts, in 1802.

Both resigned in 1827. Sometimes university rearrangements are both necessary and painful.

The Isaac Royall endowment annually yielded a little over $400. The Corporation may have doubted whether Parker's drawing power for students was worth what it cost. Ability to attract students has been one prime qualification for a professor since the Middle Ages, and the Law School, like the rest of Harvard, needed students badly. In the fall of 1827 the Corporation may have been thinking, quite correctly as events finally demonstrated, that it could use its resources better on some professor other than Parker. "As a first step, the Royall Professor must devote himself to teaching professional students; and since Judge Parker could not spare time for it, some one else must be found to take his place." [43]

Harvard is officially discreet. The records of the Corporation do not give any explanation for the following letter, dated November 6, 1827.

To the President and Fellows of Harvard University.
Having understood from one of your body that it is desirable that the office of Royall Professor of Law now held by me should be vacated, I hereby resign the same.

> Respectfully your
> obedient servant
> Isaac Parker.

On November 15, 1827, the Corporation records show this decorous entry: "The resignation of Chief Justice Parker, Royall Professor of Law, being laid before the Corporation, it was thereupon voted that in accepting the same, this Board express their full sense of the benefits which the Chief Justice has conferred on the University and on the public by the lectures which he has delivered at Cambridge, and that the Treasurer pay his salary as Professor till next Commencement." Within three months thereafter Judge Story was writing from Washington to a friend: "I am at this moment a good deal perplexed by an application to me to accept the Royall Professorship of Law at Harvard University, and to remove to Cambridge, and devote my leisure to the advancement of the Law School there. The offer is made unofficially, but in terms of considerable earnestness, and in a pecuniary point

[43] This is the judgment, in 1918, of the authors of the *Centennial History*; see page 8.

of view it is eligible. What to do puzzles me exceedingly . . . What to decide I hardly know, there are so many *pros* and *contras*.[44] Harvard had been trying for eight years to get Story as a Law School professor — the first time in 1820, the next in 1825.[45] In March 1828 he refused this third proposal. He gave his reasons in a letter to Ticknor dated March 6, 1828.

I have fears that my health would not hold out against the inroads of such additional labors. If I were there, I should be obliged to devote *all* my leisure time to drilling, and lectures, and judicial conversations. The school cannot flourish except by such constant efforts; and I should not willingly see it wither under my hands. The delivery of public lectures alone might not be oppressive; but success in a law school must be obtained by private lectures. I have yielded reluctantly to what seems to me, on the whole, the dictates of duty.[46]

Meantime the Corporation was engaged in a general program of financial retrenchment. In January 1828 that body directed its secretary to lay before the Overseers at their next meeting a statement of the pecuniary affairs of the college. President Kirkland, sick and weary, was trying to cut costs without reducing services. On January 17 he reported to the Overseers on his economy campaign:

Harvard College — January 17, 1828.
To the Honourable and Reverend the Board of Overseers. —
The income of the College having been much lessened during a few years past by the discontinuance of the annual grant of ten thousand dollars from the State and by other causes, several important changes in the management of its pecuniary concerns have been adopted by the Corporation. Some of these have already received separately the sanction of the Board of Overseers. But the Corporation ask leave now to submit a statement of the most important in order that their connexion and operation, as parts of a system, may be seen at one view. Besides the plain obligation of bringing the expenses of the College within its income which has been lately much exceeded, the Corporation found a motive for retrenchment in the conviction that it is of great importance to reduce the necessary expenses of the Students.
In conformity with the advice of the Overseers as Professorships

[44] Story to Rev. John Brazer, *Life and Letters of Joseph Story*, I, 532. Mr. Brazer, minister of the Unitarian Church in Salem, was a close friend and correspondent of Story's.
[45] Details and documentation appear in Warren, *Harvard Law School*, I, 340, 349.
[46] *Life and Letters of Joseph Story*, I, 537.

became vacant, they have been united with others or their duties assigned to other Departments; and in every such case the amount paid to one Professor has been saved. The University Professor of Metaphysics has been chosen Alford Professor, and is to perform all his former duties excepting such as were deemed inconsistent with the Statutes of the founder, which latter have been assigned to the Professor of Rhetoric and Oratory.

The University Professor of Greek has in like manner been chosen Eliot Professor of Greek. The instruction in Latin formerly given by the University Professor of that language is now given by the Professor of Hebrew and other Oriental languages, and the duties of the University Professor of Mathematics are required to be performed by the Hollis Professor of Mathematics and Natural Philosophy and the Tutors in that Department. And thus all the four University Professorships,[47] those of which the salaries were paid wholly out of the general funds of the College, are abolished. The above mentioned officers have consented to perform the new duties thus assigned to them, although the Corporation do not allow them any additional compensation. In this respect they have varied from the former usage of the College Government, which was to grant additional pay whenever new services were asked of any officer of the College. But they are of opinion that the Salaries allowed to the Professors ought to be considered an adequate compensation for the devotion of their whole time and talents to the service of the institution. The stated salaries of two of the College officers, the Hersey Professor of Anatomy and Surgery and the Smith Professor of modern languages have been reduced by consent.

In the year 1813 a grant was made of three hundred dollars per annum to the President and of two hundred dollars per annum to each Professor in addition to their salaries to continue during the pleasure of the Corporation. This grant has been repealed.

The Treasurer of the College has declined receiving any compensation beyond the actual expenses which he shall incur in discharging the duties of his office.

On the resignation of the late Erving Professor of Chemistry his former duties were connected with those of the Mineralogical Department. The vacancies which have lately occurred in the Rumford Professorship and in the Royall Professorship of Law have not been filled, but their funds are specially appropriated by the donors, and cannot be applied to the general expenses of the College.

President Kirkland's letter went on to detail other economies: some, he hoped, might lessen the cost of the student's education. The college's printing establishment, which ran at a net loss, had

---

[47] Not including Stearns's professorship. Harvard could have made Stearns Royall Professor thus using funds no longer paid to Parker. Was the Corporation already planning to dismiss Stearns?

been sold. Some scholarships, previously given outright, were replaced by appointments to perform useful tasks as proctors and monitors, thus saving money and encouraging in the young a commendable sense of self-help. Signing for the Corporation, Kirkland closed this communication expressing hope that these measures would bring Harvard's expenses within its income.

Still not everyone was convinced that the President's financial reforms were stringent enough. On March 27, 1828, during a Corporation meeting the Practical Navigator, annoyed with Kirkland because he resisted some cutback, delivered a sharp criticism at the President. Dr. Kirkland resigned next day. He was still suffering from the effects of a mild stroke which had hit him a year earlier; perhaps, at long last, he was glad to be relieved of responsibility for trying to amend the sorry state of Harvard's affairs. The university's students, moved at the departure of a friend, passed a farewell resolution affecting even now, after a century and a third.

We thank you for the honors which your award has made more sweet, and we thank you for the reproof, which has been tempered with love. We thank you for the benignity of manners which engaged our confidence, for the charities which secured our hearts. We thank you, sir, for all the little, nameless, unremembered acts of your kindness and authority. We are deeply in your debt, but the obligation is not irksome; it is a debt of gratitude we are well pleased to owe.
We should have been happy, had your connexion with the University, at least, subsisted until we had been dismissed from its walls . . . But it has been ordered otherwise, and we can only now assure you, sir, that though you have ceased to stand to us in the relation of President, there are other tender relations between you and us, which will terminate but with life, and it is our prayer to God, that your years may be very long protracted amid pleasant recollections and troops of friends.[48]

Kirkland was a kind, gentle man, an accomplished scholar, a devoted clergyman, an example of urbanity without unctuousness. He taught more than books. Even when he had occasion to chide students he seemed more amused by their human shortcomings than wrathful at their sins. Young men loved him. Perhaps he was not quite tough enough for a crisis in Harvard affairs, not ruthless enough to hurt the people who had to be hurt.

The Law School had been marginal from its beginning, and in

---

[48] Morison, *Three Centuries of Harvard*, p. 221.

this unhappy time the shrinkage in the number of law students should surprise no one. Parker's departure in November 1827 must have hurt the School's reputation. Even though the Chief Justice had not as Royall Professor been a major intellectual contributor to legal thought at the university, still his unexplained resignation may have led to the unjust belief that he sensed failure of the experiment and irresponsibly chose to desert his post. Students do not flock to what their elders consider failures. Stearns continued to struggle singlehanded through 1828. His term report of December 24, 1828, could not be addressed to the university president; Harvard had no president. Stearns wrote to the Corporation. "The number of students attending the Law School during the greater part of this time was only four. Near the close of the term, the number was increased to five — they have been generally attended to separately in their exercises . . . It is due to the students to state that, while all of them have manifested a laudable spirit of industry, two in particular have pursued their studies with great ardor and perseverance and have made very gratifying progress."

During winter terms the number of law students in residence had usually declined, and a student body of four or five does not leave much margin for shrinkage. We have no record of attendance during the winter of 1828–29. One tradition has it that the School finally shrank to one student; Mr. Justice Story, in whose later years recollection of detail could be inaccurate, recited still a worse story in his 1842 Will: "When I came to Cambridge [in August 1829], and undertook the duties of my Professorship, there had not been a single law student there for the preceding year." [49] Whatever the precise fact, the School seems to have reached the lowest point in its history in the winter of 1829.

Then in January 1829, almost ten months after the resignation of President Kirkland, the Governing Boards found Harvard a new president in Josiah Quincy. Quincy was well equipped to revitalize the university after its difficult years. He was a lawyer, a former congressman, and a former mayor of Boston, not primar-

---

[49] *Life and Letters of Joseph Story*, II, 532. O. W. Holmes wrote to Phineas Barnes in September 1829: "the Law School has increased from one solitary individual to twenty six." John T. Morse, Jr., *Life and Letters of Oliver Wendell Holmes* (Boston, 1896), I, 62. The future professor of medicine had graduated from Harvard College with the class of 1829, and entered the Law School in September of that year.

ily a scholar though he had ample intelligence and cultivation. He had judgment of men, essential to political success; he was tough, was willing to do what had to be done even if it hurt those who were worthy but inadequate — a quality without which the administrator of any enterprise may fail.

And during Stearns's last months, help, financial and human, was being arranged for the Law School, though no one told Stearns about it. In the late summer of 1828 Nathan Dane of Beverly had written to Judge Story, a Fellow of the Harvard Corporation, asking that Story discuss with Dane a new endowment for the School, which Dane was ready to provide. Story and Dane, and later Quincy and Dane, discussed the form that Dane's foundation should take. Apparently the Corporation felt that Stearns must leave the School if the new arrangements were to succeed; but Harvard has a long tradition of decent discretion about the departure of university officers, and has no record of the discussions about dismissing Stearns. As in some other similar cases, no one now knows the details.[50]

On March 18, 1829, the Corporation appointed a committee "to consider the status of the Law School and to make a report thereon." As Josiah Quincy had not yet been formally inaugurated as president, the acting head of the Corporation was its Senior Fellow, the Reverend Dr. Porter. Dr. Porter had a painful interview with Professor Stearns, probably early in April 1829; Porter said the Law School was an experiment which had failed, and he blamed Stearns for it. On April 7, 1829, less than four years after Harvard had made him an honorary Doctor of Laws, Stearns wrote to the Senior Fellow a dignified letter of resignation, giving his estimate of the causes for the School's decline. Justice to a good and conscientious man requires that Stearns's letter be quoted in full.

Cambridge April 7th 1829.

RevD Sir,

In the interview which I had with you in relation to the dissolution of my connection with the college, my feelings were expressed without reserve and I am anxious that they should not be misunderstood.

You will readily believe that if I could have foreseen this result at the time I was solicited to accept the appointment of Professor of

[50] Professor Morison, in his *Three Centuries of Harvard*, has pointed out that as to the departure of Presidents Hoar in 1675 and Langdon in 1780, "it is now impossible to get to the bottom of the matter" (p. 161). So, too, for Stearns.

Law, I should have declined the proffered honor. The failure of the experiment as you were pleased to call it, must doubtless have been a severer disappointment to me, than to any other person, however anxious he may have been for the interest and honour of the College. And I must say that it was equally unexpected and painful to me to find that I was considered answerable for this failure.

You will readily believe that my interest in the success of the Law School must have led me to watch the progress of events with solicitude; and so far as I was capable of judging, it may be supposed that I possessed the means of tracing effects to their causes. I trust, therefore, that I shall be pardoned for alluding to some of the chief causes which have operated to the injury of that institution; and these appear to me sufficient to account for what I have so long witnessed with regret, while it could not be prevented, but by the fostering aid of the Corporation.

1. I may mention in the first place the great diminution in the number of law students in the State, which, I understand, in the country (however it may be in the city) is but about half as large as formerly.

2. The establishment of similar institutions elsewhere, particularly in Virginia (which for some years furnished full one third to our number) and at Northampton where the saving of expenses in board and especially in room rent, fuel, etc. (which are understood to have been furnished gratuitously to those who were poor) have held out powerful inducements in addition to local advantages. To this I may add, that several gentlemen who sent their sons there, have assured me that they should have preferred Cambridge but for their desire to separate their sons from particular associates.

3. The great convenience to professional gentlemen, especially in the country, of having a law student in their offices has induced them to give gratuitous instruction in many more cases than formerly.

In many instances, this circumstance has induced young gentlemen to change their determination to study at Cambridge, and to leave the place sooner than they had intended.

4. Perhaps the want of a convenient and respectable building for the Law School has had quite as much influence as any of the circumstances alluded to, since the erection of the theological college has led the law students to contrast their situation with that of the students of theology.

In making these remarks, I hope I shall not be misunderstood. This is not offered as an apology; for I am not conscious of needing one. My only desire is to have facts known that correct inferences may be drawn. I wish to have it distinctly understood that I claim to have discharged my official duty faithfully and conscientiously and to have conducted the business of instruction in my department in as acceptable and satisfactory a manner both to my pupils and their friends as any department of the College. I have therefore only to request (what certainly will not be refused by my judges) that the case shall be examined and understood before any censure is cast upon me.

You did not intimate, sir, that any complaint had been made, or any unfavorable representation presented to the Corporation. But as it has been stated to me that a report has been circulated by one person that two or three students from Virginia had expressed some dissatisfaction with regard to the Law School, it is possible that report may have come to the knowledge of the Corporation or some of the members. I therefore beg leave to state that I have in my possession letters from those gentlemen, introducing their friends to the Law School, and containing such expressions as render it in my view utterly incredible that they can have made the statements imputed to them.

Though this letter has extended so much beyond the limits to which I intended to confine myself, I must still beg your indulgence for one further remark. From something you let fall I was led to suppose that some of the gentlemen of the Corporation regarded the money expended upon the Law School, as an appropriation which had produced little or no public benefit. A different opinion must, I think, be entertained by the professional gentlemen of that body. I am sure they cannot but be aware, that the effect which the Law School has had in raising the general standard of professional education, by introducing a more methodical and thorough course of instruction, has of itself (if no other benefit had resulted) more than compensated for the expenditure. The course of instruction pursued here, which was drawn up under the eye of some of the present members of the Corporation, has not only been adopted in other law schools, but more than 60 professional gentlemen in this and adjoining States have applied for copies for the use of their students. And what is still more important, students in law offices have been more attended to and better instructed in consequence of the establishment of the School.

I cannot but hope, sir, that these suggestions will be received in the spirit of candour, and that however they may fail to establish any claim to the respectful consideration of the Corporation, they may at least shelter me from censure, and that I may still indulge the belief that the respect and attachment manifested by my pupils was in their opinion not wholly undeserved. This is the first occasion which I have had to speak in my own vindication; perhaps you may think I should rather say my own commendation. If the occasion cannot excuse it, it must go unexcused.

You will please to consider me, sir, as hereby tendering my resignation of the chair of University Professor of Law which I shall not consider myself as holding after this day.

I shall rejoice at all times in the respectability and welfare of the University and especially to see the Law Department revive and flourish in more competent and more favored hands, however keenly I may feel the unkindness I have experienced.

You will please to accept my acknowledgment for the personal courtesy I have experienced in my interviews with you, and to be assured I am, as ever,

Your obedient servant,
Asahel Stearns.

Revd Dr Porter, Senior member
of the Corporation of Harvard College.[51]

On April 16, 1829, the Corporation accepted Stearns's resignation with a vote that was no more than his due.

Voted. That the Corporation accept this resignation entertaining a respectful sense of his distinguished attainments in legal science and of his diligence and fidelity in performing the duties of his office and a sincere wish for his future happiness.

Voted. That the Treasurer in settling his account with Professor Stearns allow him usual tuition fees up to close of the present College year for the students in the Law School at the time of his resignation.

Voted. That Dr. Stearns be requested to retain the use of the rooms now occupied by him and of the Law Library in his possession till the end of the present term, if this be any accommodation to him.

After a century and a third one cannot be sure whether in these resolves the Fellows were simply doing justice to a worthy but unlucky professor, or were also evidencing troubled consciences at dismissing, for unconvincingly asserted reasons, a deserving but commonplace servant to make way for more promising successors, already selected without Stearns's knowledge. We do not know. The three men most active in the rebirth of the Law School in the fall of 1828 and the forepart of 1829 were Story, Dane, and Quincy. Their conversations were private. Could the three have taken Stearns into their confidence, pointed out that though he had done his best, the School had not under his care become the focal center of legal "science" of the time? Could they have given him a chance to leave with the honors of war, with him making an explanation of the pressure of public duty as district attorney, with some *emeritus* appointment to smooth out the rasping dismissal? Was Porter too untactful to do this? Was there some asperity between Story and Stearns, or Dane and Stearns, or Quincy and Stearns? Was Stearns too hurt to see that, after all, he was not a great man and that the School needed great men to become great? We shall never know; but even after all these years

---

[51] Harvard College Papers, vol. III, 2nd series; Warren quotes it in full, *Harvard Law School*, I, 366–368.

one regrets that these scholars and gentlemen did not order it better.

Among all the *curiosa* one detail stands out. When the Corporation accepted Stearns's resignation it gave him "usual tuition fees up to close of the present College year for the students in the Law School at the time of his resignation." The plural connotes at least two. If no students at all were in the Law School (as Story wrote in 1842) the Corporation's minute giving him their fees was a crude piece of sarcasm. But the letter sounds kind, not sarcastic. Such a loutish cut as to award to Stearns fees paid by nonexistent students would have been out of character, inconsistent with the university's tradition of somewhat formal urbanity in official dealings. The obvious is more inherently probable than the arcane in human affairs, and on the sixteenth of April 1829 the Corporation seem to have referred to more than one student actually in residence at the School nine days earlier. The Corporation's resolve suggests that these young men had paid in advance for their spring tuition. Did Harvard pay the students back for instruction they were not to get; did the President and Fellows then pay Stearns out of the corporate pocket? Did Stearns, good man that he was, go on teaching his pupils in the rooms the Corporation allotted to him, until the term was over? Neither the records of the School nor of the Corporation tell anything about Stearns's career, or his students, after April 7, 1829.

Harvard dismissed the University Professor of Law in a manner not entirely suave; perhaps there was no way to make it so. A fundamental revision of the School was essential. No book had come from Stearns during his professorship which reached the scholarly level of Hoffman's *Course of Legal Study,* of Dane's monumental *Abridgment,* or of the brilliant series of books that Story struck off, year after year, during his Dane Professorship. Stearns's *Real Actions* was good, but was only plain cookery. Even if Harvard, despite its depressed resources, had been able to free Stearns from some of his daily drudgery, one doubts that he would have seen, as Story did, a vision of the university as a center of innovation and inspiration in the legal order. But men have to have a place to begin; improvement of a system is much easier than originating one; Stearns left his successors a system to improve.

He lived ten more years, and died in Cambridge in 1839; but

except for some correspondence about his repurchase of a few books he had sold to the library, he disappears from the School's chronicles after his last spring at Harvard. He must have felt disgusted and depressed by the whole business; his hard work had gone for nothing; his students had left him; his university had discarded him like an unfashionable and worn-out shoe. The Law School has now done well to put his portrait in the Langdell entrance hall, facing the painting of Isaac Royall. Royall and Stearns were both founders of the School.

IV

Joseph Story: 1829–1845

Early in September 1828, when Harvard University had no President, when its Law School had no Royall Professor, when the School's few students were leaving one by one, when Asahel Stearns was struggling to keep the School alive — in that sad time Nathan Dane of Beverly wrote to an old friend and neighbor in Salem, a Fellow of the Harvard Corporation and a Justice of the Supreme Court.

Beverly, Sept. 6, 1828.

Dear Sir

When shall you be at leisure that I can convene with you for a few moments respecting the Law Branch in Harvard University? You have known my intentions respecting that branch from my first consulting you in relation to my Abridgment — that I meant the net profits for it — they have been calculated by Mr. N[1] to be such that about two years since I put into an instrument that I keape by me for fear of accident ten thousand dollars for the benefit of that branch, but my intention is to settle the matter while I live — the material question with me now is how to apply that sum in order that the greatest benefit may result to that institution which may be produced by the addition of this sum to its law funds — At present I am not informed of the condition of that branch, so cannot Judge what is best to be done with the aid I intend — the copy right I have not as yet disposed of.

Yours sincerely
N. Dane

Hon. Judge Story

P.S. to go with the copy right I have almost a ninth volume of select decisions, English and American in law and equity made almost entirely in the last seven years.[2]

[1] I do not place "Mr. N."
[2] To Dr. Edith Henderson go the author's thanks for discovery of this letter

Nathan Dane was born in 1752 and lived until 1835. His generation saw the winning of Independence; he served in Congress during the period of the Articles of Confederation; he had a hand in drafting the Northwest Ordinance, and wrote its clause forever barring slavery from the Northwest Territory. Although Dane was twenty-seven years older than Story, the two came to be closely associated. Dane read his law in Judge William Wetmore's Salem office. Story married Wetmore's daughter, and named his son William Wetmore Story. Dane practiced in Beverly; Story practiced in Salem. There was a brotherhood among Essex County lawyers even when they joined different political parties. In 1809 Dane and Story were cocounsel for the defendants in a wonderful case about distraining cattle damage feasant.[3] The cattle had escaped from Rust's badly fenced field, had strayed across lands of two intermediate owners and had blundered into the badly fenced field of Low, Dane's and Story's client; Low held the stray cattle to ransom for the harm they had done to his field and crops — Low, that is to say, distrained Rust's cattle. The indignant owner of the cattle, Rust, sued Low the captor for this distraint. Certainly this was no simple case. In the Massachusetts Supreme Judicial Court Dane and Story cited Fitzherbert's *Abridgment* of 1514, Viner's *Abridgment* of 1742–53, and the Massachusetts General Laws and Liberties of 1642. They also mentioned such modern stuff as the Massachusetts statutes of 1785, 1788, and 1794. Chief Justice Parsons wrote the Court's opinion upholding Low's right to impound the cattle, thus sustaining Dane and Story. The Chief Justice supported his decision with citations from *Cro. Jac.* and Salkeld's Reports.[4] One wonders what, in 1809, was the customary charge by the hour in Essex

---

among Harvard Law School manuscripts. Neither W. W. Story, the Judge's son and biographer, nor Charles Warren, the School's historian of 1908, appear to have seen it. W. W. Story has Dane's decision to endow a Chair occurring "in the latter part of the year 1829." Warren has Dane writing to Story "early in 1829, shortly after President Quincy's inauguration." Warren may have relied on W. W. Story's account, which in turn may reflect an oral reminiscence told by Judge Story to his son many years after the event, when the Judge's memory of dates was inaccurate. The early date of the September 1828 letter is significant; it shows negotiations for alleviating the Law School's distress going on for months before Stearns was dismissed with no whisper to him about the improved prospect, or the pending discussions about the School's future. The letter is quoted by permission.

[3] *Rust. v. Low*, 6 Mass. 90.

[4] For the uninitiate, we explain *Cro. Jac.* as a collection of law reports made by Chief Justice Croke in the time of James I; Salkeld's Reports covered cases in the King's Bench between 1669 and 1712.

County for research by such counsel as Nathan Dane and Joseph Story into the law of stray cows.

Both Dane and Story wrote books on the law. In 1805 Story, twenty-six years old, published an annotated *Selection of Pleadings in Civil Actions*. At about the same time he began a digest of American law, intended to resemble Comyn's *Digest* of 1762–1767; but Story gave up the enterprise after completing three large manuscript volumes.[5] At the same time Nathan Dane was working on the materials for his *General Abridgment and Digest of American Law, with Occasional Notes and Comments*, the first really great systematic treatise on the general law of the United States. It was, Dane wrote in his Introduction, "exclusively, calculated to be useful to American lawyers, especially to students, and to those of the profession who cannot possess many law books." Dane planned and carried to completion something like a forerunner of today's *Corpus Juris Secundum*, or *American Jurisprudence*. His work also suggests the collective *Restatements* of the American Law Institute. His book is remarkable for its idea that there was something which could be called "American" law, a collection of common concepts, embodied in separate state statutes and decisions and in "federal law." "By Federal law," Dane wrote in his Introduction, "is meant the Federal constitutions, acts of the Federal legislature and of the Federal executive, and judicial decisions thereon; and, in a broader sense, is meant by Federal law, any law that pervades the whole Federal territory, whether of English or American origin." Dane arranged his material by subject matter: contract and the remedies connected with contractual obligations; torts; evidence; and so on. He pointed out to his readers that an alphabetical arrangement like that in the old digests presents a student with material out of its logical order; "it leads the student, in many cases, to read law first, which in its nature is last"; an index serves every purpose of alphabetical arrangement without its disadvantages. Dane preferred to arrange his treatise in what he considered a logical sequence of topics.

He worked forty years on his *Abridgment*. He published the first eight volumes in 1823, and another, his last, in 1829. Dane's letter to Story of September 6, 1828, as well as the inherent

[5] Story gave the unpublished manuscript to Harvard; it is now in the Law School's archives.

probabilities of the situation, suggest that Dane may well have discussed his work with Story long before its publication. They lived near one another. In 1814 they were two of the three editors of an edition of Massachusetts colonial and provincial laws.[6] Surely Dane must have discussed his *Abridgment* with these co-editors. Perhaps Story abandoned his partly finished *Digest* when he realized the scope and quality of Dane's *Abridgment*. Story's admiration for Dane's work is apparent from his review of it under the title "Digests of the Common Law," in the *North American Review* of 1826.[7] Years afterward, in 1842, Story's opinion in *Swift v. Tyson* [8] echoed Dane's idea that there was a general "American law."

While Dane was laboriously compiling his *Abridgment*, Story for a few years turned to editing for American readers standard English lawbooks of the preceding generation. In 1809 he brought out a new edition of Chitty's *Practical Treatise on Bills of Exchange and Promissory Notes*; in 1810, an edition of Charles Abbott's *Treatise on the Laws Relative to Merchant Ships and Seamen*; in 1811, an annotated edition of Lawes's *Practical Treatise on Pleading in Assumpsit*. Story, after his appointment to the Supreme Court in 1811, continually wrote opinions of great erudition. He wrote a good deal for the *North American Review*, which published much more material on American law than one would find in today's equivalent journals, if indeed there be any. He contributed a number of articles to the *Encyclopaedia Americana*. He was a conspicuous figure in American letters.

As the years went on Story became more and more occupied with Harvard's affairs. In 1819 he became an Overseer; in 1825, a Fellow of the Corporation. Some time during the years before 1828 Dane began to discuss with Story a plan to devote the proceeds of Dane's *Abridgment* to the Harvard Law School. So in September 1828 Dane invited Story to his house in Beverly to discuss Dane's foundation. W. W. Story wrote in 1851 of his father's interview with Dane. Dane told Story

that, in his belief, the establishment of a Law College at Cambridge, at which the principles of jurisprudence should be taught systematically, as a science, would not only extend the influence of the Univer-

---

[6] Judge William Everett of Salem was the third editor.
[7] Reprinted in Story's *Miscellaneous Writings*, p. 379.
[8] 16 Peters 1.

sity, but would render effectual service to the country and the profession. He then proceeded to say, that as the profits he had received from his Abridgment were now sufficient to enable him to carry out these views, he proposed to bestow upon Harvard University the sum of ten thousand dollars, as a foundation for a Professorship of Law, on one condition, that my father should become the first occupant of the Professorial Chair. My father, having already declined to accept the Royall Professorship of Law at Cambridge, was at first wholly indisposed to treat the proposition with favor, as far as it related to him; but as his acceptance of the office was urged, as the indispensable condition of the donation, he was prevailed upon to take the matter into consideration. Several interviews succeeded, during which, the amount of compensation, the duties to be required, and all the details of the scheme were discussed, until finally, my father became so much interested, that, despite his many doubts, he concluded to accept the office. Several considerations conspired to induce this conclusion: his enthusiasm for education; his love of the law as a science; the peculiar scope which this position would give to his powers, as an extempore lecturer; the interest he took in the young; the filial feeling with which he regarded the University; — but the leading motive, and that which was the keystone of all others, was, that his refusal would deprive the University of a useful and honorable foundation. On the other hand, many considerations operated to induce a refusal, so many indeed, that, as we have seen, he had previously declined a similar position. The acceptance of this new office would, he well knew, crowd his leisure time with labor; and the removal from Salem, by breaking up his family associations, and the social circle which had gathered around him, and to which he had become greatly endeared, might materially interfere with his happiness. But after balancing all arguments, for and against the proposition, he concluded to accept it. If Mr. Dane is entitled to the honor of being the founder of this Professorship, to my father is due the honor of being the *fundator perficiens*, since, without his acceptance the donation would have failed. It will, I think, also clearly appear, in the course of the future pages, that the creation of the School, the great enlargement of its funds, and the erection of the building itself, are mainly due to my father.[9]

More conversations followed, between Story and the other members of the Corporation, and, at some time, between Quincy and Dane.[10] In the course of the winter and spring 1828–29 be-

[9] *Life and Letters of Joseph Story*, II, 2–3. Compare Dane's letter to Story dated September 6, 1828, above. Clearly W. W. Story's account refers to the events initiated by Dane's letter of September 1828, which Story's son evidently had not seen. At this time no good end is served by speculation as to whether hen or egg came first; whether Dane, as he wrote Story, had long before decided to benefit the School, or whether Story in 1828 was indeed *fundator perficiens*. They both did well.

[10] Quincy to W. W. Story, August 20, 1851, quoted *Life and Letters of Joseph Story*, II, 564.

tween them all they shaped the future of the Law School. On May 19, 1829, about six weeks after Stearns had resigned his professorship of law, Story wrote to the Corporation a formal letter evidently stating the substance of many *pourparlers*.

Mr. Dane proposes to establish a new Law Professorship in Harvard University for the delivery of lectures on the subjects of Natural Law, Commercial and Maritime Law and Constitutional Law. He proposes to give as a foundation $10,000, the income of which is to be applied to the maintenance of the Professor. He wishes me to take the professorship, and wishes that it should be a fundamental statute of his foundation that residence at Cambridge should not be required of the Professor; but that it should depend upon his own choice. As an inducement to my accepting this professorship, he expresses a willingness to have the other statutes of the foundation framed according to my wishes; and he also expresses a contingent determination to add $5,000 more to the foundation to be applied in the same way. I am given to understand that the Corporation wish to ascertain under these circumstances whether I will accept the professorship, and upon what further terms I am willing to remove to Cambridge. I have thought much upon the subject and have great reluctance in quitting Salem. I cannot do so without a considerable sacrifice of property. I have stated to Mr. Dane that I will accept his Professorship, if non-residence is allowable, the statutes of his foundation are satisfactory to me, and the duties thereof are so arranged as not to interfere with my judicial duties, which are and ever must be with me of paramount obligation and interest. I shall deem it indispensable, therefore, to my acceptance of the office, that it shall be explicitly understood that I shall not be bound to perform any duties incompatible with my judical duties, and that my leisure only, allowing reasonable periods for recreation and health, shall be devoted to the professorship. I have no objection to the delivery of oral or written lectures or both, as from time to time may be thought most advisable by the Corporation. My written lectures I should ultimately propose to have published, which indeed the founder explicitly wishes me to understand is his principal object.

I should be willing to remove to Cambridge, if the Corporation deemed it advisable, if the following terms could be complied with.

(1) That the Corporation should guarantee to me an annual income of $1,000, including in this sum whatever I might receive from the Dane Professorship.

(2) That I can sell my real estate in Salem (which has cost me at least $8,000 and is now in perfect repair and the best order) for $7,000. A greater sacrifice than this difference, I could not consent to make, as the estate is now well suited to my wants and condition.

(3) That the Corporation erect a suitable house on land owned by the College at Cambridge for my residence, at an expense in the whole not exceeding $7,000, in such form and with such accommodations as

might be mutually agreed on. That I should take a lease of the same for five or seven years, and pay an annual rent equal to six per cent per annum upon the amount expended, with a clause that upon my removal from Cambridge or resignation of all duties excepting the Dane Professorship or the Professorship itself, I should be at liberty to surrender the lease. My object in this clause is to provide against the possibility of the office interfering in the future with my judical duties or my health, so that I could not or ought not to retain it.

(4) That at least one permanent University Professor shall be appointed with a constant residence at Cambridge, whose duty it should be to perform, throughout the year, the common duties of Professor and Instructor. He ought to receive a larger compensation than myself, because he will be called to perform duties throughout the year, whereas mine can be occasional only. I think he ought to receive $1,500 per year; if I receive $1,000. If the Law School should succeed, so that the income should be more than sufficient to pay both our salaries, the residue to be divided equally between him and myself, unless the Corporation should think it better to establish a third professorship. In that event, the surplus income, to an amount not exceeding $1,500, might be devoted to such third professorship. The surplus, if any, to be divided between the second professor and myself. But in no event, should I desire, as my services cannot be constant, more than an annual income of $1,500, whatever might be the success of the School. Situated as I am, and must be, I should not choose to be deemed by the public to seek a compensation beyond the reasonable value of my services.

(5) I should be willing to take a general superintendence of the Law School, that is to visit it and examine the students occasionally, and to direct their studies, and to lecture to them orally on the topics connected with the Dane Professorship from time to time in a familiar way. But I should rely on the permanent Professor, for what I may call the drill duty and a constant attention to the students, giving them my advice and assistance as far as I could. I could not undertake to be with them in their ordinary studies, but rather to aid them by occasional explanations and excitements. In short, to put them upon the means of instruction, rather than to see that they only get them. This is a sketch of my views and I put them on paper, that my objects may be distinctly understood; and that my promise may not exceed my performance.[11]

Story was able to write his own ticket at the university. He would move to Cambridge if Harvard would provide for him a house comparable to the house he would have to give up in Salem. Otherwise he would hold the Dane Professorship as a nonresident. Harvard must provide a "permanent University Professor" to do

[11] Harvard College Papers, vol. III, 2nd series, p. 239, quoted in Warren, *Harvard Law School*, I, 417–418.

Joseph Story. "There never was a man who did more work than he . . . With a body that seemed incapable of fatigue, he had the alertness and vivacity of youth, and imparted his own enthusiasm to his pupils." Andrew Preston Peabody in *Harvard Reminiscences* (1886). This portrait was painted by Charles Osgood in 1837.

Story was a versatile man. Sometimes he wrote poems. At a Harvard dinner in 1823 he proposed a toast to Kent saying the Chancellor's judgments on the law of the land had made New York the Land of the Law. Kent in return gave "Massachusetts, the land of Story as well as song." Auguste Edouart made this silhouette about 1842.

"drill duty" at the Law School and to give constant attention to the students. Story would give the School "general superintendence," and from time to time would lecture "in a familiar way." His judicial work was to have priority. Evidently the Corporation found this memorandum quite satisfactory, for its relevant terms appear in a subsequent formal letter from Dane to the Corporation, dated June 2, 1829,[12] proposing Story for the new professorship; the letter was laid before the Corporation at a special meeting held the same day, just before the inauguration of President Quincy.

On that early June evening there was a great inaugural dinner with six hundred guests. Someone announced Dane's gift to the assembly. Harrison Gray Otis arose to express gratitude, and quipped, "Non timeo Danaos et dona Ferentes." The Corporation met again next morning, June 3. Nobody was surprised when the President and Fellows named Story Dane Professor. Eight days later, on June 11, the Corporation elected for the vacant Royall chair John Hooker Ashmun, talented but ailing teacher at Judge Rowe's law school in Northampton. The Overseers disregarded their general rule that nominations must lie before them seven days, and on June 12, 1829, confirmed both appointments. The university authorities were understandably worried about getting enough students to enroll; evidently some people hoped that Ashmun would bring a number of his pupils with him from Northampton.[13]

Story and Ashmun spent the rest of the summer preparing for the revitalized School. On August 25, the day before Commencement, Harvard inaugurated the two new professors in the old Meeting House, which then stood in the southwest corner of the Yard, near the westerly end of the present Lehman Hall. President Quincy made an address in Latin. Professor Hedge read the statutes of the two professorships. The new professors replied in Latin, and signed the statutes. Story delivered an inaugural discourse in English, entitled "Value and Importance of Legal Studies." [14] The moment was not apt for a playful speech,

---

[12] Dane's letter is copied in the Corporation's minutes of June 2, 1829. It is quoted in Warren, I, 418–421.

[13] *The Boston Daily Advertiser*, writing of eighteen admissions by September 7, spoke of additional men "expected from the School at Northampton." See Warren, I, 432. (Did they come?)

[14] Published in *Miscellaneous Writings*, pp. 503f.

and Story's was a trifle heavy. He outlined the subjects assigned to him by Mr. Dane's foundation, the law of nature, law of nations, maritime and commercial law, equity, and the constitutional law of the United States; in much that he said he forecast some of the books he published during the following sixteen years. Perhaps some of the audience felt a little relieved when the long ceremony was over and they could adjourn for dinner at Porter's Hotel.

Early in September Story moved from Salem to a square brick house in Cambridge on the corner of Brattle and Hilliard streets, which Harvard rented for his use. He lived there for the rest of his life.[15] Story moved his personal law library to the lower floor of College House Number 2, and on September 1, wrote Quincy that the School needed a number of copies of Blackstone and half a dozen copies of Kent's *Commentaries* for student use.

Nobody need have worried about enough enrollments to keep going. Story and Ashmun turned out to be a wonderfully attractive combination; Ashmun was a steady and methodical teacher; Story was a brilliant extempore lecturer. At once Story began writing the books Dane had prescribed. In the four years of Ashmun's Harvard life the number of law students in residence rose from twenty-seven to more than forty. Once the enrollment reached fifty-three. From the opening of classes in the fall term of 1829 down to the present day there has never again been any serious doubt of the School's viability.[16]

2

The Law School's record of students admitted between 1817 and 1840, their previous education, their time of departure, their LL.B. degree if it was granted, and their admission to practice,

[15] The house still stood a century later. Then frequented by law students from Yale, it was familiarly called Eli. The drive of progress has now replaced it with an apartment house.

[16] When Ashmun died, on April 1, 1833, the registration immediately fell from a little over forty to thirty-one. It then began a steady increase until Story's death, on September 10, 1845; that month one hundred and forty-five students registered. Thereafter their numbers declined sharply until 1849–50, when the School had only ninety students. During the next decade registrations rose to one hundred and sixty-one; but the Civil War cut this number to ninety-two in 1862–63. Peace brought an immediate increase to one hundred and seventy-seven in 1865–66. These figures are taken from the reports of the faculty of law to the President and from the annual President's reports.

appear in a bound notebook, probably kept by student clerks, in which students are listed alphabetically. From September 1829 on, the entries became more complete than they had been earlier. Generally the notations are purely formal, though now and then the chroniclers put in a bit of drama. John Sullivan Fraser, of Savannah, Georgia, entered the School in 1835, stayed three years, and took his degree in 1838. Of him the chronicler noted "Shot at Blount's Ferry, Flor. Nov. 19 and died Nov. 30, 1845." Opposite the name of Richard Hightown Hayes of Tennessee who came in 1834 and left in 1835 is the note "Killed in a Street fight in Columbus, Tenn. by Wm. Polk, December 4, 1838." Watts Sherman Lynde of Homer, New York, a Yale A.B., entered the School in 1839 and left in November 1840. The recorder noted opposite his name, "Lost on board the Steamboat Erie, burnt on Lake Erie August 9, 1841." Kaled Ellis Sumner of New Hampshire, a Dartmouth A.B. entered the School in August 1834 and departed in December 1835. He "Left for a farm."

The page of names beginning with H shows that in September 1829 "Oliver Wendall Holmes" of Cambridge enrolled in the Law School. Young Holmes, so he wrote his Harvard College classmate Phineas Barnes in September 1829, had thought of going somewhere else to study law.

> September je ne sçais pas quoi, 1829
>
> Dear Barnes.
>
> . . . I am settled once more at home in the midst of those miscellaneous articles which always cluster around me whenever I can do as I please, — Blackstone and boots, law and lathe, Rawle and rasps, all intermingled in exquisite confusion. When you was here, I thought of going away to study my profession but since Judge Story and Mr. Ashmun have come, the Law School is so flourishing that I have thought it best to stay where I am.

On January 13, 1830, Holmes wrote to Barnes "I will tell you honestly that I am sick at heart of this place and everything connected with it. I know not what the temple of law may be to those who have entered it, but to me it seems very cold and cheerless about the threshold." [17] The record book shows that Holmes left the Law School in August 1830; opposite his name is the laconic entry "Deserted to the enemy (Medical)." He was also

---

[17] These letters of O. W. Holmes, Sr., can be found in Morse, *Life and Letters of Oliver Wendell Holmes*, I, 62, 65.

launching a third career; on the sixteenth day of the following month, the *Boston Daily Advertiser* carried a poem of his that kept from destruction for scrap lumber the U.S.S. *Constitution,* "Old Ironsides," now the Navy's oldest vessel still in commission.

The class that entered the School in 1829 had other great names. Benjamin Robbins Curtis, LL.B. 1832, was destined to become a justice of the Supreme Court of the United States, to resign his seat after a difference with Chief Justice Roger B. Taney over *Dred Scott's Case,*[18] and to serve as successful chief counsel for President Andrew Johnson during his trial on impeachment. On September 1, 1831, Charles Sumner of Boston enrolled. He had just taken his Harvard A.B. and during his years at the School he faithfully corresponded with college classmates. Sumner's letters are full of insights into student life. He lived in 10 Divinity Hall during the first year. Then new, it stood in a patch of woods, the most outlying dormitory at Harvard. Sumner took his meals in the Commons. After the Dane Law College was built, he moved to its Room 4, a perquisite of his office as student librarian, "the pleasantest room in Cambridge" he thought,[19] where he lived from October 1832 until December 1833. He took his LL.B. the following August.

A few days after the fall term of 1831 opened, on September 25, Sumner wrote to his college classmate Jonathan Stearns of Bedford.

Come to Cambridge and see me. I room at Divinity Hall, No. 10, on the lower floor . . . You will not disturb me; for, though I try to seize every moment of time, yet our law-studies are so indefinite that no number of hours cut out will be missed. We recite but three times a week; and one forenoon will master our lesson, though days can be given to it with profit. . . . I like living here, for I can be by myself. I know hardly an individual in the school. Days of idleness must be atoned for; the atoning offering is at hand, and it is a steady devotion to *study.* Late to bed and early to rise, and full employment while up, is what I am trying to bind myself to. . . .

I have not yet methodized my time, — and, by the way, method is the life of study, — but I think of something like the following: The law in the forenoon; six hours to law is all that Coke asks for (*sex horas des legibus aequis*), and Matthew Hale and Sir William Jones and all who have declared an opinion; though, as to that matter, I

[18] *Dred Scott v. Sandford,* 19 Howard 393 (1857).
[19] So he told a classmate who had returned to Harvard as a resident graduate. Edward L. Pierce, *Memoir and Letters of Charles Sumner* (Boston, 1877), I, 104.

should be influenced little more than a tittle by any opinions of others. We all of us must shape our own courses; no two men will like the same hours or manner of study. Let each one assist himself from the experience of others; but let him not put aside his own judgment. Well, six hours, — namely, the forenoon wholly and solely to law; afternoon to classics; evening to history, subjects collateral and assistant to law, &c. I have as yet read little else than law since I have been here: but the above is the plan I have chalked out.

On September 29, 1831, Sumner wrote to another Harvard classmate, Charlemagne Tower, of Waterville, New York: "I am now a regular member of the Law School, have read a volume and a half of Blackstone, and am enamored of the law. Tower, we have struck the true profession." On January 31, 1832, he again wrote to Tower.

Judge Story is at Washington, with the Supreme Court, for the winter. Of course the school misses him. Our class, as yet, has had nothing to do with him. Those who do recite to him love him more than any instructor they ever had before. He treats them all as gentlemen, and is full of willingness to instruct. He gives to every line of the recited lesson a running commentary, and omits nothing which can throw light upon the path of the student. The good scholars like him for the knowledge he distributes; the poor (if any there be), for the amenity with which he treats them and their faults. Have you determined never again to return to the shadows of Cambridge? By the way, the judge has a book in press, which will be published within a week, which you must read. I mention this because I doubted whether you would hear of it immediately. It is called "Commentaries on Bailments," and will entirely supersede the classic work of Jones. The title of "Bailments" is of but a day's growth. It is hardly known to the common law. Jones's work was written about forty years ago. Since then it has gained a much completer conformation. Story's work will supply all deficiencies, and, I suspect, be an interesting book; certainly a useful one.[20]

3

The Story period divides into two parts: four years with Ashmun as day-by-day executive of the School, and after Ashmun's death, twelve years with Simon Greenleaf doing the same sort of duty. Story and Ashmun followed Stearns's regime in general method, but they much expanded and modernized Stearns's reading list. President Quincy's report for 1828–29, dated January 1830, shows that Story and Ashmun had laid out a plan of instruc-

[20] *Ibid.*, I, 109–112.

tion to be completed in three years, during which a student could follow a "Regular Course" or a "Parallel Course," intended for those able and willing to give extra hours to their legal education." [21] The reading lists were divided into categories of subject matter. In 1829 students began with introductory instruction in Blackstone, Kent, and Wooddeson's Lectures. Then came personal property; commercial and maritime law; real property; equity; "Crown" (that is, criminal) law; civil law; the law of nations; and constitutional law. All the reading lists on American law subjects include texts and "Select Cases." Thus by 1829 there are discernible the beginnings not only of courses in the modern sense, but also of the study of these courses from judicial opinions. The stated norm of three years was not observed. People actually took degrees in two years, and the statement of required residence was amended accordingly in the report of 1832–33.

Story and Ashmun, as one would expect, carried on the tradition of moots for the arguments of questions of law which Stearns and Parker had carried over from their predecessors in England. Story, with a flair for imaginative improvisation, adapted questions from his judicial experience for these exercises. And he went beyond arguments of law to trials of fact — a form of instruction revived at Harvard in 1949. Story's son, who took his LL.B. in 1840, later wrote:

Twice a year there were jury trials, the counsel in which were appointed by lot among the Law Students; twelve of the undergraduates acting as a jury. On these occasions, there was a sort of a festival at the School. The ordinary exercises were suspended; the Library, where the trial took place, was crowded with members of the University; and the contests between the parties were long, sharp, and earnest. In all these trials my father took great delight, and his interest stimulated the young men in their efforts. He delivered elaborate oral judgments, and they, in their turn, prepared their cases with great zeal. He used to say of their arguments, that they were often quite as good, and sometimes better, than those of the counsel engaged in the real cases. It would have seemed only natural, that, under the pressure and excitement of his judicial duties, these fictitious questions, wanting the stimulus of actual litigation, and unaffected by the passions and interests of real parties, would have seemed to

[21] On August 29, 1831, two days before Sumner's Harvard College Commencement, he wrote to his classmate Tower: "I am stiff in the determination to commence the coming year in the study of law at Cambridge . . . I intend to give myself to the law, so as to read satisfactorily the regular and parallel courses."

him stale and flat. But it was not so. He entered into them with the same zest and gusto as if they had been real, — nay, even with more unfeigned satisfaction. He loved to see the young, ardent minds of the students, first measuring their strength in argument. There was all the interest, with none of the responsibility of his judicial life.

The benefit which the students derived from these "moot-court" trials was very apparent, and their progress in all their studies greatly encouraged and gratified my father. He entered into his professional duties with his whole heart, and all other subjects became secondary in interest to the Law School.[22]

Story had to spend the winter and early spring of each year on the bench in Washington; and during other months his academic program must have suffered some interruptions by his duties as circuit justice at terms of court in Maine, New Hampshire, Massachusetts, and Rhode Island.[23] Ashmun at first tended to everything when Story was away. Later student librarians and young instructors came to help out. The best known of these was Charles Sumner.

Story, among his other high talents, could effectively use odd moments of free time. During the intervals of judicial duty he wisely put his principal intellectual efforts on writing his books instead of preparing formal lectures. His classroom method, though it was predicated on assigned readings in texts rather than on judicial opinions, was fundamentally the dialectic which we have come to ascribe to Langdell, Ames, Keener, and their successors. Story's son later described his father as he had seen him in the lecture room.

Instead of reading a series of formal and written lectures, his method of teaching was by familiar discourse and conversational commentary. A stated portion of some textbook was allotted at every exercise as the subject to be treated at the next meeting. In this the students prepared themselves. My father commenced by making general remarks upon the subject, and sketching broadly the principles . . .

[22] *Life and Letters of Joseph Story*, II, 53.

[23] In Story's day justices of the Supreme Court sat every year in the circuit courts of the circuits to which they were assigned. The circuit courts tried cases as courts of first instance; they also had an appellate jurisdiction to review certain district court judgments. The travel involved was no small burden. Justice Iredell termed his life that of a "travelling postboy." Warren, *Supreme Court in United States History*, I, 86.

In January 1841 Story apologized for his tardy response to a letter. "I am but just off my Circuit Court duties, having been employed therein for nearly the whole of the last three months with many very difficult questions of law to dispose of in my brief leisure." *Life and Letters of Joseph Story*, II, 356.

Questions were then proposed to the students, who, in turn, whenever any difficulty presented itself, freely questioned the professor.
The recitation was not at all confined to the text-book; but the
general principles laid down in it formed the theme of a full and free
commentary, in the course of which their various modifications and
exceptions were brought out, and copiously illustrated in every shade
of differences. The book constituted merely the starting-goal, from
which wide excursions were made into every cognate province of the
law, from which matter for elucidation, ornament, or interest could
be gathered. My father's untiring enthusiasm, his copious learning,
and his extraordinary fluency, enabled him to carry out this plan
with comparative ease to himself. Roger North, in his Life of Lord
Keeper Guildford, describes him as a "good put-case." My father was
entitled to the same praise. His readiness of invention was peculiarly
exhibited in the rapidity with which he created fictitious cases for
the illustration of the question under consideration, and the facility
with which, after having supposed a case, to illustrate a general principle, he shaped its circumstances so as to expose the various modifications and exceptions to which it was subject. The figure changed
with every turn, like the pattern in the kaleidoscope. He twisted the
familiar incidents of the day, into illustrations of legal principles, —
began by telling a story, and then suddenly asked how the law would
apply to it; so that oftentimes the student, who thought he was
listening to a tale found himself in the midst of a legal discussion.
Thus he attracted the mind along, instead of driving it. Alive himself,
he made the law alive.[24]

Nathan Dane had prescribed a series of publications as part
of his professor's functions; he had written to the Corporation
on June 2, 1829: "In the first place it shall be his duty to prepare
and to deliver, and to revise for publication, a course of lectures
on the five following branches of Law and Equity, equally in
force in all parts of our Federal Republic, namely: The Law of
Nature, the Law of Nations, Commercial and Maritime Law, Federal Law and Federal Equity." Proposing Story for the new
Chair, Dane had asked "that time shall be allowed him to complete, in manner aforesaid, a course of lectures on the said five
branches, probably making four or more octavo volumes; and
that all the lectures and teachings of him, and of every professor
so to be appointed, shall be calculated to assist and serve in a
special manner, law students and lawyers in practice, sound and
useful law being the object." [25]

[24] *Ibid.*, II, 35–37.
[25] Dane's letter is copied in the minutes of the Corporation's meeting of June 2,
1829.

A published "course of lectures" such as Dane proposed would have been analogous to Blackstone's *Commentaries,* and to Kent's *Commentaries* of 1826. Dane's letter of June 2 was a statement of Story's ideas as well as Nathan Dane's. Story may have been remembering his law student days in Samuel Sewall's Marblehead office, three decades earlier, when he had wept over *Coke Upon Littleton.* He knew the need for suitable texts for students. In March 1830 he had written to Ticknor from Washington: "I shall be glad to return home, and work with the Law Students. I am impatient for leisure to prepare some written lectures, for there is a terrible deficiency of good elementary books." [26] Fortunately Story was sensitive, intelligent, imaginative. As soon as he started teaching he perceived that oral instruction is an art wholly different from the reading of formal set pieces. Lectures written both for classroom and for publication would probably serve neither well. Communication of connected logical doctrine is more efficient by printed page than by dictation in the lecture hall. A lecture read for reproduction in student notes, designed for later study as if it were a printed book, might far better be printed in the first place. But Story could extemporize *pro re nata;* could immediately adapt the matter of his discourse to the thought of his hearers; could respond provocatively to their questions, producing new examples on the spot; could induce his hearers to perceive wisdom for themselves. So he undertook the two functions separately, turned to good account his talent for extemporized lectureroom conversation, and devoted his scholarly, closeted hours to writing books on matters germane to Dane's original program. His books were not edited lectures.

4

In January 1832 Story brought out the first of his series of *Commentaries,* a book on *The Law of Bailments.* A year later he finished his *Commentaries on the Constitution,* dating the preface January 1833. In 1834 he published the world's first treatise on conflict of laws and, in addition, a secondary-school textbook for instruction in government, called *Classbook on the Constitution.* In 1835 came *Equity Jurisprudence;* in 1838, *Equity Pleading.* In 1839 he brought out *Commentaries on Agency;*

[20] *Life and Letters of Joseph Story,* II, 35.

in 1841, *Partnership*; in 1843 came *Bills of Exchange*; and in 1845, just before he died, appeared his last work, *Promissory Notes*.[27] This authorship was an amazing performance, undertaken and completed by a man between his fifty-second and sixty-seventh years of life, in the intervals of judicial duty on the Supreme Court and on circuit, in addition to classroom teaching at Harvard and to the duties of a Fellow of the Harvard Corporation. He planned, so he told Sumner before he died, to follow his *Commentaries on Promissory Notes* by a book on the law of shipping; then one on insurance; then a third book on equity, *Equity Practice*. Next he proposed a book on admiralty "embracing the Prize and Instance branches,"[28] in their history, jurisdiction, and practice . . . as it had never yet been presented, with completeness and symmetry." After that Story planned a treatise on the law of nations. Finally, a suitable summation, he planned a book of "reminiscences of his times and contemporaries."[29] Perhaps one misses this last more than any of the other unwritten books.

Story was able to produce the books he did write, covering so large a part of the private American law affecting commerce, of the growing public law of the United States, and of private international law, only because of his unique qualities and the fortunate circumstances of his life. When he began his series of *Commentaries* he had studied law continuously for more than thirty years. And from the time he was thirty-two in 1811, he had seen the passing procession of American law from the bench in Washington and from the cities on his circuit. Ever since the beginning of his student days at Harvard College he had practiced the art of using time; and in his twenties he had acquired the difficult self-discipline of promptly committing to a printer what

[27] The *Promissory Notes* manuscript is in the School's archives. One reads Story's minute, almost illegible pages, and wonders what a 1967 typesetter would say about it.

[28] "Instance branch" may be somewhat strange to a lawyer of 1967 who is not an admiralty specialist. The "Instance" jurisdiction is the ordinary admiralty field — collisions at sea, salvage, and so forth. The "law of prize" consisted of the rules of international law which permitted an armed ship, either of the line or a vessel under letters of marque and reprisal, under certain circumstances to capture another vessel *vi et armis*, put a prize crew aboard her, and sail her to some port where she could be condemned and sold as prize. The "prize money" was then divided among all hands of the captor ship's company. For a World War I case see *The Appam*, 243 U.S. 124 (1917). Prize litigation, frequent in 1800, has now disappeared.

[29] See *Life and Letters of Joseph Story*, II, 573–574.

he had written, not tarrying unduly over details, making due use of his predecessors' work, accepting whatever hazards of later criticism there might be, and turning cheerfully to the next job.

Nathan Dane's original program of writing for the Dane Professor had contemplated "four or more octavo volumes" on what he called five "branches" of the law: the "Law of Nature, the Law of Nations, Commercial and Maritime Law, Federal Law and Federal Equity." At this day no one knows just how Dane counted his five branches among these six. Quite likely Dane's list resulted from a talk with Story, before Story had carefully planned his books. At any rate what Story finally produced turned out to be somewhat different from Dane's prescription, and probably Story's series was the better for that. By the time he came to write he had subjected Dane's proposals to the imperative scrutiny required by blank paper and a pen. The law of nature receded into the background.

Story wrote his Harvard books [30] on four general subjects: commercial law, the Constitution, conflict of laws, and equity. The largest group concerned commercial law, his books on bailments, agency, partnership, and bills and notes. He saw the need for this subject in a country turning from agriculture and sailing ships to a society based on the industrial revolution and on the economic organization which accompanied it. A few days before Story died he heard that some Boston merchant proposed to erect a statue in his honor; Story suggested instead that they found in the Law School a chair of commercial law. Story's proposed books on the law of shipping, the law of insurance, and admiralty would have completed this commercial law series.

Bailment, at first glance, seems oddly narrow for Story to choose for his first *Commentaries*; but his table of contents demonstrates that in his mind that title covered a large part of the law governing the economic processes of his time, including an analysis of the concepts of negligence, which was to govern so large a part of common-law thinking as the nineteenth century grew older. He covers the orthodox subjects of "deposits" and "mandates," stating with a candor which must have relieved students in 1832 that he could see little difference between the two. Gratuitous loans, pawns and pledges, hire of things, bail-

[30] The term is not here used from pure vanity, but to designate those books written while Story was Dane Professor.

ments for work done on the thing bailed, all have a faintly archaic sound, but behind them the reader can see legal antecedents
of many modern practices.[31] Story goes on to a long essay on the
liability of innkeepers and a longer exposition of the law of
common carriers of goods; in his second edition (1840) he includes the responsibility of "rail cars." [32] He discusses carriers of
passengers for hire, and ends the book by treatment of what he
calls "quasi-Bailees for Hire" such as revenue agents, court officers, salvors, and prize agents.

Commentaries on the Law of Bailments was on the whole a
promising book though technical. It demonstrates that Story was
writing not for the past but for his own day, and even for the
future. Characteristically he makes much use of Roman and civil
law materials; in his introduction he ascribes this not only to his
own inclination but to the example of Kent and the wishes of
Dane. One reason for Story's choice of a subject may emerge
from his introductory discussion of Sir William Jones's *Essay on
the Law of Bailments,*[33] which he praises while undertaking
to correct defects. He was used to preparing new editions of
standard English texts. Perhaps even Story still felt more at ease
writing his first *Commentaries* with an existing book as a guide.

Story's second Harvard book was not the first published work
on the Constitution of the United States. The Federalist Papers
were, and still are, classics. The appendix to volume one of St.
George Tucker's 1803 edition of Blackstone contains a 237-page
"View of the Constitution of the United States." Thomas Sergeant
in 1822 published in Philadelphia the first edition of his *Constitutional Law, being a View of the Practice and Jurisdiction of the
Courts of the United States and of Constitutional Points Decided.*
Story knew and cited Sergeant's book, which had appeared in a
second edition in 1830, three years before Story published his
Commentaries on the Constitution. Like Story Sergeant saw the
desirability of an account of colonial antecedents of our constitutional system; in his 1830 edition he added an introduction with

[31] Secs. 219–420. "Hire of things" today includes the lease of immense quantities of machinery and fleets of vehicles. See *United Shoe Machinery Corp. v.
United States,* 347 U.S. 521 (1954), affirming per curiam 110 F. Supp. 295 (D.
Mass. 1953), and *Cintrone v. Hertz Truck Leasing and Rental Service,* 45 N.J.
434, 212 A.2d 769 (1965).

[32] Secs. 496–499, "Rail Cars." Story cites *Camden and Amboy Rail Road Co. v.
Burke,* 13 Wendell R. 611 and 2 Kent Comm. 240.

[33] London, 1781.

Joseph Story

a brief survey of that period. Sergeant saw nothing extraordinary in *Marbury v. Madison*; he cites the case at a number of points; and under his discussion of the Supremacy Clause, article 6, paragraph 2, simply states that "An act of Congress, contrary to the constitution of the United States, is null and void." [34] Sergeant's book is comparatively short; essentially it is a practitioners' manual on constitutional matters.

William Rawle's *View of the Constitution of the United States of America*, published in Philadelphia in 1825, was, like Sergeant's book, a much briefer survey than Story's. Rawle, writing "Of General Tribunals, and first of the Supreme Court," polishes off *Marbury v. Madison* in nine lines of terse approval. Today Rawle's thirty-first chapter "Of the Union," has a melancholy interest because of incidents that occurred a generation after the book appeared. Rawle expressed the view that any state of the Union could constitutionally secede if it so determined through the unequivocal voices of its people. West Point used Rawle's book as a text when the general officers who led the Confederate armies were cadets. To blame poor Rawle for the Civil War is an absurdity. What his book demonstrates today is the fact that men's ideas of the bond holding the United States together have changed profoundly between 1787 and 1967; and that the change came about at different times with different men. General Robert E. Lee's ideas of the Union in 1861 were not those of Lieutenant Oliver Wendell Holmes, Jr.

Story had other predecessor constitutionalists. Dane's eight-volume *Abridgment* of 1823 and his 1829 ninth volume contained much constitutional theory and precedent; Kent's *Commentaries* of 1826 had still more. But Story's two-volume work gave so much the best exposition up to his time that it deserves to be thought a pioneer treatise of constitutional history and theory; it is more than an extrapolation of preceding books.

Story's preface, dated January 1833 acknowledges "two great sources from which . . . I have drawn by far the greatest part of my most valuable materials. These are, the Federalist, an incomparable commentary of three of the greatest statesmen of their age; and the extraordinary Judgments of Mr. Chief Justice Marshall upon constitutional law." We have not, to this day, found any better guides to our constitutional origins, and Story's

[34] Thomas Sergeant, *Constitutional Law* (Philadelphia, 1830 ed.), p. 401.

opportunities to follow them were unequaled. He had been a young lawyer, eccentrically Republican in Federalist Salem, when Marshall decided *Marbury v. Madison* in 1803. The Boston newspapers discussed the case at length; [35] young Story must have devoured them. While Story had allied himself politically with Jefferson, he was a constitutionalist of the Marshall school, and in his *Constitution* he vigorously supports the *Marbury* decision.[36] In 1810 Story had successfully argued *Fletcher v. Peck* for the defendant; the judgment, upholding the validity of Georgia land grants against a supervening Georgia statute established the dominance of the federal Constitution over inconsistent state law.[37] As a justice, Story had participated in *Fairfax v. Hunter's Lessee* of 1813 and *Martin v. Hunter's Lessee* of 1816; [38] *McCulloch v. Maryland* of 1819; [39] *Cohens v. Virginia* of 1821; [40] *Gibbons v. Ogden* of 1824; [41] *Willson v. Black Bird Creek Marsh Co.* of 1829; [42] the *Cherokee* cases of 1831 and 1832.[43] When he wrote his 1833 book on the Constitution he could know all the cases ever decided by the Supreme Court, reported in its thirty-one volumes of opinions. Marshall, the original architect of constitutional law, was Story's closest friend on the Court; to Marshall Story dedicated his *Constitution*. He wrote it from firsthand knowledge.

The *Commentaries on the Constitution* is a combination of American constitutional history, of analytical theory of political science, and discussion of adjudications in the formative era of the Constitution. Story starts his book with the origins of European claims to American territories, gives a useful account of the founding and history of each of the thirteen colonies, and describes the beginnings of the federal government in the Revolution (a term Story uses without apology). He gives an account of the weaknesses of the Confederation, and the convocation of the Constitutional Convention of 1787; his history of the con-

[35] For references to Boston papers see Warren, *Supreme Court*, I, 246. The *Marbury* case is reported I Cranch 137.
[36] Secs. 1575f.
[37] 6 Cranch 87.
[38] 7 Cranch 603; 1 Wheaton 304.
[39] 4 Wheaton 316.
[40] 6 Wheaton 264.
[41] 9 Wheaton 1.
[42] 2 Peters 245.
[43] *Cherokee Nation v. Georgia*, 5 Peters 1; *Worcester v. Georgia*, 6 Peters 515.

vention seems surprisingly brief. Story so frequently cites Pitkin's *History of the United States* [44] and Marshall's *Life of Washington* that the modern reader is led to suspect that Story may, quite sensibly, have taken these two books as outlines of our constitutional origins, filling in such details as he needed from whatever other sources he could find.

Two of Story's expositions of doctrine concerned ideas destined to be momentous. He approved of judicial review of federal legislation, exemplified in his day only by *Marbury v. Madison.*[45] It was, he wrote, supported by clear and convincing reason.[46] And he vigorously opposed at some length the theory that the Constitution was a mere "compact" between states, from which any state might lawfully withdraw whenever it should choose to do so.[47] In the 1830's judicial review of Acts of Congress was a comparatively minor feature of our constitutional system and Story's brevity is understandable. But state defiance of the Union was ominous. When Story wrote the preface to his *Commentaries on the Constitution* in January 1833, Georgia's resistance against the federal government and South Carolina's nullification movement must have been fresh in his mind. Had he lived sixteen years after 1845 he would have seen his horror of secession confirmed by the Confederacy.

In the first three years of Story's term as Dane Professor he had thus produced two notable treatises, one on private law, one on public law. By the winter of 1833 old Nathan Dane could see his intellectual aspirations for the School turning into excellent reality.

One of Story's great traits was his habit of continuing to write. He had no sooner finished his *Commentaries on the Constitution* than he started his *Commentaries on the Conflict of Laws, Foreign and Domestic, in regard to Contracts, Rights, and Remedies,*

[44] Timothy Pitkin, *A Political and Civil History of the United States* (New Haven, 1828).

[45] And perhaps by *U.S. v. Todd* (1794), reported only in a note to *U.S. v. Ferreira,* 13 Howard 40 (1851), and *Hodgson v. Bowerbank* 5 Cranch 303 (1809).

[46] Sec. 1569. Story in a footnote quoted at length from Marshall's opinion in 1 Cranch; his footnote, he wrote, was intended as "a corrective to those loose and extraordinary doctrines, which sometimes find their way into opinions possessing official influence."

[47] Story was here rejecting the ideas of St. George Tucker in his 1803 edition of Blackstone's *Commentaries.* Judge Tucker had stressed the idea of the Constitution as a compact between the states. See Story's bk. III, chap. III, "Nature of the Constitution — Whether a Compact."

and Especially in Regard to Marriages, Divorces, Wills, Successsions, and Judgments. The preface of this third "portion of the labors appertaining to the Dane Professorship of Law in Harvard University" he dated January 1, 1834. Previous Anglo-American scholarly writings on conflicts were few and slight. Story prints after his table of contents a list "of some of the more important Authors, whose works have been cited [which] may assist the student in his researches." Of the forty-five writers there listed all but three are continental jurists. Two are Scottish, Erskine and Kaims; none is English. Only one writer in Story's list was an American, Samuel Livermore of New Orleans, who in 1828 published his little book *Dissertations on the Questions which Arise from the Contrariety of the Positive Laws of Different States and Nations.*[48] The rest were continental writers. As Nadelmann [49] has pointed out, however, beside those few Story had other Anglo-American sources of conflicts law. His own unpublished manuscript digest contained a collection of relevant decisions; Esek Cowen, reporter of the New York Supreme Court in 1825, had digested *Lex loci and lex fori* in an eleven-page note to a conflicts decision in 4 Cowen; Kent and Wheaton had references to conflicts matters; Jabez Henry's work *On Foreign Law* appeared in London in 1823. American courts had been deciding conflicts cases since the time of the first volume of Dallas' reports which appeared in 1790. In the Anglo-American field Story did not start entirely from scratch; he had civil law antecedents by the dozen.

Story goes at the law of conflicts in a modern way. His chapter headings are not strange today: domicile, capacity of persons, marriage and divorce, "foreign contracts," personal property, realty, wills, successions, guardianships, jurisdiction and remedies, foreign judgments, penal laws, matters of evidence. Some modern headings one misses. He does not discuss torts in general, though "torts on ocean, of foreign vessels, by what law governed in case of a conflict of laws" appears in the index to the second edition of 1841. Foreign corporations get bare mention in the second edition, none in the first. Jurisdiction to tax has no place

[48] Livermore gave Story a copy, now in the Harvard library.

[49] A perceptive and learned evaluation of Story's work on conflicts is the paper of Kurt H. Nadelmann of the Harvard Law School faculty, "Joseph Story's Contribution to American Conflicts Law: A Comment," *American Journal of Legal History,* 5:230 (1961). I have here drawn much from it.

in the index, nor does *renvoi*, nor "characterization." Many aspects of the law of tort have become important only because of modern technology; their absence from Story's topics is understandable. Some of his omissions are probably terminological. His book, for its time, was so far ahead that it was a new creation rather than a development of the existing state of the literature. One would not turn to Story's *Conflicts* for guidance in a question arising in 1967, but the book marked a great advance in the learning of its day. On April 11, 1834, Kent wrote to Story from New York:

> . . . There would be plenty of matter for us to chat about if we were together. I have now read and studied thoroughly your admirable Commentary on the Conflict of Laws. You are, as usual, full and perfect in every part, and have left no collateral, as well as no direct point unexamined . . . You have interested and delighted me exceedingly, and I have perceived and felt the want of precision in every instance in which you have intimated it, and have endeavored to correct my own passages. I say there is no such book extant in any single branch of the Law, so full and clear and perfect; and there was no head of the Law which stood more in need of such a production, giving us all the principles and reasoning of all the great Jurists of Europe on the subject . . .
>
> Believe me, truly and affectionately yours,
> James Kent [50]

In December 1835, nearly two years after the appearance of his *Conflict of Laws*, Story brought out his *Commentaries on Equity Jurisprudence as Administered in England and America*; [51] and after still another two years, in 1838, he published his *Commentaries on Equity Pleadings*. Story once told Sumner he intended, in time, to write a third book on equity, treating of its practice.[52] The equity books he did write still have historical value; the chapters in the *Equity Jurisprudence* dealing with trusts, charities, and implied trusts show the state of those sciences in the 1830's. Today's lawyer, reading the *Equity Pleadings*, may feel a bit relieved to learn what he no longer has to know. Story wrote in his preface: "As the present work is confessedly one of a purely technical character, and many of the rules are

---

[50] *Life and Letters of Joseph Story*, II, 167–168.

[51] The author's preface and the letter dedicating the book to William Prescott are both dated December 1835. We do not know the date when the first printed copy became available.

[52] *Life and Letters of Joseph Story*, II, 574.

either of an arbitrary nature, or of a conventional form, it is not easy, in a great variety of instances, to find the exact reasons on which they are built, or by which they are sustained." Perhaps the unwritten book on practice would have been a commentary on any American vestiges of the system which gave rise to *Bleak House*. It is a pity that few authors write legal history in advance, consciously describing their own regimes for readers who may find them curious a century and more later.

On July 18, 1839, Story signed the preface of his *Commentaries on the Law of Agency, as a Branch of Commercial and Maritime Jurisprudence, with Occasional Illustrations from the Civil and Foreign Law*. He intended this book as the first of a series in that field. He wrote in his preface:

The present volume is the commencement of a series of Commentaries, which, in pursuance of the original scheme of the Dane Professorship, it is my design, if my life and health are prolonged, to publish upon the different branches of commercial and maritime jurisprudence. The task is truly formidable, and full of difficulties; and I approach it with a diffidence, proportionate to the public sense of its importance, and to my own consciousness, that its perfect execution will require a leisure, and learning, and ability, which are very far beyond my reach. So various are the topics to be discussed, and so numerous the authorities to be consulted, that a whole life might well be spent in collecting and mastering the materials . . . What I propose to do, therefore, I beg may be treated as an approximation only towards the accomplishment of such a desirable object.

Story's *Agency* of 1839, his *Commentaries on the Law of Partnership* of 1841, his *Commentaries on the Law of Bills of Exchange* of 1843, and his last book, *Commentaries on the Law of Promissory Notes, and Guaranties of Notes, and Checks on Banks and Bankers*, its preface dated "Cambridge, near Boston, June, 1845," were all parts of his intended series on commercial law. With his first treatise, *Bailments*, those four covered most of the law of Story's time affecting the operations of the national economy. He projected further treatises on shipping, on admiralty, and on insurance which he never wrote. One misses any plans for a treatise on sales; and though he treats briefly of corporations in his *Conflicts*, and though manufacturing, banking, and other private corporations were becoming frequent [53] and were oc-

[53] See E. Merrick Dodd, "Corporations in Massachusetts" in *Harvard Legal Essays*, Roscoe Pound, ed. (1934), p. 65.

casioning some litigation, corporations do not appear in the chapter headings or the indexes of his books on agency and partnership. But a modern man should wonder more at what Story completed than at what he omitted.

5

Story not only wrote books; all his life he collected them, at first for his own library, then for the Law School. He and Ashmun, from their first days as the School's faculty, understood that the renewed and enlarged library could not run itself. In the time of Stearns and Parker the books in College House Number 2 had sat on the shelves without systematic new acquisition or care — necessarily so, for the revenue from the tuition was entirely inadequate to buy books and employ a librarian in addition to paying Stearns a few hundred dollars a year. The Royall fund brought Professor Parker a yearly income of only about four hundred dollars. As a practical matter Stearns had not been able to carry out his burdensome duties at the School, act as Middlesex district attorney, and keep very close track of the books as well. But the increase in enrollments which came with Story and Ashmun in the fall of 1829 immediately opened better possibilities. The Dane and Royall funds together yielded about $900 annually. Tuition fees brought in more than $3000 each year. Story's salary was $1000, Ashmun's $1500, leaving a yearly surplus of about $1500,[54] which permitted the university to advance the cost of improving the library against reasonably expected income. In December 1829 the university bought Story's set of law reports for $2212, about half its market value. On February 4, 1830, the library Visiting Committee recommended to the Overseers that the Law School collection be built up to constitute "a complete, American Library." In July 1831 the university bought the rest of Story's law books for $1400. By the time of the President's sixth annual report, for 1830–31, the university had spent over $6000 on the law library. The President and Fellows had paid out for the Law School, including its library, $3485.01 more than the School had taken in; but as enrollments were increasing this was a prudent investment.

[54] Warren abstracts from the President's and Treasurer's reports the income and expenses during Story's early years as Dane Professor. *Harvard Law School,* I, 467f.

Story and Ashmun began the practice of appointing student librarians. The President's report for 1830–31 shows no salary for them, but certainly after 1832 these young men got the advantage of a room in Dane Hall. George Thomas Davis was student-librarian in 1830–31; Wheelock Samuel Upton in 1831–32. In 1832–33 the librarian was Charles Sumner, who took his LL.B. in 1834; he was destined to serve the School in many ways. The Law Library by 1832 had grown to 3000 volumes. Sumner prepared its second catalogue for which the Corporation voted him a payment of $150. On December 31, 1833, he completed its preface with a valuable history of the library, noting that as he was writing the last page, word had come of "a splendid bequest, by the late Samuel Livermore, Esq. of New Orleans, (the able author of the *Treatise on the Law of Principal and Agent,* and of the *Dissertations on the Contrariety of Laws*) of his entire library of works on the Roman, Spanish, and French Law." The School's comparative law collection began early.

In September 1832 Asahel Stearns's proposal of 1825 came to realization, and the Law School moved into a house of its own. On July 15, 1830, the Corporation had voted that the Treasurer consider a Law School building, and on August 19 it directed the President and Treasurer to prepare a plan with estimates of cost, and to select a site. Story was worried about the financial uncertainties involved; he was still in doubt of the ultimate success of the School. On January 11, 1831, he wrote to Ashmun from Washington.[55]

Washington, January 11th, 1831

My dear sir:

. . .

In respect to a Law Building at Cambridge, I expressed to President Quincy, a few days before I left home, some doubt whether it was not a premature project. I would not have a dollar expended on our account, which would ultimately prove a loss. It would mortify me beyond measure. I would rather live in the old house, and work our way there through its dark lecture-rooms. It is perhaps yet uncertain how far our success may be permanent, and there is some danger, at least, that some of the profession, as well as other dignitaries, may not take a liberal interest in our success. At all events, it will be well to resist, rather than to invite expenses, until we find assurance doubly sure. As a temporary arrangement, I should not object to remain as

[55] *Life and Letters of Joseph Story,* II, 42.

we are, or to take a part of Massachusetts Hall, though I feel a good
deal of repugnance to the latter course . . .

Believe me, most truly, your obliged friend,

Joseph Story

President Quincy, however, on September 12, 1831, wrote to
Nathan Dane a letter which, Warren says, "as an example of art-
fulness and tact, could not be excelled." [56]

The Law School in Harvard University in its present flourishing
state is justly considered a creation of your own. As its founder, I
deem it my duty to keep you apprised of any intentions concerning
it, which may have a tendency to affect its prosperity and usefulness,
to the end that any views you may entertain in relation to it may not
be counteracted by any acts done without your knowledge; or that
should they differ from your plans or be less adequate or appropriate
than your anticipation, you may know our reasons, before they take
the form of acts, and be varied or abandoned by any wishes you may
have or may see fit to indicate.

The School is flourishing beyond all expectation. It already consists
of thirty-five members. Five or six more are anticipated. We think
ourselves justified in calculating with certainty on 40 members, and
I have reason to think it will exceed that number; in this state of
things a serious question is pressed upon us. The Corporation have
completed the purchase of the whole of Judge Story's Library. The
cost of it, with books previously purchased, have stood the College
in stead the sum of $8000. The Library is too large for any single room
we can appropriate for it, and is consequently distributed into two or
three, and is consequently very inconvenient for arrangement or
research, and extremely exposed to injury and dilapidation.

Besides which, none of the rooms at present possessed by the College are suitable for public lectures, moot courts and occasional
meetings of the students and professors.

A temporary and unsuitable wooden structure, Quincy told Dane,
would cost $2000; a brick Law College "suitable to contain a
library, professors' rooms, lecture rooms and every convenience
the institution now demands" would cost $7000. The Corporation
had already spent on the School $4000 more than it had received;
the President thought that $2000 for a Law College was the most
he could hope to get from the Corporation. If erected, such a
building, he wrote,

[56] *Harvard Law School*, I, 469. Warren cites this letter in "Harvard College
Archives — Quincy Papers." It is no longer there, nor in the Law School
Archives among Warren's papers. Fortunately Warren quoted the letter in full
(I, 470–472); I here copy Warren. Dane's reply is in vol. V, Harvard College
Papers.

must unquestionably bear your name. If not given to it by the Corporation as it would be, it would be done by the public voice. Now such a building, if erected, ought to be fully adequate to our wants, and to have some feature of permanence, and bear some affinity in material and effect to our benefactor's distinguished bounty. Now a building of wood to cost $2000 would do neither the one nor the other. My opinion of the inadequacy and inexpediency of erecting such a building is so strong that I have contemplated attempting a subscription for the difference between the sum I deem adequate and the sum I find those influential individuals of the Corporation with whom I have conversed are alone willing to appropriate. I am deterred from this measure from considerations of a general character, which in the judgment of the friends of the University render an application of this kind to the generosity of the community at this time peculiarly inexpedient. I have thus taken the liberty, sir, to present to you a simple statement of the prosperity, the prospects and the exigencies of the School your liberality has founded. My purpose has been simply to make a distinguished benefactor know precisely the relations of the object of his bounty. I consider the moment to be somewhat in the nature of a crisis in respect of the progress of the School. If nothing is done by the Corporation, the tendency to check the growth to which it seems destined is unquestionable. A temporary wooden building seems to me neither suited to our exigencies, nor yet worthy of the Institution or its founder.

Before taking any step, therefore, I have thought that my duty required I should apprise you of facts, that if any views or wishes exist in your mind on the subject, they may be known, should you see fit to communicate them; and that should you have any reason to be dissatisfied with any of our proceedings, you should have no occasion to complain of our intentions not having been previously communicated. This communication you will consider confidential, or otherwise, at your pleasure, and should you see fit to make any reply to it, any restriction you may choose to impose on the subject matter of it shall scrupulously be observed.

Dane replied at once.

It has never been my wish the Law School should be a charge on the funds of the Corporation or on public charity. In my donation 1 allude to an addition. This I have put into a paper I always have by me. It is no present aid — as your meeting will be as soon as this letter can reach you, I write in a hurry. I can only say at present, I should be unwilling to have a mean building erected or have the Law School ultimately any charge on the funds of the Corporation or aided by a subscription. As things appear at present I see no need of it. Perhaps I shall be willing to erect the building at an expense of $7000, provided it can be at my disposal when erected.

A structure built in Harvard Yard but at the "disposal" of a benefactor suggested strange possibilities. President Quincy tactfully replied to Dane that the grateful Corporation would of course accept any of his conditions. To be sure the fee simple of the land did belong to Harvard, but the Corporation could certainly arrange matters.[57]

President Quincy's handling of this generous but somewhat opinionated old gentleman was a model for administrators. After some correspondence Nathan Dane finally gave up his idea of buying part of Harvard, and offered to pay over to the university $5000 immediately. The university was to pay $250 interest to Dane each year for six years, and then add $5000 to the endowment of the Dane Professorship without further obligation to Dane. For the six years of annual interest Dane agreed to look solely to the surplus income of the Law School. He also undertook to lend $2000 more for six years at 5 percent interest, but the university was to repay the principal of this loan to Dane or to his estate.[58]

The final estimate for Dane Hall was $10,000; university buildings are apt to cost more than people first think. The Corporation nevertheless went ahead and built it "north of the Meeting House," that is, in the Yard in the space between the present southern entries of Straus and Matthews halls. The Dane Law College was a two-story Greek Temple, forty feet wide and sixty deep. Four Ionic pillars adorned the front. The ground floor provided a library with a reading room, and studies for the two professors. On the second floor were a lecture room and two smaller rooms; one was for the librarian's dwelling, Sumner's "pleasantest room in Cambridge." Dane Hall was enlarged in 1845, and remained the home of the School for a half century until Austin Hall superseded it. Then the Harvard Cooperative Society used part of Dane until 1904; Professor Münsterberg had his psychological laboratory there from 1892 to 1905; Harvard used it for various offices until 1918 when it burned. Thinking of that once splendid house one might imagine Story, brushing snow from his face as he came into its lecture hall after a walk against a blustering December storm, and remarking, "Gentlemen, this is one of the days when I'd rather *facit per alium* than

[57] President Quincy's reply is in the Harvard College Archives, Quincy Papers.
[58] For documentation see Warren, I, 471f.

facit per se" [59] It is pleasant to think of him hurrying into Dane Hall when he came back from Washington in the spring, the students crowding around him while he told of the Court's work at the term just adjourned.[60]

So astonishing progress marked the first four years of the re-constituted School. In early 1829 Stearns, the Law School's surviving teacher, had been trying to keep it alive with its pitiful remnant of students; by the spring of 1833 the School had three times as many students as it had had in the most prosperous days of Parker and Stearns. The curriculum had been expanded and brought up-to-date. Justice Story, the Dane Professor, had written and published two admirable books, one on private and one on public law, and had become famous for his brilliant and stimulating classroom teaching. John Ashmun had provided steady continuity of instruction whether Story was in Cambridge or in Washington. The library had grown to a conspicuous collection of American and foreign books with some system in cataloguing and care. The School was beautifully housed. Story and Ashmun had done great work.

On April 1, 1833, Professor Ashmun died, while Sumner, his student-friend, sat at his bedside. Ashmun's work during the preceding four years had been essential to the revival of the School. He had long suffered from tuberculosis; his friends knew his life could not be long; but as often happens, his death at thirty-two was a shocking surprise when it came. The law students attended his funeral together, and Story delivered a eulogy in the university chapel. On Story's recommendation the Corporation on April 23, 1833, elected in Ashmun's place as Royall Professor Simon Greenleaf of Maine, a studious and increasingly successful practitioner and author, fifty-one years old.

Simon Greenleaf demonstrated that without either college or law school education, a man could acquire a "scientific" conception of the law and could become both a successful teacher and a learned author. He was born in a Newburyport parsonage in 1783 and got his only formal schooling in the Latin School of that town. When he was sixteen he moved to New Gloucester,

[59] *Centennial History*, p. 12. For those unfamiliar with conventional English pronunciation of Latin in their great-grandfather's day, I point out that in *facit* the letter "a" was pronounced as in "case"; "c" was pronounced as "s."

[60] Story must have been a joy in the School's moot courts. We have his manuscript notes of a student argument of *Swift v. Tyson* in 1842. See 16 Peters 1.

Maine, where his parents preceded him, and at 18 he started to read law in Ezekiel Whitman's office. Five years later he was admitted to the Cumberland County bar, and began twelve years of small-town practice, most of it in Gray, near New Gloucester. His business was slight enough to give him leisure for deep and wide reading, and he began work on *A Collection of Cases Overruled, Denied, Doubted or Limited in Their Application*. In 1818 he moved to Portland, and when Maine attained statehood in 1820 he was appointed reporter of its Supreme Court. Volumes one to nine of the Maine Reports are his products. In 1821 he published his volume of *Cases Overruled*. His reputation for sound, methodical learning brought him increasing numbers of retainers and in 1832 he found himself too busy with his practice to go on with his work as reporter. The following year on Story's nomination he became Royall Professor to succeed Ashmun.

Greenleaf, like any other busy and responsible practicing lawyer, had duties to clients whom he could not abandon in a moment. After his appointment in April 1833 he needed three months to close out his practice. Story called in James Church Alvord of Salem to perform Ashmun's duties in the interval. Alvord had been an able student at the School in 1830, though like many men of that day he had left without a degree. He had been called to the Essex bar in 1832, and was already marked as a man who would make a name for himself. Alvord was the first alumnus to be called to teach in the School. Like other later brilliant young men, called in to help when need arose, he acquitted himself well.

Story and Greenleaf, with some help from such occasional junior faculty, ran the School until Story died in 1845. Student enrollment quadrupled in those twelve years — at Story's death the School had more than 140 students. In 1833–34 the professors divided the School into three classes according to the students' state of learning. Admissions and departures began to coincide more generally with the beginning and ending of terms. However, the rule, in force since 1817, that a candidate with no previous degree must study law five years for the LL.B., although a graduate could in fact take a professional degree in less than two, proved too rigorous for the times. In 1834–35 this difference in required residential study was dropped. And for a number of years no more was heard of an examination as a degree requirement.

Sometime after 1820 this procedure had quietly disappeared, and there remained as the only criteria for the LL.B. the faculty's certificate that the candidate had pursued the required course of study and, based on that, the vote of the Governing Boards. From the early 1830's to 1870 the full curriculum occupied four terms, or two years. But few men stayed for the entire four terms; any students who remained eighteen months in residence acquired the LL.B. without more formality.

As the 1830's moved toward the 1840's the student population at the Law School rose beyond fifty; in 1839 sixty men were studying there. Story being necessarily in Washington for three months of each year, Greenleaf found, as Stearns had already found with far fewer students, that lectures, the oral quizzes called "examinations," preparation for and attendance at moot-courts, and the general administration of the enterprise were far too much for the effective attention of one man alone. From 1835 on, Sumner served as instructor during the first three months of each year when Story was sitting with the Supreme Court. On February 9, 1835, Story wrote to Sumner

> I rejoice that you have gone through the ordeal of your inaugura-
> tion, and fairly through, and are now acclimated in the Law School.
> I never had any doubt upon the subject. Your success (for so I learn
> from Mr. Greenleaf) has been complete, and every way gratifying.
> I hope this is but the beginning, and that one day you may fill the
> chair which he or I occupy, if he or I, like autocrats, can hope to
> appoint our successor . . .
>
> Your affectionate friend,
> Joseph Story.[61]

Greenleaf continued some practice in addition to his teaching, which presented to the President and Fellows a difficult choice. Should they continue in the future as in the past to look with favor on active professional commitments of professors of law? A teacher training young men for careers at the bar may well gain effectiveness from some continued participation in the contemporary realities of that profession. But both the practice of law and the teaching of law are jealous mistresses. Each can consume all a man's powers. Wise instruction in the law requires much time for thought. Instruction also requires, however, that the instructor understand from his own observation the actual operation of the

[61] *Life and Letters of Joseph Story*, II, 189–190.

governmental process. We have never achieved a wholly satisfying reconciliation of these two requirements.[62]

This antithesis of objectives presented itself somewhat dramatically in 1837 when the Charles River Bridge case [63] was argued a second time, with Story on the bench and Greenleaf as counsel for the successful rival Warren bridge. Harvard owned a share in the older Charles River toll bridge, a share which President Quincy estimated as worth over $35,000 — a large sum for the university. The earlier bridge and Harvard's stake in it were worth nothing if the Commonwealth could later charter the parallel Warren bridge which would shortly become toll free. Could the owners of the older bridge use the contract clause of the federal Constitution to block the charter of the new bridge, on the ground that it would impair the contractual obligation of the older charter? Story, Dane Professor and Fellow of the Corporation, gave Greenleaf permission to be away to argue as counsel for interests opposed to Harvard's. Much turned on the case — not only Harvard's financial stake. Perhaps the future of the nascent steam-railroad industry could be gravely affected if a charter granting a monopoly to one railroad could be made worthless by a later charter providing ruinous competition.

With both professors away, Sumner was left in sole charge of the Harvard Law School. Greenleaf was held in Washington for two weeks before the case was reached for argument, and six days more for the argument. Counting travel time he must have been away from Cambridge for nearly the entire month of January 1837. Sumner tried to reassure him.

BOSTON, Jan. 25, 1837.

MY DEAR FRIEND, — Many thanks for your cordial letter of the 11th from Washington; and much pardon do I need at your hands for the lugubrious, hypochondriacal epistle which I inflicted upon you. I write now to greet you on your way home. Pray stay, as long as your affection requires, with your daughter, and banish all thought of the Law School. All are cheerful, respectful, and contented, and seem to receive the law with perfect faith from their *pro tem.* professor. A murmur, slight as that of a distant brook, has reached me from a counsel against whom I decided in a moot-court case, with an expression of an intention to appeal to Cæsar on his return. The parties

---

[62] See, for example, pp. 71–73 of the Centennial History. A half-century after Story's appointment this problem was to be much on the minds of President Eliot and Dean Gurney, Eliot's principal executive assistant. See pp. 186f, below.

[63] 11 Peters 420 (1837).

were, however, entirely respectful, and none have given me any reason to be uneasy. Starkie I hear three days in the week, while Kent I encounter every day. This week I have held two courts, and decided the question of partnership and statute of limitations; and also that of the Hindu witness. I held, in the first case, that the admission of one partner after a dissolution did not take a case out of the statute; and I took a technical distinction, which enabled me to evade the force of the late Massachusetts and English cases, so as to decide the case independent of them. The venue being laid in Rhode Island removed it from their influence; but I put it on grounds which may be maintained in Massachusetts even in the face of those cases. In the other case I held that the deposition of the Hindu priest was admissible, for reasons which I will explain fully when I have again the joy of your countenance.

The students inquire of me daily when you will be back, and enter earnestly into your forensic contest. I have explained again and again the nature of the question you have argued, and endeavored to enforce and illustrate your views: in short, to make the school "*Warren-Bridge men*." I have been with you in your labors, and have hung with anxious confidence upon the accent of your lips. I have hoped that some of your points might reach our dear judge's prejudices, and bear them away. If such be the case, I shall have great joy with you. To convince him would be a greater triumph than to storm a citadel . . .

The students attend all the exercises promptly and constantly, and seem to take an unabated interest in their studies, studying the cases referred to in the marginal notes. I endeavor to stimulate them as much as possible, and flatter myself that I have at least kept the old breath in the body, if I have not succeeded in breathing into it any new afflatus. We shall all welcome you back; and we have long ago said — "Ducite ab urbe domum, mea carmina, ducite Daphnim".

Ever yours affectionately,   C. S.[64]

6

Story undertook to provide a regime of American rather than Massachusetts law. This had been conspicuous among Dane's ideas, it accorded with Story's, and Story cordially carried it forward. The School attracted students from every part of the United States as it does today. In 1835 for example, thirty-five new men enrolled; they came from fourteen states, Maine, Vermont, New Hampshire, Massachusetts, Connecticut, Ohio, Indiana, Virginia, Kentucky, Tennessee, Georgia, Florida, Alabama, and Louisiana.[65] If the School's two most significant criteria are the students and

[64] Pierce, *Memoir of Charles Sumner*, I, 187, 188.
[65] The figures are drawn from the Law School Record Book, 1817–1840.

the teachers it attracts, Harvard's Law School was an extraordinary success in the 1830's. Young Richard Henry Dana, matured and toughened by two years before the mast, came back in 1836 for six final months at Harvard College, happy in that world so different from the sea, but feeling no real call to the law in which his grandfather [66] had been distinguished. After he graduated from the college he went over to Dane Hall and enrolled almost *faute de mieux*, like an occasional young man today. He was much surprised by what he found there.

"Free," as he expressed it, "from all the details, chicanery and responsibilities of practice, we were placed in a library under learned, honorable and gentlemanly instructors, and invited to pursue the study of jurisprudence, as a system of philosophy. From the very first recitation it became exceedingly interesting to me, and I have never yet found it dry or irksome."

Of the surpassing excellence of the Cambridge Law School at this period, and of the high professional spirit there fostered, Dana always spoke with warm admiration. Of some of the young men then associated with him he a year or two later wrote as follows: —

The most successful speech made at the school during the whole time I was there, was made before a jury of under-graduates, Judge Story on the bench, by Wm. M. Evarts. A law argument which he introduced into it, addressed to the Court, was the most complete, systematic, precise and elegantly spoken law argument I have ever yet heard, including many arguments of our most distinguished counsel before our highest courts. Evarts' jury argument was very well done, but Wm. Davis of Plymouth, who was his opponent, did quite as well to the jury. Evarts' was the best law and Davis' the best jury argument I heard in the school. When charging the jury, Judge Story said he must rule the law in certain points against the defendant's counsel (Evarts) though they had been argued to him "in a manner to which I cheerfully do homage." Judge Story always complimented liberally, but never went so far as in this instance. Indeed, Evarts has been a peculiar young man at school, college, and in his professional studies. If he does not become distinguished, he will disappoint more persons than any other young man whom I have ever met with.[67]

Young Dana, like many of his successors, paid part of his way at the Law School by teaching in the college — in his case teaching "elocution." He declined a proctor's post since he disliked supervising student conduct; but in his spare time he wrote a book about his years at sea, which turned out to be one of the most

[66] Francis Dana, chief justice of Massachusetts, 1791–1806.
[67] Charles Francis Adams, *Richard Henry Dana* (Boston, 1891), I, 22, 23.

successful American writings of the nineteenth century. Harpers paid him $250 for the copyright of *Two Years before the Mast*! He took his LL.B. in 1839 and went on to a notable career at the bar. After Dana had argued the *Prize Cases* [68] for the United States in February 1863, a friend of his met Judge Grier in a corridor of the Capitol. The Judge, filled with enthusiasm, burst out most injudicially "Well, your little 'Two Years Before the Mast' has settled that question; there is nothing more to say about it!" [69]

Another student in the 1830's who gave some time both to literature and law was James Russell Lowell. Lowell took his A.B. at Harvard in August 1838, enrolled in the Law School on the last day of that month, and then fell to doubting whether he had chosen the right profession. He thought of the Church, but that career, too, had difficulties. To his friend G. B. Loring he wrote on September 22, 1838,[70] about the desirability that a minister have some independent means of support. "I have been led to reflect seriously on the subject since I have thought of going into the Divinity School . . . I don't feel as if I ought to have any time now "vacare Musis." And yet I hardly like to bid the "swate deludering cratures" farewell. A plan has been running in my head for some time, of writing a sort of dramatic poem on the subject of Cromwell." On October 11, however, he wrote to Loring, "I am reading Blackstone with as good a grace and as few wry faces as I may." On some unnumbered day in October he wrote to the same friend:

> Elmwood, Oct., 1838.
>
> . . . A very great change has come o'er the spirit of my dream of life. I have renounced the law. I am going to settle down into a business man at last, after all I have said to the contrary. Farewell, a long farewell to all my greatness! I find that I cannot bring myself to like the law, and I am now looking out for a place "in a store." You may imagine that all this has not come to pass without a great struggle. I must expect to give up almost entirely all literary pursuits, and instead of making rhymes devote myself to making money. If I thought it possible that I ever could love the law (one can't make a lawyer without it) I wouldn't hesitate a moment, but I am confident that I shall never be able even to be on speaking terms with it.

[68] 2 Black 635 (1863).
[69] Adams, *Richard Henry Dana*, II, 269.
[70] The Lowell correspondence here quoted appears in Charles Eliot Norton, *Letters of James Russell Lowell* (New York, 1894), I, 32f.

I have been thinking seriously of the ministry, but then — I have also thought of medicine, but then — still worse!

But on November 8 he again wrote Loring; he had visited a United States Court in Boston, and had heard Webster in action. He wrote "I had not been there an hour before I determined to continue in my profession and study as well as I could." On February 27, 1839, Lowell wrote Loring that he was at "the office." What office is not clear from the letter — apparently not a law office, for later in the same letter he announces "I have quitted the law forever." Forever was not long. Ten days later Lowell wrote another letter to Loring. "The more I think of business the more really unhappy do I feel, and think more and more of studying law . . . I'm afraid people will think me a fool if I change again, and yet I can hardly hope ever to be satisfied where I am. I shouldn't wonder if next Monday saw me with 'Kent's Commentaries' under my arm. I think I might get to take an interest in it, and then I should not fear at all about the living."

The future successor in Longfellow's Smith Professorship at Harvard, later minister to Spain and then to the Court of St. James, did became sufficiently interested to take his LL.B. at the Law School in 1840 and to gain admission to the Massachusetts bar; but his career in literature has made almost everyone forget his early, indecisive ventures into the law.

The School's only graduate to became President of the United States was Rutherford Birchard Hayes, LL.B. 1845. He had a much happier time studying law than James Russell Lowell did. Hayes graduated from Kenyon College, in Ohio, in August 1842, when he had not quite reached his twentieth birthday.[71] On the following October 17, he began the study of law in an office in Columbus, Ohio. Like other men, Hayes found his own limitations his most difficult obstacles. He wrote in his diary — "my chiefest obstacle is within myself. If I *knew* and could *master myself*, all other difficulties would vanish."

In August 1843 Hayes entered the Harvard Law School. He had a fine time, not only in the routine work and in moot courts over which Story presided, but also attending lectures in history and in literature by Longfellow, Bancroft, and Sparks — in which he was not subject to examination. He went to hear Webster,

[71] This account of Hayes's student life and the quotations from his diary and letters are taken from Williams, *Life of Rutherford Birchard Hayes*, I, 28f.

Choate, Adams, and Winthrop make political campaign speeches. Perhaps we crowd today's students with too many compulsions. The autumn sessions began early.

Cambridge, August 29, 1843. — Yesterday we heard the introductory remarks of our learned professors. After speaking of the object of our assembling, Judge Story proceeded to remark on the requisites of a finished legal character. He spoke at some length of the advantage and necessity of possessing complete control of the temper, illustrating his views with anecdotes of his own experience and observation. His manner is very pleasant, betraying great good humor and fondness for jesting. His most important directions were: "Keep a constant guard upon temper and tongue. Always have in readiness some of those unmeaning but respectful formularies as, *per ex.*, 'The learned gentleman on the opposite side'; 'My learned friend opposite,' etc. When in the library employ yourself in reading the titles, title-pages, and tables of contents of the books of reports which it contains, and endeavor to get some notion of their relative value. Read Blackstone again and again — incomparable for the beauty and chasteness of its style, the amount and profundity of its learning.

Cambridge, September 1. — I have now finished my first week in the Law School. I have studied hard and I am confident that my real gain is as great as I should have had in two weeks in an office. Our lectures have all the advantages of recitation and lectures combined without their disadvantages. We have no formal lectures. Professors Story and Greenleaf illustrate and explain as they proceed. Mr. Greenleaf is very searching and logical in examination. It is impossible for one who has not faithfully studied the text to escape exposing his ignorance; he keeps the subject constantly in view, never stepping out of his way for the purpose of introducing his own experience. Judge Story, on the other hand, is very general in his questions, so that persons well skilled in nods, affirmative and negative shakings of the head, need never more than glance at the text to be able to answer his interrogatories. He is very fond of digressions to introduce amusing anecdotes, high-wrought eulogies of the sages of the law, and fragments of his own experience. He is generally very interesting, and often quite eloquent. His manner of speaking is almost precisely like that of Corwin.[72] In short, as a lecturer he is a very different man from what you would expect of an old and eminent judge; not but that he is great, but he is so interesting and fond of good stories. His amount of knowledge is prodigious. Talk of many "irons in the fire"! Why, he keeps up with the news of the day of all sorts, from political to Wellerisms; and new works of all sorts he reads at least enough to form an opinion of, and all the while enjoys himself with a flow of spirits equal to a schoolboy

[72] Hayes always admired Thomas Corwin (1798–1865). He was governor of Ohio from 1840 to 1842, and was later United States senator, secretary of the treasury, and minister to Mexico.

Dane Hall, the School's first separate home, cost $10,000, most of which Nathan Dane provided in 1832. It stood in the Yard "north of the Meeting House," between the present southern entries of Straus and Matthews halls, and was the Law School's home for a half-century until Austin Hall superseded it in 1883.

in the holidays. So ho! the pleasures of literature are not so small after all!

September 16. — "Pleading and evidence," said Judge Story, "a lawyer should always have at his tongue's end. Chief Justice Marshall was the growth of a century. Providence grants such men to the human family only on great occasions to accomplish its own great ends. Such men are found only when our need is the greatest. Four great judges I have known in my time. I could not say that one was greater than another, but either was a head and shoulders taller than any man now living.

"When a young lawyer," said Judge Story, "I was told by a member of the bar at which I practiced, who was fifteen years my senior in the profession, that he wished to consult me in a case of conscience. Said he: 'You are a young man and I can trust you. I want your opinion. The case is this: I am engaged in an important cause; my adversary is an obstinate, self-willed, self-sufficient man, and I have him completely in my power. I can crush his whole case; it is in my hand, and he does not know it, does not suspect it. I can gain the case by taking advantage of this man's ignorance and overweening confidence. Now, the point is, Shall I do it?' I answered, 'I think not.' 'I think not, too,' he replied. 'I have determined to go into court to-morrow, show him his error, and set him right.' He did it. This was forty-five years ago, but I have never forgotten that act nor that man. He is still living, and I have looked upon him and his integrity as beyond all estimate. I would trust him with untold millions, nay, with life, with reputation, with all that is dear" . . .

September 20 . . .

Judge Story said: "A liberal allowance for a lawyer's library would be $10,000; for convenience merely $3000 would suffice; for necessity $300 might answer, and many eminent lawyers have commenced with less. My library was worth $300. All my means were contained in that and it exhausted all my means. The reports have quadrupled and elementary treatises are ten times as numerous now as in my day.

"Thomas Jefferson said: 'When conversing with Marshall I never admit anything. So sure as you admit any position to be good, no matter how remote from the conclusion he seeks to establish, you are gone. So great is his sophistry you must never give him an affirmative answer or you will be forced to grant his conclusion. Why, if he were to ask me if it were daylight or not, I'd reply, "Sir, I don't know, I can't tell."'

"A lawyer should never resort to petty tricks to increase his business. He should not leave 'a celestial bed to prey on garbage.' Courts will not unravel the threads that are good from the threads that are bad, but will leave the whole fabric exactly as it was woven."

September 26. — Judge Story in his lecture remarked that, as a body, lawyers, so far as his observations extended, were more eminent for morality and a nice sense of honor than any other class of men. They have the most important and delicate secrets entrusted to them; they have more power of doing mischief, and are more instrumental in healing family dissensions, neighborhood feuds, and general ill-blood, than any other profession. He considers the man who lays a wager on the result of an election as more an enemy, or rather more dangerous to public liberty, than the avowed adversary of our institutions. Wagers tempt men to use corrupt means to gain power, and power corruptly gained is sure to be corruptly used; the result is a continual sinking in the scale, worse than despotism, for it is for the interest of despots to make matters no worse, while corruption must increase to secure its ends.

Cambridge, November 15. . . . I argued my first cause in Moot Court, and though my success was not flattering, yet I see nothing to discourage a man in earnest in this matter, as I am. Greenleaf says you might as well attempt to abolish light as the principles of pleading. A clear statement of a man's case often wins the battle. "Commend me to the lawyer who can make a short, lucid statement of the grounds upon which rests his case."

December 21. — Judge Story delivered the most eloquent lecture I have ever heard, yesterday morning, on the duty of American citizens to adhere honestly and implicitly to the Constitution. The application was particularly directed to the abolitionists. "There is a clause in the Constitution which gives to the slaveholders the right of reclaiming a fugitive slave from the free States. This clause some people wish to evade, or are willing wholly to disregard. If one part of the country may disregard one part of the Constitution, another section may refuse to obey that part which seems to bear hard upon its interests, and thus the Union will become a 'mere rope of sand'; and the Constitution, worse than a dead letter, an apple of discord in our midst, a fruitful source of reproach, bitterness, and hatred, and in the end discord and civil war; till exhausted, wasted, embittered, and deadly foes have severed this Union into four, six, or eight little confederacies, or the whole shall crouch under the iron hand of a single despot. Such must inevitably follow the first success of those mad men, who even now are ready to stand up in public assemblies, and in the name of conscience, liberty, or the rights of man, to boast that they are willing and ready to bid farewell to that Constitution under which we have lived and prospered for more than half a century, and which I trust may be transmitted, unimpaired, from generation to generation for many centuries to come. It was the result of compromise and a spirit of concession and forbearance, and will end when that spirit dies from the hearts of this people. Let no man think to excuse himself from a duty which it enjoins. No mental reservation can save his honesty from reproach. Without perjury, no public officer can ever be false to his trust by refusing to execute the duties enjoined by that glorious instrument.

In the case between the States of Pennsylvania and Maryland I delivered the opinion at the solicitation of my brothers, who adopted unanimously my first draft."

Cambridge, January 4, 1844. — Judge Story delivered his last lecture for the term to-day. His parting advice was good, and his farewell to those who were about leaving the school feelingly eloquent . . .
"To those who now leave the school I would say, you carry with you my best wishes. I may live to see some of you able advocates before me. I may hear of the success of others. You know not how I am rejoiced to hear of your success, and what a lively interest I take in your welfare. When I go from among you, the proudest inscription I would ask upon my tomb would be the fact that while I was professor in the law school of Harvard College so many thousands graduated from it." Pshaw! how my haste (indecent) spoils the old man eloquent . . .

January 31. — To-day I attended a club composed of the members of the Law School who are remaining here during the vacation.[73] The subject debated was the admission of Texas into the Union. I advocated the negative on constitutional grounds. Public speaking is no more difficult than I expected to find it after so long a disuse. Connected trains of thought and logical reasoning must be the end of all my efforts. These are more useful and more difficult of attainment than fluency or grace of manner. No man of clear conceptions and logical habits of mind can fail to be fluent, and practice, careful practice, will remove those faults of manner which are to be avoided.

February 26. — The summer session of the Law School commenced to-day. One hundred and six students made their appearance. Professor Greenleaf made the opening address. The only thing in it worthy of remark was his idea of a lawyer: "A lawyer is engaged in the highest of all human pursuits — the application of the soundest reason and purest morality to the ordinary affairs of life. He should have a clear head and a true heart, always acting at his fingers' ends."
Moot cases were given out. Mine is to come up in three weeks. I have read the first chapters in Cruise and Kent. The respite afforded by the vacation seems to have had a very salutary influence. The law is quite interesting. I hope it may so continue. At all events I shall endeavor to profit by this session, as it may be my last in the school. . . . I must try to acquire greater mildness of temper and affability of manners . . .

Cambridge, May 12. — For many days I have been very busily engaged. The study of the law of real property, preparation for the performance of duties in clubs, the weather, and the political movements of the day, have, altogether, kept me from paying the proper attention to other affairs.

[73] The autumn term of the School began late in August. This may explain a January–February vacation.

I heard Webster make a political speech in Faneuil Hall, Thursday evening. He supports the nominations of the Baltimore convention of May 2, Clay and Frelinghuysen. But his speech was poor for him. His course for the few months he remained in the Cabinet was a serious injury to his reputation.

I heard Walker preach twice to-day. What a powerful reasoner he is! How solemn and impressive are his appeals! His subject in the forenoon was taken from the 26th chapter of Proverbs, 16th and 17th verses: Cruelty for sport, false wit, ill-timed jests, sarcasm, ridicule, and all the means of wounding the feelings of a fellow creature wantonly. Let me bear it in mind. I need such admonition . . .

Cambridge, May 18. — We have had a little excitement here for a few days past, occasioned by a skirmish between some of the Southern law students, and the members of the senior class in college. It has resulted in a few slight bruises, the loss of a few soap locks, and the expulsion of one or two from each department. *Sic transit, etc.*

I am progressing slowly in the acquisition of the learning of real property. I shall be glad when this term is through. My health requires more attention than can be given it while engaged in study. In six weeks the vacation begins. Then I shall throw aside my books entirely for a season. Since I commenced the study of the law, I have taken no sufficient recreation.

June 12. — Judge Story has been lecturing for the last week on the Constitution . . . [Hayes abstracted these lectures at some length in his diary.]

Cambridge, January 1, 1845. — This is the beginning of the new year. In two or three weeks I shall leave the Law School, and soon after shall begin *to live.* Heretofore I have been getting ready to live. How much has been left undone it is of no use to reckon . . .

7

Story reached his sixty-fifth birthday on September 18, 1844. He passed the year as usual, sitting with the Supreme Court in Washington, doing circuit duty in New England, teaching at the Law School, and writing in his minute, compact hand the manuscript of his treatise on *Promissory Notes* which came out in June 1845. But time was catching up with him. He had great plans for books still to be written, but he had come to realize that he could not complete his writing and also do judicial work. He no longer needed his pay as a justice; his books were bringing him $10,000 a year, and Harvard stood ready to increase his salary as a professor if he should resign his judgeship and devote all his time to his professorship. He was nearly sixty-six years old; he had sat on the Supreme Court almost thirty-four years. He was the last survivor of the Court as it was when he was appointed. Marshall, his beloved chief, had died in 1835; Story's 1837 dissenting opinion in *Briscoe v. Bank of Kentucky* [74] had noted that if Marshall had lived, things would have been different. There had arisen up a new king over Egypt which knew not Joseph. Story was ready to quit the judgment seat and turn to his books. On August 5, 1845, he wrote to Francis Bassett, clerk of his Circuit Court, who was resigning:

I, also, am about to retire from the seat, which I have occupied for nearly thirty-four years, and to leave to others the labors and anxieties, which are necessarily incident to a situation of so much responsibility, and requiring so many qualifications. I hope that my country may derive more benefit from the diligence and learning and talents of my successor, than I have been able to bring to the task. I claim nothing for myself, but the consciousness of earnest endeavor to administer justice, however imperfectly, according to my best understanding of the true spirit of the law.

Believe me, my dear sir, with great respect,

Truly, your obliged friend,

Joseph Story.[75]

He spent the rest of August clearing the Circuit Court's docket. Early in September he fell ill; on the tenth he died. We shall not look upon his like again. On the two hundred and fiftieth anniversary of Harvard, in 1886, Holmes told the Harvard Law School Association:

There are plenty of men nowadays of not a hundredth part of Story's power who could write as good statements of the law as his, or better. And when some mediocre fluent book has been printed, how often have we heard it proclaimed, "Lo, here is a greater than Story!" But if you consider the state of legal literature when Story began to write, and from what wells of learning the discursive streams of his speech were fed, I think you will be inclined to agree with me that he has done more than any other English speaking man in this century to make the law luminous and easy to understand.[76]

Roscoe Pound, in an address composed for the celebration of the centennial of the Harvard Law School, appraising the contribu-

---

[74] 11 Peters 257 (1837).
[75] *Life and Letters of Joseph Story*, II, 545–546.
[76] Oliver Wendell Holmes, *Collected Legal Papers*, (New York, 1952), p. 41.

tions of the School to the common law, spoke of two events which determined that the common law of England would be a system rivaling that of Rome for the legal allegiance of modern peoples.

Those events were persistence of medieval English law into the seventeenth century through the influence of law teaching in the Inns of Court, and reception of seventeenth-century English law as the law of the English-speaking new world, and the development and making over thereof in the courts of that new world, even as the Roman law was developed and made over in the continental universities. Maitland has told us how taught law was the controlling factor in preventing a reception of Roman law in sixteenth-century England. Taught law was no less a controlling factor in insuring the reception of the common law as the law of America. In truth that reception was in no small part the work of Joseph Story as Dane Professor at Harvard . . .

Truly the stars were in a happy conjunction when the Dane professorship was founded. The tradition of the Inns of Court had insured that an Anglo-American academic law school, established and conducted by common-law lawyers, would be a professional school. The philosophical ideas of the time in which Story had been trained had insured that a school under his guidance would be a school of law, not of the rules of law of this or that time or place. The necessities of the time when the school was founded had made it a school of Anglo-American law; and Story's zealous exposition of the dogmas of that law, in the light of a natural-law philosophy and of comparative law, as declaratory of universal principles of natural reason, enabled it to remain a school devoted to the system of the common law that shares with Rome the legal allegiance of the world of today.[77]

What were Story's general theories of law and the state? He was not primarily a philosopher but a practical man, systematizing what needed arrangement in our law but not pondering abstractions. He reached intellectual maturity when Bentham's thought had become available. His program of writing *Commentaries* was conceived while Austin was lecturing at University College, London; and Austin's *Province of Jurisprudence Determined* appeared in 1832, the same year Story published his first Harvard book. But nowhere in his systematic plan for writing did Story make a place for theoretical jurisprudence. He dedicated his greatest efforts to bringing order in the law governing the American economy, and in this he was a man of his time. He felt and preached the constitutional necessity for the rule of that economy by a well-knit national government clearly predominant over the states, a line

[77] Pamphlet, *The Law School and The Common Law, Address by Dean Roscoe Pound.*

of thought which was evident not only in the acceptance, in his *Commentaries on the Constitution,* of judicial review of legislation [78] as obvious, but also in his decision in *Swift v. Tyson,*[79] which took as its predicate the existence of a federal decisional law governing the national economy, and superior to the local law of the several states. He saw the necessity of a unified theory for the choice of laws to govern a controversy involving the law of more states than one, or the law of a foreign nation and the United States, and finding no English writer to guide him used his deep knowledge of civil-law sources to construct his theory. He saw that for a legal order to function smoothly, unyielding rules of law need an orderly and effective system of equity to adapt them to individual needs, and he expanded such a system clearly and usefully. And in all the busyness of his life he was able to build up a school to which talented young men came from every part of the nation to absorb his ideas, carry them back, and put them to work in men's daily lives. This is enough achievement for any man.

Simon Greenleaf became Dane Professor in August 1846 and, somewhat ailing, nevertheless kept things going at the Law School in a sort of postscript for three academic years after Story's death. Steadiness was Greenleaf's great trait. The coruscating Story was wonderful, but he was away several months each year. Though Greenleaf did keep up some practice after he began to teach in 1833, he was almost always present at the School for duty, and he performed it systematically and thoroughly. He did not possess Story's facility in authorship. He brought out only one book in his fifteen years of teaching, his *Treatise on the Law of Evidence,* which appeared in 1842. It was a useful manual, much in demand; before Greenleaf died, eleven years later, his book had been through six editions. Greenleaf cheerfully admitted his indebtedness to Thomas Starkie, Downing Professor of Cambridge University, whose book on evidence had appeared in 1824, and to Samuel March Phillips, of the Middle Temple, whose treatise had come out in 1814. But Greenleaf restated the subject to accord with American needs in his time, and did it admirably. He well earned the place Pound gave his name on the westerly frieze of Langdell Hall.

[78] 1 Cranch 137 (1803).
[79] 16 Peters 1 (1842).

The years of Story, Ashmun, and Greenleaf saw the Harvard Law School gain in all essentials. At Story's death it had a large and largely talented body of students, and though their numbers declined during the next four years from 145 to 90, the following decade more than restored the losses. The School's library by 1841 was twice as large as it had been in 1834. William R. Woodward, student librarian in 1841, prepared a new edition of the catalogue, in which he wrote that the acquisitions since 1834 "nearly complete the collection of European law, both British and Continental, from the earliest times down to the eighteenth century." The *American Jurist* of October 1841, reviewing the new catalogue, mixed praise with criticism.

The publication of this catalogue enables us to judge, in some sort, of those means of obtaining a law education, in the Law School at Cambridge, which are independent of the personal labors of the distinguished professors of that institution. In the departments of English and American law, little perhaps is wanting; but, in some departments of general jurisprudence, much is to be desired. In the department of Roman law, for example, we find none of the modern works, with the exception of the unfinished English translation of Savigny's history, by Cathcart, and a French translation of the same work, and the newly discovered fragments of Gaius; and yet in no department of jurisprudence, has the present century produced more, or more valuable works.

During the next five years some of those gaps were filled and others which the commentator mentioned. For Harvard to have achieved by 1841 a library where "in the departments of English and American law little perhaps is wanting" was not a small achievement. By 1846 a new catalogue had become necessary; the law school library, with about 12,000 volumes, had nearly doubled its size since 1841. Throughout the School's history it has been outgrowing its quarters. By 1844 Dane Hall, new in 1832, was already too small. In 1845 the university completed a new transverse addition across the rear of Dane Hall; so housed the Law School made do for nearly four decades. The prospects seemed pleasing. As the School entered the third period of its history, it had students, teachers, books, and a house.

A Harvard era ended in the mid-forties, and not at the Law School alone. President Quincy resigned by letter of March 19, 1845, six months before Story died. Though Emerson could write that the President had been "a lubber and grenadier among our clerks," the university missed his vigor and imaginative common sense. During the next twenty-four years Harvard had five presidents and one acting president. Among them were men of high scholarship and devotion, but their successive brief tenures produced no great developments in the university. The Law School for a quarter-century attempted to do as Story had done, but without Story's spark. Perhaps institutions need such fallow periods in which unseen preparation precedes the next growth. But the next quarter-century was to raise questions whether the School had sufficient vitality to change with the times, or whether without Story it could only repeat, unquestioning, the rituals of Story's time; whether the School was content "to rest upon a formula" in "a slumber that, prolonged, means death." [80]

[80] Holmes, in "Ideals and Doubts" (1915), *Collected Legal Papers*, p. 306.

Parker, Parsons, and Washburn: 1845–1870

In 1866 John Chipman Gray and John Codman Ropes, two young men who had taken the LL.B. at Harvard five years before, launched a new journal, the *American Law Review*, published by Little, Brown and Company in Boston. They immediately made their *Review* the most significant legal periodical of its generation. In 1870 Oliver Wendell Holmes, Jr., and Arthur G. Sedgwick, both Harvard LL.B.'s of 1866, took over the editorial direction from Gray and Ropes. The October 1870 issue, the first under the new régime, carried this entry in a section called "Summary of Events":

Harvard University. Law School. For a long time the condition of the Harvard Law School has been almost a disgrace to the Commonwealth of Massachusetts. We say 'almost a disgrace' because, undoubtedly, some of its courses of lectures have been good, and no law school of which this can be said is hopelessly bad. Still, a school which undertook to confer degrees without any preliminary examination whatever, was doing something every year to injure the profession throughout the country, and to discourage real students. So long as the possession of a degree signified nothing except a residence for a certain time in Cambridge or Boston, it was without value. The lapse of time insured its acquisition. Just as a certain number of dinners entitled a man in England to a call to the bar, so a certain number of months in Cambridge entitled him to a degree of Bachelor of Laws. So long as this state of things continued, it was evident that the school was not properly performing its function. We were glad to learn, therefore, that the old system has been abandoned, and are glad to find convincing evidence of the fact in a circular just issued by the Faculty. The circular states that "The degree of LL.B. will be conferred upon students who shall pass satisfactory examinations in all the required subjects, and, in at least seven of the elective subjects, after having been in the school not less than one year." [1]

[1] Howe in his *Justice Oliver Wendell Holmes: The Shaping Years* discusses the authorship and merits of this criticism. See his chap. 5.

This stern judgment came from the *Review* twenty-five years after Story's death had called forth panegyrics on the School he had rebuilt. During that quarter-century the School's welfare had been principally guided by three men: Joel Parker, Royall Professor for twenty-one of those years; Theophilus Parsons, for twenty-two years Dane Professor; and Emory Washburn, who from 1855 to 1876 was successively lecturer, University Professor, and the first Bussey Professor. If the *Review's* criticism was just, those three men should bear the major blame.

In that quarter-century the School fluctuated in its enrollment, never going much above the 145 students of Story's last year, once declining to about 90, once to 78. When the *Review's* paragraph appeared, the School had 154 members. The best men who came in the twenty-five years after 1845 were equal to the best any school of law has ever attracted. Holmes and Sedgwick, the editors of the *Review*, were themselves examples. Among those who studied law at Harvard in these years were Horace Gray and Melville Weston Fuller, who became justices of the Supreme Court of the United States; Walbridge Abner Field of the Massachusetts Supreme Judicial Court; Professors James Bradley Thayer, Jeremiah Smith, and Christopher Columbus Langdell, who, in the last part of the century, demonstrated that the School of Parker, Parsons, and Washburn contained the means of its own regeneration. The roster of students bears names of advocates who carried forward the best traditions of the American bar, lawyers of the quality of James Coolidge Carter, president of the American Bar Association, who founded the Carter Professorship of General Jurisprudence; Joseph Hodges Choate, ambassador to England; and scores of other men who won notable distinction in practice and in public life.

Memoirs of students during that time have told of the stimulus which the post-Story School could give to alert men. George Frisbie Hoar of Worcester, Massachusetts, later a leading member of the United States Senate, who had taken the LL.B. at Harvard in 1849, wrote in his autobiography [2] fifty-four years after his graduation:

I spent two years at the Law School after graduating from the College. I cannot state too strongly my great debt to it, and to Frank-

[2] George Frisbie Hoar, *Autobiography of Seventy Years* (New York, 1903), I, 129–130.

lin Dexter,[3] Simon Greenleaf, Joel Parker, and Theophilus Parsons. I have no remorse for wasted hours during those two years. The time in a Law School is never likely to be wasted if the youth have in him any spark of generous ambition. He sees the practical relation of what he is learning with what he has to do in life. The Dane Law School was then, and I suppose that it is even more true of it now, a most admirable place for learning the science of law and preparing for its practice. The youth breathed a legal atmosphere from morning till night all the year round. He had the advantage of most admirable instruction, and the resources of a complete library. He listened to the lectures, he studied the text-books, he was drilled in the recitations, he had practice in the moot courts and in the law clubs. He discussed points of law in the boarding-house and on his walks with his companions. He came to know thoroughly the great men who were his instructors, and to understand their mental processes, and the methods by which they had gained their success. The title of old Nathan Dane to a high place on the roll of his country's benefactors, and to the gratitude of the profession of the law, and of all lovers of jurisprudence throughout the country cannot be disputed.

Senator Hoar's warm recollections could be ascribed to retrospective sentimentality, but this afterglow cannot explain away exuberant letters written in student days. In 1863 John Fiske entered the School. He was destined to write half a shelf of books, among them a history of the United States under the Articles of Confederation which justices of the Supreme Court have more than once cited to justify their construction of the Constitution.[4] Fiske found the School wonderfully stimulating, though he liked some subjects and professors more than others. On October 7, 1863, he wrote [5] to Abby Brooks, the girl he was to marry.

Cambridge, October 7, 1863.
Dear Abby:

I have pitched into work in good earnest. Yesterday after you had gone, I entered my name with Judge Parker, and with the steward, as a member of the Law School, took from the Library Vol. I of Blackstone, Vol. I of Washburn on "Real Property", and Story on "Bailments". I then went in to hear Parker lecture; the lecture room was very pleasant but I didn't know enough law to understand much

[3] Lecturer at the School on constitutional and international law and the jurisprudence of the United States, 1848–1849.

[4] John Fiske, *The Critical Period of American History* (Boston, 1896). See also the dissenting opinion of Justice Jackson in *Independent Warehouses v. Scheele*, 331 U.S. 70 at 94 (1947), and *Hood v. Du Mond*, 236 U.S. 525, 533 (1949).

[5] The correspondence can be found in *The Letters of John Fiske* (New York, 1940), edited by his daughter Ethel. It is quoted by permission of Miss Susan W. Flint, heir of Ethel F. Fiske. John Fiske took his LL.B. in 1865.

of the lecture and I decided not to go to any more lectures until I had done some preliminary reading which is necessary in order to understand them. At noon I came home and spent the hour before dinner in acquiring a few notions about "Bailments", and in drinking the other bottle of ale which I got when you were here yesterday; I couldn't help thinking how much more I enjoyed it 24 hours ago.

Four days later he wrote again —

Cambridge, October 11, 1963.

Dear Abby:

I am perfectly enraptured, carried away and *electrified* with Blackstone; as much as ever I was with the "Opium-Eater". I scarcely ever read anything so interesting in my life, I get so engrossed in it that I can hardly bear to leave it to go to bed. I never knew what I was talking about when I professed a dislike for the law, I am inclined to think that this notion that it's "dry" is all humbug and that I shall find it as attractive as any study I ever pursued. The subject of "Contingent Remainders", is said to be one of the driest in the whole science, but from what I get of it in Blackstone I think it perfectly fascinating; and as for Bailments, it is as pretty reading as Trigonometry. I have been so completely absorbed that I have not had time to be lonely. I started with the intention of reading 100 pages of law every day, my record for the past five days is 423 pages in Blackstone.

Tomorrow and Tuesday I shall hear Parsons lecture on Blackstone and Wednesday I shall hear Parker on the subject of Bailments. I shall not go to hear Washburn until next week, he lectures on Real Property, and when I enter upon that subject you may expect to hear me swear.

Fiske's letters to Abby overflowed with praises of Herbert Spencer, unenthusiastic comment on the study of the law of real property, and occasional comment on the Civil War. He wrote to her on November 7, 1863.

Dear Abby:

"The tenant cannot in an avowry avoid the lord's possessory right, because of the seisin given by his own hands. This writ does not lie for tenant in tail; for he may avoid such seisin to the lord by plea to an avowry in replevin. The writ of mesne lies when upon a subinfeudation the mesne lord suffers his tenant paravail to be distrained upon by the lord paramount. In such case the tenant shall be indemnified by the mesne lord; and if he make default therein, he shall be forejudged of his mesnalty, and the tenant shall hold immediately of the lord paramount." (!) What do you think of that Abby? Nice reading isn't it? Darn nice!

Two days before Christmas he wrote:

December 23, 1863.

Dear Abby:

I am doing great things in these days. Since Sunday I have read 349 pages in Washburn on "Real Property". Washburn is detestable. His style is clumsy, obscure, inelegant, ungrammatical, lame, feeble, inaccurate, systemless, metaphysical and ambiguous. While his thinking is but little more lucid than his style. Today I piled into Parsons and read 112 pages on "Contracts" in less than three hours! Nothing like a wedding in prospect, to make a fellow work! I find Parsons very pretty and very clear and easy, almost like a novel. He is very far superior to Washburn as a writer. I am in the highest imaginable spirits and in vast good humour. Nothing agrees with me like a regular furious set-to at books. If I keep on until Sunday, this will have been the biggest week's work of my life.

The Vedas, inculcating forgiveness, say: —
"The tree withdraweth not its shade
from the woodcutter."

On New Year's Day, 1864, Fiske discovered a great book. He rhapsodized about it.

Cambridge, January 3, 1964.

Dear Abby:

I have passed through an Era and entered upon a new Epoch of my Life. Thursday evening I began Sir Henry Sumner Maine's "Ancient Law" and read it all New Year's, *finishing* it at exactly midnight. No novel that I ever read enchained me more. I consider it almost next to Spencer. It has thrown all my ideas of law into definite shape. It has suggested to me many new and startling views of social progress. It has confirmed many new generalizations which were beginning to arise in my mind as faint suspicions. I scarcely ever read a work so exceedingly *suggestive*. In fact it *suggests* far more than it *says*. Almost every proposition in it may be made the foundation of a long train of thought. But beside what it hints at, what it explains is wonderful.

He lays open the whole structure of ancient society; penetrates into the ideas of primitive men; discovers the origin of International Law; explains the notion of succession to property, and shows how wills arose; points out the origin of the idea of Property; shows the progress of the idea of Contract, and of our moral notions of Obligation; shows how Criminal Law has grown up; illustrates the progress of men's ideas of Justice; lays bare the whole structure of the Feudal System, and exhibits the condition of society in the Middle Ages; traces the history of Roman jurisprudence; shows up the social condition of India, Russia, and Austria; explains the influence of Roman law on theology, on Morality and on Metaphysics; shows the way in which national thought depends on its language — it is perfectly GLORIOUS! I am going to read it over and over until I know it by heart.

Intellectual excitement was available in the School for those who looked for it.

One purpose of examinations is their compulsion on the student to review and to systematize the material gleaned from readings and lectures. For some men in the School of 1845–1870, bar examinations performed this function.[6] John Fiske wrote to his mother as he girded himself for this ordeal.

Cambridge, May 18, 1864.

Dear Mother:

Abby has given me the gist of all that was said in New York in relation to our marriage. I am very well satisfied with Mr. Stoughton's proposal that I enter the Boston Bar as a condition precedent. The performance of such a condition will not delay our marriage after the middle of September. I have already read more law than most of these fellows do in two years; and the librarian says that I can without doubt enter by September 1st. I have abandoned my article-work for the present, and shall give 11 hours per day to law until I am admitted. I entertain no fears of being rejected: I know I can answer any question which it will be fair to ask, in spite of the fact that when I sounded Judge Curtis a little, asking him if it was possible to pass the examination with a year's study, he assured me very positively that it was not — such a thing had never been heard of, and the examination was much more thorough now than formerly. So I see that there will be no use in asking him to propose me in July. I shall keep quiet and read law at the rate of 250 pages a day.

By July 1st he was about ready. He wrote to Abby:

Cambridge, July 1, 1864.

Dear Abby:

I saw Judge White this morning, and procured from him a certificate that I had studied law *two years*: (not a bit worse than taking a feudum novum, habendum et tenendum ut feudum antiquum, and a good many other legal fictions!) I also procured a certificate from Parsons that I had attended the Law School two terms, been regular at lectures and was a most exemplary chap generally. Judge White then drew up a petition to the most worshipful judges of this Commonwealth that John Fiske, being of full age, a native of U.S. and citizen of Cambridge, having graduated at Harvard University, and studied law two full years, be admitted to practice as an attorney: which I signed. We then took this petition with the two certificates,

[6] Howe describes Holmes' self-disciplined bar review and his examination in *The Shaping Years*, pp. 260f.

and deposited them with the clerk of the Superior Court, paying $1.40 for so doing.

All the preliminary formalities are now over; I have nothing to do but to be examined. I have told George Roberts and he is tickled to death; thinks it is "GRAND, old fellow". I am beginning to feel rather tired with work but there is only one week more of it. I do not propose to issue forth from the little end of the horn. My time is all too short; the Statutes to be finished and a large part of Kent to be reviewed — that is a heavy job for 5 days.

I tell you what, Petersham hills will look pleasant if I am a member of the Bar when I next see them!

And on July 13th Fiske wrote to his mother in triumph.

Petersham, July 13, 1864.

Dear Mother:

Last week Tuesday, I went into Court and passed an 8 hours' written examination, answering every question at length and correctly. There were 39 questions.

On Monday morning I was admitted to the Bar, took the oath of office and received my certificate — Judge Russel saying I had passed "a most excellent examination".

Since October 7 I have read 37 volumes in preparation. I feel as if I could bid goodbye to law with a good will until the autumn. The day before my examination I got tired out with the Statutes and went to Waltham to see the Walkers. Played several games of croquet with the girls and had a big saucer of wild strawberries off the place, with cream too thick to pour! Otherwise I have had no sprees.

After receiving my certificate Monday I gathered up my duds and started off up here with Abby, in a recently provided express train which leaves at 5.30 P.M. We reached Athol in a heavy thundershower and drove over in a covered carryall with a horse that was afraid of the lightning, getting to the Brooks's at 10 o'clock.

I shall not read much this summer except Scott's novels.

John Fiske, Attorney at Law.

Fiske's attitude toward the Civil War seems curiously detached, today. He writes of it as though it were an exciting spectacle, which moved him to Union partisanship, but he does not once in his published correspondence suggest that he considered trying to enlist. He apparently was not alone in this reaction. The lowest attendance at the Law School during the Civil War was 78, about half the peak enrollment during the twenty years 1847–67. In contrast, in World War I the School shrank from 857 men in 1916–17 to 70, all physically unfit, just before the armistice in 1918.

Parker, Parsons, Washburn

Oliver Wendell Holmes, Jr., one of the young editors of the *American Law Review* in 1870 when that journal excoriated the Law School, became a lecturer on jurisprudence at Harvard in 1871–72, author of his celebrated *Common Law* in 1881, and professor of law in 1882. He resigned his Harvard chair after a few months to take a seat on the Supreme Judicial Court of Massachusetts. Despite the hard words of his *Review* in 1870, Holmes looked back with warmth on the Law School of his student days. He told the Harvard Law School Association in 1886:

> The aim of a law school should be, the aim of the Harvard Law School has been, not to make men smart but to make them wise in their calling — to start them on a road which will lead them to the abode of the masters. A law school should be at once the workshop and the nursery of specialists . . . It should obtain for teachers, men in each generation who are producing the best work of that generation. Teaching should not stop, but rather should foster, production. The "enthusiasm of the lecture room", the contagious interest of companionship, should make the students partners in their teachers' work.

He spoke of the change in teaching methods we associate with Langdell's name and then added:

> I pause for a moment to say what I hope it is scarcely necessary for me to say — that in thus giving my adhesion to the present methods of instruction I am not wanting in grateful and appreciative recollection (alas! it can be only recollection now) of the earlier teachers under whom I studied. In my day the Dean of this School was Professor Parker, the ex-Chief Justice of New Hampshire, who I think was one of the greatest of American judges, and who showed in the chair the same qualities that had made him famous on the bench. His associates were Parsons, almost if not quite a man of genius, and gifted with a power of impressive statement which I do not know that I have ever seen equalled; and Washburn, who taught us all to realize the meaning of the phrase which I have already quoted from Vangerow, the "enthusiasm of the lecture-room". He did more for me than the learning of Coke and the logic of Fearne could have done without his kindly ardor.[7]

For men like Fiske, or Holmes, the School of Parker, Parsons, and Washburn served well. The professors conducted it "as if it were a graduate school for men of responsible maturity"[8] who

[7] "The Use of Law Schools," address delivered at the celebration of Harvard's two hundred and fiftieth anniversary, *Collected Legal Papers* (1920), p. 35. Karl Adolf von Vangerow, 1808–1870, of Heidelberg University, was an extraordinarily popular professor of Roman Law.

[8] Howe, *The Shaping Years*, p. 185.

had no need of pedagogical discipline to compel them to study. But this assumption was ill founded. Of 106 men who in 1869 completed their longer or shorter periods of study at the School, 62 took LL.B.'s. Of the 62, less than half — only 27 — had taken any previous degree. In 1868–69, that is to say, the Harvard Law School was not entitled to consider itself an institution for graduate study of a profession.

One should not too hastily assume that a student with an undergraduate degree more worthily earns a degree in laws than a nongraduate. And perhaps no firm demonstration underlies an asumption that evil results came from the lack of degree examinations during the Parker-Parsons-Washburn regime. The significance of examinations, graduate or undergraduate, is more often taken for granted than demonstrated. No one can be sure that the average Harvard LL.B. of 1885 when admission to the School had been mostly limited to A.B.'s and when the LL.B. was conditioned on examinations, was a more learned and wiser man of the law than the average graduate of 1865. Means of measurement are lacking. Brave men lived before Agamemnon. But some acute observers, who wished the School well, thought in 1869 that its quality had declined under the three professors. The existence alone of that impression of decadence called for reappraisal.

2

A university must not only have brilliant students but also have outstanding scholar-teachers if it is to achieve greatness. Sometimes after a dominant figure has left the Harvard scene, the university has for a time hesitated, in doubt as to its next step. After Story died the School passed through such a doubting season in which the Governing Boards were uncertain as to what sort of teacher they sought. A successor for Story the judge was easier to find than a successor for Story the professor. Charles Sumner, forty-four years old, had taught successfully in the School. He was a powerful orator, but his speeches had irritated some of the Boston establishment. He was not eminent in the practice of law; Harvard sought professional eminence in a permanent professor. The university temporized by naming as instructors Sumner, and John Clark Adams, a brilliant young man, who had taken his LL.B. at the School in 1843. The Corporation persistently and vainly continued to look for another Story. Meantime Simon Greenleaf held things together.

It occurred to Greenleaf that maybe a Kent could repeat the Story miracle. In October 1845 he recommended to the Corporation that it appoint as permanent professor William Kent, son of the Chancellor. The younger Kent was cultivated and urbane, forty-three years old, an office lawyer rather than an advocate. In 1838 the Law School of the University of the City of New York had made him professor of the law of persons and personal property. In 1841 he had become a judge of the New York Circuit Court.[9] Harvard sounded him out; Justice Benjamin R. Curtis urged him to accept. But Kent, somewhat dominated by his father's greatness, waited for the aged Chancellor's consent. Meantime he had resigned from the Circuit Court in 1845 and gone to Paris for his health. (One reads the memoirs of the first half of the nineteenth century with increasing wonder at the number of men who sickened in America and sought health in Europe.) In the summer of 1846 Kent finally accepted the Royall professorship, and the Corporation made Greenleaf Dane Professor.

Kent's Harvard career was short. He moved his family to Cambridge, and 1846–47 gave courses on insurance, sales, agency, partnership, Kent, and Blackstone. Greenleaf lectured on equity jurisprudence and pleading, common-law pleading, evidence, and real property. Kent made a happy impression on students and on the university faculty. But in September 1847, he found that his father needed him in New York and, sacrificing his professorship to filial duty, resigned as Royall Professor. The Law School, its faculty again reduced to Greenleaf, recalled as a temporary lecturer John Clark Adams, and as another lecturer obtained George Ticknor Curtis, who had attended the School in 1833–34 but had never taken his degree in law. So shored up, the School got on until November 1847, when the Corporation elected as Royall Professor Chief Justice Joel Parker of New Hampshire, fifty-two years old, brilliant, hard-minded, precise — perhaps too precise to write freely, for he produced no book during his pro-

[9] At this time, New York had a system of circuit courts sitting in eight circuits. See Rev. Stat. 1836, pt. III chap. I, title IV. For a sketch of Judge William Kent's life see Benjamin D. Silliman's memorial of him in the Appendix to 34 Barbour's (New York) Reports, at page 640.

fessorship of twenty years. Parker continued to hold his chief-justiceship until June 25, 1848, when he resigned from the New Hampshire Court. By that time the faculty of law had again fallen to one professor, for Greenleaf had resigned on June 10. Story's death had been the first of a train of difficulties, and for the third time in two years the Corporation had to find a new professor.

It now turned to Rufus Choate of Boston, who had been a student at the Law School in 1820 but had never taken his degree. Choate felt unable to abandon his distinguished trial and appellate practice. On July 15, 1848, the Governing Boards elected as Dane Professor Theophilus Parsons, fifty years old, son of the late Chief Justice of the Supreme Judicial Court of Massachusetts. Parsons had taken his A.B. at Harvard in 1815, and had qualified for the bar by two years' study in William Prescott's office. In 1817, like other well-to-do young Bostonians of his day, he went to Europe for the good of his health; he spent a few months visiting William Pinckney, minister to Russia, and returned to practice law first in Taunton and then in Boston. He went to Harvard after conspicuous success in practice.

Parsons was a Story type, talkative, gregarious, a ready author, less of a detail man than Parker. But Parker and Parsons could not by themselves handle a hundred and forty students who were demanding instruction in specialties. The School then, as it often has since, turned to the Boston bar for temporary lecturers. In 1848 the Corporation appointed Franklin Dexter of Boston lecturer on international law and patents, and Luther S. Cushing [10] lecturer on civil, parliamentary, and criminal law. In 1849 these gentlemen decided not to continue; to take up the slack Frederick Hunt Allen of Bangor, Maine, was appointed University Professor for one year. Despite all this chopping and changing, things went better than one might expect. A Visiting Committee of the Overseers in 1849–50 reported "kindly and instructive social relations among the students, and also between the students and their instructors. Young men engaged in similar pursuits are professors to each other." But at the close of 1849–50 the Corporation decided not to reappoint Allen as professor, and instead reappointed Cushing as lecturer. Among all this shuffling of instructors

[10] Cushing's student lecture notes, taken under his uncle, Professor Asahel Stearns, in 1824–25, are preserved in the Law School archives.

of different ranks emerged an evident fact — that two professors could not carry the load, that a series of short-term part-time lecturers would not do, and that some better, more permanent establishment was necessary.

Anti-slavery feeling was running high in Boston, which further complicated the already complex problem of restaffing the School. In 1852 the university appointed Edward Greely Loring of Boston lecturer in law. He was a capable lawyer and teacher, was judge of probate and United States commissioner. As commissioner he had under the Fugitive Slave Law the duty of ordering the return of any fugitive slaves who might be discovered in Boston — a duty obnoxious to anti-slavery people. Loring impressed the Corporation, who wanted to appoint him professor of law; but in 1854 pursuant to his clear legal duty, Loring ordered that a fugitive slave named Anthony Burns be returned to his Virginia master.[11] A majority of the Overseers thereupon refused their consent to Loring's appointment as professor. The School was still in trouble.

In 1855 the Law Faculty proposed as lecturer former Governor Emory Washburn, born in 1800, A.B. at Williams in 1817, student at Harvard Law School in 1819–20. He had practiced law in Worcester, had been in both houses of the General Court, had been a judge of the common pleas. Rumor said Washburn had favored Loring in the Overseers' vote. The Governing Boards duly elected him lecturer, and next year they created for him a third chair, another university professorship.

Washburn served for twenty-one years. In May 1862 he became the first Bussey Professor. Benjamin Bussey was born in the reign of George II, was a private soldier in the War of Independence, became a Boston merchant, and by the time of his death in 1842 was one of the richest men in the United States. He left his property to Harvard, half for a school of agriculture and horticulture,[12] the remainder in equal shares for the use of the

[11] The Burns affair is described in a pamphlet, *The Boston Slave Riot and Trial of Anthony Burns* (Boston: Fetridge and Company, 1854).

[12] In 1872 the Governing Boards established the Bussey Institution to carry out the donor's intention respecting agricultural science. It still exists as a Harvard research organization, closely affiliated with the biological laboratories and with the Arnold Arboretum. In 1965 the university established a Bussey Professorship of Biology of which in 1966 Carroll Williams became the first holder. The Divinity School for a time had two Bussey chairs; both have been discontinued; in 1956 they were succeeded by the Bussey Theological Fund, for the general purposes of the Divinity School.

Theological and Law schools in such manner as the Corporation should direct. By 1862 the Law School had available from the Bussey gift the income on more than $100,000. The Corporation created some prizes, and changed the name of Washburn's chair from the university professorship to the Bussey professorship. The financial relief to the School was more than welcome.

Thus for ten years after Story's death the School had got on with a mixed bag of teachers until it finally settled on Parker, Parsons and Washburn. These three gave the School its tone from 1855 to 1868. Parsons was a copious author. His celebrated *Contracts* appeared in 1853; in 1856 he published *Elements of Mercantile Law*, and in 1859 his *Maritime Law*. They were solid, useful books on solid, useful subjects. They helped students learn; they told practitioners what to do. Emory Washburn was amiable, experienced, and outgoing. In 1860 he published his *Real Property*, a book which became the foundation of modern instruction in property law at Harvard. In his monumental *Cases on Property*, John Chipman Gray, in 1888–92, followed Washburn's arrangement of real property subject matter *mutatis mutandis;* Edward H. Warren followed Gray's lead; in 1947 James Casner and Barton Leach skillfully reshaped and brought to date the work of their predecessors. Each book was fresh and new in its time; the authors built on the general thought of Washburn. Parker was the most learned of the professors of 1855–1868. He was witty, brilliant, satirical; but he produced no books.

All three, Parker, Parsons, and Washburn, interested and challenged the best students, which is the optimum test of any teacher. What, then, gave rise to the irritated criticism fired by the *American Law Review* in 1870? Fundamentally the critics deplored a lack of change. The three professors' concept of education was not unworthy. On the contrary, their motivating ideal was the same that Abbott Lawrence Lowell was later to expound — the concept that free study, free discussion, student with student and student with instructor, was the most important element in graduate study, perhaps transcending courses and examinations. In his President's Report for 1908–09 Lowell wrote of training candidates for the doctorate of philosophy. "Courses there should be in the sense of scholars' contributions to knowledge, but neither attendance on them, nor examination thereon, should be required, and the idea of credit for courses should be

left as far behind as supervised study in a school room." [13] President Lowell's concept of brilliant young men, left free to study
as they would, reached its apogee in his Society of Fellows, given
all the privileges of the university, furnished maintenance during
their term of three years, subjected to no academic regulations
concerning candidacy for a degree. The record in scholarship of
these men has been brilliant; they have needed no apparatus of
pedagogy because they have been so well chosen.

Parker, Parsons, and Washburn conceived of the Law School
as a place where similar processes could occur; where eager young
men could, if they would, read law, educate one another by talk
with their fellows, feel the excitement of the lecture hall, meet
older lawyers in easy friendship. The three professors were well
equipped to produce this atmosphere among a student elite, but
the Law School students were taken run-of-the-mine; the School
accepted all comers without even the uncritical barrier of a
previous undergraduate degree. Self-directed scholarship only
serves for rare intellectuals. To select such a distinguished and
necessarily small corps Parker, Parsons, and Washburn had
neither patience nor inclination; and Harvard could not easily
do without the tuition fees of the less gifted majority. Proverbially
the poor cannot be fastidious.

The records the professors have left us show little consideration
of possible improvement in the instruction or in the quality of
the student body at the Harvard Law School. Their reports are
monotonous recitals of educational statistics. In 1853–54 the
faculty reported "No changes have taken place in the arrangements of the exercises since the last Report." In the 1854–55 and
1855–56 reports occur statements that "no important changes"
have occurred. During the three years 1856–59 the reports are
silent on change in instruction; in 1860–62 the faculty assure the
reader: "There have been no new arrangements in relation to the
organization of the School or the course of instruction." From
1862 to 1864 the faculty comforted those interested by assurance
that the organization of the School and the course of instruction
remained unchanged and that they had nothing to add to previous reports. From 1864 through 1868 the faculty incorporated, and
then annually reincorporated by reference in identical words, their

[13] Henry Aaron Yeomans, *Abbott Lawrence Lowell* (Cambridge, 1948),
pp. 527f.

previous statements of unchanged education. "As there have been no new arrangements in relation to the organization of the School or the course of instruction, the Faculty have nothing to add to their previous reports on these subjects, and therefore adopt the language of their last report."

One cannot be sure, of course, that the three gave no thought to constructive change. They were intelligent and conscientious men, and perhaps each year they scrutinized their system of instruction and decided that the School offered all that was best in the law. But such a combination of self-scrutiny and self-delusion is improbable. Inborn aversion to change is more likely than fatuous self-satisfaction. Probably Parker, Parsons, and Washburn had an unconscious reluctance to experiment, even to ask whether experiment was desirable. After all, things were going reasonably well. Why risk novelty? Conservatism is natural to man.

One defensive remark that recurs in the faculty reports of this period does suggest conscious, resolute opposition to uncomfortable change. On June 12, 1846, the Corporation appointed President Everett, Chief Justice Shaw, and Charles G. Loring [14] a committee to revise the statutes of the Law School. The committee spent six months at it; then in February 1847 the Governing Boards proclaimed new regulations. The tenth general regulation provided that "No person shall be recommended by the Law Faculty to the Corporation for the degree of Bachelor of Laws in the University or for any certificate or diploma unless he shall have been exemplary in his conduct, diligent in his studies and attendance upon the lectures and exercises of the Law School and have passed an examination satisfactory to the Professors." For twenty-three years thereafter the faculty stubbornly refused to comply.

"An examination" was the key expression in the tenth regulation of 1847. The Corporation, their committee, and the Overseers must have long been familiar with what the Law faculty ambiguously called "examinations" — frequent oral quizzes on assigned

---

[14] Two of the three were distinguished lawyers. Lemuel Shaw was Chief Justice of the Commonwealth. Charles Greely Loring, 1794–1867, A.B. Harvard 1812, studied law in Litchfield and in Samuel Hubbard's office, and practiced many years in Massachusetts. He was active in public affairs and a longtime Fellow of the Harvard Corporation. Everett as President bore the university's principal responsibility for the standards and well-being of all its parts.

text material, conducted by the professors of law from the School's earliest days. To have "passed an examination" must have connoted some much more formal ordeal. The President's annual report for 1845–46 listed in the School's exercises *"Reviews and examinations* of the Students in the Text Books. These are held twice a day, five days in the week, and the time occupied with each Class is one hour." Surely the new regulation intended more than these daily interrogations. Yet only this same statement, with minor textual changes, taking no note of the new tenth general regulation, appears in the reports from 1846 to 1850. There is no provision for either an oral or written degree examination.

The 1850–51 report, after a remark about "the usual examinations upon the matter of the text books and the presentation of cases connected therewith for opinions by the students," adds: "The application of the subject-matter of the lectures in this mode is believed to be even more beneficial and satisfactory than direct examinations, which test the memory of the student, rather than aid him in applying what he has learned to actual practice." The reports for 1851–52 [15] and 1852–53 add, "Experience has confirmed the Faculty in the belief, that this is the most useful method of examination." The professors' statement suggests men defending a position. Was a Committee to Visit the Law School nudging the professors? Pushed or not, the faculty dug in their heels and wrote in their 1853–54 report: "Longer experience has more firmly convinced the Faculty that no other mode of examination would be so well adapted to the wants of the School." After all, the School in that year had 148 students and gave 60 LL.B.'s. A large enrollment offered a good argument for resistance to change. In 1854–55 the faculty used the same phrase about examinations prefacing it by the words "We repeat." The enrollment of the School that year had slipped a little, to a roster of 125 students, and Harvard had granted 58 LL.B.'s. At that time Bussey's bequest was not yet yielding any income and the faculty may have been reluctant to risk frightening away students by stiffening requirements. The sad days of 1828 were not beyond memory. In 1855–56 the School had only 117 students and only

[15] Christopher Columbus Langdell entered the Law School on November 6, 1851. He must have been questioned in the classroom as to his opinion on "cases . . . framed to illustrate the principles stated." See page 20 of the 1851–52 report. His case method was not wholly novel in 1870.

47 men earned LL.B.'s A declining enrollment also furnished a good argument for resistance to change. The professors held the examination line with the same phrase that year and the next, and did the same in 1857–58 when enrollments rose to 143 and degrees to 59. Perhaps the Mexican War had accounted for the temporary decline in the number of students. At any rate, through the hard days of the Civil War and on to 1868–69 the same entry concerning examinations continues.

The reluctant faculty of law felt no spur from the administration. Andrew Preston Peabody, that kindly teacher, in his report, dated October 1, 1869, on his year as acting president, commented on the undesirability in the college of "that spasmodic and unhealthy industry which is commonly termed cramming for examinations." Though Peabody conceded that college honors would depend more and more on the result of examinations, he would have dropped no students for poor performance in annual tests. Dr. Peabody saw advantages in retaining the low-ranking men. "Their defect of memory will always keep them near the foot of the class; and by occupying that position they sustain the self-respect and ambition of those next above them. The ninetieth scholar in a class of a hundred has an appreciable rank, which he will endeavor at least to maintain." By the time of the Peabody report Parker had resigned [16] and Nathaniel Holmes [17] had been appointed as the third professor. He with his seniors Parsons and Washburn continued to oppose degree examinations, in the teeth of the 1847 regulation. Dr. Peabody was neither by nature nor by belief the man to override them. The only change he suggested in the Law School was establishment of a student loan fund. The School's 1868–69 record, he said, "was one of success and prosperity." But the good-hearted clergyman did not speak for everyone.

Times were changing. On May 19, 1869, the Governing Boards of Harvard elected as President Charles William Eliot, thirty-five years old, professor of chemistry at the Massachusetts Institute of Technology. Eliot was inaugurated on October 19, 1869; his inaugural address made evident to all who heard it the new

---

[16] On February 29, 1868.

[17] Nathaniel Holmes, A.B. 1836, LL.B. 1839, had practiced in St. Louis from 1840 to 1865, had been a judge of the Supreme Court of Missouri from 1865 to 1868, and was appointed Royall Professor to succeed Parker in 1868. He resigned in 1872.

President's energy and progressive intentions. He was full of ideas for university reform. His spirit spread. A report of the Overseers' Committee to Visit the Law School disclosed concern for the School's condition. The report is discreet; like so many Harvard documents it suggests more than it discloses. It appeared shortly after the professors of law had blandly reported to the Overseers on October 21, 1869, that "the condition of the School at the present time is eminently satisfactory." The Visiting Committee on the other hand, wrote

The condition and prospects of the Law School have been the subject of much discussion by the Committee, but they have found the subject too important and too difficult to mature and agree upon any recommendations for change which they can offer to the Overseers. They therefore make no further report, but say only in conclusion that in their opinion the whole subject should be carefully considered by a committee so constituted as fully to represent and command the respect of the legal profession as well as to have weight with the Corporation, the Overseers and the public.[18]

A threat of reform in the Law School, imposed from outside its faculty, with some adverse reflection on the old order, must have been discouraging to the aging Professor Parsons. On December 11, 1869, he submitted his resignation of the Dane professorship, to take effect on the first of the following March. He was seventy-two years old and had devoted his best years to teaching and writing at Harvard. Certainly he had done his duty as he saw it. Now sensing discontent with his efforts of twenty years Parsons must have felt saddened as he ended his teaching. Of the three professors who had dominated the span between Story and Langdell, only Emory Washburn was left. The time was ripe for a shake-up, and Eliot was the man for it.

In his first President's Report, Eliot wrote kindly of Professor Parsons: "His teachings and writings have done much to maintain and build up the reputation of the Law School." But perhaps the new President was not displeased to see two of the three old-time professors of law out of the way. Sweeping reforms would be much easier under a new regime. Eliot's judgment of the School as Parker, Parsons, and Washburn had carried it on was not undiscriminatingly adverse. Sharp eyed as he was, he saw in the Law School wholesome vigor along with resistance to re-

[18] Both reports appear in Warren, *Harvard Law School*, II, 358–359.

form. In his second annual report covering 1870–71 the new President wrote of the School that "The common life or sympathetic association of the body of students, all in eager pursuit of the same end, is a very valuable part of the training which the school supplies. The incessant discussions and contests which go on among them, and in fact the whole tone and atmosphere of the place are most stimulating and wholesome." [19] These traits were not developed in a year; Eliot must have known that he was describing a tradition that grew up long before he assumed the presidency of Harvard.

3

A century afterward what should be our judgment of the School of Parker, Parsons, and Washburn? On balance we can take much pride in it. During those years the School performed its essential function. It graduated annually a half-hundred or so Bachelors of Laws; of these a great percentage were useful and honorable lawyers, and some were lawyers in the grand manner. Probably the School never produced a larger proportion of these latter, either before Story's death in 1845 or since Langdell's coming in 1870. Langdell himself was a product of the *anciem régime* of Parker, Parsons, and Washburn. So was John Chipman Gray, LL.B. 1861, who came to the Law School before Langdell; so was James Bradley Thayer, LL.B. 1856, who came to the faculty in 1873; so was Oliver Wendell Holmes, Jr., LL.B. 1866, who came to the School as lecturer in jurisprudence in 1871, and who in 1882 became a professor of law before he went on to other and probably greater things.

Justice Holmes once told of a man who deducted five dollars' from his valet's wages "for lack of imagination." Perhaps the three professors shared the valet's defect. One reads the annals

[19] Eliot's 1870–71 comments on the schools of Divinity and Medicine were much harsher than his report on the Law School. As to the Divinity School he said that "There is reason to hope that in that year (1869, when the requirement of a knowledge of Latin and Greek was abolished) the school touched bottom." Of the Medical School he wrote: "It seems almost incredible that the grossly inadequate training above described should be the recognized preparation of aspirants to a profession which was once called learned and which preeminently demands a mind well stored and a judgment well trained, a profession in which ignorance is criminal and skill a benefaction, a profession on which penetrates the most sacred retreats of human love, joy and sorrow and deals daily with the issues of life and death."

of the Law School with no sense that its teachers were idle. Their fault was a lack of vision, of perception, of an eager aspiration to make a good School better. No one thing was gravely wrong. Some talented students came, were excited about their study, educated one another. Eliot said so in 1886 when he told the Law School Association how he found a new Dane Professor in 1870, who, eighteen years before that, was already inspired, and could inspire others, with his conceptions of law.[20]

Then I remembered that when I was a Junior in College in the year 1851–1852, and used to go often in the early evening to the room of a friend who was in the Divinity School, I there heard a young man who was making notes to *Parsons on Contracts* talk about law. He was generally eating his supper at the time, standing up in front of the fire and eating with good appetite a bowl of brown bread and milk. I was a mere boy, only eighteen years old; but it was given to me to understand that I was listening to a man of genius. In the year 1870, I recalled the remarkable character of that young man's expositions, sought him in New York, and induced him to become Dane Professor. So he became Professor Langdell. He then told me, in 1870, a great many of the things he has told you this afternoon: I have heard most of his speech before. He told me that law was a science: I was quite prepared to believe it. He told me that the way to study a science was to go to the original sources. I knew that was true, for I had been brought up in the science of chemistry myself; and one of the first rules of a conscientious student of science is never to take a fact or a principle out of second hand treatises, but to go to the original memoir of the discoverer of that fact or principle.

Essential to the success of study of law as a science, with the connotations Langdell and Eliot gave to that expression, was a body of eager, highly intelligent, well-prepared students. But if Parker, Parsons, and Washburn ever considered the financially risky venture of admitting to the School only such talented candidates for degrees, and refusing the applications of commonplace people, the proposition never appeared in their annual reports. The three old-timers were good, steady men, aiming to carry on in the accustomed way. So they did.

The library grew but little between 1845 and 1870. Here, too, the trouble was lack of imagination for what a library could be. The librarian was a student without power to buy books who helped earn his way by keeping track of the existing collection;

[20] *Record of Commemoration, 250th Anniversary, 1886, of Harvard College.*

Langdell was such a student librarian from 1852 to 1854. A subcommittee of the University Library Visiting Committee observed with acidity in 1861 that when the librarian was pursuing his studies or was otherwise unavailable the Dane Hall janitor was "the executive officer of the Law Library as well as the factotum of the Law School." [21] In 1846 the Law library contained about 11,000 volumes; in 1869 the number had grown to 15,000, but 4,000 of these were textbooks for the use of students in day-by-day class work. Students, professors, and library all were housed in Dane Hall throughout the quarter-century, and indeed so continued until 1883.

The School, that is to say, after 1845 went along unchanged for twenty-five years. In 1845 it had been an excellent institution, and it continued to have excellences. What it lacked was self-scrutiny by professors with minds open to the possibility of improvement. Allotment of blame for this unchallenged continuity is a futile exercise. The crisis which came to a climax in the Civil War, long smoldering before it burst into flames in 1861, occupied much of the professors' attention during at least half of the Parker-Parsons-Washburn era. The Law School was not alone in its quiescence during the middle years of the nineteenth century; the rest of Harvard walked in old ways too; so did the rest of academic America. Perhaps the changes that began with Eliot's Presidency were part of a nationwide reinvigoration of higher learning that came shortly after the end of the war.

The significant warning of that time for our time is the ease with which the familiar becomes inevitable. Essential to continued well-being in any human organization, including a uni-

---

[21] The janitor was John Sweetnam, a recruit of President Quincy. "He had come to this country and fallen upon evil days, being glad to get a job at street digging. President Quincy, passing one day, was amazed at a red head emerging from a trench and quoting, in excellent Latin, the lines from the Bucolics concerning the pleasures of the husbandman. He took the orator into his own service, but finding him perhaps too much of a handful, turned him over to the Law School. Here he became an autocrat. His professional duties, as popularly understood, he limited to opening the doors in the morning and locking them at night. He was deeply aggrieved if asked even to replace library books left on the tables, and seizing on the maxim so frequently used in Torts, modified it to suit his own purposes thus: 'Sic utere libris ut me non laedas.' But he invented other and higher duties. He attended all the lectures, and subsequently gave the speaker the benefit of his criticism on both delivery and doctrine. He exercised a general supervision over all matters connected with the School, and in his later years became a terror to every one in or near it. But he was at last displaced by the wave of reform that swept over the School about 1870." Warren, *Harvard Law School*, II, pp. 317–318.

versity school of law, is continued inquiry as to its appropriate functioning, and that inquiry must not be too much constrained by what has been habitual. Still, Parker, Parsons, and Washburn had run a reasonable enough School by the standards of the 1840's. They had allowed their School to become unimaginative, this is evident. But they had run it well enough to inspire a generation of younger teachers who could refit and reinvigorate it. They had provided the means for regeneration of their own work. When a balance is struck, we are much in their debt.

VI

The Langdell Era: 1870–1895

Langdell became Dean of the Law School in 1870 and resigned in 1895. Ames carried the deanship from 1895 to 1910. Between 1870 and 1910, in the forty years of the Langdell and Ames deanships, Harvard developed a modern Law School. By 1910 it had come to resemble today's School much more than it resembled that of Story in 1845, or the Parker-Parsons-Washburn School in 1868. Granted, between 1910 and 1967 the student body has more than doubled; there are in 1966–67 five times as many teachers as in 1910; the library collection has multiplied by seven; all this is housed much more amply and more beautifully than it was when James Barr Ames laid down his books. But between 1870 and 1910 the School changed, in degree and in kind, much more rapidly than it did between 1910 and 1967.

When the academic year 1869–70 opened only 120 students or so came to register, about twenty fewer than in Story's last year. The office of dean did not exist. The three professors still gave instruction on Story's plan. They had all come to teaching in middle life; Nathaniel Holmes, youngest of the three, had reached his fifty-fifth year. The library, still in the charge of a student librarian and a janitor, remained essentially as Story had left it. The School was housed in Dane Hall, standing where Story had built it in the southwest corner of Harvard Yard.

By the close of 1910 the School had grown to 750 students. Two extraordinarily talented deans, Langdell and Ames, in two-score years had transformed it in every way. In 1910 courses were taught by a faculty of fifteen, nine professors, an assistant professor, and five lecturers. The curriculum had been entirely revised. Admission to the School required an undergraduate de-

Christopher Columbus Langdell, aged sixty-six, painted in 1892 by Frederic
Vinton in the twenty-second year of Langdell's deanship. His white beard and
cane may suggest an old, timid, unworldly scholar, probably ineffective. But
during his deanship Langdell was determined, courageous, forceful, and got his
way. The portrait hangs in Langdell Reading Room.

gree. Harvard now granted its LL.B. only after three years of rigorous study, tested by annual examinations which excluded the unsuccessful with impersonal severity. John Himes Arnold, the full-time librarian, and his assistant librarian, Robert Bowie Anderson,[1] supervised the revived and much expanded library. The immortal John McCarthy ruled the stacks and delivery desk. Richard Ames, LL.B. 1909, was secretary of the School, predecessor of today's administrative staff. The *Harvard Law Review* and the Law School Association were a quarter-century old. Dane Hall, abandoned by lawyers, standing in the Yard near the Square, now housed only college offices. The School had migrated to the north side of Kirkland Street and was quartered in Austin Hall and Langdell Hall. Students fortunate enough to find university rooms mostly lived in Hastings Hall and Gannett House. In 1910 Roscoe Pound was Story Professor; he only stopped writing in 1964. In 1910 Samuel Williston, Joseph H. Beale, Eugene Wambaugh, and the two Warrens, Edward H. and Joseph, were teaching and writing. Austin Scott, now Dane Professor *Emeritus* had already joined the faculty. As these words are written he is busy with proofs of a new edition of his casebook on trusts and is publishing a new edition of his treatise on the same subject. Royall Professor *Emeritus* John MacArthur Maguire,[2] who now comes regularly to his office in Langdell Hall, was halfway through his law-student days. Among the students in 1910 were other men who in 1967 often revisit the School. The Conference of Commissioners on Uniform State Laws had come into being fifteen years earlier, and professors from Harvard had written or contributed to important Uniform Acts, as they do today. Be-

---

[1] He became assistant librarian of the Law School on November 23, 1903; he resigned on December 1, 1942, then associate librarian. He died in 1949 in Melrose, Massachusetts. Such devoted men have kept the School going.

[2] John MacArthur Maguire was born in Denver, Colorado, in 1888. He received his A.B. from Colorado College in 1908, his LL.B. from Harvard in 1911, and his LL.D. from Colorado College in 1949. He was engaged in law practice from 1911 to 1917, and from 1917 to 1919 served with the war emergency division of the Department of Justice. He was a partner in the law firm of Hale and Dorr, Boston, from 1919 to 1923, and became counsel to that firm in 1957 on his retirement at Harvard. In 1923 he was appointed professor at Harvard Law School. He became Royall Professor in 1950 and in 1957 became Royall Professor Emeritus. Professor Maguire took leave from Harvard to serve with the United States Treasury Department in 1938, and again in 1943. In 1942 and 1943 he was assistant reporter of the American Law Institute Federal Income Tax Statute project. He has written casebooks on taxation and casebooks and a treatise on evidence.

tween 1870 and 1910 Langdell and Ames had presided over this complete transformation of the School.

An extraordinary presidency of Harvard coincided with this dramatic period of growth and change. Charles William Eliot became President in 1869, and guided the university for forty years while Langdell and Ames were deans. Eliot retired only in 1909, just before Ames died. Eliot's energy, his unflagging and understanding interest in the progress of the Law School through four decades, his insight into the qualities its teachers required, his willingness to risk innovation, his continuous support of Langdell and Ames, all were essential to the transformation effected in their deanships.

Langdell, backed by Eliot, in 1873 chose Ames as assistant professor. Ames was as great an innovator as Langdell. He was a new sort of law teacher, a man comparatively young, whose professional accomplishments all were to be in writing, teaching, and in educational administration, with no preliminary experience in practice or on the bench. Ames was Langdell's disciple; he used Langdell's methods better than Langdell himself. Much subsequent history of teaching law in America so turned immediately and mediately on President Eliot's choice of Christopher Columbus Langdell as the School's first dean in 1870. In retrospect the forty years, 1870–1910, the years of Langdell *cum* Ames, seem a single unit in the School's history.

But that forty-year span was divided in two segments by change in the society and government of the United States. A university school of law which serves the country as it should must in the learning of its professors and in the instruction of its students be part of the social and governmental movements of its time. The society and government and law of this nation underwent a dramatically accelerated evolution between 1895 and 1910. No change in a society, no development of governmental institutions, occurs in a moment; each involves changes in the habits of thought and the mode of existence of great numbers of people, and these changes are gradual, like all human growth. But perception of change may be sudden. Around the turn of the century the United States, somewhat surprised, saw dimly that it had turned from a society of homesteads to a world of intricate machines; from an isolated nation which could, if it would, live by itself to a republic intimately involved with the affairs of the whole world, for which isolation was no longer possible. It became conscious that its geometrically increasing millions of people who had never been really docile, who had never been peasants ready to accept want and pain as inevitable, were now turning more and more to getting by political means what they wanted from life,[3] more and more to governmental rather than private action, more and more to action by national rather than local governing power. The fifteen years of Ames's deanship, from 1895 to 1910, saw the School begin to reflect these great movements, which have accelerated dramatically as the twentieth century has been passing. So the era we can conveniently name for Ames requires a separate chapter. Langdell's quarter-century from 1870 to 1895 was a period of its own sort; the story of Langdell's School must have a chapter named for the first dean.

Langdell, born in 1826 in New Boston, New Hampshire, worked his way through Exeter, and entered Harvard College as a sophomore in the fall of 1848. He was then twenty-two years old, an age when many university students had already graduated. He stayed at Harvard College only a year and a half, and left without a degree. Then, after supporting himself as a private tutor for a few months, he returned to the town of Exeter where for a year and a half he read law in the office of Stickney and Tuck. In November 1851 he entered the Harvard Law School, where he stayed three years, twice the conventional three terms. His means were slender. At first a fellow student let him sleep on a spare cot; twenty dollars kept him in food for most of a term. Then the faculty, sensing his value, employed him as student librarian. Parsons gave him work on *The Law of Contracts* which first appeared in 1853. With his talents, and by means of the work they brought him, Langdell ultimately lived in comparative ease as a student and became a sort of oracle to his fellow students at the School. Fifty-six years later one of these, Charles Phelps of Baltimore, wrote:

> The Librarian was no less a personage than C. C. Langdell, a book worm if there ever was one. He always wore over his eyes a dark shade with a green lining. I don't remember ever seeing him without it.

[3] In a little book of Holmes Lectures at the University of North Carolina, under the title *Apology for Uncomfortable Change, 1865–1965* (New York: Macmillan, 1965), I have offered some observations on these matters.

There were about a dozen of us who took our hash together at a boarding house on Brighton Street, and of these Langdell was the presiding genius. At table, nothing was talked but shop. Cases were put and discussed, and I have sometimes thought that from these table discussions Langdell got the germ of the idea that he later developed into the case system of instruction which has made his name famous both here and abroad.[4]

Judge Phelps said another time: "From these table-talks I got more stimulus, more inspiration, in fact, more law, than from the lectures of Judge Parker and Professor Parsons." [5] In 1853 Langdell took his LL.B., and Phi Beta Kappa elected him an honorary member. The next year, when his college classmates were receiving the A.M. in regular course, Harvard gave Langdell that degree *honoris causa*. Later Harvard gave him his A.B. as of 1851, the year of his college class.

For sixteen years following 1853 Langdell practiced law in New York City. He was a lawyer's lawyer rather than a business-getter, but the leaders of the bar greatly respected him. Still unmarried, he lived in a bedroom over the law offices of Stanley, Langdell and Brown, and devoted himself to practice. On January 6, 1870, Eliot brought him to Harvard as Dane Professor of Law. The rest of Langdell's life belonged to the Law School. One may ask why Eliot made this choice, so fruitful in its results. The reason was Eliot's and Langdell's common intellectual commitment to the scientism of the day.

2

On April 8, 1870, the Corporation adopted a set of University Statutes and Laws, some new, some re-enacted. Two of these deeply affected the Law School. This time the School obeyed both.

7. The Faculty of each Professional School elects a Dean, whose duty it is to keep the Records of the Faculty, to prepare its business and to preside at its meetings in the absence of the President . . .

12. The ordinary degrees of Bachelor of Arts . . . Bachelor of Laws . . . are conferred after recommendation with the concurrence

[4] From a letter written in 1908 by Judge Charles E. Phelps, LL.B. 1853, to Charles Warren, quoted in *Harvard Law School*, II, 181–182.

[5] Quoted in James Barr Ames, "Christopher Columbus Langdell," in *Great American Lawyers*, vol. VIII (Philadelphia, 1909), reprinted in *Lectures on Legal History* (Cambridge, Mass., 1913), p. 467.

of the Overseers. It is required that no candidate for these degrees be recommended except after thorough public examination.

On September 27, 1870, the Faculty of Law held its first formal meeting, in President Eliot's office. Eliot presided, and present were the professors, Washburn, Nathaniel Holmes, and Langdell. On Washburn's motion they elected Langdell as first Dean of the School.

The Dean's duties, as the statutes defined them, were formal and trifling. Whatever Langdell's ideas of reform might be, he could only effect them by persistently and patiently working to make the deanship a power and, with Eliot's backing, using it powerfully. What were Langdell's ideas? His "case method" of instruction has attracted so much interested attention and comment that it may have diminished notice of more fundamental reforms. The four basic requisites of a school of law, conducted in the grand manner, are a talented body of eager students; a faculty both learned and wise; a great collection of writings on the law, and a beautiful house in which these may coexist and may react, each on the other. In Langdell's deanship Harvard gained in all of these, but its most significant advance concerned the quality of its students.

Eliot and Langdell came to Harvard when the Law School accepted as a student any man whose "moral character" was good. The new President and Dean began a change toward insistence that only men of high intelligence and industry could enter the School; [6] that only students who demonstrated those qualities in the study of law could remain in the School; that only those who had achieved a reasonable mastery of method and principle, demonstrated by stringent examination, could proceed to the university's degree in laws.

From the beginning the best of the men who sought the law at Harvard had been as intelligent, as wisely studious, as any men can ever be. But a School open alike to the excellent and to the mediocre, to all comers without regard to talents or performance, tended to devaluate its degree and to impair the learning process. The School has always given its most effective instruction by producing interaction between student and student, between eager

[6] Warren, *Harvard Law School*, II, 397, tells of the adverse reaction to this requirement among some Overseers.

intelligence and eager intelligence, by contagious excitement of discussion, dissection, argumentation, carried on outside as well as inside the classroom. This reaction prospers in direct proportion to the high quality of the mass. Slate in coal impedes combustion.

The Langdell School at first undertook to discourage the attendance of non-ignitable men by barring them from degree candidacy,[7] thus putting a premium on intelligence. Only those were to be accepted as prospective Bachelors of Laws who had already demonstrated reasonable energy and intellect by achieving a previous degree, or those who could make an equivalent demonstration by passing a somewhat formidable qualifying examination. In 1875 the law faculty and the Corporation established the necessary regulation:

> The course of instruction in the School is designed for persons who have received a college education, and Bachelors of Arts will be admitted as candidates for degrees on presentation of their diplomas; but for the present, young men who are not Bachelors of Arts will also be admitted to the School for a degree, upon passing a satisfactory examination, as follows:
>
> 1. In Latin, in which subject candidates will be required to translate (without the aid of grammar or dictionary) passages selected from one or more of the following books: *Caesar's Commentaries; Cicero's Orations* and the *Aeneid of Virgil.*
>
> 2. In *Blackstone's Commentaries* (exclusive of Editor's notes)
>
> Proficiency in French representing an amount of preparatory work equivalent to that demanded of those who offer Latin will be accepted as a substitute for the requisition in the latter language. Candidates will be required to translate (without the aid of grammar and dictionary) passages from standard French prose authors, and also to render into French, passages of easy English prose.
>
> The Faculty will in their discretion permit some other language to be substituted for Latin or French, but a satisfactory examination in some language other than English will be insisted upon in all cases.[8]

The ensuing examinations were not by any to be entered into

---

[7] Then, as now, admission to the bar in many states was open to any man who had studied law for a period prescribed by state law, if only the candidate could satisfy the bar examiners. Achievement of an academic law degree was not essential for admission to practice. See Alfred Z. Reed, *Training for the Public Profession of the Law* (New York, 1921), p. 91. Thus work as a special student, regardless of eligibility for a degree, had a practical value. Still the degree carried a cachet, and Langdell made candidacy a privilege.

[8] Quoted in Warren, *Harvard Law School*, II, 395.

lightly or unadvisedly. In 1878 candidates for admission were required, among other Latin exercises, to render these lines into English:

> Sacra Dionaeae matri divisque ferebam
> Auspicibus coeptorum operum, superoque nitentem
> Caelicolum regi mactabam in litore taurum.
> Forte fuit iuxta tumulus, quo cornea summo
> Virgulta et densis hastilibus horrida myrtus.
> Accessi, viridemque ab humo convellere silvam
> Conatus, ramis tegerem ut frondentibus aras,
> Horrendum et dictu video mirabile monstrum.
> Nam, quae prima solo ruptis radicibus arbos
> Vellitur, huic atro liquuntur sanguine guttae
> Et terram tabo maculant.

Perhaps during the next dozen years attention to classical studies in American universities was already declining; by 1900 the language questions seem to have become a little easier. But by way of compensation the Blackstone questions had become harder.

BLACKSTONE.

1. What were the different kinds of guardian at common law? What were the duties of each?

2. What are the principal powers of a corporation? How may a corporation be dissolved?

3. What were the principal incidents of an estate tail?

4. A, owner of land in fee simple, wishes to give the following estates: to B for ten years, followed by an estate to C for C's life, followed by an estate to the eldest son of D, D being at the time a bachelor. How can A create these interests? What interest will each person have?

Suppose D does not marry until a year after the termination of the interests of B and C; what is the result?

5. What is an executory devise? Give examples.

6. Give two examples of redress of private wrong by mere act of the parties. What other remedy would have been available in either case?

7. What is a writ *de homine replegiando*? When is it used?

8. What was wager of law?

9. Name and explain three offenses against public trade.

10. What was the law as to arrest of offenders by a private individual? [9]

[9] 1900 Examination Pamphlet, page 63.

One may speculate as the faculty's reasons for choosing questions on a foreign language and on an eighteenth century Oxford professor's treatise to judge the fitness of young men seeking the law at Harvard in Langdell's day. Ability to write suitable glosses on difficult matters in Blackstone's *Commentaries* demonstrated general intellect, including an ability to get to the bottom of concepts in English legal history. The Latin, too, could serve as a general intelligence test. Selection of young men for the British civil service, so they say, was once based, at least in part, on high academic standing in education largely classical, on the theory that a youth who could learn to make Greek verses could learn to do anything.

Until 1909 admission to law-degree candidacy continued nominally possible on passing an entrance examination, without completing the work for a previous undergraduate degree, though the number of admissions on this system declined to insignificance. In 1909 the School ended even this possibility.[10] In the academic year 1910–11 of 766 students in residence, sixteen had completed all their college work though their degrees had not yet been conferred; only three others were special students with no previous degree.[11]

The Langdell School progressively stiffened requirements in still other ways, which in turn required still abler students. In 1871 the course of study for the LL.B. was lengthened from eighteen months to two years. In 1872 the School prescribed examinations at the end of the first year's study as a condition of admission to the second and, at that time, final year. In 1876 the School lengthened to three years the period of study for the LL.B., but for a while allowed regular students who had been in residence for two years to pass their third year without attendance at classes. Special students, to qualify for a degree, had to stay in

[10] Through the academic year 1908–09 a man could become an LL.B. candidate without a previous degree, if he was admitted as a special student upon examination in Latin and French, and Blackstone, and obtained Law School grades within 5 percent of those required for the degree *cum laude* — in effect requiring the special student to make B grades to take the LL.B. See *Official Register of Harvard University: The Law School,* 1908–1909, p. 9. The 1909–10 register states that Special Students "to obtain a degree, must hold a degree from a college or law school"; the 1910–11 register makes the terse announcement "Persons admitted as Special Students are not eligible for a degree."

[11] See *Official Register of Harvard University: The Law School,* 1910–1911, page 51.

residence three years. Two-year men qualified for the degree by returning to Harvard for final examinations at the end of the third year.[12] This system ended in 1899 when Harvard required of all students three years in residence for the LL.B., with satisfactory performance in course examinations at the end of each of the three years.[13]

The course examinations at Harvard Law School have passed through a long evolution since they began in 1871. They have increasingly required students to analyze complex fact situations before applying principles of law. The early questions required much less preliminary analysis than those of the 1960's. For example, Langdell in June 1871 put as the first question of his "General Paper" on Contracts: "What are the necessary elements of a contract under seal; of a contract not under seal?" He posed more complex problems in a "Special Paper"; the tenth question was: "An offer is sent from Boston to New York by mail on Monday, and an answer accepting it is received on Wednesday at 10 a.m., but in the meantime another letter withdrawing the offer has been sent on Tuesday, and received on Wednesday at 9 a.m. Is there or not a contract between the parties, and why? If there is, what was the *punctum temporis* at which it was completed?" The School's publications do not explain the reason for the difference between the general and special papers. The record of grades shows that some students were given two grades in Contracts for 1870–71, one set being apparently a half-credit. Perhaps the special paper was optional. Professor Gray's first question on First Year Real Property in June 1878 was: "What is the distinction between a right *in rem* and a right *in personam*? Give an instance of each."

One might contrast with these early examinations a June 1965 question in Contracts and one in Real Property.

---

[12] See Warren, *Harvard Law School*, II, 383f, and the Centennial History, p. 32, for the added requirements, 1871–1876. The third year spent *in absentia* may have been intended to permit a student to pass the year in a clerkship required under state laws. See Dean Langdell's Report to the President for 1876–77 annexed to the President's Annual Report for that year. And see Reed, *Training for the Law*, p. 261.

[13] In 1898 the School required residence for all students for three years, including regular students who had entered the first-year class since May 1, 1897, adding in its published announcements, "In rare cases and for cogent reasons submitted to the Faculty, regular students may be permitted to be absent from the School during one of the last two years" (*Announcements, 1898–1899*, p. 12). The next year even this exception disappeared.

The Langdell Era

CONTRACTS
Section 3
Professor Braucher
2–6 P.M.

You should have with you Fuller & Braucher, Basic Contract Law, and you may also use any other material, whether prepared by you or otherwise.

Unless otherwise stated, all events take place in Massachusetts, where the Uniform Commercial Code has been in effect since October 1, 1958 . . .

1. The Acme Folding Box Company, on April 30, 1965, wrote the following letter to the Barnes Aircraft Rental & Sales Co.:

"Our company has decided, for reasons of economy, to discontinue the use of our own private aircraft. Because our relations in the past have been so cordial, we are pleased to be able to make you a special offer of two used, single-engine, four-passenger planes, a Cardinal and an Egret, at $4,500 each, 20% in cash, with a purchase-money mortgage for the remainder. We would be glad to have you inspect these planes at the Meredith airport at your convenience, and to let any of your prospective customers inspect them, but we must have your reply in 15 days."

A Barnes representative, after traveling to Meredith and inspecting the planes himself, brought a Mr. Alfred Corben to look at them, told him that the planes belonged to Barnes, and said that Corben could purchase them for $5,500 each. Corben, a flying instructor and owner of a small private airport, said he would think it over and on May 12, wrote Barnes that he had decided to accept the offer for the Cardinal and would be willing to pay $2000 in cash. He enclosed a check for $500 as a deposit.

On May 13, the same day it received this letter, Barnes also received a letter from Acme stating that all of Acme's stock had just been sold and that the new owner of the company had decided to keep the planes. Barnes, seeking to protect itself, immediately wrote to Acme stating that "your offer of April 30 is hereby accepted." On May 25, not having heard from Acme and being pressed by Corben for immediate delivery, Barnes came to your firm for advice and you have been asked to prepare a memorandum discussing your client's rights and liabilities.

PROPERTY I
Section 4
Professor Leach
2–6 P.M.
VII

Suggested time: forty minutes. Maximum: Six bluebook pages or three pages double-spaced typescript.

The Langdell Era

CG in 1907 purchased a large area in the State of Ames, laid out streets, and sub-divided it into lots of about one-half acre. He began selling off these lots immediately. The sixth sale was made in 1908 to A (who will become plaintiff in this case). The forty-seventh was made in 1920 to B. All lots were sold by a printed form of deed which contained a covenant by the grantee on behalf of himself, his heirs and assigns, with CG, his heirs and assigns that the premises should never be used for any purpose except a residence. There were no words in the deed by which CG made any covenant. As the lots were sold, the owners erected residences on them. In 1940 B sold his lot to X (who will become defendant in this case); the deed contained no covenants by either party. All deeds were promptly recorded. X knew of the covenant in the deed from CG to B, but had no actual knowledge of the terms of any of the prior deeds. X announced in 1941 that he was going to establish an ice cream parlor accommodating 75 persons to market the products of Dutchland Farms, Inc. A immediately brought a bill in equity against X to enjoin this intended use of X's lot.

A statute in Ames, passed in 1900, provides as follows:

"Conditions or restrictions, unlimited as to time, by which the title or use of real property is affected, shall be limited to the term of thirty years after the date of the deed or other instrument or the date of the probate of the will creating them. . . ."

X claims the protection of this statute, and asserts that he is not bound by any covenant which A can enforce.

a. State, in no more than one-half bluebook page or equivalent typescript, the substance of X's defense based on the statute.

b. As counsel for A, outline a brief on his behalf.

(You will note that the fact situation is somewhat similar to Snow v. Van Dam, Casner & Leach p. 1126. However, the present case arises in the State of Ames where, by the rules of the game, there are no locally binding precedents. The quoted statute is a Massachusetts product which has been severely criticized; and the statute was relied on in that case in a portion of the opinion not included in the case-book.) [14]

As the School makes available to students printed copies of examinations of past years, study is thus to some extent guided by requirements of recent examination questions. Probably the modern form is more exacting. It adds to the requirements of the 1870's a test of ability to untangle complex skeins of fact which the lawyer meets in practical affairs. But one can easily underrate Gray's 1878 inquiry concerning the nature of *in rem* and *in per-*

[14] In the 1965 examinations appear some multiple-choice questions. The author of this history, being nonadept in this type of examination, discreetly withholds comment.

sonam rights. It invited more than a simple call for memory work. In response to Gray's challenge a scholar of mature insight could write an essay in depth,[15] while a superficial youth could glibly repeat formulas he had read in a book. Perhaps Gray's questions served to sort the men from the boys as effectively as the questions put nine decades later; but possibly today's examinations are better educational devices. One cannot be sure.

Steady increases in the average quality of the School's students and in the requirements for its degree were the work of many people — these were corporate decisions of the School and of the university. The "case method" was Langdell's own. He left few statements about his theories of the law and of the best way to teach it, about his case method. He explained himself best in the preface of his 1871 *Cases on Contracts*, and in his address at the meeting of the Harvard Law School Association held in 1886 at the university's two hundred and fiftieth anniversary celebration. He wrote in his preface:

Law, considered as a science, consists of certain principles or doctrines. To have such a mastery of these as to be able to apply them with constant facility and certainty to the ever-tangled skein of human affairs, is what constitutes a true lawyer; and hence to acquire that mastery should be the business of every earnest student of law. Each of these doctrines has arrived at its present state by slow degrees; in other words, it is a growth, extending in many cases through centuries. This growth is to be traced in the main through a series of cases; and much the shortest and best, if not the only way of mastering the doctrine effectually is by studying the cases in which it is embodied. But the cases which are useful and necessary for this purpose at the present day bear an exceedingly small proportion to all that have been reported. The vast majority are useless, and worse than useless, for any purpose of systematic study. Moreover the number of fundamental legal doctrines is much less than is commonly supposed; the many different guises in which the same doctrine is constantly making its appearance, and the great extent to which legal treatises are a repetition of each other, being the cause of much misapprehension. If these doctrines could be so classified and arranged that each should be found in its proper place, and nowhere else, they would cease to be formidable from their number. It seemed to me, therefore, to be possible to take such a branch of the law as Contracts, for example, and, without exceeding comparatively moderate limits, to select, classify, and ar-

---

[15] Some interesting contrasts between rights *in rem* and rights *in personam* occur in Chief Justice Holmes's opinion in *Tyler v. Court of Registration*, 175 Mass. 71 (1900).

range all the cases which had contributed in any important degree to the growth, development, or establishment of any of its essential doctrines; and that such a work could not fail to be of material service to all who desire to study that branch of law systematically and in its original sources.

Langdell told the 1886 audience:

[It] was indispensable to establish at least two things; first that law is a science; secondly, that all the available materials of that science are contained in printed books. If law be not a science, a university will best consult its own dignity in declining to teach it. If it be not a science, it is a species of handicraft, and may best be learned by serving an apprenticeship to one who practices it. If it be a science, it will scarcely be disputed that it is one of the greatest and most difficult of sciences, and that it needs all the light that the most enlightened seat of learning can throw upon it. Again, law can be learned and taught in a university by means of printed books. If, therefore, there are other and better means of teaching and learning law than printed books, or if printed books can only be used to the best advantage in connection with other means, — for instance, the work of a lawyer's office, or attendance upon the proceedings of courts of justice, — it must be confessed that such means cannot be provided by a university. But if printed books are the ultimate sources of all legal knowledge; if every student who would obtain any mastery of law as a science must resort to these ultimate sources; and if the only assistance which it is possible for the learner to receive is such as can be afforded by teachers who have travelled the same road before him, — then a university, and a university alone, can furnish every possible facility for teaching and learning law . . . We have also constantly inculcated the idea that the library is the proper workshop of professors and students alike; that it is to us all that the laboratories of the university are to the chemists and physicists, all that the museum of natural history is to the zoologists, all that the botanical garden is to the botanists.[16]

In 1870 the word "science" carried connotations quite different from its eighteenth century meaning. In 1870 "science" was a term no longer widely used to describe any organized body of knowledge; Langdell evidently thought of the "science of law" as analogous to the sciences of chemistry or botany. Natural science was all around him. Harvard had chosen for her president a pro-

[16] *Record of the Commemoration, November Fifth to Eighth, 1886, on the Two Hundred and Fiftieth Anniversary of the Founding of Harvard College* (1887), pp. 97, 98. Search for sources was a favorite theme of Langdell's. On the flyleaf of his first casebook he printed Coke's maxim "Melius petere fontes quam sectari rivulos," It is better to go up to the wellsprings than to follow rivulets downhill.

fessor of chemistry, who had brought Langdell to the Law School. Eliot was "quite prepared to believe" Langdell.[17] He told the same audience in 1886: "Out of these two fundamental propositions, — that law is a science, and that a science is to be studied in its sources, — there gradually grew, first, a new method of teaching law; and secondly a reconstruction of the curriculum of the School."

In the years that followed the Civil War a system of thought then described as "positivism," the concept that knowledge is based exclusively on the methods and discoveries of the physical or "positivist" sciences, was deeply moving young Harvard intellectuals — Oliver Wendell Holmes, Jr., William James, John Fiske, Henry Adams, and Brooks Adams who "came to history seeking science." [18] Langdell has left no such record of his reading as Holmes left, but he cannot have escaped the deep intellectual currents of the time. His gospel was the application of the method of the natural sciences to the science of society. To him proper study of the law, like the study of chemistry, physics, zoology, and botany, consisted in the careful observation and recording of many specific instances, and then from these instances derivation of general conclusions that the qualities of the phenomena or specimens observed would hold constant for other instances of the same classes.

Langdell's specimens were opinions of judges, collected in a library. The student of law, he thought, like the student of chemistry or biology, must learn the arts of close scrutiny and discriminating classification. The student of law, that is to say, must continually study, compare, and classify judicial opinions. Recourse by many students to the same book of reports would soon destroy the book; each student needed his own collection of selected opinions which he could conveniently carry away and study.[19] But even when thus given a book of opinions for study, the untrained student would still need help in learning to classify the cases, to distinguish like from unlike despite superficial similarity, to reject as useless opinions which were ill reasoned,

[17] See above, p. 159, for Eliot's account of Langdell's belief in the "scientific" character of law and Eliot's acceptance of the idea.

[18] See Howe, *Justice Oliver Wendell Holmes: The Shaping Years*, chap. 6.

[19] The Harvard Medical School now furnishes a beginner in the study of histology with his own collection of microscope slides, which he can carry away and study with his own microscope.

based on bad logic, and hence were flawed specimens, unsuitable for generalization. Learning this art of analysis and discrimination requires first careful study of the material, then discussion with others, submission to questioning, justification of the student's judgment, or confession of error when error becomes apparent. Such dialectic, though carried on between a teacher and only one student, can educate as many men in a lecture hall as are well prepared and eager to follow with critical interest the dialogue between instructor and student. This process, with variations *pro re nata,* was Langdell's "case method." Under it lay a philosophy. It was no mere classroom scheme of debate.

No human procedure can be perfect, and Langdell, a modest man, would have been the last to claim perfection for his. A man who studies Langdell's case method in the light of nearly a century of subsequent legal development can wonder whether it suggested too persuasively to the beginners that the legal process was principally adjudication by logical reasoning deriving from immutable general principles. There is more to the law than lawsuits; more to it than opinions — sometimes wise opinions, sometimes not — in which judges give their reasons for deciding lawsuits this way or that. The law is legislative as well as adjudicative; men not only study law, they make it. But in 1870 the great rush of legislation, state and national, which constitutes so large a part of our present law, was mostly in the future. Administrative regulation was in its early infancy. The individual's welfare was far less a governmental concern than it has since become. Langdell was training young men in the law as he had seen it, not as it would be in a day which he and his contemporaries foresaw dimly, if indeed they could foresee it at all.

Neither Langdell nor his disciple Ames was stubbornly and exclusively insistent that each student construct for himself his own corpus of legal doctrine solely by arranging in order a mass of decisions as one might sort a basket of sea shells. Neither Langdell nor Ames sought to dissuade a student from studying another man's arrangement of case law — that is to say, a text, or some other compendium. Indeed many judicial opinions are textual essays on some area of the law, and the study of cases can be a sort of textbook study. When Langdell became dean, and the faculty of law prescribed entrance examinations for non-degree men, they set a doctrinal text — Blackstone's *Commen-*

taries — as part of the subject matter on which to examine applicants for admission to the School. Once admitted, the student was
invited to study other compendia. Langdell added a summary,
a sort of restatement of contracts, at the end of his 1871 casebook.
The index of his 1872 *Cases on Sales* is a statement of doctrine as
well as a guide to the contents of the book. Ames, when he prepared his massive *Cases on Bills and Notes* in 1881 added a textual
summary of that law at the end. Langdell and Ames, that is to
say, prescribed doctrinal reading as well as study of opinions.

But Langdell insisted that the student examine any text critically, using his own evaluation. Essential to Langdell's case
method was not only the material studied but the requirement
that the student judge all material for himself, scrutinize instances
closely, accept no other man's judgment until he had judged its
logic for himself, judged its soundness, its wholesomeness.

A weakness in the philosophy of Langdell's method lay in its
assumption that the social science of the law was fundamentally
like a natural science; that its essential process was observation
of phenomena and derivation from that observation of constant
"laws" like the "laws" of chemistry or physics. Langdell was a
perceptive man, not naive; he knew, of course, that men could
change their enacted or decisional laws to suit their convenience,
whereas they could not amend the law of gravity. Perhaps the
scientism pervasive among intellectuals during his youth and
early middle years had constrained him to express the analogy
of law to natural science as though it were an essential likeness,
even when he knew it was not really so. But whatever error of
perception he may have entertained, still his insistence on scrupulously exact examination of legal materials, on their classification
according to essential likenesses and differences, were disciplines
of great value. The early casebooks provided admirable material
for such training in the hard-eyed scrutiny of any writing, in perception of the relevant and rejection of the irrelevant, in logical
progression from premise to conclusion. Men rigorously schooled
in such intellectual processes could use them in any phase of
the life of the law.[20]

---

[20] For an evaluation of the case method made by an Austrian professor of law
on the invitation of the Carnegie Foundation for the Advancement of Teaching see
Redlich, *The Common Law and the Case Method in American University Law
Schools* (New York, 1914). The late Judge Jerome Frank wrote a somewhat ad-
verse estimate of Langdell's reforms in "A Plea for Lawyer Schools," *Yale Law
Journal*, 56:1301 (1941).

The Langdell Era

Langdell's portrait on the wall of the School's reading room emphasizes his white beard, his wrinkles, his cane; these symbols of age may suggest that during his deanship he was an old, timid, unworldly scholar, probably ineffective. The fact was quite the contrary. Langdell was determined, courageous and forceful. The School might well have evolved the institution of the casebook without Langdell. But Langdell's administrative talents, demonstrated in the results of his quarter-century of deanship, were essential to the School's transformation. Men are remembered by tag descriptions. Langdell's case method is his popular memorial; perhaps we should rather remember his strict policies of admission and examination.

His dialectic at first displeased most of his students. He converted neither Professor Washburn nor Professor Nathaniel Holmes who continued to lecture on the old plan. Edmund H. Bennett, Judge Charles S. Bradley,[21] and St. John Green, during the early 1870's part-time lecturers on their several specialties in practice, could hardly be expected to use Langdell's novel technique. The process appeared chaotic to most students, who were used to continuous, logically arranged doctrinal lectures. Langdell would first ask a man to "state a case" — tell what the facts were, how the litigation developed, what point was at issue, what the court had decided, and the court's reasoning. Then he would ask whether the student agreed with the result, and why; whether the case followed others which the class had read, or was inconsistent; whether it could be "distinguished"; and so on. The process confused members of his first classes in Contracts. When he asked questions some of his hearers thought he was ignorant. Nobody seemed to be "learning law" in the usual way. Langdell acquired a few supporters, a larger number of critics. One day Edgar Morris Warner, LL.B. 1872, one of the pro-Langdell men, cornered his Dean in a classroom dialectical exchange, rousing mingled claps and boos from the class. Few of them at that moment understood Langdell's triumph as a teacher when he thus stimulated Warner to effective reasoning.[22] Attend-

[21] Judge Charles Smith Bradley became Bussey Professor in 1876 and resigned in 1879. He was perhaps the last Harvard law professor entirely unaffected by Langdell's method of teaching.

[22] Professor Washburn's grandson, S. F. Batchelder, tells this story in a sketch of Langdell in *Green Bag*, 18:437 (1906). Batchelder must have got the story at second hand for he came to the School twenty-five years after the event. Perhaps the story grew better with age, as good stories will. *The Green Bag*, which described itself as "A Useless but Entertaining Magazine for Lawyers" began

ance at Langdell's class dwindled to a faithful handful, called "Kit's Freshmen" by their skeptical classmates. But one of these persistent followers was James Barr Ames, who himself joined the faculty of law in 1873, who became the second teacher at Harvard to use the case method, who was a better classroom dialectician than his master, who became a scholar of international reputation and who in 1895 succeeded Langdell in the deanship.

Another disturbing innovation was a rise in tuition, which had remained unchanged for fifty-three years. In 1817 Boston lawyers by custom charged a student an "established fee" of $100 for office tuition, and the Law School then established the same sum as the tuition for a full year's study. In 1870–71 the Corporation announced that this charge would be raised to $150 for the first year, remaining at $100 for the second, and dropping to $50 for each subsequent year.[23] One object of this diminishing scale of fees was to encourage students to stay more than a single year.

The School had a comparatively small endowment, and depended for existence on tuition fees. Heightened standards of scholarship as a condition of continuance in the School, extension to two years of the period of time required to earn the degree, adoption by the Dean of a new and puzzling method of instruction which had not yet demonstrated its usefulness, appointment of James Barr Ames as an assistant professor when he was only a year out of the Law School and Ames's adoption of Langdell's novel teaching procedure, substantial increase in the annual charge for instruction, all occurring within the three years 1870–1873, did somewhat cut down the number of enrollments as President Eliot later pointed out. In 1870–71, the year of Langdell's appointment as dean, enrollment, which then fluctuated considerably during the year, rose to a yearly average of

---

publication at Boston in 1889 and flourished for a generation. The name was drawn from the green cloth container in which, even today, some Boston lawyers and some law students at Harvard still carry miscellaneous professional papers and books.

[23] These figures are discussed in Warren, *Harvard Law School*, II, 382. I find it difficult to understand Warren's explanation. In Boston in 1817 did a student or his parents pay a lawyer $100 once for all, as Miss Trotwood paid Mr. Spenlow a "premium" of a thousand pounds (stamp included) when David Copperfield was articled to Spenlow and Jorkins in Doctor's Commons? Warren thought that in the early days at Harvard a law student's fees were measured by quarter-years of active attendance — probably a reasonable plan where periods of study were so diverse.

136 from 119 the previous year.[24] But by 1872–73 the average number of law students had shrunk to 113. After that year enrollment began to rise again, and only once in the next thirty-five years was the numbers of students below 150. That dip occurred in 1882–83, perhaps because by that time the requirement of three years' study for a degree, adopted in 1876, had had its full impact. President Eliot, in his 1879–80 report, wrote: "the resort to the Law School has somewhat narrowed of late, chiefly in consequence of a loss of students from the Southern and Middle States . . . There are very good reasons, partly external and partly internal, for this exceptional, and probably temporary, tendency in the Law School. Since 1850 thirty-one new law schools have been established in the United States, the whole number previously existing having been but nine." Of the Harvard law students who registered in 1880–81, 49.3 percent were Massachusetts residents. New England as a whole contributed 61.5 percent of the total. Of the remaining 38.5 percent the West sent 16 percent; the southern states, 7.7 percent; the middle states, 10.9 percent. The remaining 4 percent — six men or so — came from elsewhere.[25]

The effect of competition in delaying the growth of the Harvard Law School is hard to gauge. The population of the United States was increasing. Industry and commerce greatly expanded

---

[24] See President Eliot's report for 1878–79. The "number of students at Harvard Law School" in any year in the early 1870's is hard to answer concisely. The student population fluctuated during the year much more than it now does. Langdell wrote in his report as dean for 1870–71: "The whole number of different students connected with the school during the year 1870–71 was one hundred and sixty-five. Of these one hundred and seven were in the school the whole year, ten for three-quarters of the year, and nine for one quarter of the year; making an average of one hundred and thirty-six students for the entire year."

[25] Eliot added an informative table to his 1879–80 presidential report.

RESIDENCES OF LAW STUDENTS AT FOUR DATES COMPARED

	NUMBER				PERCENT			
	1865–66	1870–71	1875–76	1880–81	1865–66	1870–71	1875–76	1880–81
Massachusetts	52	57	69	77	29.4	37.	43.	49.3
New England	78	83	82	96	44.1	54.	51.	61.5
Middle States	27	26	15	17	15.2	17.	09.	10.9
Southern States	24	7	11	12	13.5	05.	07.	07.7
Western States	43	33	38	25	24.3	21.	24.	16.
Other Places	5	5	15	6	3.	03.	09.	4.0
Total	177	154	161	156				

Descriptive essays on a number of early law schools appear in the first two volumes of *The Green Bag*, for 1889 and 1890.

after the war of 1861–1865, and the need for lawyers grows with the economy. Study in a lawyer's office to qualify for the bar continued frequent until well into the twentieth century. Other more organized institutions were training lawyers. Professional instruction in an expanded private law-office school began at New Haven in the early 1800's under the guidance of Seth P. Staples of the New Haven bar. In 1824 his students were listed in the Yale catalogue; and in 1843 Yale began awarding the LL.B. Tulane began professional instruction in law in 1847, Pennsylvania in 1850, Albany in 1851, Columbia in 1858, Boston University in 1872. The characteristic Law School faculty of the middle and latter part of the nineteenth century was staffed by active judges and practicing lawyers who gave part of their time to teaching. Schools often depended for their library resources on the libraries of courts or legislatures. One senses that perhaps the rivalry of 1880 was less between Harvard and other schools, than between any academic schooling and the "practical" virtues of law-office apprenticeship. Perhaps some sort of rivalry did exist between Harvard — with part of its teachers using the case method, with the nonpracticing Ames as a prominent professor — and other schools which kept strictly to the practitioners and judges for their faculties, which supplied their students with lectures on the law, which avoided the irritating and sometimes ridiculed dialectic of Langdell and Ames.

At any rate the rivalry did not gravely damage Harvard. Despite the competition of other schools and increased rigor of Harvard's requirements, enrollment in 1882–83 only fell to 140, the size of the School at Story's death. Excellence of instruction and the prestige of the degree obtained under rigorous requirements soon began to raise the number of students again. By 1895 the School had 400 students. Langdell's reforms not only brought an able student body; they brought a large one,[26] which put the School on a sound financial basis. President Eliot in 1895, reviewing at a Harvard Law School Association meeting Langdell's quarter-century of achievements as dean, mentioned first his case method; next his pioneer choice of Ames as a teacher despite Ames's lack of experience in practice. Eliot then continued:

And now I come to a third of Professor Langdell's achievements,

[26] A striking exposition of the School's fluctuation in numbers of students during its first century is a graph at page 344–345 of the Centennial History.

one which, I venture to say, has greatly commended itself to his Scotch nature. I refer to the extraordinary pecuniary success of the Law School. He never shrank from any measure that would obviously diminish temporarily the number of students in the School. But when in time the success of his work was demonstrated; when, as years went on, a strong and united Faculty worked with him in the School, and the number of students began to increase, and that of late years quite rapidly it was a sincere delight to the Dean that the Law School became the most prosperous of all the departments of the University . . . This pecuniary success of the School is the third of the achievements on which we congratulate the Dean.[27]

An intellectual success must not be evaluated by its cash balance. But the School had found out in 1828 that it could not finance itself without plenty of students. Langdell saw that the School paid its way.

3

Langdell was as successful in attracting distinguished professors as he was in assembling a brilliant student body. In 1870 he had joined a faculty with two professor colleagues — former Governor Emory Washburn, seventy years old, first occupant of the Bussey chair, and Nathaniel Holmes, fifty-five, onetime judge of the Supreme Court of Missouri. Washburn had joined the faculty as a Lecturer in 1855 and had been with it ever since. He had written an admirable treatise on real property, foundation of teaching materials used in the School today. Louis Brandeis later wrote that Washburn was the most beloved instructor in the School's annals. At his age, with his background, he could not undertake to change his teaching methods when Langdell came. Judge Holmes had been elected Royall Professor in 1868 to succeed Joel Parker. Holmes served only four years. He resigned in 1872, perhaps because he felt uneasy at the prospect of drastic change under Eliot and Langdell. At any rate his resignation left the Royall chair vacant, and provided an opportunity for the appointment of a teacher who would eagerly follow Langdell's lead.

[27] In Eliot's annual report for 1894–95 he wrote: "Professor Langdell's administration has been remarkable for four things: First, for the invention and adoption of a new method of teaching law; second, for the adoption of a new mode of training teachers of law; third, for a great, though gradual elevation of the standard of the degree in Law; and fourth, for success in regard to number of students, increase of endowment, improvement of equipment, and income from tuition-fees."

Eliot and Langdell for the moment left the Royall chair unfilled and in 1873 proposed as assistant professor for five years James Barr Ames, who had taken his LL.B. in 1872, the same year Holmes resigned. Ames had stayed on in 1872–73 for additional study in the Law School.

Ames was a born teacher. While still a candidate for the LL.B. he taught modern languages in Harvard College; and during his graduate year in the Law School he foretold his later interest in legal history by teaching two history courses in the college: one in medieval institutions and one in the seventeenth century history of England. In 1895 Eliot told the Law School Association the circumstances under which, on June 2, 1873,[28] the Governing Boards had appointed Ames assistant professor of law.

Professor Langdell early advocated the appointment as teachers of law of young men who had had no experience whatever in the active profession. What a venture was that, gentlemen; what bold advice was that for the head of the School to give! This School had never done it; no school had ever done it; it was an absolutely new departure in our country in the teaching of law. I remember very well how reluctantly the Corporation and the Board of Overseers consented to the first experiment on this point, namely, the appointment for a limited term of five years of Assistant-Professor James Barr Ames. (Prolonged applause.) You may well applaud now, gentlemen, when the success of that experiment has been absolutely assured; but what was the courage which first suggested the experiment! Now, that experiment, too, has not only been extended in our own Law School with perfect success, but it has been adopted by various other law schools throughout the country.

And what does it mean? What is to be the ultimate outcome of this courageous venture? In due course, and that in no long term of years, there will be produced in this country a body of men learned in the law, who have never been on the bench or at the bar, but who nevertheless hold positions of great weight and influence as teachers of the law, as expounders, systematizers, and historians. This, I venture to predict, is one of the most far-reaching changes in the organization of the profession that has ever been made in our country.

The two contrasting policies — that of appointing young scholar-teachers with little or no experience in practice "to breed professors of law by the same gradual process by which competent teachers are trained up in other departments of the University"; [29] and that of appointing men who have already, for years, experi-

---

[28] *Report of the Ninth Annual Meeting, in Especial Honor of Christopher Columbus Langdell*, p. 70.

[29] The phrase is that of Eliot in his presidential report for 1873–74, at page 27.

enced the practical application of the law which they were later called to teach — were to present to the School difficult choices for many generations.

On December 8, 1873, the Corporation followed what was then the more traditional course of electing as Royall Professor James Bradley Thayer, nearly forty-three years old, a graduate of Harvard College in 1852 and of the Law School in 1856. He had practiced law in Boston for seventeen years, making at the same time a reputation for scholarly writing. Shortly before his election to the Law School Harvard had unsuccessfully sought him as a professor of English. Thayer did not begin to teach in the Law School until the autumn of 1874, when he gave the courses on evidence and trusts. He was not yet converted to Langdell's case method, and taught by the older system of doctrinal lectures.

On March 14, 1875, the Corporation created the Story chair, and four days later elected to it John Chipman Gray, LL.B. 1861, a brilliant young cavalry officer in the Civil War, one of the first editors of the *American Law Review*, founder with John C. Ropes of the Boston law firm which still bears their names, and lecturer at the School since 1869. For a time after Gray's appointment the School discontinued the use of part-time lecturers; in 1875–76 all the courses were given by the four professors and Assistant Professor Ames. Washburn taught real property, criminal law, and criminal procedure. Langdell taught equity and civil procedure. Thayer taught evidence, trusts, and parts of equity not covered by Langdell. Gray taught sales, partnership, and other titles in mercantile law. Ames taught contracts, torts, and bills and notes. Langdell and Ames used the case method; the other three lectured as usual.

On April 1, 1876, Governor Washburn resigned, effective the following September 1. He was seventy-six years old, the last of the three professors who had carried most of the School's work in the interval between Story and Langdell. Kindly, always at the service of his students, cheerfully carrying his full load of teaching far beyond the usual age, Professor Washburn evoked from his students, from his colleagues, and from President Eliot a farewell of genuine affection and gratitude. Now Langdell, with only six years of service, had been teaching at the Law School longer than any of his colleagues. In seven years the School had entirely changed its faculty.

During the first fifteen years of Langdell's tenure, while the

Law School's student population fluctuated around 150, the number of permanent professors continued small. The Corporation created three new chairs during those years. The first was the Story, founded in 1875, appropriately commemorating its eponymous teacher, judge, and author; Gray was the first Story Professor. The Bemis professorship dates from 1878, when George Bemis, LL.B. 1839, bequeathed a sum to found a professorship of "public or international law in the Dane Law School"; the chair remained vacant for twenty years, until Harvard chose its first Bemis Professor, Edward Henry Strobel, in 1898. The delay occurred because under the terms of Bemis' will Harvard would not receive the fund until the expiration of a life estate in the Bemis fund, which did not terminate until 1892. The Corporation then sought for six more years until it found in Professor Strobel a man combining the scholarly qualities and experience in international affairs which the donor had prescribed. Another new chair, the Weld professorship, was endowed in 1882 by William F. Weld of Brookline; its generous donor desired anonymity during his lifetime, and the chair was unnamed until his death in 1893. The first professor under this foundation was Oliver Wendell Holmes, Jr., appointed in 1882.

Young Louis D. Brandeis, who came to the Law School as a student in September 1875, was an enthusiastic advocate of Langdell's case method, but in 1876 he wrote his brother-in-law Otto Wehle expressing some surprise at Ames's toplofty criticism of judges engaged in the practical application of legal principles to men's affairs.[30] Ames's academic attitude disturbed some other academics, but Eliot staunchly upheld him. In his report of 1881–82 Eliot called Ames's appointment "a conspicuous success" and suggested that as the selection of such younger men was a general practice in the law faculties of continental Europe, Harvard might extend it "without, however adopting it as a policy." On the other hand Ephraim W. Gurney, the first Dean of the Faculty of Harvard College and Eliot's general right-hand man, wrote a letter of protest to the President sometime in the spring of 1883, when the Governing Boards had under consideration the appointment of William Albert Keener, LL.B. 1877.[31] Keener had prac-

[30] For Brandeis' student correspondence see Alpheus T. Mason, *Brandeis: A Free Man's Life* (New York, 1946), pp. 34f.

[31] Mrs. Merle Fainsod kindly called to my attention Dean Gurney's letter filed

ticed only four years; Gurney saw with dismay a prospect of gradually recruiting for the faculty of law a group of men relatively inexperienced in the law's practical application. Eliot was evidently drafting an annual report repeating the theme — appointment of young scholars of law rather than older practitioners — which he had discussed in his 1881–82 report. Dean Gurney wrote:

Private
Dear Eliot,

I am sorry to say that I did not sleep last night as well as usual, and, as I lay awake, I found my mind revolving about the Law School problem and what you said about it in the part of your report which you read me.

I did not see clearly as you read why you should make the argument as you did from the statistics you had collected; — at any rate I did not see as clearly as I seemed to do in the night that you were indicating in advance a policy in the management of the school which has not yet been adopted; which was practically decided the other way in the nomination of Holmes;[32] which there has been but a month to reconsider and which I suppose is still to be considered or under argument. Is this right policy? Is it giving the interests of the University fair play for its head to commit himself in print — to go out of his way to commit himself in print upon a point on which the arguments are not yet closed and a decision reached?

So much upon a point of administration I think it not impertinent to say, as a looker-on interested in the welfare of the University as a whole.

If I go on to say something of what occurred to me in the night as to the policy of the Law School, it certainly comes nearer an impertinence, on the other hand you know that no person connected with

---

with President Eliot's papers in Widener Library. A photocopy is now filed in the Law School archives. It demonstrates the active concern of the principal officers of Harvard in a question which three quarters of a century later is still under occasional debate.

[32] Oliver Wendell Holmes, Jr., LL.B., had by 1882 been practicing law in Boston for fifteen years. He had been an editor of the *American Law Review*, and of the twelfth edition of Kent's *Commentaries*. He was the author of a book still read today for its style and its jurisprudential insights — his *Common Law* of 1881. He had been a lecturer on constitutional law in Harvard College in 1870–71, and in the Law School on jurisprudence in 1871–73. He became a professor of law on January 23, 1882, and resigned January 8, 1883, to take his seat on the Supreme Judicial Court of Massachusetts.

Dean Gurney obviously wrote his letter to President Eliot after Holmes's resignation and before Keener's appointment to replace him became final on May 14, 1883. Keener had taken his LL.B. at Harvard in 1877 and had practiced law in New York City only four years when Harvard made him an assistant professor of law. Roscoe Pound, many years later, told of Keener's effective teaching. See below, page 203.

the University outside of the Law Faculty except yourself has followed the workings of the Law School so closely or taken the same interest in it which I do. You know, too, that no one is more friendly to all the persons and the general policies advocated in the School. If I seem in any way critical concerning Langdell or Ames, you know that it is not because I am not a hearty admirer and believer in them both, to whom belongs the credit, as I have at all times and in all company maintained, of making the School the admirable one it is. To Langdell especially the School will owe such a monument as belongs to a founder.

Believing all this, I believe less firmly only because it is a matter of the future instead of the past that Langdell, running the School at his pleasure, would wreck it. He is as *intransigeant* as a French Socialist, and his ideal is to breed professors of Law, not practitioners; erring, as it seems to me, on the other side from the other schools, which would make only practitioners. Now to my mind it will be a dark day for the School when either of these views is able to dominate the other, and the more dangerous success of the two would be the doctrinaire because it would starve the School. In my judgment, which you may well say on such a matter is not worth much, if the appointment of Keener — of whom I never heard till yesterday, and of whom I am ready to believe all the good which is said — means that the School commits itself to the theory of breeding within itself its Corps of instructors and thus severs itself from the great current of legal life which flows through the courts and the bar, it commits the gravest error of policy which it could adopt, and I hope you will think many times and consult with persons who, unlike myself, have professional qualifications for judging of it before you announce it in print.

The whole tendency of the system would be, to build up a great school of law as an exact science, and divorce it more and more from its actual administration. One hardly needs more evidence of this tendency than the contemptuous way which both Langdell and Ames have of speaking of Courts and Judges — not simply those of the day, but the men of the past whom the profession looks up to as its great ornaments. The trouble in their mind with those judges is that they did not treat this or that question as a philosophical professor, building up a coherent system would have done, but as the judges before whom the young men are going to practice will do. I pardon this in Langdell, who has a right to knock bigwigs about; but it seems to me to sit with an ill grace on Ames as yet, and I can easily understand some prejudices against the School, if an old lawyer hears some youngster in his office fresh from the School take this tone. Doubtless Langdell and Ames from their point of view are right in their criticism of this or that decision; it is only the attitude of mind, as following almost necessarily from a too academic treatment of a great practical profession which I do not wish to see control the School.

Another feature to my mind of the same tendency is the extreme unwillingness to have anything furnished by the School except the pure science of the law. It seems to a layman that when the School exacts a year more than any other of study for its degree, it might concede something, at least at the start, of their time to such practical training as might be given successfully in such a school. I have never been able to see why this should be thought belittling to the School or its instructors, nor why the young men should be left to call in a Wellman [33] to give them what they felt they needed. If you[r] LLB at the end of his three years did not feel as helpless on entering an office on the practical side as he is admirably trained on the theoretical, I think he would begrudge his third year less. But I dare say this would be pronounced foolishness by Thayer and Gray no less than by Langdell and Ames.

One word more about Choate [34] and you shall be released. Whether he is a learned lawyer or not, I do not know; but it will be easy to learn. That he is fit to be Chief Justice anywhere I have not a doubt; and that he is among the few men I have fallen in with who might be trusted to rise to the height of any case however great I feel sure. That he would have any charm as a lecturer I do not believe; but I am confident that he would have great weight with the men.

In view of what was said last evening, may I suggest two considerations. One is that one can not safely argue from the work of a professor who remains in active practice, like Bradlee [35] or several men at the Boston law school to that of a man who, like Choate probably, would give himself up to the work of the school. To Bradlee the School was but one care of many he had in hand.

As to your point made against the man of fifty, I certainly wish he were forty; though I should not readily choose between fifty and thirty. The ripeness of experience counts for much in my view of the qualifications of a teacher of a great practical as well as theoretical subject like the law and especially in the impression teaching makes upon the Young.

When you quoted Leidy,[36] one must remember also that he was not only fifty, but was fifty as a teacher. The freshness of the younger man is to be ascribed to the novelty of his work as well as to his youth. In myself I feel that it is not so much my fifty years or the twenty-five years round of teaching which tends to make me stale. Once more, that the training of a judge is no ill qualification for the teacher.

I had some other things to say, but I will spare you. The one lesson I should draw from all my experience in the University is not systems, but men. Wait for a man at any temporary inconvenience, rather than run the risk of taking on a man who will not be satisfactory. Not, of

[33] "Wellman" here is a puzzle. Francis Lewis Wellman, 1854–1942, author of *The Art of Cross-Examination* (1903), would probably have been too young at 29. Perhaps not.

[34] Joseph Hodges Choate, LL.B. 1854.

[35] Charles S. Bradley, Bussey Professor from 1876 to 1879.

[36] I have not identified Leidy.

course, that risk can be evaded, but time is always on the side of a great institution.

Always affectionately,

E. A. Gurney

I need hardly say that this long scrawl calls for no reply.

Gurney.

The change from a faculty mainly staffed with old hands at the bar came only gradually. At the end of Langdell's deanship in 1895 the faculty consisted of seven professors, an assistant professor, a lecturer, an instructor, the librarian, and the secretary. Of the full-time teaching staff of eight, three had come to the faculty young, without much experience in practice. These were Ames, Assistant Professor Joseph Henry Beale, LL.B. 1887, and Professor Samuel Williston, LL.B. 1888. Beale and Williston had both joined the faculty in 1890. The other five had had years of practice. Judge Jeremiah Smith, in 1895 the Story Professor, had studied law at Harvard in 1860–61, and had never taken his LL.B. He came to the School in 1890, when he was fifty-three years old, after many years at the bar and after seven years on the Supreme Court of New Hampshire. Eugene Wambaugh, LL.B. 1880, practiced at the bar in Cincinnati for nine years and then was professor of law at Iowa State until 1892, when he became professor of law at Harvard. Thayer and Gray were experienced lawyers when they came to the School, and Gray continued to practice law actively for the rest of his life, the only professor since 1870 to do so.[37] His *Rule against Perpetuities* of 1886 and his *Nature and Sources of the Law* of 1909 are both masterpieces. His teaching was elegant and witty — and effective. Gray is hardly classable as a part-time teacher. He and Story both led double professional lives, and were able to achieve a mastery of both. Gray somehow managed to be a full-time teacher and a full-time lawyer simultaneously. Langdell had had sixteen years of practice in New York before 1870 when he came to the Law School; from that day forward his profession was solely academic law at Harvard.

From the composition of the faculty of 1895 one cannot convincingly demonstrate a general conclusion either that teachers

[37] The *Centennial History* of the School contains a series of biographies of men who have taught law at Harvard. They are unsigned. Gray's biography, beginning at page 205, is so sensitive, so appreciative of Gray's quality and style as a man and a scholar-lawyer, that it deserves special mention here.

of law with considerable previous experience in practice are the most useful, or that the best prospect is a man like Ames, who comes to teaching directly from university study. One cannot even be certain that the man who combines teaching with practice or judicial duty will necessarily be second-rate at one or the other — though men like Joseph Story and John Chipman Gray will be rare in any generation. The faculty Langdell had assembled by the end of his deanship demonstrated the truth in the point Gurney made in his letter to Eliot: "The one lesson I should draw from all my experience in the University is not systems, but men."

4

Administration of the School's library by student librarians, supplemented (or directed) by that distinguished janitor John Sweetnam, the system which obtained prior to 1870, was defective in at least two respects. One defect, the less serious, was inadequate protection of the books. A shortcoming which over the years since Story had much more gravely affected the library's welfare was lack of a vigilant and responsible librarian, a scholar learned in the law, whose duty was to assure that the School always had the most comprehensive collection of legal literature within its means.

Langdell and Eliot were as wise in the renovation of the library as they were in the selection of faculty. In 1870 the Corporation appointed the School's first full-time librarian, William Abbott Everett. After a year Everett resigned, and in 1872 in his place came John Himes Arnold, the father of the present library. John Arnold remained as librarian for more than forty years; when he became librarian emeritus in 1913 the collection had grown from 15,000 to 150,000 volumes, rivaled in size only by the law collections of the Library of Congress and the Supreme Court. The mere number of books is, of course, a superficial basis of evaluation. Arnold saw to it that the collection was well chosen.

In his dean's report for the academic year 1889–90 Langdell reviewed the progress of the library during the preceding two decades.

In 1869–70 the library was so nearly a wreck that it required to be reconstructed almost from its foundations. Now it is believed to be larger (referring only to law books proper, and excluding statutes), more complete, and in a better condition than any other law library in the United States, with the possible exception of the national library at Washington . . . Prior to 1870–71 the only persons employed to care for the library were a student-librarian and the janitor of Dane Hall . . . Now, a permanent librarian, a permanent assistant librarian (both of whom have held their present positions for the last eighteen years), and three assistants are constantly employed in the care and administration of the library and in other administrative duties. Prior to 1870–71, and subsequently to the time of Professor Greenleaf, no one connected with the School took much interest in the subject of purchasing books for the library. The practice was for the booksellers with whom the School kept an account to send to the library a copy of every new book received by them; and, as to each book so sent, one of the Professors decided whether it should be kept or not. As to the purchase of other than new books, there was no system whatever; and such books were seldom purchased unless for some special reason; and when it was decided to purchase any such books an order for them was given to a bookseller. Under this practice the library seldom received any accessions of old books; and, even had this been otherwise, it would almost inevitably have happened that most of the accessions received would represent some person's hobby, and so would improve the library only in some one direction. Moreover, old books purchased in such a way are sure to cost two or three times as much as they need cost. There are thousands of law books without which no library is perfect, and which yet have no fixed market value, and which may be said to be more or less rare in the sense of being more or less difficult to find, but very few of which are rare in the sense of commanding a high price in the market. The only way, therefore, to purchase such books to advantage is to seek opportunities of purchasing them at a low price, and to purchase them, as a rule, only when such opportunities offer. It was therefore decided, about seventeen years ago, that the Librarian should make it a part of his duty to follow up auction sales of law books in all the principal cities of the United States. Accordingly, on the 22d day of January, 1874, he attended an auction sale for the first time and purchased 36 volumes . . . Prior to 1870–71 there was never, so far as is known, any collation made of books purchased for the library for the purpose of ascertaining whether or not they were perfect. Indeed, the practice of collating books was not begun until January, 1874; but since that date every book purchased for the library, whether new or old, and whether purchased at private or public sale, has been collated, page by page, before being accepted. Soon afterwards the work was begun of collating, page by page, all the books that were in the library prior to the date just mentioned; and this work has since been prosecuted with as much rapidity as possible; and no money has ever been spent in rebinding or otherwise repairing a book until it was first collated . . . Prior to

1870–71 the library was as little cared for in respect to the binding and repairing of the books as in other respects. Binders were employed with little regard to their ability to do good work, and little pains were taken either to give them proper directions or to see that they did their work in accordance with such directions as were given them, or that they did it properly; and the results were deplorable. In no case was the work what would now be regarded as good; in many cases it was shocking in respect to the work done and the materials employed; and in many other cases books were actually ruined by the binder. Since 1870–71 the most strenuous efforts have been made to improve the administration of the library in respect to the binding and repairing of books; and, though the success of these efforts has not been all that could be desired, yet it has upon the whole been gratifying; for the library may now safely challenge comparison in respect to its condition with any other law library in the United States.

By the 1890's the School's library had gained an international reputation. Albert Venn Dicey, Vinerian Professor of English Law and Fellow of All Souls at Oxford, wrote in the *Contemporary Review* of 1899 concerning the School's Anglo-American material:

It constitutes the most perfect collection of the legal records of the English people to be found in any part of the English-speaking world. We possess nothing like it in England. In the library at Harvard you will find the works of every English and American writer on law; there stand not only all the American reports — and these include, as well as the reports of the Federal courts, reports from every one of the forty-five states of the Union — but also complete collections of our English reports, of our English statutes, and of the reports and statutes of England's colonies and possessions. Neither in London nor in Oxford, neither at the Privy Council nor at the Colonial office, can one find a complete collection, either of American or even astounding as the fact sounds, of our Colonial reports.[38]

At the end of Langdell's first decade the inadequacies of Dane Hall had become intolerable. Langdell wrote in his report for 1878–79:

Little has been said heretofore, in the annual reports upon the Law School, of the need of a new building. It is not, however, because the inadequacy and unfitness of Dane Hall for the purposes of the School have not long been severely felt that silence has been kept upon the subject, but rather because it seemed undesirable to excite discontent with what we have, so long as there was no immediate prospect of our

[38] Warren, *Harvard Law School*, vol. II, chap. 47, gives a detailed account of the development of the library, 1869–1907.

being able to get any thing better. It is unnecessary to speak of the architectural shortcomings of Dane Hall, for they are so great and so notorious as to be a discredit to the entire University. Regarding it, however, from a purely practical point of view, it has never been a good building. First, its means of ventilation are wholly insufficient for such numbers as have frequented it for several years past. This evil of insufficient ventilation has been much aggravated in the lecture-room by the great increase in the number of lectures. For many years after Dane Hall was built there were never more than two lectures in a day; and hence it was not necessary — though it was the practice — to occupy the lecture-room two hours in succession. Now, however, there are almost six lectures a day upon an average; and hence it is necessary, during four days of each week, to occupy the lecture-room four hours in succession each day; namely, from 9 A.M. to 1 P.M. The occupation of the room, however, for a single hour by a large class, and with the windows closed, makes the air of the room very foul; and yet there are no means of changing the air between two lectures which occupy successive hours except by opening the windows during the ten minutes' recess; and that renders the room uncomfortably cold during at least two-thirds of the academic year. Perhaps these things would be true, in some degree, of any room that could be constructed; but, assuming that to be so, it only shows that the Law School is in pressing need of more than one lecture-room. Secondly, the library and lecture-room are each lighted from four different directions; and it would probably be safe to say that a year has never passed in which the cross-lights of these two rooms have not ruined, or seriously injured, the eyes of one or more persons. Thirdly, by reason of its being so low studded and so near the roof, the lecture-room is a very uncomfortable place in warm weather. The difference in temperature between the lecture-room and the library, for example, on a warm day is very striking. Fourthly, when Dane Hall was erected, its location was as good as could be desired; but since it was moved sixty feet to make room for Matthews Hall, what with the paving of Harvard Square and the great increase of traffic, its location has become one of the worst that could be found in Cambridge. The noise, for example, is so great that it is impossible to make one's self heard in the lecture-room with the windows open; and yet the atmosphere of the room frequently becomes suffocating with the windows closed. Fifthly, regarded as a repository for books, the accommodation afforded by Dane Hall is very bad in quality, and in the near future it will be absolutely insufficient in quantity. During the summer, when it is necessary to keep the windows open, the books suffer greatly from dust, while during the cold weather they suffer greatly from heat. The evil arising from excessive heat is greatly aggravated by the necessity of utilizing for the storage of books all the space from the floor to the ceiling. The books also suffer from gaslight during all seasons of the year. Again, the danger to the books from fire is so great as to be a

Austin Hall, gift of Edward Austin of Boston in 1882. It was a good house for the School, pleasant for study by professors and students, convenient for lectures. The high-ceilinged reading room with Richardson's wild boars and dragons carved in the hardwood beams and with the vast open hearth that sometimes held a fire of massive logs; the light, pleasant library stacks; the professors' studies graced by fireplaces which lent an air of reflective leisure — have we anything better now?

Gannett House, seen through one of Austin Hall's romanesque arches. Once the dwelling of Caleb Gannett, eighteenth century tutor and Steward of the College, it appeared in the 1905–06 Law School catalogue as a student dwelling. Gannett now houses the Law Review, the Legal Aid, and the Voluntary Defenders.

cause of constant anxiety. If the library should be destroyed, it is probably safe to say that a hundred thousand dollars would not replace it; and its value is increasing rapidly. Bad, however, as is the quality of the accommodation afforded for the storage of books, an increase in its quantity is the most immediate and pressing need of the library. Already the Librarian has been compelled to remove large quantities of books from the library into private rooms; and even this resource, to say nothing of its inconvenience, will soon be exhausted. Sixthly, within recent years loud and bitter complaints have been made of insufficient room for study in the library, and of inadequate ventilation; and though the grounds of these complaints, as regards the students, were in a measure removed two years ago, there is still no proper accommodation for the professors and instructors. Formerly, each professor occupied a private room, and it was not the practice of the professors to do any work in the library. In this respect, however, there has been a total change. The five instructors have only two private rooms at their disposal, and even these are so far removed from the library that they are unavailable for ordinary working purposes. All the work, therefore, done by the instructors in Dane Hall is now done in the library; and yet they have no suitable accommodation whatever. Behind the railing there is space for only one person to work comfortably, and that space is properly occupied by the Librarian's desk. Two professors can find places to sit, such as they are, but when more than two are present at the same time, some of them must content themselves with standing-room; and whether sitting or standing, they are a constant inconvenience to the Librarian and his assistants.

In his presidential report for 1879–80 Eliot endorsed Langdell's complaint. Dane Hall, the President wrote, "is inadequate in every respect. There is but one lecture-room, so that two classes have been this year obliged, at great inconvenience, to resort to lecture-rooms which chanced to be temporarily vacant in University Hall; the very valuable Library is exposed to destruction by fire; the situation of the building is such that the lectures are much disturbed by the noise from the streets; and neither professors nor students can be properly accommodated in the Library. A new building upon a new site is urgently needed."

These reports may well have brought Austin Hall. Edward Austin of Boston, born in 1802 or 1803, was nearly eighty years old at the time of Langdell's report of 1878–79 and Eliot's of the following year. Austin had been a successful supercargo for a Boston shipping firm in the 1820's, had come back to Boston and made a fortune in cotton, railroads, and insurance. In early 1881 he offered Harvard $100,000 to build a Law School building in memory of his brother Samuel Austin, though he stipulated at first that the source of the gift be kept secret. H. H. Richardson designed the brownstone Romanesque building for its site on Holmes Place — a street now no longer existing, which then ran westerly into Massachusetts Avenue just south of Gannett House as that structure then stood. Gannett House now stands in what used to be Holmes Place.[39] When the estimated cost for Austin Hall exceeded by more than one-third the available $100,000 (as estimates will), Austin raised his offer to include the extra $35,000. Construction began in the spring of 1882, and at that time the university announced the donor's name. In September 1883 the librarian began moving books to the new stacks. Classes began in Austin Hall on October 1, 1883.

Austin was a good house for the School, pleasant for study by professors and students, pleasant and convenient for lectures. The great high-ceilinged reading room [40] with Richardson's wild boars and dragons carved in the hardwood beams and with the vast open hearth that sometimes held a fire of massive logs; the light, pleasant library stacks; the professors' studies graced by fireplaces which lent an air of reflective leisure — have we anything better now? Granted, Austin Hall alone could not begin to provide for today's sixteen hundred and more students, seventy-odd teachers, administrative staff, essential secretaries, library people, a photocopying team and its machinery that in a year now turns out over five million pages.[41] But we have been obliged to sacrifice some values by our inevitable magnification and multiplication — an idle reflection characteristic of men of a certain age.

5

When the School moved from Dane to Austin it came to modern times. The new Austin was the prologue of today. In 1883

[39] Gannett House in 1883 stood where the Hemenway gymnasium now stands, between Walter Hastings and the present position of Gannett House. Gannett House was moved southerly to its present site in 1924.

[40] Now refitted as the James Barr Ames Courtroom.

[41] At page 16 of his report for 1879–80 Eliot wrote: "Both in recitations and lectures the practice of taking notes prevails; but various devices are employed by instructors and students to lighten the labor of notetaking. Some professors place upon the blackboard before the exercise begins the references, titles, tables or diagrams which they wish the students to copy; others distribute to the class all such matter in manuscript, reproduced in sufficient quantities by some of the cheap copying processes." Surely there is no new thing under the sun.

John McCarthy began as kindest and most diligent of book boys his service to the School and its library which ran through more than half a century. Pictured, steel spectacles and all, benign, as he used to preside at the delivery desk in Langdell Hall, he now looks in speaking portraiture on the students busy in today's great reading room.

In 1883 the graph of student population, after forty years around 150, began its sharp rise to 750 a third of a century later. In 1889–90 the university built Walter Hastings Hall a few yards from Austin. Then, as now, it offered living quarters with generous space, fireplaces in studies, a sense of ease. Law students soon made it a School preserve. Gannett House, once the dwelling of Caleb Gannett, eighteenth century tutor and steward of the college, appeared in the 1905–06 Law School catalogue as a student dwelling, with the appealing and revealing comment, "Room No. 9 and Room No. 4 which serves as bedroom for No. 3, are heated by steam."

The academic year 1886–87 saw two other new features of the School which have worked powerfully for its good. On September 23, 1886, one hundred and fifty former members of the School met in Boston and organized the Harvard Law School Association under the secretaryship of Louis D. Brandeis.[42] By November 5 the association had proved to be so popular that about 400 members assembled to join in the observance of the two hundred and fiftieth anniversary of Harvard College, to hear addresses from the association's first President, James C. Carter of New York, from President Eliot, Justice Holmes, Dean Langdell, and others. There was evident in that gathering the community of interest, lasting through life, which has tied together the School's members in a continuing fellowship, and which has contributed so much, in so many ways, to the well-being of the institution.[43]

On April 15, 1887, appeared the first number of the *Harvard Law Review*, with John Jay McKelvey as editor-in-chief, and with a board which included Joseph H. Beale, Jr., Julian W. Mack, and John H. Wigmore. The *Review* was an innovation —

[42] See *Record of the Commemoration, 1886, on the Two Hundred and Fiftieth Anniversary of the Founding of Harvard College*, pp. 55f.

[43] In the School's archives is a printed proposal, dated May 1850, to form a Story Association of the Law College. Another paper dated June 25, 1868, signed by a number of the School's distinguished former students, proposes an association substantially like that of 1886. The dates are significant though neither group lived long. Evidently the School of Parker, Parsons, and Washburn could generate alumni loyalty.

a journal edited by students in a professional school, attracting papers written by noted mature academic jurists, by judges, and by scholarly lawyers in practice. The editorial work by students has proved to be an outstanding part of their legal education; mature professional writing published in the *Review* has brilliantly contributed to American law during the last eighty years. Other university schools of law rapidly followed the example of the *Harvard Law Review.* University law journals have collectively become a nationwide academic institution scrutinizing American justice.

One may well ask what students of the Langdell era thought of the School. Two particularly notable men have left us their impressions: Louis D. Brandeis wrote letters about the School during the mid-1870's, and Roscoe Pound later told his colleagues about the School of 1888–89. Brandeis was an acutely intelligent boy from Louisville, Kentucky, who had studied at the Annen-Realschule in Dresden before he came to the School in 1875 at the age of nineteen. He had done no undergraduate work in any American college, but his Law School record was not less brilliant for that.[44]

Brandeis found Ames and Gray the rising lights of the faculty of law. The frank differences of opinion his professors expressed about legal matters excited his surprised admiration. On November 12, 1876, he wrote to his brother-in-law Otto Wehle: [45]

Last year, it seemed to be Ames's great aim and object to convince us that nine-tenths of the Judges who have sat on the English Bench and about ninety-nine-hundredths of the American Judges 'did not know what they were talking about' — that the great majority of Judges were illogical, inconsistent, and unreasonable, that there had been in fact only one man who understood his trade and profession, i.e., Baron Parke — that even the great Mansfield was a fraud, who stood convicted of the inexpiable crime of having introduced equity doctrines into the sacred and immaculate Common Law, of having been the first to prepare for the eventual victory of the Roman Law in England . . . Under Bradley all this is different. He never lets an opportunity escape him for lauding the English and especially American Judges. Story and Marshall, Nelson and Grier, Mansfield and Eldon

---

[44] Tradition gives to Justice Brandeis the highest grades ever attained at the Harvard Law School. Notation of excellence on a scale of 100 has varied over the years, so that a grade of 90-odd in 1878 is not convertible into the same figures in 1967; the astonishingly high quality of Brandeis' work is still entirely evident.

[45] See Mason, *Brandeis,* pp. 34f, for Brandeis' Law School correspondence.

are repeatedly the subject of his praise. Ames would set up his own reasoning against that of a legion of Judges and scores of text-writers. Bradley in his deference to "His Honor" even goes so far as to avoid offering any criticism on what has become settled by decisions, however unsupported by reason.

Brandeis was elected to the Pow Wow Club, one of the most celebrated of the student groups which as early as the 1820's began to be organized to brief and argue moot cases. The clubs, he thought, were "grand institutions, a great incentive to labor, and the work for them is a pleasant change." In the autumn of 1876 Brandeis was working up an evidence point for Pow Wow arguments. He wrote to Otto Wehle:

I have spent a great deal of my time for several weeks on the subject of "Declarations forming a part of the Res Gestae" as I was of counsel on two cases involving that branch of the law of Evidence. One of the cases that we tried in our Club-Court was *Insurance Company v. Mosely*, Wall. 489 [46] which was decided, as is usual in Supreme Court (U.S.) cases, by a divided Court. I was counsel for the Company and am fully convinced of it, that the decision is utterly wrong, and I expect our Court, like that learned Judge in the English Exchequer,[47] to decide that the case of the Plff (Mosely) so far as it relies on authority fails in precedent, and so far as it rests on principle fails in reason!

Harvard was still a fairly close-knit society, and as in Langdell's student days, a Law School man interested in people met scholars of different disciplines. Brandeis delighted in it all. In 1911 he said of his days as a law student. "Those years were among the happiest of my life. I worked! For me the world's center was Cambridge." [48]

Roscoe Pound came to the Law School in the autumn of 1889, fourteen years later than Brandeis. He was not quite nineteen years old and already had an A.B. and an M.A. from Nebraska. The decision that the young man should study law seems to have been made by his father who was a judge of the Nebraska Circuit Court. Young Roscoe Pound had already completed a year's graduate study in botany, and wanted to be a scientist. Seventy-

---

[46] Brandeis is probably referring to *Travelers Insurance Company v. Mosley*, 8 Wallace 397 (1869).

[47] I have been unable to identify the learned and epigrammatic Baron of the Exchequer.

[48] Mason, *Brandeis*, p. 47.

three years later he told a friend at Harvard the story of his conversion.[49]

"Dean Pound, how did you come to pick out Harvard?"
"I expect my father did. I'd have to stop to think about that."
"Was the reputation of our Law School high in Nebraska in your young days?"
"No. The reputation of law schools generally wasn't particularly high out there at that time. There was a very strong cult of local law. I can well remember one of the first law books that I read was Walker's *American Law*. My father told me to read Walker and to read Blackstone; that was the way he'd started. Well, Blackstone made me very tired. I didn't appreciate the first volume a bit. Then, as to Walker's *American Law*, I discovered that law was just a matter of rules. It didn't make any difference about what theories, you had, or what philosophical ideas — there was 'the law,' and it was your job to learn 'the law,' and the law could be found in certain books, and you were to get outside of those books. Well, that didn't stimulate me very much.

Young Pound told his father what he thought of Blackstone and Walker; Judge Pound considered the matter awhile and then announced that his son was right, that the books were out of date and that the boy had better go to the Harvard Law School. Meantime, the judge set him to reading opinions of the New York Court of Appeals and the Supreme Court of the United States. The boy still hankered, a little wistfully, for a scientific career.

I wanted to be a botanist. My mother was a very good botanist, and I'd been brought up to collect plants and to collect insects. I had a very fine collection as a boy. But those were the days when a boy did what his father told him to. Father said I was to go to the Harvard Law School and that settled it. I came here with the idea in the back of my head that this was a botanical Mecca. Farlow, the great man on fungi in those days, was here at Harvard, and old Dr. Watson was the great man on the flowering plants; he was at the Herbarium. I had a notion that I could probably work into a botanical atmosphere. But the Harvard Law School is quite a compelling institution. I hadn't been here a week before I saw that I belonged here.

When Pound came to Harvard, in September 1889, the faculty of the Law School numbered eight men. Langdell was Dane Professor and Dean, John Chipman Gray was Royall Professor, James

---

[49] Pound was so kind as to allow me to record this conversation on tape, now in the School's archives. I am grateful to the *Harvard Law Review* for their permission to reprint part of my paper "One Man in His Time," *Harvard Law Review*, 78:7 (1964), which contained this account of Pound's student days.

The Langdell Era

Barr Ames was Bussey Professor, William A. Keener was Story Professor, James Bradley Thayer was professor of law, Heman Chaplin lectured on criminal law, William Schofield was instructor in torts, John Arnold was librarian. There were 254 students. Austin Hall, new, architecturally radical, wonderfully convenient, housed the School.

"When you came here, Dean Pound, who on the faculty particularly struck your attention?"

"Well, there were great men, Langdell, Ames, Gray, Keener — they were outstanding. You couldn't talk with any one of them three minutes without seeing that you were talking to an exceptional man. I saw very little of Langdell. I attended his lectures on equity pleading because I wanted to practice in Nebraska, and I knew that in the federal court they had equity practice, and that the local lawyers didn't know anything about it and stayed out of the federal court as much as they could. So I thought I'd take equity practice. Well, it was a curious course. I confess it bored me a little sometimes; but afterwards, when I came to read over my notes when I was in practice, I found I knew an awful lot about it. Langdell was always worried about 'Why?' and 'How?' He didn't care particularly whether you knew a rule or could state the rule or not, but how did the court do this, and why did it do it? That was his approach all the time. He did most of the talking himself; there was very little talking done by anybody else in his class in my time. What might have been before, I don't know.

"Ames was teaching common law pleading, and he wasn't teaching common law pleading: he was teaching the Hilary Rules. The Hilary Rules didn't obtain but a short time in England, never governed anywhere else; they weren't orthodox common law; they weren't modern pleading. Ames had a faculty of rational exposition that made that course tolerable. But it wasn't a fair test of Ames. When I came afterwards to go over the notes in his course in trusts. I saw that Ames in trusts was wonderful. I think he left something of a mark on Scott.

"Ames was a great teacher, and yet he wasn't a natural teacher as Scott is. Nature made Scott a teacher and made Keener a teacher. I think I have known only a few great natural teachers. Keener, Williston, Scott were outstanding natural teachers; they couldn't help teaching. They were just built that way. It was as easy for Williston or Scott or Keener to teach as it was to eat their breakfast."

"Mr. Pound, how did Harvard start off a law student in 1889? Did you start with the regular first-year work?"

"You were supposed, when I came here, to take common law pleading, contracts, torts, property, and criminal law — five. Torts was taught by William Schofield who had been one of the prize students and later became a federal judge. Property — Gray was a master of that subject. Gray was an outstanding influence with me. I think I owe a great deal to him."

"How did Mr. Gray teach? Did he use the dialectic process?"

"Well, Gray would sometimes think out loud in class. He would ask questions occasionally; he might get into a discussion; but he knew the law of real property inside and out. He was a learned scholar, a great scholar. I owe a great deal to him. He would do curious things. I have two memories of him I like to tell. During the Christmas recess in 1889 — it took four days to get back to Lincoln in those days and I stayed here all through the recess — I was up in the reading room. I had noticed in our casebook on property — Gray's old first edition — that in the first part that deals with personal property, in front of every section, there was an extract from the *Institutes of Justinian*. As a matter of fact our personal property did get a considerable start from Bracton, who was quite learned in the Roman law. I was rather interested. I knew there was such a thing as Roman law but I didn't know anything about it. So I went up to the delivery desk over in Austin, in what was the reading room then, and there was a character, a Scotsman by the name of Gordon, who was presiding. I told him I wanted a book on Roman law. Of all books on earth, he got me Lord Mackenzie's *Roman Law*, which is the Roman Law of Scotland but not the Roman law of the Romans. It was about the most impossible book for anybody who wanted to know anything about the modern Roman law or the ancient Roman law either! Well, I had that book in front of me there in the reading room. Next thing I knew I heard a rather gruff voice behind me saying, 'Don't read that!' I looked up, and there was Gray. 'Well,' I said, 'Mr. Gray' — Do we still say Mister here? That was the rule then. — 'Mr. Gray, what should I read?' He talked very abruptly. 'Do you read German?' 'Oh yes,' I said. He picked up Lord Mackenzie and walked out. Pretty soon he came back with Sohm's *Institutionen des Römischen Rechts*, which was then the standard introduction to Roman law. It's since been translated but then it was the original German. A great book. He opened it at the same spot where he saw I'd been trying to read Lord Mackenzie and said, 'Read that,' and walked off.

"That was Gray, very abrupt in his speech. I remember in class one day in first-year property — Gray would every once in a while go off on some medieval matter that hadn't been of any consequence even as late as Lord Coke — one morning he put something that depended on a case way back in the thirteenth century, on some queer question of tenure; and then he turned to a man in the front row and said, 'What do you think of that?' Well, the man floundered; so Gray then tackled another, and he went along, and finally he tackled me. I'd been thinking about it hard. I gave him an answer. He looked at me in astonishment; he would pull his beard, this way, 'Hm, Hm.' 'Well,' he said, 'that's mighty ingenious but it isn't so!' Then he quit and went on to something else. He was a great teacher, after all."

"What did you have with Mr. Keener?"

"Contracts. Dialectic was the whole thing with him. He was quick as a cat in discussion, pick you right up on a thing, get you into an argument about it, and he'd have you all twisted up like this — in no time. I had trusts with Ames. I had to teach trusts out in Nebraska many years later and I found from my notes of his trusts that it was an admirable course. He was clear as a bell: he wasn't an oracle like Gray and he wasn't a quizmaster like Keener, but he certainly did lay out trusts beautifully."

Pound used to tell with some amusement that, at the end of his year at Harvard, Dean Langdell wrote a letter to Judge Pound announcing that his son had attained in his courses an average of grades over seventy-five. Like many other parents since that time, the judge was unfamiliar with the Law School's somewhat curious conventions of grading. He said to his son, a little sternly, that if he could do no better than that, he might as well give up Harvard. Pound has not, as far as I know, left us a record of what Judge Pound said when he found that his son had achieved a high A.

Pound left Harvard after a single year; he returned to Lincoln, qualified for the Nebraska bar, and was sworn in as a full member of the calling, which he followed all his life. One wonders what Harvard had given him. For one thing, perhaps, self-appraisal. Before he was twenty he had there been able to measure his own intellectual powers against those of the then greatest American legal scholars. Roscoe Pound was acute and sophisticated, well equipped to judge himself strictly. He must have seen his own capabilities. One doubts that Harvard "taught" him anything he could not have got from books. He had already learned thoroughness in the Nebraska laboratory. At Harvard he acquired an enthusiasm for the law that rivaled, and then outran, his interest in botany — an inspiration that could well have come from seeing first-rate intellects at work on the law. Enthusiasm, rather than indoctrination, must have been Pound's most valuable endowment from his Harvard teachers.

In his ninety-third year, Pound once fell to musing aloud about the people who had taught him. His parents led the list: Pound entered his first classroom already well started toward becoming an educated person. Bessey at Nebraska gave him the discipline of science. But, reflecting after seventy-odd years, Pound said repeatedly in conversation, and suggested in the preface of his

1959 *Jurisprudence*, that John Chipman Gray had influenced him more than any other of his formal instructors. What in this relation was cause, what effect, is here, as so often elsewhere, an indeterminable mystery. Pound and Gray had many similarities. Both had vigorous and successful careers at the bar and in university scholarship. Both thought of law in the broadest, most philosophical terms. Both, as practical men, "knew a lot of law." Both were willing to master details. Both had unusual linguistic equipment, ancient and modern, which led both to explore other legal systems to illustrate their own. One wonders whether Pound from the beginning was, as he thought, led by Gray; or whether, sensing their inherent likenesses, as the years went on Pound came more and more to admire this one of his teachers. Probably both estimates are true. In human affairs the conjunctive is true more often than the disjunctive.

When Langdell was sixty-nine years old, in 1895, he asked the Corporation to relieve him of the deanship, and to cut his teaching load by a third. He asked to retain his teaching in jurisdiction and procedure in equity, and to be allowed to concentrate on that classic matter. "This suggestion," said Eliot, "being offered to the Corporation by the Dean, could receive but one answer." [50] Langdell had been dean during a third of the School's life. He joined the faculty of a school Story designed, and left a school with today's essential features. On the twenty-fifth of June, 1895, at the end of Langdell's twenty-five years' deanship, the Law School Association called a meeting in his especial honor. Sir Frederick Pollock crossed the Atlantic to deliver the principal address. President Eliot, Justices Gray and Brown of the Supreme Court of the United States, and Justice Oliver Wendell Holmes of the Supreme Judicial Court of Massachusetts spoke at the Law School dinner that evening. Eliot reviewed Langdell's achievements before five hundred and twenty-five members and guests of the association. The President mentioned James Barr Ames; the guests interrupted Eliot with prolonged applause for the man whom the Governing Boards in 1873 had somewhat reluctantly approved as an assistant professor for an experimental term. No one was surprised when Ames succeeded Langdell as dean. For

[50] See the *Report of the Ninth Annual Meeting of the Harvard Law School Association*, held in 1895, p. 72.

five years after he resigned the deanship, Langdell continued as Dane Professor. He became Dane Professor Emeritus in 1900, continuing his lifelong habit of daily study and writing. In 1903 the Corporation established the Langdell chair; two years later work began on the School's new building; in 1906 the Corporation decided to call it Langdell Hall. Langdell lived long enough to know of this recognition of his rebuilding of a great institution. On July 6, 1906, he did a full day's work, and then died without pain or expectation as one would wish he might. He was at home, quietly talking with his wife.

VII

James Barr Ames: 1895–1910

Ames came to the deanship in a time of fundamental changes in the American social and political scene, changes not wholly perceived by the American people. Technological, social, and political evolution deeply affected American law. The great industrial expansion which succeeded the Civil War had produced a concomitant increase in the nation's labor force. And in America political power goes with numbers. Felix Frankfurter used to ask classes who had been the most important law reformer of the eighteenth and nineteenth centuries; after students had suggested Mansfield or Blackstone or Bentham, Frankfurter would say it was James Watt, who invented the steam engine.[1]

The "farm vote," too, was powerful. Around the turn of the century the Granger movement had either produced or got credit and blame for state and federal legislation intended to control overgrown power of the railroads. The Sherman Act of 1890 undertook to restrict unreasonable aggregates of industrial power, a reform which President Theodore Roosevelt dramatized and re-enforced by his "trustbusting" policies in the early 1900's. In 1906 the Congress passed the Food and Drug Act. Protection and benefits that multitudes of small people wanted were prevailing over the industrially powerful few. Justice Holmes told the Harvard Law School Association of New York in 1913 that twenty years earlier "a vague terror went over the earth and the word socialism began to be heard."[2] The Supreme Court, a somewhat conservative influence in government, began to find inadequacies in the constitutional powers of legislation vested in the national

---

[1] Harlan B. Phillips, *Felix Frankfurter Reminisces* (New York, 1960), p. 197.
[2] See his speech "Law and the Court," *Collected Legal Papers*, p. 295.

government, and to find that the federal and state due process clauses prevented unreasonably drastic economic regulation. In 1895 the Court found a federal income tax unconstitutional, observing in its opinion that Article I, section 2, clause 3, of the Constitution was "manifestly designed . . . to prevent an attack upon accumulated property by mere force of numbers." [3] In 1905 the Court in *Lochner v. New York* held unconstitutional a New York statute limiting the work week of bakers to sixty hours,[4] and in 1908 in *Adair v. United States* it held unconstitutional an Act of Congress forbidding an interstate carrier to discharge employees for joining a labor union.[5] Legislatively, presidentially, judicially, the center of gravity of American government was shifting toward Washington.

A concomitant shift occurred in the scholarly activity of the School's faculty, and ultimately in the curriculum offered to students. Professor James Bradley Thayer saw the direction of Supreme Court adjudication earlier than most men. In 1893 he published in the *Harvard Law Review* a noted paper — his "Origin and Scope of the American Doctrine of Constitutional Law" [6] — which urged judicial restraint in exercising the Court's powers, and which for two generations forecast the American liberal attitude toward constitutional adjudication. In 1960 Felix Frankfurter said of Thayer:

He influenced Holmes, Brandeis, the Hands, Mr. Stimson, Joseph Cotton, and so forth. I am of the view that if I were to name one piece of writing on American Constitutional Law — a silly test maybe — I would pick an essay by James Bradley Thayer in the *Harvard Law Review*, consisting of 26 pages, published in October, 1893, called "The Origin and Scope of the American Doctrine of Constitutional Law" which he read at the Congress on Jurisprudence and Law Reform in Chicago on August 9, 1893. I would pick that essay written 67 years ago. Why would I do that? Because from my point of view it's the great guide for judges and therefore, the great guide for understanding by non-judges of what the place of the judiciary is in relation to constitutional questions.[7]

[3] See *Pollock v. Farmers' Loan & Trust Co.*, 157 U.S. 429 at 583; and see 158 U.S. 601; the clause in question reads "direct taxes shall be apportioned among the several States which may be included within this Union according to their respective Numbers."
[4] *Lochner v. New York*, 198 U.S. 45.
[5] *Adair v. United States*, 208 U.S. 161.
[6] *Harvard Law Review*, 7:129 (1893).
[7] Phillips, *Felix Frankfurter Reminisces*, pp. 299–300.

In 1909 Roscoe Pound, then professor of law at Northwestern University, wrote for the *Yale Law Journal* his paper "Liberty of Contract" [8] protesting the *Adair* case of the preceding year and foreshadowing the rise of sociological jurisprudence which during the next half-century was gradually to pervade American law. Pound wrote:

Jurisprudence is the last in the march of the sciences away from the method of deduction from predetermined conceptions. The sociological movement in jurisprudence, the movement for pragmatism as a philosophy of law, the movement for the adjustment of principles and doctrines to the human conditions they are to govern rather than to assume first principles, the movement for putting the human factor in the central place and relegating logic to its true position as an instrument, has scarcely shown itself as yet in America. Perhaps the dissenting opinion of Mr. Justice Holmes in *Lochner v. New York*, is the best exposition of it we have.

This essay, published just before Ames's fifteen-year tenure ended, may have the next year influenced the Harvard faculty to invite Roscoe Pound to join them. The School's announcement of courses for 1909–10 did not yet generally reflect the shift of emphasis of government and law from that which was parochial to that which was national and from much *laissez faire* to much economic control; but surely in the fifteen years of Ames's deanship, new wine of doctrine filled at least the School's old constitutional law bottle.

Another fundamental change in the government and law of the United States, accelerated during Ames's deanship, concerned our position in the society of nations. Americans had always recognized some of the significance of their international position to their welfare. As colonies America watched, and took part in, the armed rivalry between Britain and France. She became thoroughly versed in diplomatic and warlike maneuvering between 1775 and 1815, but her people in general continued to think that international complications were episodic, transitory, abnormal; that America could someday return to splendid isolation, moated by oceans. The war with Mexico of 1846 was a dispute concerning an immediate border, not a world war; the war of 1861–65, for all its international maneuvers, was an in-

---

[8] *Yale Law Journal*, 18:454.

ternal struggle, the decision of a question of American constitutional law by nonjudicial means. But the war with Spain in 1898 and the annexations it brought demonstrated to the American people that matters all around the world could affect them directly and intimately. The Hawaiian Islands became American territory in the same year. A Constitution written in 1787 for a row of coastal settlements on the American mainland began to concern Cuba and Puerto Rico and Hawaii and the Philippine Islands. Professor Thayer published in the February 1899 *Harvard Law Review* a paper on "Our New Possessions." He wrote:

No longer can we claim our old good fortune of being able to work out a great destiny by ourselves, here in this western world. In my judgment it was a bad mistake to throw away our wonderful inherited felicity, in being removed from endless complications with the politics of other continents. Had we appreciated our great opportunity and been worthy of it, we might have worked out here that separate, peculiar, high destiny which our ancestors seemed to foresee for us, and which with all its grave drawbacks and moral dangers, might have done more for mankind than anything we may hope to accomplish now by taking a leading part in the politics of the world. "Let not England," said John Milton to the Parliament in 1645, "forget her precedence of teaching nations how to live." So to the United States of America, before this Spanish war, — possessed as she was of this fortunate isolation, of free yet guarded institutions, of vast, unpeopled areas, of an opportunity to illustrate how nations may be governed without wars and without waste, and how the great mass of men's earnings may be applied, not to the machinery of government, or the rewarding of office-holders, or the wasteful activities and enginery of war, but to the comforts and charities of life and to all the nobler ends of human existence, — so, I say, to our country as she was before the war, that same solemn warning of Milton, "God-gifted organ-voice of England," might well have come: "Let not America forget her precedence of teaching nations how to live."

But now we are no longer where we were. The war has broken down the old barriers. First it brought us Hawaii, a colony two thousand miles away, in the Pacific Ocean. In point of distance this was much as if we should sail out over the Atlantic and annex the Azores. And now the end of the war is bringing us Puerto Rico, Cuba, and the Philippine Islands. All these strange tropical countries are likely to be on our hands. Hawaii is already actually a part of our territory. From the other islands we have driven out their sovereign, and we have loaded ourselves with great responsibilities and hazards in supplying them with government, maintaining order, and determining what shall be their fate in the future. What are we to do? That the situation is full of peril for us there is no doubt; that it is certain to involve us in great outlays and perplexities, and in constant hazard of war is clear enough.[9]

Thayer died in 1902. He was 68 years old in 1899 when he wrote this prophetic essay. His *Preliminary Treatise on Evidence at the Common Law* had come out the preceding year. In 1895 he had produced an admirable two-volume casebook on constitutional law still useful for its collection of materials hard to find elsewhere. He compiled a widely used casebook on evidence. In 1900 he felt constrained by failing health to decline an appointment to the Philippine Commission, tendered by President McKinley. His heart began to trouble him in 1901; in July he wrote to Jeremiah Smith from Mount Desert: "The head seems all right yet — so far as I can judge — but in other regions time is telling. Fast walking and mountain-climbing are for others now."[10] On Friday, February 14, 1902, he came to Austin Hall but suddenly felt too ill to meet a scheduled class. He went home, and died later the same day. Five hundred law students marched as a guard of honor from his house to his funeral services in Appleton Chapel.

Just before classes began in the preceding fall, he had prepared a memorandum. It was found in his study after his death.

September 15
For next year
Have a single plan to put through. Without that the small, everyday matters eat up all the time. They easily may, for they can be done either well enough, or *perfectly*. That plan must be the 2nd volume of Evidence. For the year following, a small Vol. on Const. Law. For the time following that, the works, writings, and life of Marshall — *and then an End.*[11]

2

Story had early shown the value of a brilliant, energetic, and versatile professor, who as a judge could take an active part in national affairs, and still plan instruction, write, teach effectively, and add to the fruitful life of the Law School. America's increasing involvement in diplomatic and other international concerns

[9] Reprinted in J. B. Thayer, *Legal Essays*, E. R. Thayer, ed. (Boston, 1908), pp. 155-156.
[10] Professor Smith quoted the letter in a short memorial of Thayer, published in the April 1902 *Harvard Law Review*.
[11] Quoted in the *Centennial History*, p. 283.

Assistant Professor James Barr Ames, aged 28, in 1874. In 1895, the year Ames became Dean, President Eliot told the Law School Association how the Corporation and Overseers had hesitated to appoint Ames an assistant professor of law in 1873 when he had had no experience in practice. The choice of Ames was one of Langdell's brilliantly successful innovations.

at about the turn from the nineteenth to the twentieth centuries evoked another type of professor-cum-public-servant: the adviser to or participant in executive government. The School was to produce many examples in the next seven decades; the first came from a bequest for international law. George Bemis, LL.B. 1839, who died in 1878, had by the terms of his will invited involvement of a professor in intergovernmental activity. His bequest created a Chair of International Law, and the testator expressed the wish that the professor might be ". . . not merely a professor of the science, but a practical co-operator in the work of advancing knowledge and good-will among nations and governments. For that object I should prefer, if practicable, that the incumbent should have had some official connection with public or diplomatic life, or at least have had an opportunity, by foreign travel or residence, to look at the United States from a foreign point of view, and so to estimate it as only one of the family of nations." [12]

An outstanding life estate in the Bemis fund delayed search for the first Bemis Professor until 1892; and the Corporation then spent six additional years finding a man who satisfied the testator's terms — Edward Henry Strobel. Strobel, a South Carolinian, took his LL.B. at the Law School in 1882, and after three years of practice in New York City became by President Cleveland's appointment secretary of legation at Madrid. He spent five years in Spain; in 1888 he went on a diplomatic mission to Morocco; and after a short interval out of the federal service President Cleveland appointed him third assistant secretary of state in 1893. He became minister to Ecuador thereafter, then minister to Chile. He was chosen the sole arbiter in a dispute between France and Chile. In the fall of 1898 Strobel accepted the Bemis professorship. He held that chair for eight years, teaching both in the Law School and in the college, and also acting in 1899 as Special Counsel for Chile before the United States–Chilean Claims Commission in Washington. In 1903 the King of Siam offered to Professor Strobel the post of general adviser to the Siamese government. His duties were to be primarily connected with foreign affairs, though not limited to that field. The university granted him leave of absence for this work in 1903 and extended that leave until Professor Strobel resigned his chair in 1906. After

[12] Quoted in Warren, *Harvard Law School*, II, 408.

Story, Strobel was the first of a long series of professors at the School to serve both the federal government and Harvard in the fields of their particular expertness.[13]

During Ames's deanship members of the School's faculty began another public activity which has continued ever since their time: the reform of American domestic law, both federal and state. A conspicuous example was the work of the Conference of Commissioners on Uniform State Laws. The American Bar Association in 1889 had proposed this organization composed of commissioners representing the several states. In that year New York by statute first provided for the appointment of its commissioners. Other states followed this lead and the national conference was so born. Its first major project was the Negotiable Instruments Law, drafted by J. J. Crawford of New York, approved by the commissioners in 1896 after only three days of debate at Saratoga Springs. During the next four years it was adopted by the legislatures of fifteen states, and enacted by the Congress for the District of Columbia.

Dean Ames was in his time the most distinguished university scholar in the field of negotiable paper in the United States, possibly in the world. His *Cases on Bills and Notes*, published in 1881 and reprinted in 1894, with an elaborate summary of the existing law, had been in use for fourteen years and more when Crawford was drafting his statute and when the commissioners were considering and adopting it. Dean Ames saw the Uniform Negotiable Instruments Law for the first time when it had already been adopted in four states. The fact that the commissioners did not call Ames into consultation in the forming of this statute, and that he did not see a draft while the project was under way before the commissioners, is an eloquent demonstration of the detachment of academic jurists from the practical science of legislation during the 1890's.

Dean Ames wrote a memorable critique of the statute, published by the *Harvard Law Review* in 1900.[14] Lyman D. Brewster

[13] Strobel's successor in Siam was his assistant adviser, Jens I. Westengard, Harvard LL.B. 1898. He had been an instructor and assistant professor of law from his graduation until he went to Siam as Strobel's assistant. When Westengard returned to the United States in 1915 he became Bemis Professor. He died in 1918. He left to the School his house on the corner of Concord Avenue and Appian Way: as Westengard House it has long served Professor and Mrs. Glueck as headquarters for their research in criminology. He also left the substantial residue of his estate as a scholarship fund for foreign students.

[14] *Harvard Law Review*, 14:241 (1900).

of Connecticut, president of the Conference of Commissioners, answered the Dean in an article in the *Yale Law Journal*.[15] Ames replied.[16] Brewster rejoined.[17] Charles L. McKeehan summed up in the *American Law Register*.[18] Ames wrote a final paper, "Necessary Amendments."[19] This once famous "Ames-Brewster controversy" formed a sort of critical treatise on the Negotiable Instruments Law. In 1902 the *Harvard Law Review* printed the statute and the Ames-Brewster papers in a pamphlet. Professor Brannan of Harvard in 1908 collected and printed, as an appendix to his edition of the statute, not only the Ames-Brewster papers but also McKeehan's essay; his book served as a text for Harvard students through many years.

Dean Ames's criticisms of the Negotiable Instruments Law reflect his incisive mind, and possibly also his slender experience with the practical business of legislation. His objections were technically acute, but the defects he criticizes made little trouble when the statute was applied to men's daily concerns. The commercial success of the Negotiable Instruments Law, and the British Bills of Exchange Act on which it was modeled, the small amount of litigation which arose over the defects which Ames discerned in its draftsmanship, demonstrate the usefulness in the legislative process not only of intellectual acumen but also of practical contact with the world of affairs. In his 1903 paper Dean Ames concluded that "it is wiser to have no code at all than to adopt the Negotiable Instruments Law in its present form." But the commissioners and the remaining legislatures wisely disregarded Ames's advice despite its sharp technical analysis. Adoption by Georgia in 1924 put the Negotiable Instruments Law in effect in every state of the Union, in the District of Columbia and in the territories of Alaska and Hawaii; Puerto Rico followed in 1930. Withdrawal of the statute by the commissioners in 1900 would at the best have resulted in some delay, and at the worst would have resulted in substantial nonuniformity, in the absence of uniform amendment by the fifteen states which by then had already enacted the law.

Still the lessons indicated by Dean Ames's careful criticisms were not lost. Massachusetts appointed him a commissioner on

[15] *Yale Law Journal*, 10:84 (1901).
[16] *Harvard Law Review*, 14:442 (1901).
[17] *Harvard Law Review*, 15:26 (1901).
[18] *American Law Register*, N.S. 41:437, 499, 561 (1903).
[19] *Harvard Law Review*, 16:255 (1903).

uniform laws in 1902, and he served most years until his death, putting his acute analytical mind to work on a mass of useful legislation. The commissioners asked Professors Samuel Williston of the Harvard Law School to draft the Uniform Sales Act, which the Commissioners approved in 1906, and which by 1941 had been adopted in thirty-eight states and federal jurisdictions. Professor Williston's 1909 treatise on the law of sales [20] was in effect a commentary on his Uniform Sales Act, and an exposition of the law as it was previous to the drafting of that statute. Williston's other contributions to American commercial law were numerous and versatile. With Barry Mohun he drafted the Uniform Warehouse Receipts Act which the commissioners approved in 1906. Between 1906 and 1909 Professor Williston prepared five successive drafts of the Uniform Bills of Lading Act which the commissioners approved in 1909. Between 1907 and 1909 Professor Williston also completed the drafting of the Uniform Stock Transfer Act which the commissioners approved in 1909. By the close of Dean Ames's life in 1910, Professor Williston had drafted uniform legislation covering a large part of American commercial law. Eight years later, in 1918, he completed the Uniform Conditional Sales Act. The uniform acts he thus drafted, together with the Negotiable Instruments Law, formed the foundation of the present Uniform Commercial Code. Professor Williston's monumental treatise on contracts, first published in 1920, rounded out his immensely useful work in this field.

3

In the academic year 1909–10, the last of his life, Dean Ames held the Dane professorship. Jeremiah Smith was Story Professor; John Chipman Gray held the Royall chair; Joseph Doddridge Brannan was Bussey Professor; Eugene Wambaugh was the Langdell Professor (a chair created in 1903); Joseph Henry Beale was Carter Professor of General Jurisprudence (a chair created in 1907); Samuel Williston was the Weld Professor; Edward H. Warren and Bruce Wyman were professors of law. There were five lecturers, one of them Joseph Warren who later became

[20] *The Law Governing Sales of Goods at Common Law and under the Uniform Sales Act* (New York, 1909).

a professor of law. The School had an assistant professor of public speaking. John H. Arnold was within three years of his retirement at the end of forty-one years as librarian. Robert Bowie Anderson was assistant librarian. The School had fourteen teachers of law for 700 students, one for every fifty — about the same ratio which had obtained in the school of Parker, Parsons, and Washburn.

In 1909 the nine teachers of professorial rank formed a close-knit society; in retrospect they seem extraordinarily diverse and colorful. Dean Ames was endowed with all the graces of scholarly existence. Perhaps his most conspicuous influence was his contribution to nationwide improvement of legal education. Teachers trained at Harvard during his deanship staffed many of the most progressive American law schools. He lived to see ten of his own pupils become deans. The bar of every state felt the influence of his thought and study. President Eliot's annual report for 1901–02 cites an instance.

At the request of the University of Chicago and of Professor Beale, the Corporation gave Professor Beale leave of absence during half of the academic year 1902–03, and the whole of the academic year 1903–04, in order that he might organize and develop during its first two years, a law school in the University of Chicago similar to the Harvard Law School in methods and aims. This original and instructive method of establishing a new law school is now being successfully carried out. It is a striking instance of effective coöperation by two universities. The older university thus puts all its experience in carrying on a law school at the service of the younger university, and lends a valued professor to serve as organizer and temporary administrator of the new school. It is evident that the common commercial motives have not governed this transaction.

Professor Brannan was precise, dry, exact, supporting every remark in his chosen field of negotiable instruments by an appropriate citation. One of his students recalls an irreverent poem current more than a half-century ago.

> Brannan got up and put on his shoe —
> (Fifty Michigan forty-two).
> He put on his coat and went out the door —
> (Twenty Wisconsin sixty-four).

Granted, superabundant verbal footnotes do not render a lecture more appealing; but a certain type of detailed work must be done by men like Brannan, willing to dedicate themselves to the precisions of the law.

Eugene Wambaugh was a versatile and witty scholar in many fields, at home alike in the archaisms of the Middle Ages and the legal technicalities of twentieth century agency. Men particularly remember him today for his work in constitutional law. His estimates of the direction of movement of Supreme Court adjudications have turned out to be perceptively sound.

Joseph Henry Beale, then teaching first-year students criminal law and third-year men conflict of laws, was as kindly as a man can be; at the same time he was a dialectical swordsman who played for classroom victory. He persuaded himself that some sort of necessity controlled law, that there existed a cosmic logical sequence which could be perceived and stated if only one could think aright. He loved to demonstrate this as a magician demonstrates the rabbit in the hat. The admirable portrait in the Treasure Room at the School is alive with his character. Older students remember his round little figure and his round pink face, his bald head emerging above the desk where he sat. We can still hear his disarmingly cordial response to a telling observation, "Oooh yes!" — followed by an unexpected thrust which would disable the student adversary. But his blade was never poisoned; he managed to win without hurting his opponent; his students could join in his pleasure at an adroit if unconvincing turn of argument. Great tales were told of him. Once, so they said, he started to demolish a student's observation on the law of some point by brashly asserting, "Show me one case, just one case, that holds what you say." Then he paused thoughtfully, and prudently ended, "and I'll show you a case that's wrong!" Probably apocryphal, but good caricature, is the story of Professor Beale's sweeping observation that a student's proposition was "not law in a single State, not in one single State!" The young man, who had done some homework, politely but firmly cited a decision in the Supreme Court of Pennsylvania. "Oooh, of course," trumpeted Beale with great good humor, not at all taken aback; "but Pennsylvania is not a state, it's a Commonwealth." *Se non é vero é ben trovato!* He was much loved.

Samuel Williston was poised, polished, his every question carefully calculated, knowingly directed to some pedagogical end. He was a master of the art of dialectical demonstration.

When he had finished with the beautiful structure of one of his platonic interchanges on the law of contracts, the student saw the inevitability of the result, as Williston had intended that he should. And if sometimes the passage of years, and some experience in the world, came to demonstrate to the onetime student that in the law very little is entirely inevitable, still this did not destroy the artistry of Williston's demonstrations, or the joy of recollecting them.

The redoubtable Edward H. Warren, then with only five years' service on the faculty, was building up a reputation for classroom truculence; students called him "the Bull." Probably in dialogue with students Edward Warren carried to great extremes the power he bore, but he treated with respect and without rancor any man who stood up to him. Like many men with a rough tongue Warren was sensitive, kindly at base. Veterans of his classes used to tell to their juniors true or legendary tales of his terrors, just as old soldiers love to boast of a long-gone First Sergeant. *Meminisse juvabit.*

Bruce Wyman was the first teacher of administrative law at Harvard Law School. In a time when commissions regulating public utilities were coming to occupy a greater and greater part in the American legal structure he performed a useful and modern duty introducing these concepts, then somewhat novel, to a generation of Harvard students. He was fated to resign his chair in 1913 in a controversy over speeches he had made concerning an investigation into the affairs of the New Haven Railroad.[21] Professor Wyman had publicly advocated a point of view favorable to the railroad without announcing the fact that he was under retainer by that corporation. The statements would have been beyond criticism had he only pointed out with a few words his professional engagement in a matter upon which the substance of what he said had a bearing. By an unfortunate mistake in judgment he permitted a possible inference that he was expressing the views of a professor with no commitment as an advocate. Half a century and more later one thinks of the episode with regret and sympathy.

In 1909–10 Jeremiah Smith and John Chipman Gray were the last two professors still active at the School whose training dated

[21] At that time the New Haven came under heavy fire for some of its corporate activities. Louis D. Brandeis was active on the anti-New Haven side.

from the days before Langdell. Professor Smith ended his teaching in June of 1910 at the age of seventy-three. A story often told about him points up the youth of the School. His father, Chief Justice Jeremiah Smith of New Hampshire, had been a soldier in the American Revolution, and had married shortly after that war. His wife had borne to Judge Smith a son who died in 1796. Judge Smith was widowed, and married again comparatively late in life; to him and his second wife was born on July 14, 1837, Jeremiah Smith, Junior, who in 1890 at the age of fifty-three became the Story Professor of Law at Harvard. Tradition has it that one day in 1896 Professor Smith, coming into the classroom, opened the hour by saying to his students, "Gentlemen, this is a sad day in my family. One hundred years ago today my brother died!" Authorities differ as to whether he made the same remark, *mutatis mutandis*, in 1906.

In 1902 Harvard made John Himes Arnold a Master of Arts. He had then finished forty years of service to the university. In the degree ceremony President Eliot saluted him as "Librarian of the Law School, through whose keenness in pursuit and skill in buying, that Library has become the best collection of common law books in existence." Arnold's education was not originally in the law. He was a graduate of the Rhode Island State Normal School, and taught in public and private schools for several years until, at the age of thirty-three, he became law librarian at Harvard. He took office just after Langdell had begun his deanship. Fifty-one years later, in 1913, three years after the Langdell-Ames era had ended, he was appointed librarian emeritus.

John Arnold was born to be a law librarian, and quickly trained himself to the point of expertise. He soon was far ahead of almost all lawyers, including academic lawyers, in his knowledge of relevant bibliography, in his talent for vigilant pursuit of rare editions, and of publications from countries whose legal collections then seemed unimportant to many of his contemporaries. As the years passed, and as more men understood the significance of foreign law to the United States, Arnold's wisdom became apparent. He knew secondhand book dealers in obscure corners of a dozen foreign countries; from time to time he made it his business to rummage through their shelves, discovering treasures which he brought home to Harvard. The library was his life. The Law School Association showed its appreciation when it presented his portrait to the School in 1913. Appropriately this gracious painting has a place in the Treasure Room, where John Arnold, scholarly, poised, wise, seems to survey the shelves full of his rarest acquisitions.

A new generation of younger teachers was on the way. Austin Wakeman Scott was destined to join the School's faculty in December 1909. He had taken a Rutgers' A.B. in 1903, just before his nineteenth birthday. Then for three years he taught mathematics in a preparatory school. He happened during that time to start reading a set of Blackstone's *Commentaries*, and through these four volumes he progressed with ever increasing delight. He went on to read Cooley on torts, Harriman on contracts, Stephen on pleading, and Austin's *Jurisprudence*. So inspired, he began to think of law school. He spent a summer in a law office in New Jersey and then entered Harvard in the autumn of 1906. Young Scott wrote twice a week to his father, Austin Scott, who was President of Rutgers. When President Scott died, many years afterwards, among his papers were his son's letters written from the Law School. They begin early in the younger Austin Scott's first term at Harvard.

September 28, 1906
The second day of work is finished and now I am beginning to see what the work is going to be like. It certainly seems mighty interesting and I enjoy it immensely . . .

September 30, 1906
I think I see why in a way it is advantageous to know no law when one comes here. The object in the system of the school is to take a case, study it and extract from it the real point decided which of course is often mixed up with other unimportant matters. The text book of course merely gives the result of the decision. So the Professors say that reading the text book first is like looking up the answer before solving the problem, and advise us not to read the text book until we have ourselves extracted the ratio decidendi from the cases. Then the text books may be looked at to check the result. I think however that the reading I have done will be of great service to me. I am sure that for the present I should have but little understanding of the cases without it. The perplexity at the first when students are unfamiliar with the technical terms is one of the great drawbacks of the case system. But as I begin to understand the working of this system it seems to me more and more to be the correct way not so much to acquire the rules of the law but the power of "legal reasoning" to which you remember our friend Thayer gave so much attention.

October 2, 1906
I have just . . . returned from a lecture on Contracts which is

probably the most important subject we have. Assistant Professor Wyman has charge of this work; he is young — he looks not much over thirty — and not quite as sure of himself apparently as some of the older Professors, but still he is quick and talks interestingly. Professor Smith is capital, though he speaks very rapidly and rather indistinctly at times. Prof. Beale, who lectures on Criminal Law is quick and sharp and they say rather sarcastic and not over-courteous when excited — but he has not yet of course shown this characteristic. Prof. Ames, the Dean, and Prof. Wambaugh I have not had long enough to know much about.

October 9, 1906

I am most interested just now in Torts and Contracts, though the course in Criminal Law is very good too. Prof. Beale is rather sarcastic and points out in no gentle terms the absurdity of the answers given. "He has a dampening effect on my conversational ability" as one of the fellows put it . . .

October 15, 1906

The work is as interesting as ever — more so if anything. I have been reading at odd times a book which I have often seen quoted, and which some of the professors have alluded to from time to time, Holmes on "The Common Law." It is very interesting, and goes quite deeply — though it is rather a small book — into the theory and logic of the common law, rather than merely telling the principles as does our old friend Sir W. B. The author seems to have a fine power of analysis. [A subsequent letter shows that Austin Scott knew all about Roosevelt's appointment of Holmes.]

November 14, 1906

The work and all go well; I think I enjoy it as much as ever, as I settle down and the novelty wears off. I have nearly gotten over the stage where I dream law every night as I did at first, just as when I first went to the Trap I used to dream x^2 and y^2 . . . ["The Trap" was a house for students and masters in the school where Scott had taught.]

December 12, 1906

I find the Contracts which we have three times a week more interesting than any of the rest. It is great . . .

December 16, 1906

Prof. Beale has been absent for nearly a week. Rumor has it that it is twins but I have heard no authentic report as yet. He has also just been reelected alderman of Cambridge and perhaps he is celebrating the triple event.

January 30, 1907

I have enjoyed the Real Property which we have just finished, particularly the law of Uses; I had a good foundation in Blackstone, though I have had more real understanding of the logic and principles underlying it than I imagined existed . . . But the other day he [Prof.

W.] [22] called for an abstract of one of the cases; the student gave a
case which we had just finished, entirely different in principle, and he,
i.e. Prof. W. never noticed it; I think most of the class failed to notice
it either though one or two did.

April 28, 1907

Professor Williston has as I told you taken the class in Pleading,
though we have it now only once a week. With all due respect to the
Dean it does seem to me that Williston can teach the subject better.
The Dean spent about half the time answering foolish questions which
the askers had they stopped to think could easily have answered
themselves; so that only about half of the time was there any use in
taking notes. But with Professor W. we get new ideas every moment;
and he presents them in such a way that we have to discover them for
ourselves.

4

When Professor Edward H. Warren published his memoirs in
1942, he chose for a title *Spartan Education.* The name well described the effect of comparatively liberal admission policies combined with stringent course examinations at the end of each year
of law study. In 1910 achievement of an undergraduate degree
from a respectable American college, passport to the Harvard
Law School, was still no very extraordinary feat of intellect. This
was the era of the "gentleman's C." As a practical matter the Law
School was open after about 1900 only to men with a previous
undergraduate degree, but this criterion involved little selectivity. Any student who came to the School's secretary with a
diploma from any one of a long list of colleges could enroll without more credentials. At the end of each year's study, however,
the School's professors undertook a surgically impersonal process
of grading the examination "blue books" from their own courses
with the signatures of the students on the covers turned back, so
as to eliminate identification while grading. Thus they cut off the
inept at the end of the first year, and thereafter dismissed some
of the survivors of that ordeal at the end of the second year, and
refused degrees to some at the end of the third year. The wastage
often amounted to a third or more of a class.

Academic deficiencies were, of course, not the only reasons
which separated students from the Law School rolls, but still the

[22] The 1905–06 Announcement shows that Ames and Wambaugh taught first-
year property.

figures of declining numbers in the successive years of a Law School class were eloquent of Spartan education. In the academic year 1896–97 there were two hundred and twenty-two first-year, one hundred and thirty-nine second-year, and ninety-five third-year students. In the academic year 1901–02 there were two hundred and forty-eight first-year, two hundred and four second-year, and one hundred and forty-three third-year students. In the academic year 1909–10, the last year in which Ames served as dean, there were two hundred and forty-three first-year, two hundred and eight second-year, and one hundred and seventy-two third-year students.

Much could be (and was) said for this system of liberal admission followed by strict scrutiny of the subsequent performance of the men admitted. One member of the faculty has said of the process what was said of the pioneer men and women who went out in wagon trains to settle the far west, "The cowards never started and the weak died on the way." Yet a man who had done badly in college but still had courage and natural aptitude was given a chance to demonstrate his ability in the Spartan Law School.

Nevertheless for a substantial portion of every entering class the change from easy attainment of an undergraduate passing mark to the exhausting struggle for survival and fierce competition for grades in the Law School was a shocking experience, and for those who after a year or two or three were impersonally severed because of inadequacies in examinations, the wound was deep. The School to a certain extent, like an old drill sergeant, tended to pride itself on its rigor, and yet there was here perhaps less reason for pride than for sorrow. Selection of able people in advance was possible. The waste of teachers' energy and attention, diverted from the able to the slow, and the waste of student time called for justification; in retrospect the grounds are not convincingly apparent.

Search for better screening of applicants found no place in the annual reports of that day. Instead of applying more stringent requirements for admission, the School admitted larger and larger classes. A more rigid admissions testing, a system of "flunking them out before they come," was an institution of a far later date, adopted, perhaps, only when applicants for admission became so numerous that the School could surely be filled to capacity with excellent students. Only then, late in the 1930's, did a merciful selectivity replace the policy of an open door to almost anyone carrying a college diploma.

5

In 1883 Eliot and Langdell expected Austin Hall to house the School for a half-century. At that time the number of students had only increased by about fifty since Story died, and Austin could easily have accommodated a similar increase during the next two score years. Restriction of admission to degree men, the requirement of course examinations, the lengthened course of study, would, Eliot and Langdell thought, inhibit any unusual rise in membership.

This forecast proved quite wrong. From one hundred and sixty-five men in 1885, student membership in the School rose to seven hundred and sixty-four in 1904, an increase of 364 percent; more students must have more space. John Arnold vastly expanded the library collection; more books require more stacks. Enlargement of Austin Hall proved impracticable; but the spectacular increase in students and the consequent increase of income had by 1905 built up a Law School surplus fund of several hundred thousand dollars, which made possible a major new building. On the faculty's recommendation, the Corporation then employed Messrs. Shepley, Rutan, and Coolidge [23] to design what is now Langdell Hall. The Corporation and its architects wisely foresaw that the School would continue to grow, and so planned a building intended ultimately to extend northerly almost as far as Langdell does today.[24] However, the construction then undertaken included only the southerly portion; the bobtailed structure ran north a little less than half the extent of the present reading room. Even so it cost more than $400,000, which was a far larger sum in 1906 than it would have been sixty years later.

The faculty and the Corporation was foresighted in 1905, but not foresighted enough. By 1928 the partly completed Langdell

[23] This firm of architects was the successor of Henry Hobson Richardson who had designed Austin Hall.

[24] A drawing of "Proposed New Building: Langdell Hall" made by Shepley, Rutan, and Coolidge appears at page 480 of Warren's 1908 *History of the Harvard Law School*. At page 56 of the *Centennial History* is a photograph of the original portion of Langdell as it stood from 1906 to 1928.

Hall had become so overcrowded that the building was extended still farther north than the architects had planned twenty-one years before; and the west wing was an additional new feature. Still Ames had been wise in 1905; he foresaw much growth and made provision for it which proved adaptable to even more growth than he foresaw. Today his portrait, on the wall above the delivery desk in the Langdell reading room, hangs at the line of division between the Langdell Hall he built, and the additions Pound made in 1928–29.

In November 1909 when Dean Ames was sixty-three years old he suddenly found himself unable to apply his mind to his work. His mental processes, for so long so acute, so readily at his command, no longer obeyed his will. The small faculty of law in those days used to lunch together each week. At the conclusion of one of these gatherings Dean Ames leaned forward in his chair and quietly said:

I am very sorry to say that I must leave the Law School. It may be only for a short time, till June or next year or I may not be able to come back at all. I have been examined by three physicians, and none of them can tell me what is the matter with me. But I find I can't remember names. I can't recall the name of any one of you here without extraordinary effort. It has taken me three hours to prepare a lecture that I've usually prepared in half an hour. I must go away at once. Now I don't want any of you to be unhappy about this. I am not at all unhappy myself. If I never come back, it will not make me unhappy. If this is the end, I shall have had long years of service, and far more in my life than most men ever have. I must leave you to make provision for the School.[25]

He died a few weeks later on the eighth day of January 1910, in Wilton, New Hampshire.

Austin Scott had graduated from the Law School in the June preceding Dean Ames's death, and was appointed instructor in December 1909 to take over Ames's courses in pleading and in equity for the rest of the year. Nearly sixty years later Professor Scott's recollection of the dean of his student days is still warm; his admiration is undimmed; he still delights to tell of Dean Ames's gentle greatness. James Barr Ames was an understanding

---

[25] Professor Edward H. Warren wrote these words for the Boston *Transcript* of January 15, 1910, a week after Dean Ames died. His warmhearted appreciation of the Dean he reprinted in his *Spartan Education* (1942) at page 32.

and effective teacher, a talented scholar, a man of generous kind-liness and quick moral sensitivity. He taught students the law by dialectic; by his presence he taught them the obligation of honor-able uprightness. To remember him, to learn of him, is warming and reassuring.

VIII

Thayer and Pound: 1910–1936

Giving a name to any period in the Law School's life is a puzzling enterprise. The School is compounded of many men's work, hopes, and aspirations; no one man in any era, be he dean or professor, can rightly have all the praise or take all the blame for its character during his time. Those of us whose life is in the School resemble other men in our tendency to limit our view to nearest things, and so we may overlook or underrate the influence of the university's presidents. We speak of the years from 1870 to 1910 as the era of Langdell and Ames, but the epoch of the School's development during those deanships could very well be named the age of President Eliot; the School would not have been the same without the direction of that wise and persistent man.

Eight months before Ames died, Abbott Lawrence Lowell, A.B. 1877, LL.B. 1880, replaced Eliot as president of Harvard. His only graduate degree came from the Law School. Lowell was not the first lawyer-president. John Leverett, president from 1708 to 1724 and Josiah Quincy, president from 1829 to 1845, had both been men of the law. Lowell held office until the end of the summer of 1933 when James Bryant Conant succeeded him. Lowell admired the Law School's intellectually acquisitive spirit, the determination which it aroused in its students; he hoped to stimulate some of the same attitude in the undergraduates of Harvard College.[1] He stoutly supported the School as his times required, just as Eliot had supported it during his presidency. Notably in the troubled days following the close of World War I, when various alumni criticized Zechariah Chafee, Felix Frankfurter and

---

[1] See Henry Aaron Yeomans, *Abbott Lawrence Lowell* (Cambridge: Harvard University Press, 1948), pp. 123f.

even Roscoe Pound as obnoxious radicals, Lowell gave them his courageous backing. His presidency lasted until the beginning of the New Deal, lasted until three years before Pound ended his deanship. Perhaps it would be just to name the twenty-six years of Thayer and Pound as the age of Lowell.

Or, if we had sufficient nomenclatural ingenuity, we might name the School's years from 1910 to 1936 for their social and governmental trends. During those years the movements of the preceding two decades continued with dramatic acceleration. The Constitution and state and national law changed accordingly. The scholarly concern of the School's professors, and ultimately the School's curriculum, followed these developments. During that third of a century inventive talent continued to produce more and more intricate and fascinating machines, and the machines more and more drastically revolutionized life. They made possible the growth of greater and greater cities, supported by fewer and fewer farmers. Because machines could produce goods faster than men could save money, the machines gave rise to new schemes of merchandising by which more and more men bought on the strength of earnings they hoped to make in the future. Williston's Uniform Conditional Sales Act, approved by the Commissioners on Uniform State Laws in 1918, was no mere coincidence; it responded directly to the social demands of its time. The motor car, in 1900 a rare luxury for economic aristocrats, became through the ingenuity of Henry Ford a possibility for millions of average citizens by the early years of the century's second decade. With this proliferation came higher wages in Ford's factories, which helped induce higher wages in other areas of industry. The American people, who had been learning to buy on the installment plan since the close of the Civil War, received a new vigorous stimulus to that procedure by the sale of Liberty Bonds during the war of 1917–1918, paid for out of wages a few dollars at a time. The Conditional Sales Act arrived at an appropriate moment. The School's curriculum adapted itself to these development.

The election of 1912 put a professor in the White House. Woodrow Wilson dedicated himself to a vigorous "progressive" program. Many of these reforms involved more federal intervention in the nation's economy. Wilson urged his ideas on the Congress and succeeded in bringing about the Federal Reserve

Act, the Federal Trade Commission Act, and the Clayton Anti-Trust Act which favored labor interests by limiting injunctions in labor disputes and by exempting labor associations from anti-trust laws. Wilson's progressive legislative achievements duly appeared in the School's courses. In 1913 came the Sixteenth Amendment giving the Congress "power to lay and collect taxes on incomes, from whatever source derived, without apportionment among the several States, and without regard to any census or enumeration." The resulting tax, comparatively light at first, growing heavier ever since, and accompanied by federal and state taxes on inheritances, affected American corporate and individual existence in a great many different ways. Concomitantly, it has produced important changes in the curriculum and researches of the Harvard Law School. The increasing time devoted to study of taxation during the half century after 1913 has been one of the most striking developments in the School.

The international concerns of the United States increased from the comparatively slight insular involvements of 1898 to our national anger at Germany in 1916, and our declaration of war in 1917. Student sentiment at eastern American universities strongly favored the Allies from 1914 on. Before the United States entered the war young men from Harvard enlisted in the Royal Flying Corps or went to drive ambulances in the French army. By 1916 the German submarine campaign and German successes in northern France were putting all American domestic concerns in the background. Early in the following year war with Germany mobilized the United States with a completeness previously unknown to Americans. Harvard became a sort of barracks. Professor Scott was a major in a battalion of the Harvard College Reserve Officer Training Corps regiment.[2] The Law School's registration shrank by more than 90 percent. A number of professors took leave for military or other wartime duty.

Despite peace in western Europe, the following year, 1919, brought widespread social disturbances in many parts of the United States, which some observers, with varying degrees of error and correctness, ascribed to influence of the Communist revolution in Russia. The name of A. Mitchell Palmer, Wilson's Attorney General, was ascribed to a series of raids by federal

[2] To his regret he had been rejected for field service because of his eyesight; the army refused to waive his disability.

officers on radicals of diverse varieties. These "Palmer Raids" evoked denunciations from liberals in and out of American universities, and consequent outcry against professors by indignant alumni.

During the decade following World War I the Supreme Court declared unconstitutional some federal and rather more state legislation regulating the economy, provoking outcry by those who disagreed. Causes still not understood brought economic depression. By 1926 business had begun to slow down, and this slowdown became alarming between 1929 and 1932. It brought the election of Franklin D. Roosevelt whose New Deal of 1933 and the following five years profoundly altered American government, American law, and American law schools. The Thayer deanship occurred in an era of social reform in America and during the first stages of the war in Europe. Pound's deanship stretched through America's part in that war, through the economic acceleration and deceleration of the 1920's, through the first years of the New Deal, and ended in the midst of the Supreme Court crisis of the mid-1930's.

The life of the Harvard Law School reflected all these national movements. In the troubled years immediately after the war Professor Zechariah Chafee came under criticism for his support of causes thought radical. Felix Frankfurter expressed himself about the Sacco-Vanzetti case and prospective contributors to the School announced their withdrawal of support. Unsigned editorials in the New Republic, which people said Frankfurter wrote, aroused similar criticism for what some thought an ultraliberal trend.

The 1920's brought the complaints about administration of criminal justice perennial since Fielding's 1751 *Enquiry into the Causes of the Late Increase of Robbers*. Pound and Frankfurter took part in the Cleveland survey of 1922; the School sponsored a survey of criminal justice in Boston. Pound was a leading member of the Wickersham Committee appointed by President Hoover which made a similar survey of federal criminal justice between 1929 and 1932.

Meantime in 1929 the School organized as a sort of annex an Institute of Criminal Law, which briefly ran a training curriculum for correctional administrators. Steady work proceeded on other domestic law. Samuel Williston worked in the field of commerce;

ENQUIRY

Into the CAUSES of the late

Increafe of Robbers, &c.

WITH SOME

PROPOSALS for Remedying this GROWING EVIL.

IN WHICH

The Prefent Reigning VICES are impartially expofed ; and the Laws that relate to the Provifion for the POOR, and to the Punifh-ment of FELONS are largely and freely ex-amined.

Non jam funt mediocres hominum libidines, non humanæ auda-ciæ ac tolerandæ. Nihil cogitant nifi cædem, nifi incendia, nifi rapinas. CIC. in Catil. 2da.

By HENRY FIELDING, Efq;

Barrifter at Law, and One of His Majefty's Juftices of the Peace for the County of *Middlefex*, and for the City and Liberty of *Weftminfter*.

LONDON:

Printed for A. MILLAR, oppofite to *Katharine-Street*, in the *Strand*. M. DCC. LI.

[Price 2 *s.* 6 *d.*]

Austin Scott in the field of trusts; Joseph H. Beale in conflict of laws. Eugene Wambaugh, succeeded by Thomas Reed Powell in 1925, wrote and taught about constitutional law.

About 1925 the School began a process of intense self-scrutiny, giving rise to a series of reports prepared by its faculty concerning its function and operation, which have continued to the present time.

To invent a chapter title which, in some epigrammatic phrase, summarized all these twenty-six years of public development and the academic reaction to it, would be an admirable feat, unfortunately beyond man's powers. I come back to naming the chapter "Thayer and Pound."

2

Ezra Ripley Thayer in 1910 came directly from the practice of law to the deanship.[3] His father was Professor James Bradley Thayer; he was born in Milton, Massachusetts, on the twenty-first of February 1866, was graduated A.B. from Harvard in 1888 and took his LL.B. at the Law School in 1891. He spent a year as law secretary to Mr. Justice Horace Gray of the Supreme Court of the United States, and then returned to Boston to practice, first with Brandeis, Dunbar and Nutter, and then as a partner in Storey, Thorndike, Palmer and Thayer. In practice he was brilliant, meticulously careful, and conspicuously successful. The School had tried to recruit him for a faculty post when he graduated in 1891, and had again invited him in 1902 when his father died. Both times he declined. But when Ames died and the School proposed the deanship to Thayer, the task appeared to him a necessary duty and he undertook it. He abandoned his practice and during the remaining five years of his life turned himself entirely to the university. In his years at the bar he had always hoped for appointment to his state's Supreme Judicial Court; an offer of a seat on that bench came to him in 1913. He had by that time fully committed himself to the Law School and, probably with some regret, he declined the judicial post for which he had once wished.

Dean Thayer was a perfectionist — a trait perhaps associated

[3] He was appointed dean on March 28, 1910, to take effect September 1 of that year.

with some wholly unnecessary self-questioning as to his fitness for the academic work he had chosen. In hours of depression he sometimes asked colleagues whether the School really needed him. After classes, he would dictate to his secretary accounts of his dialectical interchanges with his students, followed by summaries of student interviews in his office, with his own commentary, and suggestions for his own further study. Sometimes he would write a long letter to a student discussing a knotty problem the man had raised in class. This careful and detailed self-scrutiny inevitably impeded writing for publication. Despite Dean Thayer's wisdom and experience in the law, we have only a few published bits of his writing. Characteristically he used to say, "After all, the reputation of the School will suffer no injury from what I do not write." In 1916, after his death, the *Harvard Law Review* printed a pamphlet containing four of his essays, with a sketch of his life, and the proceedings on the dedication of his portrait to the School.[4] The few essays which he left show his clarity, his care, his meticulous attention to detail.

Early in 1915 Dean Thayer fell ill of a nervous depression so serious as to keep him from his work during most of the spring. He braced himself to return and finish his year's teaching and conduct final examinations; then came a complete collapse. On September 14, 1915, his body was found in the Charles River.

Professor Pound in a memorial essay written for the November 1915 *Harvard Law Review* pictured Thayer as sometimes quite different from the intensely earnest, self-questioning man he generally seemed. "His wit was Greek in its gracefulness and playfulness. Indeed the reading of Greek,[5] which he kept up to the last, had left its mark upon him and one might think of him as one of the well born, well bred, well taught, widely cultured youth with whom Socrates practiced his dialectic." Deprived of Thayer Harvard was less graceful, was a university with a diminished human endowment.

The School did not greatly change in numbers between the beginning and ending of Thayer's deanship. In his first year, 1910–11, 790 students registered; in his last year, 1914–15, the School enrolled 730. Notable in his administration was the insti-

[4] *Ezra Ripley Thayer. An Estimate of His Work as Dean of the Harvard Law School, a Sketch of His Life and Reprints of Certain of His Writings* (1916).

[5] While Thayer was preparing for college he spent a year in Athens studying the Greek classics. Throughout his life he read Greek with pleasure.

tution of a possible fourth year of study, with the doctoral degree as an objective. Probably even more significant were several brilliant new appointments to the faculty.

For some years before Dean Thayer had assumed his duties the faculty had been considering the addition of an optional fourth year. In 1909 it had voted to recommend to the Corporation the grant of a doctoral degree in law, but Ames's sudden illness and death in January 1910 delayed the adoption of this plan. The register of the Law School for 1910–11 for the first time announced that the School offered a post-baccalaureate degree, Doctor of Law. Graduates of the Harvard Law School or of other schools qualified to be members of the Association of American Law Schools could earn it by one year's resident study after receiving the bachelor's degree in law, and by passing with distinguished excellence examinations in courses open to fourth-year students requiring ten hours of lectures a week during the entire year. The doctoral candidate was required to include among these courses Roman law and the principles of the civil law, and in addition at least two hours of lectures a week from other courses open exclusively to fourth-year students. On June 20, 1912, the university admitted its first doctoral candidate, Eldon Revare James,[6] "ad gradum Scientiae Juridicae Doctoris."

The School's announcement of degrees continued to describe the requirements and availability of the degree "Doctor of Law" through the academic year 1923–24. The Register for the following year, 1924–25, announces instead two graduate degrees, the higher called in English "Doctor of Juridical Science," intended primarily for teachers of law or for students preparing to become teachers. The announcement states that "it is usually inadvisable to become a candidate for the Doctor's degree without at least three years of experience in the practice or in law teaching after receiving the first degree in law." The same Register announced another graduate degree, Master of Laws. Both degrees required an academic year's study of twelve hours per week, including Roman law, civil law, and some other course work of graduate level. The doctoral candidate could, however, in place of four hours' of course work per week, do distinguished research or

[6] On September 1, 1923, Harvard appointed Eldon James professor of law and librarian of the Law School, a position in which he served the university with great distinction until he became professor and librarian emeritus in 1942.

guided study under a professor. The prospective Doctor was required to pass his course examinations "with distinguished excellence." The would-be Master had only to pass his examinations in course work "with high rank." In describing the difference between the requirements for the two degrees, the faculty of law coped as best they could with the perennial difficulty of describing a higher and a lesser ranking of scholarly endeavor by words which, by their nature, are general and indefinite. The requirement of a thesis embodying the results of research for the doctoral degree, imposed in 1928, to some extent clarified the distinction. For doctoral candidates entering in 1935 and thereafter the School required a "dissertation" in publishable form accepted by the Committee on Graduate Studies as a "significant contribution to legal literature."

Thayer began his deanship with eight full professors in addition to himself, with Assistant Professor Scott, and with four lecturers on law. His last academic year, 1914–15, began with ten professors, including himself, and three lecturers. During Thayer's tenure three professors left active duty; Jeremiah Smith at the age of seventy-three became Story Professor Emeritus in June 1910; John Chipman Gray, last of the pre-Langdell faculty,[7] became Royall Professor Emeritus on January 13, 1913; Professor Bruce Wyman resigned on December 22, 1913. Harvard filled the three professorial vacancies thus created by appointing Roscoe Pound in 1910 as Story Professor; by promoting Joseph Warren from instructor to professor in 1913; and by appointing Felix Frankfurter as professor of law in 1914. Austin Scott's promotion from instructor to assistant professor, Roscoe Pound's appointment as Story Professor, and Thayer's appointment as Dean and Dane Professor all took effect on September 1, 1910.

Professor Scott in a letter to a colleague later told how he first came to join the faculty.[8]

After I was graduated in 1909, I became, at the instance of Felix Frankfurter,[9] a clerk in the office of Winthrop & Stimson in New York.

[7] Gray was appointed a lecturer on December 24, 1869; thirteen days later Langdell became Dane Professor.

[8] This letter, written in 1962 to W. Barton Leach, appears in *Perspectives of Law: Essays for Austin Wakeman Scott*; Pound, Griswold, and Sutherland, eds. (Boston, 1964).

[9] Frankfurter was a great recruiter of talent, governmental, academic, and other. Austin Scott was an obvious prize for any law firm.

At that time I had no thought of teaching law. But in December Dean Ames suddenly became ill and had to leave the school, and a month later he died. I remember that old Professor Wambaugh (though actually he was not old then according to my present standards) [10] came to the office and told me that the faculty of the Law School wished me to take over Dean Ames's courses in Pleading and in Equity for the rest of the academic year. I accepted the invitation, as who would not? For the rest of that year I commuted from New York to Boston, preparing for my classes during the train rides. Fortunately at that time the trains were pretty slow, so that I had time enough. I remember that at Christmas time the other law clerks received an increase in their pay, $15.00 a week instead of $10.00 Since I was necessarily absent for two days of the week, I continued to receive $10.00 until the academic year was over. However, I was told that I would receive at the Law School the salary of an assistant professor, although I was only an instructor, which I think at that time was $2500.00 or $3000.00. But there was a little catch in this. Since I did not start until December, I was later told that I would have two-thirds of the salary, and, since I was giving only four hours a week whereas the standard was six, I would receive only two thirds. Hence, my take home pay was two thirds of two thirds of an assistant professor's salary. Having majored in mathematics, I knew that this was four ninths of the full salary of an assistant professor. I am not complaining of this. I think that it was all soundly mathematical. But after deducting the railroad fares and the cost of a room in Cambridge, I was not exactly a plutocrat.

In the spring, I was invited to join the faculty as a real assistant professor. This was all so unexpected that I hesitated for a time whether to burn my bridges, leave New York and come to Cambridge. Having had some experience in teaching and having thoroughly enjoyed it, I accepted the invitation. Hence, on the same day, to wit May 9th, 1910, Roscoe Pound and I were appointed to the faculty of the Law School, he as Story Professor and I as Assistant Professor.

When I was an assistant professor, indeed *the* assistant professor, the then dean, Ezra Ripley Thayer, frequently quoted a maxim, *labores ad juniores.* Whenever it was necessary to have someone take over a course, I was asked to take it. I once boasted to Professor Seavey that I had taught a dozen different subjects, but he, who had taught in many law schools, told me that he had taught more than twenty subjects. All this was good for me if not good for the students. But finally I settled down and devoted myself to Trusts and Procedure, and ultimately to Trusts alone.

[10] Eugene Wambaugh was then fifty-three. Students used to ascribe phenomenal age to him, despite his alert, almost elfish wit, and his wholly up-to-date estimate of constitutional matters. In 1925 a classmate told me, with affection and appreciation, that Wambaugh had been a drummer boy in the Wars of the Roses.

Roscoe Pound was another portentous faculty recruit in 1910. He had left Harvard Law School in June 1890 without an LL.B., after one academic year studying law; he was admitted to the Nebraska bar later the same year. Busy beginning practice in his home town, Lincoln, Pound still wavered a bit between professions. Nebraska was an agricultural state. A scientific survey of her plant life was highly desirable, and only Pound's age, now twenty-two, stood in the way of his selection as director of the state survey.[11] Professor Bessey who had taught Pound as an M.A. candidate in botany at the University of Nebraska nevertheless selected him for this responsibility, and between 1892 and 1903 Pound carried out the task in addition to his practice. By 1897 he had completed his "Phytogeography of Nebraska," a dissertation which earned him Nebraska's doctoral degree in botany.[12] Meantime Pound was trying jury cases in cow towns, writing briefs with his father, who had resigned from the bench to practice law, and arguing appeals in state and federal courts. He happily married Grace Gerrard in 1899, and in the same year the University of Nebraska made him an assistant professor of law — an avocation that he carried on along with the consuming demands of a courtroom practice and the administration of the botanical survey.

In 1901 the Nebraska legislature, to relieve docket congestion in the state Supreme Court, provided for nine commissioners of the Supreme Court, to be appointed by that body, who should conduct hearings and perform duties as the court should direct. Pound, at the age of thirty, was appointed a commissioner; in the next two years he wrote about two hundred and fifty reported opinions.[13] They generally concerned pedestrian controversies — as do most opinions of most courts. Pound showed himself a sound competent workman, as he was all his life. His opinions were not intended to be epigrammatic; they were well adapted to their purpose, solid, suitable to persuade his fellow commissioners and the reviewing court. The statute creating the commission dis-

---

[11] Roscoe Pound died in the summer of 1964 when this book was under way. At the request of the *Harvard Law Review* I wrote for the November number of that year a biographical sketch of Dean Pound, intending it for later inclusion here. The material which follows is part of that article.

[12] Revised and published in 1898 as Pound and Clements, *Phytogeography of Nebraska*.

[13] Reported in volumes 61–69, Nebraska Reports. See Reuschlein, "Roscoe Pound — the Judge," *University of Pennsylvania Law Review*, 90:292 (1942).

qualified a member from the practice of law during his tenure of office but did not prohibit academic activity, and while he was a commissioner, Pound was able to continue teaching at the university and to direct the botanical survey.

Somehow, despite all this, he found time to prepare with awe-inspiring thoroughness the first edition of his *Outlines of Lectures on Jurisprudence*, originally published in 1903. One interested in Pound's intellectual tendencies does well to consider the nature of this book. It suggests his *Phytogeography of Nebraska*; it is a book of scientific ordering, of minutely detailed nomenclatural terms. Here is a botanist, explaining the taxonomy and nomenclature of justice. The American and foreign bibliography in the *Outline* reveals an amazing depth of jurisprudential reading; and this evidence of omniscience increased as editions succeeded one another.

In 1903 Pound gave up his judicial duties to become the dean of the University of Nebraska College of Law. This school had somewhat less than two hundred students; the faculty consisted of three full-time professors and a part-time instructor.[14] Dean Pound immediately made changes. He increased the required course from two to three years, providing time to instruct by the case method. He also pressed for a richer offering of electives so that, for the student who saw himself able to acquire practical subjects by office experience after graduation, there might be available at the university such broad cultural offerings as international law, Roman law, and legal history. The Law School for the first time instituted as a prerequisite for admission a full high school course, although it expected a decrease in enrollments. One stands in awe of the Nebraska high school graduate of 1903, who brought to Pound's course in jurisprudence an ability to cope with such matters as "Development of the conception and definition [of law] from Grotius to Kant," via Montesquieu, Hobbes, Burlamaqui, Rousseau, Savigny, and Ihering.[15]

All his life, Roscoe Pound felt urges both to scholarship and to effective public activity. To both he gave expression in August 1906, when at St. Paul, Minnesota, he unfolded to a somewhat startled American Bar Association the causes for dissatisfaction

[14] See *Report of the Dean of the College of Law*, in University of Nebraska Board of Regents Report, 17:37–41 (1905).
[15] Pound, *Outlines of Lectures on Jurisprudence* (Lincoln, Nebraska, 1903).

with American justice. Half a century later his speech seems mild enough, though it evoked some indignant oratory from the audience at the time. It resulted in the appointment the next year of an association committee, of which Pound was a member, to consider needed reforms in the administration of justice.[16] Another consequence was the organization of the American Judicature Society in 1913. A bronze plaque on the wall of the Minnesota Capitol Building and an impetus to reform in the administration of justice inspired on that August evening now memorialize Pound's address.

Dean Wigmore of the Northwestern University School of Law heard Pound's learned and forceful speech; the following spring he invited Pound to join its faculty. The decision must have been difficult for Pound; his roots were deep in Nebraska. His father and mother lived in Lincoln; his sister Louise was now a professor of English at the university; and his younger sister Olivia was a teacher and administrator in the Lincoln public schools. But Northwestern was a wider stage and had a larger audience than the University of Nebraska. Pound moved to Northwestern. He had stayed there only two years when the University of Chicago invited him to move again, to what he thought a still more notable faculty. To Wigmore's great annoyance, Pound accepted Chicago's invitation. He stayed only one year at Chicago. Pound's last months at Northwestern had been marked by the publication of his respected paper "Liberty of Contract," [17] in which he deplored constitutional decisions on dogmatic grounds without regard to the practical effect of such decisions on daily life. It was a resounding statement that the law must be made for man's needs, and a firm restatement of James Bradley Thayer's doctrine that the Constitution must tolerate economic reform.[18] Thayer's son, Ezra Ripley Thayer, practicing law in Boston, noticed Pound's paper with admiration. On March 28, 1910, Ezra Ripley Thayer was appointed Dean of the Harvard Law School. On May 9, 1910, Roscoe Pound was appointed Story Professor of

[16] The report of this committee may be found in *American Bar Association Reports*, 3:542 (1908).
[17] *Yale Law Journal*, 18:454 (1909). This paper protested the decision in *Adair v. United States*, 208 U.S. 161 (1908), invalidating a federal statute forbidding discrimination by interstate railroads against employee membership in unions.
[18] See Thayer, "The Origin and Scope of the American Doctrine of Constitutional Law," *Harvard Law Review*, 7:129 (1893).

Law in place of Judge Jeremiah Smith who had resigned. Tradition has it that Dean Thayer urged Pound's appointment because of Pound's "Liberty of Contract." [19]

The first fruit of Pound's Harvard professorship was his 1911–12 paper "The Scope and Purpose of Sociological Jurisprudence." [20] This was a sort of confession of faith, a summation of Pound's studies in jurisprudence up to that time. Characteristically, the paper was taxonomical, dividing the field of jurisprudence with a minuteness that to the nonadept in that science appears overrefined and a little wearying. But when he comes to sociological jurisprudence in the last part of his paper, even the casual reader senses Pound's warm enthusiasm. Here, evolved, is the theme of his "Liberty of Contract" paper of 1909. He traces the influence of science on law in the late nineteenth century and observes:

It has been felt for some time that the entire separation of jurisprudence from the other social sciences, the leaving of it to itself on the one hand and the conviction of its self-sufficiency on the other hand, was not merely unfortunate for the science of law on general considerations, in that it necessitated a narrow and partial view but was in large part to be charged with the backwardness of law in meeting social ends, the tardiness of lawyers in admitting or even perceiving such ends, and the gulf between legal thought and popular thought on matters of social reform. Not a little of the world-wide discontent with our present legal order is due to modes of juristic thought and juridical method which result from want of "team-work" between jurisprudence and the other social sciences.

That law must serve men's interests is now so commonly accepted that most men are unconscious of any other conceivable point of view. Yet Pound, an extremely practical man, felt the need to demonstrate the point in 1911, using all his somewhat ponderous apparatus of jurisprudential learning. His is a large part of the credit for making this point of view obvious. And even in our day the dean of a great law school has felt it necessary to restate the same point.[21] In 1913 Pound was made Carter

[19] Paul Lombard Sayre in his biography of Pound tells how Pound's "Liberty of Contract" helped bring Pound to Harvard. See Sayre, *The Life of Roscoe Pound* (Iowa City, 1948), p. 155. The chronology is there a little confused. In 1964 Mr. Justice Frankfurter told Professor Mark DeWolfe Howe that Pound's article had helped persuade the Harvard faculty to invite Pound to join them.

[20] Parts 1–3, *Harvard Law Review*, 24:591, 25:140, 25:489.

[21] Eugene V. Rostow, "American Legal Realism and the Sense of the Profes-

Professor of General Jurisprudence, most appropriately in view of his dominant interest.

On April 7, 1913, Harvard's Governing Boards promoted Joseph Warren from instructor in law to professor of law. He had for four years been either a lecturer or an instructor, and for part of that time had been both at once. Students of his day remember with awe his third-year course in future interests.[22] They remember with admiration the formal morning coat and high stiff collar he wore for lectures; they recall the urbane courtesy which earned him the sobriquet of Gentleman Joe. They are grateful for the kindly hospitality of his house in Milton. Joseph Warren was destined to be vice-dean and acting dean of the School at various times in his long career. He became Weld Professor Emeritus in 1942 and died later that year.

On September 1, 1914, Felix Frankfurter became a professor of law at Harvard. He continued a member of the faculty until 1939 when he became a justice of the Supreme Court of the United States. During that quarter-century he injected into the Harvard corporate personality a new dash of color. Of course every man of strong and confident intelligence is quite different from every other, but some are more different than others and Frankfurter was more different than most. He was a complex man, at once intellectually humble and intellectually arrogant; a gentle man and an irritable scold; open-minded and opinionated. He could and did attract disciples who worked valiantly in his seminars, hoping for the reward of his approval. For brilliant men he was a strong stimulant. He was a gadfly and a patron. One seeks other, equally inconsistent figures of speech to describe this coruscating person.

Frankfurter was born in Vienna in 1882, came to New York when he was twelve years old, and grew up in that city's public schools. He graduated from the College of the City of New York

sion," in his collected essays published as *The Sovereign Prerogative* (New Haven, 1962), p. 3.

[22] For the enlightenment of any reader without the law, we here explain that sometimes a man may wish to give property by deed or by will, but give it far in the speculative future. This farsighted benefactor might, for example, wish to endow his future grandsons, though not yet married himself. Here are many intricate mysteries stemming from an ancient feudal policy to have only fighting men hold land, and from a much more recent social interest in keeping all property freely salable. Unborn grandsons can neither go forth to war nor sign deeds. Some of these complications W. Barton Leach has simplified by drafting up-to-date legislation; but enough remain to provide a tidy income for those medical specialists in gastric ulcers who have lawyers for patients.

at twenty, worked for a year in the New York City Tenement House Department to save a little money, and went up to Cambridge to enroll in the Harvard Law School. Like everyone else he was somewhat frightened at first, deciding that the pace was too fast for him to compete; the students were too bold for him. He changed his mind on both points; the School soon delighted him. He led his class, was an editor of the *Law Review*, and during the summer after his graduation helped Professor Gray with volumes five and six of Gray's *Cases on Property*. Then he went off to New York to work in the busy and prosperous office of Hornblower, Byrne, Miller and Potter at a yearly salary of $1000. However, Frankfurter's law school record here intervened. President Theodore Roosevelt had just appointed Henry L. Stimson [23] United States attorney for the Southern District of New York; in 1906 Stimson, canvassing the ablest graduates of good law schools to staff his office, offered Frankfurter $750 a year as an assistant district attorney. Frankfurter hesitated, and then went with Stimson; it was the first demonstration of his lifelong fascination by federal government. At the end of Roosevelt's term in March 1909 Stimson returned to private practice, taking Frankfurter with him. In 1910 Taft appointed Stimson secretary of war; Stimson took Frankfurter along to Washington as law officer of the War Department's Bureau of Insular Affairs, the agency in overall charge of Puerto Rico, San Domingo, the Panama Canal, and the Philippines. Young Felix Frankfurter could be uncommonly valuable in the government of these new overseas possessions; furthermore he was available for miscellaneous emergencies whenever Secretary Stimson might call on him. Such bright young men are useful to have around.

Frankfurter enjoyed Washington. He lived in a house he and some congenial friends rented at 1727 19th Street, where they entertained interesting celebrities with brilliant and witty talk. Frankfurter argued in the Supreme Court of the United States six or eight appeals from the Supreme Courts of Puerto Rico and the

[23] Stimson studied at the Harvard Law School from 1888 to 1890. Like Roscoe Pound, his contemporary at the School, he left without an LL.B. However, in 1889 Stimson took an A.M. The 1888–89 Harvard University catalogue (p. 184) provided that a Bachelor of Arts who for one year pursued appropriate courses in the Law School might become a Master of Arts; but the student must have "no intention or expectation of counting the same study toward the degree of Bachelor of Laws." If he took the full course for the law degree and passed his examinations "with high credit" he could take both the LL.B. and the A.M. Stimson followed the first alternative.

Philippines; he began to feel quite at ease in the old Supreme Court Room. When Theodore Roosevelt began his Bull Moose campaign for the presidency in 1912, Frankfurter offered to resign, telling Stimson that he proposed to support Roosevelt. But Stimson on his own initiative got Taft's authority for Frankfurter to stay on in the Department, and so he stayed, openly supporting the President's Progressive opponent. Undoubtedly both Taft and Stimson saw that Frankfurter's usefulness as an able public servant outweighed his defection as an amateur politician. His allegiance to the Bull Moosers would make little or no difference in the campaign. Frankfurter was welcomed by all three sides of the 1912 political triangle: when Woodrow Wilson took office in 1913, his Secretary of War, Lindley M. Garrison, got Frankfurter to continue in the Bureau of Insular Affairs. His party reliability was questionable but his brains and energy were beyond doubt.

Then one day early in 1914 a letter from Edward H. Warren, redoubtable young professor of law who had been a particular friend of Frankfurter's in law school, tendered him the School's invitation to join its faculty as a full professor. The prospect was both attractive and worrisome. All his life Frankfurter was drawn between activism and scholarship. Now friends advised him against Harvard. Justice Holmes reminded him of the intellectual dangers of developing his opinions in a cloistered community with no practical responsibility for conclusions. Stimson, too, thought the move would be a mistake; he said Frankfurter was unusually well equipped for work in government, and that able public servants were in shorter supply than legal scholars. Obviously Frankfurter was a man to prize. Stimson told Dean Thayer of the larger available stock of potential professors; Thayer invited Stimson to name a few. Frankfurter disregarded Holmes's and Stimson's advice and accepted Harvard's invitation. His formal appointment came immediately, to take effect the following September. He left Washington early in the summer of 1914 and spent the next weeks in the Law School stacks, catching up with the judicial decisions reported since 1906 when he had graduated. In September he began teaching the second-year course in public service companies, and in the spring semester he taught first-year criminal law.[24]

[24] Most of this account of Frankfurter's early career comes from Phillips, *Felix Frankfurter Reminisces*, a book of Frankfurter's memoirs recorded on tape.

"Roscoe Pound was perhaps the last great generalist of the law . . . His green eyeshade was . . . made necessary, he said, by the weakness of his eyes — though they served him as the window to millions of words for more than ninety-three years." Dean Griswold, July 7, 1964.

Pound chose Coke's bold admonition to King James — NON SVB HOMINE SED SVB DEO ET LEGE — to inscribe in 1928 over the portal of the enlarged Langdell Hall.

Thayer and Pound

Between Ames's disabling illness in November 1909 and Thayer's death in September 1915, the most important events in the School's life were these three new appointments to the faculty — those of Austin Wakeman Scott, Roscoe Pound, and Felix Frankfurter. The names speak for themselves.

3

Thayer died September 14, 1915, leaving the School without a dean, two weeks before the fall term was to open. The Corporation named Professor Scott, then thirty-one years old, as acting dean, but for the permanent deanship, on the following January 10, they selected Roscoe Pound. He took up his duties on the fourteenth of February 1916. The task he undertook was a heavy one; prophetically he had described the duties of a dean in a graceful, brief paper memorializing Dean Thayer.[25] If Pound had taken time to write a longer analysis of his new duties as he took them up, he undoubtedly would have divided the task with scientific minuteness, preparing a sort of phytogeography of deanship. To foster and maintain a great school, a dean must ensure that it attracts great scholar-teachers, who, to be sure, are drawn by talented students. And, like any other leader, he must continually demonstrate his own intellectual achievements. At least as early as 1916 the Law School had become far more than a place where students learned a calling; it had become a place of leadership in the policies of government. Thus its dean inevitably takes a significant part in American public life. With all this he must provide and administer an expensive, complex physical plant. He must maintain and increase a library adequate to scholarship in any field of man's law and government. He must house all this activity, not only conveniently, but with sufficient grace to show that in his school men study the law, as Holmes put it, "in the grand manner." All this Pound, with an astonishingly small staff of administrators, did well at Harvard.

He took over Thayer's complete administrative staff of two persons. One was May McCarthy, the Dean's secretary, who typed the countless manuscripts which he wrote in pencil; filed his papers and then found them again; presided with benign severity over the admission of visitors; and was still faithfully

[25] *Harvard Law Review*, 29:9 (1915).

serving Roscoe Pound when he died forty-eight years later. The other administrator was Richard Ames, LL.B. 1909, Dean Ames's son. As secretary of the School, Ames handled all admissions and records. His bright charm was the new student's first introduction to the School.

Immense energy enabled Pound to get through his incredible array of work. He came to his Langdell Hall office at seven o'clock in the morning to grind the day's administrative grist. He made time for omnivorous reading and continuous writing. He prided himself on his ability to teach the courses of any professor who fell ill. He ran an informal student loan fund. At any hour of the day or night he would appear in a police station on behalf of any one of his students so unfortunate as to become involved with the Cambridge guardians of the peace. He was tireless in student activities. After a gruelling day he would judge an evening moot court with gruff severity, or attend a student dinner with wholehearted enjoyment. He loved to sing. Sometimes after dinner young men could persuade him to sound out the verses of his song about Dives who under trying circumstances asked the Devil for a "brandy and sodium," only to be told,

> "Just 'cause you were on the stock exchange up in Jerusalem,
> You needn't think that you can run this ancient institutium."

The company would shout the chorus

> Ho Azuram
> Ho Azuram
> Halle-alle-ooia.
> Ho Azuram!

In April 1917, only a little over a year after Pound took over the deanship, Congress declared war on Germany. War hit the School hard. Eugene Wambaugh at the age of sixty-three went on duty in Washington as an Army judge advocate. The Secretary of War, Newton D. Baker, telegraphed Felix Frankfurter to come to Washington for the weekend. Frankfurter packed his bag and caught a train; the weekend lasted until the fall of 1919. Frankfurter became assistant to the Secretary of War, secretary and counsel to the President's Mediation Commission, assistant to the Secretary of Labor from 1917 to 1918, and in 1918 chairman of the War Labor Policies Board.[26] Professor Hill [27] too went on leave for the duration of the war. Wambaugh and Frankfurter came back when the war was over; but Arthur Hill never returned to academic existence.

The war demonstrated the faculty's potential usefulness for emergency government service, and the United States has ever since continued using Law School professors in peacetime and wartime. Of course this has made administrative complexities; rearrangement of teaching duties or provision of a replacement is often difficult. But the faculty to which the professor returns is strengthened by his new experience and judgment; and the availability of wise and detached experts, indifferent to political bounty, has added to government a resource otherwise unavailable.

War changed student life much more than the life of professors. Young men fight wars. In September 1916 the School had 850 students. In September 1918 seventy men, none physically fit for field service, constituted the School's total enrollment. The Armistice of November 11, 1918, brought a rush of veterans returning from the services. The faculty kept registration open until December 1 to take care of them, and fifty-eight students enrolled during this extension. Obviously demobilization was going to continue for many months and students would be coming back at irregular times. The faculty held a special session of the School from February through August 1919, and for this term permitted registration as late as the first of March. In the Register of the Law School announcing the special sessions appears a regulation, repeated with a minor change in the Register of 1919–20, admitting as candidates for the LL.B. "Students who have completed three years of the prescribed course of a college of high grade and left college to enter the military or naval service of the United States or of one of the countries allied with the United States, upon producing certificates of their college work and proper evidence of furlough or discharge from the service." [28]

[26] Many things concerning the School of 1903–1960 can be found in Phillips, *Felix Frankfurter Reminisces.*

[27] Arthur Dehon Hill, LL.B. 1894; professor of law, 1916–1919. He came, after long trial experience, to teach evidence; the war called him away on leave after a short professorship, and he resigned his chair in 1919.

[28] The 1919–20 register offers admission to nondegree men only if they were in the service at least six months.

Three hundred and seven students enrolled by March 1, 1919, and many more would have done so but for the necessity of fixing that cut-off date. The total number of men in the regular session 1918–19 and the special session from February to August 1919 came to 435, a bit over half the prewar registration. The faculty of the School, which had thus run two partly concurrent programs of instruction in 1918–19, finished the summer session on August 30, 1919, and began the regular fall schedule three weeks later at the usual time, September 22, 1919. In 1919–20 the School had 883 students, and in 1920–21, 946.

Student life in the 1920's had fewer amenities than it has since acquired. In 1924–25 the School had increased to 1201 students; in 1925–26, to 1325. Of these only a minor fraction could find dwelling space in Hastings Hall, though law students had first call on its rooms. A few men could live here and there in other Harvard buildings. Some found pleasant quarters in the Episcopal Theological School's Winthrop Hall, but when these resources were exhausted there were still far too many men who, each summer and early fall, were obliged to trudge Cambridge streets and ring doorbells, looking for rooms to rent. Sometimes they did find quarters that were charming. A student of that time remembers two elderly ladies who then rented rooms in their dwelling on Brattle Street, now taken over by Radcliffe College. They looked after their young tenants with gentle kindness, which in cold weather prompted them to maintain a hard-coal fire in each student's fireplace. The luxury of coming in from a bitter winter night to find a glowing mass of coal in an iron grate! A fireplace, in those days, was still standard equipment for university rooms; the Harvard houses [29] built in the late 1920's and early 1930's have a fireplace in each undergraduate's study. Law students quartered in Hastings or Winthrop could, too infrequently, find time to sit for an hour in front of a wood fire, doze or talk with a friend, or read a novel, and forget for a little while the nagging urge to make the most of every minute, to read and abstract cases, or to make a connected summary of a mass of classroom

[29] To those who may be unfamiliar with Harvard, I might explain that beginning with the later years of the Lowell presidency, each Harvard College student, after his freshman year, has become a member of one of nine colleges within the college, called houses, where student lives are centered, where students take meals together, study, and live with some junior faculty. The houses are, to a degree, analogues of the Oxford and Cambridge colleges.

notes. Young men who had to watch every penny, or who applied too late for college rooms, were apt to end up in moldy or rickety quarters in a deteriorated lodging house whose depressing effect was not entirely alleviated by the fact that most waking hours were spent at work in the Langdell or Austin reading rooms. Few students were married compared to the substantial numbers since World War II.

After 1924–25 there was no provision for university meals near at hand, such as the Harkness Commons have provided since 1950. Memorial Hall, until the end of 1924–25, still served anyone who wished to sign on. Its Great Hall had a certain sentimental magnificence, with its high pseudo-Gothic beams, stained glass, refectory tables of varnished wood, its reminders of a war then remembered by few living men. For $8.50 a week students could there indulge themselves in the luxury of food served by waiters. Law students dined in Memorial Hall with men from many other parts of the university — a decided advantage in an academic community whose segments tended too much to departmental parochialism, and in which a broader acquaintance was wholesome for everybody.

Memorial Hall dining ended in June 1925; law students thereafter could board at the Union, but it was a long way off. Still, at noon a good many men rushed just as far to the Square for lunch. A favored spot was the Georgian Cafeteria on Dunster Street, long-since disappeared. It was then known to an elite among its patrons as "Holt's," perhaps because of some predecessor restaurateur of that name on the same spot. Use of the name gave cachet to the user. The theory that the establishment had been founded by Lord Chief Justice Sir John Holt, who lived 1642–1710, advanced by some legal historians among its patrons, has unfortunately never been authenticated. With Holt's is associated a pleasant memory in the mind of one habitué, a picture of a noonday in 1924 — young Professor Zechariah Chafee serving lunch to several small Chafees and hurrying to and from the counter to bring the innumerable glasses of milk demanded by the rising Chafee generation.

A less elaborate but equally famed victualler was Jimmie's Lunch, then on Massachusetts Avenue about where the Holyoke Center now stands. A man in a hurry could find a place to stand at Jimmie's counter, bolt something to eat, and hurry back to

Langdell and ever waiting work. Dean Pound and a number of apprentices of the law used to frequent Jimmie's establishment. Francis Plimpton in classic numbers simultaneously immortalized the Lunch and the Dean.[30]

CAP. V

Now first upon the list comes Pound,
  Like ancient Sacrobosco,
Who was a learned man, and sound —
  No sounder than our Roscoe.

The common law's most shining light,
  They herald him — the bunch
With whom he takes a frugal bite
  Each noon at Jimmie's Lunch.

In Jurisprudence you should hear
  Him talk in manner quizzic
Of Pufendorf, DeGroot, Beaussire,
  All jurists metaphysic.

He knows the laws from nuts to soups,
  And classifies decisions
In eighteen heads, and forty groups,
  With ninety subdivisions.

The Lincoln's Inn Society, named by youthful arrogation for its more revered English predecessor, is the oldest and was then the only student dining club. At that time it occupied a pleasantly worn bow-windowed house on Brattle Street near Appian Way, where Albert the steward took excellent care of the members. There they found occasional half hours of relaxed friendship in rare intermissions of the mingled ambition, anxiety, and dog-weariness that then made up a large part of the sensations of student life.

In the year 1925–26 the first-year class had 575 students; in its second year, that class numbered 363; 351 survived into 1927–28. In June of 1928, 320 of these took their LL.B. degrees. The risk of failure was real; the prizes for the successful were proportionately great. The *Law Review* Board when the first-year

---

[30] *In Personam. A Lyrical Libel* (1924). Plimpton took his LL.B. in 1925. In addition to the acknowledged distinction of membership in that remarkable class, he has more recently represented his country at the United Nations as ambassador. Plimpton's poem, privately and elegantly printed, he deposited in the Law School library in April 1925, with a dedicatory inscription "To the Harvard Law School Library as a slight revenge for the hours spent there."

grades of 1925–26 came in, took the top 14 men as members. If
Review men could hold their rank in the examinations at the
end of their second year, they knew they were probably headed
for graduation with honors.[31] Five during their third year became officers of the *Review*. Top men, on graduation, had their
pick of places with leading law firms. Two would get secretaryships with Supreme Court Justices Holmes and Brandeis. An
occasional man on his graduation was invited to join the School's
faculty. Classmates knew and envied the grades of all these
magnates. But for each such brilliant success, about ten men
were dismissed as failures; sometime in the summer of 1926 over
200 men, almost 37 percent of the class who had entered the
preceding September, received letters informing them that because of academic failure they could not return to the school.[32]
For these, admission had been a mistake.

The School's faculty were entirely conscious of this sad situation and were attempting to correct it. A larger and larger number
of students sought to enter the School each year and the School
attempted to keep down enrollment by stiffening requirements.
In 1924 the faculty had required that, for admission, graduates
of "first-list colleges" must have "meritorious college records,"
standing in the upper three quarters of their classes, while
graduates of "second-list colleges" must stand in the upper
fourth. Despite this, the entering class in 1926 numbered 694. The
faculty also made new regulations requiring better performance
to remain in the School after admission. Up to 1920 a student
could continue under "conditions," despite two failed courses,
which obviously he had to make up to get his degree. Beginning
in 1920–21 a student could not remain if he failed in more than
one course. In 1925–26 and thereafter a student who failed in
one course could remain in the School only if he had an average
5 percent better than the passing grade, or had at least two C's.[33]

[31] *Cum laude* through 1926. Thereafter honor degrees were awarded as in
the college, *summa*, *magna*, and *cum laude*.

[32] The figure of 37 percent, 212 men, seems to include all first-year students
not returning in September 1926, without allowance for students leaving voluntarily; thus the percentage of "failures" may be a little lower than 37. But in any
event it was large. See the discussion of the serious problem of failures in the
Dean's report for 1925–26, pages 185f; his report for 1927–28, pages 204f; and the
report of 1928–29, page 184. The whole subject was explored at length by the
Committee on Curriculum of 1934–35, in a report now in the School's archives.
The Dean's reports are included in the Harvard University Annual Reports.

[33] See the Dean's report for 1927–28; page 205 of the Harvard University

One result of this stringency was the 37 percent cut of first-year men at the end of the year 1925–26.

The School continued to struggle for at least a decade thereafter with this matter of academic casualties. The problem involved, of course, a conflict in policies. The policy effective in 1925 provided for comparatively open admissions, followed, after a trial year, by competitive examinations to decide who could stay to profit from the school's limited facilities. On the other hand conceivably the School could admit students on competitive examination, selecting only those men who could profit by the School's offerings, and thereafter retain all students save those few who, as it later developed, had been unwisely admitted. Throughout Pound's twenty years of deanship, the first, more Spartan policy obtained. In the Register for 1935–36 appear the records of the student population in 1934–35. In that year the School had 593 first-year students, 417 second-year, and 374 third-year men. Quite evidently many more still entered than could survive.

A resulting sentiment among survivors was a predictable but not entirely wholesome bravado. Survival gave a man a somewhat brutal pride; he repeated to himself "Cowards never started and the weak died on the way." The School did sort out strong men, as their record in the practice of law and in government service later demonstrated. Students learned to pace themselves; they slept, took exercise, ate, and studied on a system. There was still room in it all for great friendships, based on common respect for achievement, attained through intelligence and endurance under shared stress. And the School's faculty never sank into complacency after the fashion of 1850's, never accepted the accustomed as a demonstrated optimum. Throughout the School's records there recurs, after 1925, a theme of self-appraisal. The faculty were continually asking themselves whether they could not find better ways to select students, and better ways to teach them.

4

The Russian revolution which began in 1917 gravely disturbed many Americans, who thought they saw Russian Communist in-

---

Annual Reports for that year; and the Law School Register for 1925–26, page 11. If the School were a medieval monastery these publications would be its annals.

fluence in the United States, and wanted it put down by vigorous measures. Academic defense of free speech and free political advocacy fell under much suspicion. Obviously a man could not support the right to advocate doctrine unless he liked the doctrine. Symptomatic of much in American law that was to develop during the next forty years was a reaction evoked from some readers of three articles which appeared in the *Harvard Law Review* in 1919, 1920, 1921, written by Professor Zechariah Chafee, Jr. Chafee was born in Providence in 1885, was a Brown A.B. of 1907, and a Harvard LL.B. of 1913. He was one of the most charming of men. He had been an undergraduate classicist at Brown with a graceful talent for rendering Latin verse in English. When his first-year Harvard Law School grades were so high that a *Review* Board editorship was a matter of course, he declined that awe-inspiring honor because the prospect bored him. He practiced law for three years in Providence; then while Austin Scott was acting dean in the fall of 1915 the faculty voted to invite Chafee to return to the Law School as an assistant professor. To young Dean Scott fell the honorable duty of going to Providence and persuading Zechariah Chafee to begin his forty years of service on the Harvard faculty.

In 1916, despite the war in Europe, an afterglow of the Wilson domestic humanitarianism still shone in the United States. Chafee wrote in 1950 of those days a third of a century earlier:

forward-looking men and women were still engaged in rethinking our traditional political, economic, and social conceptions and considering how they could be best altered to meet the new needs of an industrial and highly developed country. All possibilities were open to examination, under the guiding principle, "Prove all things; hold fast that which is good." Men's minds moved with a freedom which is now incomprehensible, for thinking had not yet been hardened into queer shapes by the emotions aroused by war and conflicting reactions to the Russian Revolution.[34]

This happy state of affairs ended early in 1917; the United States declared war on Germany, and a wave of patriotic intolerance swept over the country. The Congress passed the Espionage Act of June 15, 1917,[35] and reinforced it with amendments of May 16, 1918. The 1917 act was not limited to espionage; it

[34] Chafee, "Harold Laski and the Harvard Law Review," *Harvard Law Review*, 63:1398 (1950).
[35] 40 Stat. at L. 217.

also forbade a list of disruptive statements, including attempts to cause insubordination in the military, or to obstruct the recruiting or enlistment services. The 1918 amendment prohibited obstructing the sale of United States bonds "except by way of bona fide and not disloyal advice," and penalized language intended to bring into contempt or disrepute the form of government of the United States, the Constitution, the flag, or United States military uniforms; it penalized speech urging curtailment of war production and the like. The maximum penalty was a $10,000 fine, or twenty years in prison, or both.

The federal government began a series of prosecutions under these statutes, including one case against a man named Abrams and several codefendants for distributing leaflets urging that munitions workers stop producing war material which could be used by American and Allied troops against revolutionary forces in Russia. Abrams and various codefendants were convicted in the United States District Court for the Southern District of New York. Henry D. Clayton,[36] the trial judge, announced when imposing sentence: "we are not going to help carry out the plans mapped out by the Imperial German Government, and which are being carried out by Lenine and Trotsky. I have heard of the reported fate of the poor little daughters of the Czar, but I won't talk about that now. I might get mad. I will now sentence the prisoners." He sentenced Abrams and two others to twenty years' imprisonment, and a fine of $1000. Ultimately the Supreme Court affirmed the conviction of Abrams and his codefendants, with Holmes and Brandeis dissenting.[37] This was one of the cases in which Holmes stated his "clear and present danger" standard for determining the constitutionality, under the First Amendment, of a statute proscribing public expression. Holmes concluded his Abrams dissent: "I regret that I cannot put into more impressive words my belief that in their conviction upon this indictment the defendants were deprived of their rights under the Constitution of the United States. Mr. Justice Brandeis concurs with this opinion."

In June 1919, Professor Chafee [38] published in the *Harvard Law Review*, under the title "Freedom of Speech in War-Time,"

[36] Author of the Clayton Anti-Trust Act of 1914. He had been a congressman from Alabama.
[37] 250 U.S. 616 (1919).
[38] He was appointed professor of law on June 18, 1919.

the first of his three papers on the Espionage Act cases. In April 1920 he published "A Contemporary State Trial — the United States versus Jacob Abrams et al." This was a vigorous, detailed criticism of the conviction of Abrams and the others, and of the severity of the sentences. Chafee ended his piece in the April 1920 *Law Review:*

Most of the discussion of the Abrams case has turned on the question whether the decision of the United States Supreme Court affirming these convictions was right or wrong. It seems to me much more important to consider the case as a whole, and ask how the trial and its outcome accord with a just administration of the criminal law.

The systematic arrest of civilians by soldiers on the streets of New York City was unprecedented, the seizure of papers was illegal, and the evidence of brutality at Police Headquarters is very sinister. The trial judge ignored the fundamental issues of fact, took charge of the cross-examination of the prisoners, and allowed the jury to convict them for their Russian sympathies and their anarchistic views. The maximum sentence available against a formidable pro-German plot was meted out by him to the silly futile circulars of five obscure and isolated youngsters, misguided by their loyalty to their endangered country and ideals, who hatched their wild scheme in a garret and carried it out in a cellar. "The most nominal punishment" was all that could possibly be inflicted, in Justice Holmes' opinion, unless Judge Clayton was putting them in prison, not for their conduct, but for their creed. The wife of one prisoner has been deported to Russia without even a chance for farewell, while he and his friends are condemned for their harmless folly to spend the best years of their lives in American jails. The whole proceeding, from start to finish, has been a disgrace to our law, and none the less a disgrace because our highest court felt powerless to wipe it out. The responsibility is simply shifted to the pardoning authorities, who except for the release of the unlucky Rosansky have as yet done nothing to remedy the injustice, and to Congress which can change or abolish the Sedition Act of 1918, so that in future wars such a trial and such sentences for the intemperate criticism of questionable official action shall never again occur in these United States.

Harcourt, Brace and Howe in 1920 published Chafee's book *Freedom of Speech* which reprinted much of his *Harvard Law Review* articles on the Espionage Act cases. In March 1920 Dean Pound, the Law School librarian Edward B. Adams, Professor Frankfurter, and Professor Francis B. Sayre all signed an application asking executive clemency for the prisoners.

At all institutions of learning, utterances of professors quite often disturb alumni. In May 1921 Austen G. Fox of the Board of Overseers submitted to that body a "Statement for the information of the President and Fellows of Harvard College and the Board of Overseers of Harvard College with respect to certain teachers in the Harvard Law School." On the first page was the following pronouncement:

New York, 3 May, 1921.
To:
    The Board of Overseers of Harvard University;
    The undersigned have read the accompanying statement prepared by Mr. Austen G. Fox of New York, at the request of a group of graduates of the Harvard Law School, and deem its contents of sufficient importance to request its careful consideration by the Board of Overseers.

Yours very truly,

William Byrd,	Peter B. Olney,
Guy Cary,	F. K. Pendleton,
William M. Chadbourne,	Dean Sage,
Joseph H. Choate, Jr.,	James R. Sheffield,
Russell Gray,	John S. Sheppard,
Edward Harding,	Albert Stickney,
John H. Iselin,	Archibald G. Thacher,
Camillus Kidder,	Eliot Tuckerman,
James Gore King,	Edgar H. Wells,
James B. Ludlow,	Beekman Winthrop.[39]

Mr. Fox's statement recited:

When a professor in the Harvard Law School puts forth in the *Harvard Law Review* misleading statements of fact, and writes in a petition for executive clemency, in which petition the whole truth is not stated, and repeats his misleading statements in a published book, the question is: Is he fit longer to be entrusted with the training of youth? . . .

The question is much the same, whether he knew that his statements were false or whether he made them with reckless indifference as to whether they were true or false. The question remains even if the professor be acquitted of intentional falsehood, or reckless indifference to the truth, but takes no pains to correct his misleading statements in the *Review*, even after his attention had been called to the truth . . .

Attention is invited, not only to the misleading statements of fact made by the writer of the article in the *Harvard Law Review* for April 1920, but also to the acts of other teachers in the law school who united with the author of the article and others in adopting and

[39] Quoted by Yeomans in his *Abbott Lawrence Lowell*, p. 318.

endorsing the petition for pardon prepared by the attorney for the convicted defendants and united in presenting the petition to the President of the United States for the exercise of Executive Clemency. The action of the writer of the article in the *Harvard Law Review* and the action of the other teachers in the law school who signed the petition for clemency was a perpetuation of some of the misleading statements of fact contained in the article in the *Harvard Law Review*.[40]

The Board of Overseers referred Mr. Fox's statement to their Committee to Visit the Law School. The committee had fourteen members. Francis J. Swayze, chairman, was a judge of the highest court in New Jersey. The rest of the committee was equally distinguished; it included Benjamin N. Cardozo of the Court of Appeals of New York and later of the Supreme Court of the United States, William H. Dunbar, former partner of Justice Brandeis, Robert Grant, judge of the Probate Court in Boston, Augustus N. Hand, judge of the United States District Court in New York City, Julian W. Mack, judge of the United States Court of Appeals for the Second Circuit, Langdon Marvin of the New York bar, James M. Morton, Jr., United States district judge in Massachusetts, William Thomas of the San Francisco bar, Henry N. Sheldon, retired judge of the Supreme Judicial Court of Massachussetts, Jeremiah Smith of the Boston bar, William C. Boyden of the Chicago bar, John H. Wigmore, Dean of Northwestern University Law School, and Henry L. Stimson, former secretary of war.

On May 22, 1921, the committee met at the Harvard Club of Boston and conducted what thereafter used to be called "The Trial at the Harvard Club." Three members, Messrs. Boyden, Wigmore, and Stimson, were unable to attend. President Lowell, after taking counsel with Thomas Nelson Perkins [41] of the Harvard Corporation, met with the committee. The accused faculty members appeared. Lowell took charge of the operation, which turned into a battle between Lowell and Fox. Chafee gave a calm statement of the Abrams case, and his reasons for thinking it unfair. He concluded: "I come of a family that have been in America from the beginning of time. My people have been business people for generations. My people have been people of sub-

[40] Yeomans, *Abbott Lawrence Lowell*, pp. 320–321.
[41] LL.B. 1894. He was a greatly respected Boston lawyer, a member of the firm of Ropes and Gray, with a distinguished record of public service.

stance. They have made money. My family is a family that has money. I believe in property and I believe in making money, but I want my crowd to fight fair." [42] Frankfurter, when he was nearing the end of his life, said that this was one of the most impressive sentences he had ever heard.

Years after the Harvard Club Trial, Lowell wrote to a friend:

> It is the record of an excellent chance to do some fighting in the cause of free speech; and the result was not any too certain, for we carried the day by a vote of only 6 to 5 in the committee . . .
>
> I had not intended to conduct the case; but some members of the Law School were so excited that I had to do what would naturally have fallen to them . . . The vote practically to acquit Professor Chafee was, as I have said, 6 to 5, the majority being determined by Judge Cardozo . . .
>
> If one wants to maintain free speech, and open-minded justice, one will find one's self first and last at odds with every element in the community.

Still later in 1937, he wrote to Chafee: "I wonder what would have happened if they had succeeded in getting a majority of the committee? — Probably nothing at all; for I suspect the Overseers would have laid it on the table, or otherwise refused to confirm it. If they had censured you I suspect the whole, or a large part, of the Faculty of the Law School, including the Chair, might have gone overboard." [43] The Overseers Committee to Visit the Law School reported:

> In the matter of the statement of Austen G. Fox, Esq., with respect to an article by Professor Zechariah Chafee, Jr., in the Harvard Law Review of April, 1920, entitled "A Contemporary State Trial."

REPORT OF THE COMMITTEE TO VISIT THE LAW SCHOOL

To the Board of Overseers of Harvard College:

At a meeting of the Board of Overseers, held on the 9th day of May, 1921, a statement signed by Austen G. Fox, Esq., and an accompanying letter signed by certain graduates of the Harvard Law School with respect to an article by Professor Zechariah Chafee, Jr., in the April, 1920, number of the Harvard Law Review, and with respect to a petition for pardon signed by Dean Pound, Professors Frankfurter, Chafee and Sayre, and Mr. Adams, the Librarian of the Law School, were

---

[42] Phillips, *Felix Frankfurter Reminisces*, p. 177.

[43] In addition to the other accounts of the brouhaha over Chafee's Abrams piece, readers would do well to consult Morison's *Three Centuries of Harvard*, pp. 463f. "The Chair" who "might have gone overboard" was President Lowell.

referred to this committee to consider and report its conclusions to the Board of Overseers.

This committee had a hearing on the issues raised by this statement, at the Harvard Club of Boston, on the 22nd day of May, 1921, at which were present the President of the University, Mr. Fox and several of the gentlemen who signed the letter of transmittal, Dean Pound, Professors Chafee, Frankfurter and Sayre, Librarian Adams and others.

The committee has carefully considered the issues involved and begs to report as follows:

1.   The charge of impropriety in signing a petition for the pardon of Jacob Abrams was not sustained and was abandoned.

2.   The committee are unanimously of the opinion that Professor Chafee made no statements in his article which were consciously erroneous.

A majority of the committee are of the opinion that he made no statements in his article that were culpably negligent and so far as any material statements of law or fact may have been erroneous, the errors, if any, were in matters of opinion only.

A minority of the committee are of the opinion that the article contains erroneous statements of fact which should not have been made, and having been made, should have been corrected in the Harvard Law Review.

The committee therefore recommend that no further action be taken by the Board of Overseers.

Respectfully submitted,

For the Committee.

(Signed) FRANCIS J. SWAYZE,

Chairman.[44]

Professor Chafee published in the November 1921 *Harvard Law Review* a correction of a number of errors in his April 1920 article, "A Contemporary State Trial." The mistakes were inconsequential, with little or no bearing on the merit of Chafee's original criticisms or Abrams' trial and sentence. For example, Chafee had written that the Court had directed an acquittal of one prisoner; he corrected this to state that the jury acquitted him. Chafee had stated that the Abrams matter was Judge Clayton's first Espionage Act case; he corrected this to state that Judge Clayton had tried two or three previous Espionage Act cases, unreported so far as Chafee knew. Relying on a letter from Harry Weinberger, trial counsel for Abrams, Chafee had written "The wife of one prisoner has been deported to Russia

---

[44] Quoted by Chafee, *Harvard Law Review*, 35:9–10 (1921).

without even a chance for farewell." This Chafee struck out. He had described the defendants as "youngsters"; he corrected this to read "young aliens." There were other amendments of similar weight. At the worst the mistakes showed haste in checking unimportant details.

Chafee's stand for freedom showed his greatness of heart, which won the admiration and affection of faculty and students alike. At the 1924 Lincoln's Inn Christmas Dinner, Francis T. P. Plimpton read his justly celebrated poem *In Personam*, which contained, in its Capitulum IX, some elegant verses on Chafee.

CAP. IX

And now we've reached upon our lists
    Free speech's best Messiah,
The bulwark of all Bolshevists,
    Our Chafee, Zechariah.

Free speech? He surely uses it,
    For all his class room stories
Display a most abandoned wit —
    They're *contra bonos mores*.

A man named Abrams once was seen,
    By anti-Red retrievers,
To wave his hat and cheer Lenine,
    With most seditious vivas.

The cops then clubbed him on the head —
    The sound was quite euphonious —
Judge Clayton gave him life and said
    His conduct was felonious.

It angered Zach just through and through,
    This treatment governmental,
And in the Harvard Law Review
    He said it wasn't gentle.

On reading this, some lawyers said
    "It's plain there's treason to it!"
At first they thought our Zach a Red,
    And presently they knew it.

So very wroth these Wall Street peers
    Got up a strong petition,
And thus did get the Overseers
    To hold an Inquisition.

In Boston's Harvard Club they met,
    With awful portent dire;

Thayer and Pound

In righteous wrath each face was set —
    They said to Zechariah:

"Young man, if students hear you air
    Opinions any broader,
Just think what will become of their
    Respect for Law and Order!

"And now of course we don't propound
    Of freedom any blockage;
Call anything you like unsound —
    But make it villein socage!"

Now Zach gave way before the strength
    Of those irate grandmommas,
In fact apologized at length —
    For several misplaced commas.

Another unhappy criminal prosecution, gravely affected by a wave of resentment against "reds" and "radicals," was the trial for murder, the conviction, and the execution of two Italian radicals named Nicola Sacco and Bartolomeo Vanzetti. They were charged with committing murder during the holdup of a shoe-factory paymaster and his guard, in South Braintree, Massachusetts, on April 15, 1920. There has never been any doubt that somebody shot the paymaster and guard, and took the money. There has ever since been a serious dispute about the identity of the killers, and about the justice of the Sacco-Vanzetti trial.

On May 5, 1920, twenty days after the South Braintree shootings, police officers arrested Sacco and Vanzetti. Both were carrying loaded pistols; Sacco had 23 extra cartridges; Vanzetti had in his pocket three or four shotgun shells. In September 1920 a Norfolk County grand jury indicted the two men for the South Braintree murders. They came to trial at Dedham on May 31, 1921, before Superior Court Judge Webster Thayer and a jury.

The two Italians were well known among their associates as socialists and radicals, and during the war of 1917–18 they had gone to Mexico to evade the draft. The years 1919–1920 were a bad time for "red" draft-dodgers. Since 1919 the Attorney General of the United States, A. Mitchell Palmer, stirred by a series of bomb outrages including one on his own house, had started a vigorous effort to capture and deport alien Reds. Some measures taken by federal agents in the "Mitchell Palmer Raids" were violent and lawless. In May 1920 a group of twelve distinguished

American lawyers, including Roscoe Pound, Zechariah Chafee, and Felix Frankfurter of the Harvard Law faculty, had published a document entitled *Report upon the Illegal Practices of the United States Department of Justice.* Charles Evans Hughes, commenting on the revelations in this document, spoke of "violation of personal rights which savor of the worst practices of tyranny."[45] On the other hand much public opinion hardened against "the Reds"; and this reaction deeply affected the climate of the subsequent Sacco-Vanzetti trial.

Men accused of murder with pistol shots who are arrested carrying loaded pistols are, as a practical matter, obliged to take the stand in their own defense. The prosecutor, cross-examining Sacco and Vanzetti at length, brought out their radicalism and their draft-dodging. Judge Thayer allowed this questioning to go on to an unreasonable extent, although the prosecutor was obviously seeking to arouse the prejudices of a strongly patriotic, anti-red jury rather than to explore identification of the South Braintree gunmen. The prosecution's identification of Sacco and Vanzetti as the murderers rested on doubtful evidence, much of it elicited from witnesses who saw the holdup only for a very few seconds, under circumstances where careful observation was impossible. The prosecution's proof thus was weak; and the cross-examination concerning the defendants' radicalism could have been conclusive in the minds of the jurors. The jury found Sacco and Vanzetti guilty of murder.

During the remaining six years of the lives of the convicted men, their counsel made a series of unsuccessful legal moves to obtain a new trial. In the long effort to reverse the conviction, or at any rate to avert the execution, many prominent liberal Americans were active in the defendants' cause, and among these Felix Frankfurter was conspicuous. He had been in Europe when the South Braintree murder occurred, and so had heard nothing about it until sometime later. He paid little attention to the case until 1925, when William G. Thompson of the Boston bar became counsel for Sacco and Vanzetti. Thompson, an able trial lawyer whom Frankfurter greatly respected, moved for a new trial on newly discovered evidence. He argued that the District Attorney,

[45] See, for these matters Louis Joughin and Edmund M. Morgan, *The Legacy of Sacco and Vanzetti* (New York, 1948), p. 211. The authors give documentary references.

when preparing the case, had been unable to procure from a prosecution ballistics expert, Captain Proctor, a definite statement that in Proctor's opinion the bullet found in the body of one of the dead men came from Sacco's pistol. At the trial, the District Attorney had therefore adroitly asked this expert only whether the markings on the bullet were "consistent" with being fired from Sacco's pistol. To this question Captain Proctor had given an affirmative response; a jury, unaccustomed to fine distinctions of speech, could have taken Proctor's equivocal statement as an incriminating identification of the bullet. Frankfurter, shocked by this quibbling question and answer when men's lives were at stake, undertook to study the record of the trial to make up his own mind as to the justice or injustice of the procedure. As a result of his study he wrote an article for the March 1927 *Atlantic Monthly* expressing his conviction that the trial was unjust. Later in March Frankfurter expanded the article to a little book, *The Case of Sacco and Vanzetti*. In the April 25 Boston *Transcript* Dean Wigmore of Northwestern University Law School attacked Frankfurter's *Atlantic* article. Frankfurter stoutly replied in the next day's *Transcript*; a second-year law student named Erwin Griswold hurried to Harvard Square to buy a copy. Wigmore returned to the charge in the May 10 issue. Frankfurter counterattacked in the *Transcript* of May 11.

On May 4, 1927, counsel for the condemned men presented to the Governor of Massachusetts a petition for clemency, signed only by Vanzetti. Apparently Sacco was resigned to death. Governor Fuller appointed a committee of three — President A. Lawrence Lowell of Harvard; Samuel W. Stratton, President of the Massachusetts Institute of Technology; and Robert Grant, a retired probate judge — to advise the Governor on the exercise of clemency. On July 27, 1927, the committee reported to the Governor that the two men had been properly convicted, and on August 3, Governor Fuller denied executive clemency. On August 22, 1927, Sacco and Vanzetti were executed.

Outside university circles there was much resentment against Frankfurter for the effort he had made to save the condemned men; there was some even at Harvard. At one time President Lowell was seriously concerned about clamor for Frankfurter's dismissal, but Lowell stood firm for Frankfurter, as earlier he had for Zechariah Chafee. Lowell took the position that only moral turpitude would justify dismissal of a professor, and that Felix Frankfurter had here evidenced no moral turpitude since he was clearly sincere in his belief that Sacco and Vanzetti had been unjustly convicted. Nobody ever questioned the honesty of Frankfurter's opinion; indeed the deeper his belief, the more dangerous he appeared.

The Sacco-Vanzetti affair was at its height in 1926–27, during a Harvard Law School endowment campaign. As usual, talk went round that Frankfurter's activities had diminished gifts. A third of a century after the Sacco-Vanzetti case Felix Frankfurter was discussing [46] people who during the fund-raising effort of the mid-1920's had said "they wouldn't give any money as long as Frankfurter was on the faculty." Frankfurter remembered being comforted by one of his friends, either Samuel Eliot Morison or Grenville Clark, who told him that when people were not going to give anyhow, they liked to have somebody to blame for their own lack of generosity. Perhaps some admirers of Harvard's courage made gifts which more than made up these losses.

Of course the passing of the 1920's did not end criticism of the School for harboring professors with "radical" views. This action and reaction inheres in the existence of a free university; Harvard was to hear another outburst of like denunciation in the dozen years which followed World War II. The resemblance of a private university to the Supreme Court is sometimes remarkable: both are reasonably free from compulsion to follow majority pressures; both are exempt from the influences of political party maneuver; both are primarily intellectual rather than emotional. Both, for these reasons, are fated to attract popular hostility from time to time. But with the hostility is mingled some pride, grudging admiration and respect, a sort of wistful envy.

5

Raising money has always been an essential part of educational administration. When the university built the original southerly part of Langdell Hall in 1905–06, the School had about 700 stu-

[46] In *Felix Frankfurter Reminisces*, p. 177. For the Sacco-Vanzetti case, a good review is Joughin and Morgan, *The Legacy of Sacco and Vanzetti*. See also Frankfurter's *The Case of Sacco and Vanzetti* (Boston, 1927) and Yeomans, *Abbott Lawrence Lowell*. Frankfurter discussed the *Transcript–Herald* counter-battery in *Felix Frankfurter Reminisces*, pp. 215f.

dents. Twenty years later, with the same buildings, the School had twice that many. The faculty had eleven teachers of law in 1905; twenty years later twenty-six teachers of all ranks were on the staff. Clearly the twenty-year-old plan for enlarging Langdell Hall had to be restudied and put in effect; clearly funded support for the augmented faculty was required. A major effort to raise money was necessary if the School was to thrive.

In 1917–1919 Harvard had engaged in a general university endowment-raising campaign which included in its scope some provision for the Law School. The effort resulted in total additions to the Law School's endowment amounting to a little over $64,000. This was, of course, very welcome, but it would, at most, produce only a bit more than $3000 in annual revenue; it was not a major rise in the resources available to the School. The report of the university Treasurer for 1924–25 shows capital endowments of $647,883.97 for Law School professors' salaries; for library funds, of $371,644.66; for "scholarship, beneficiary and prize," of $172,021.24 — a total endowment invested in income-bearing funds amounting to $1,191,549.87. More significant than the capital figure was the yield of income. During 1924–25 the School spent $313,000; to this tuition fees contributed about $237,000; only $66,000 came from return on endowment.[47]

On October 21, 1924, the faculty appointed as a committee to consider plans for new buildings Professor Edward H. Warren, Chairman, and Professors Beale, Joseph Warren, Frankfurter, and Scott. This committee, as one would expect, took a broad view of its mission. Three weeks after its appointment it recommended that the School be more selective in its admissions "with a view to eliminating men who are not qualified successfully to do the work of students after admission," and that the School attempt to raise $4,200,000 of endowment. Both of these objectives had some relation to inadequate space. The number of students, teachers, and books, and the efficiency of work, were limited by the size of the School's structures. Expansion of numbers had to stop; and more space was necessary even for the existing students and teachers. For new buildings the Corporation would, very likely, advance money against expected income from tuition; but

[47] These figures come from the Treasurer's report for 1924–1925, p. 57; they are here stated at the nearest $1000. The School had miscellaneous receipts of $5000; the year's operations resulted in a deficit of $5000.

a larger and thus more expensive faculty was necessary to maintain adequate teaching and research, particularly in the then conspicuous fields of criminal justice and legislation. The School's expenses consumed its income; no money was left over for research professorships or for repayment of advances to complete Langdell Hall.

The Corporation accordingly approved a nationwide fundraising campaign, with support of research in criminal justice prominent among its purposes. This was the first major organized endowment effort in the School's history, though the principle of such an endeavor had been understood ever since Josiah Quincy in September 1831 had persuaded Nathan Dane to advance the money to build Dane Hall. The School asked an outstanding alumnus, Wilson M. Powell of New York, LL.B. 1898, to act as chairman of the executive committee in charge of the campaign. Powell organized a powerful committee, mostly made up of graduates of the School who were leaders of the American bar though he also included a few such distinguished nonalumni as Bishop Lawrence of Massachusetts and John G. Milburn, Elihu Root, and George W. Wickersham of the New York bar. The committee set up headquarters at the house of the Association of the Bar of the City of New York at 36 West 44th Street. It obtained the services of Ivy Lee and Associates, New York City experts in organization and publicity of fund-raising enterprises. The committee divided the United States into eighteen regions, each with a regional chairman and committee, and undertook to solicit subscriptions from every alumnus and every other likely contributor in the nation.

The School asked for $5,400,000. The announced purposes for which the funds were desired give some indication of the faculty's judgment of contemporary movements in the law. A million dollars was intended to endow five new professorships at $200,000 each; the incumbents were to devote themselves to criminal law, legislation, judicial organization and administration, legal history, and comparative law. The School planned to allocate $500,000 to endow graduate fellowships; $500,000 to support the library; $200,000 for a publication fund. The General Education Board, a Rockefeller foundation, pledged $750,000 toward this $2,200,000, on condition that the balance be obtained from other sources. The rest of the $5,400,000 was destined for additional endowment of the Royall, Dane, Bussey, and Story professorships at $150,000 each, totaling $600,000; for buildings and land including the completion and extension of Langdell Hall, $2,000,000; for bibliographical assistance, fellowships, scholarships, publication funds, and funds for special library purposes, $600,000.

The campaign literature eloquently explained, to fund workers across the country, substantial difficulties they should expect to meet. Much of the money would have to come from persons not trained in the law. To the layman the campaign's dominant theme — the value of legal research to American society — would probably seem questionable. The law was highly technical; its reform appeared unrelated to the ordinary man's daily welfare. It sometimes seemed a mass of exasperating rules, tending to retard rather than to forward the ends of true justice. In the mid-1920's, as in most times, much published criticism of the enforcement of criminal law and of the legal regulation of business reflected these views. The growing popularity of administrative boards and commissions, vested with judicial powers, demonstrated a belief that traditional legal machinery was cumbersome, ill-adapted to the handling of highly complex modern problems calling for experts. The campaign committee sought to demonstrate to prominent and prosperous men of affairs that the School proposed practical means to improve the very condition which dissatisfied them.

Careful preliminary preparation for the fund-raising effort occupied a year and a half. The committee then launched the campaign on October 22, 1926, with dinners in Philadelphia and Pittsburgh at which Dean Pound and Professor Beale addressed alumni and their guests. Other regional dinners followed, where assembled friends of the School heard other distinguished speakers setting forth its needs and the usefulness of the expected contributions. The committee held a climactic fund-raising dinner on November 9 at the house of the Association of the Bar of New York. For this occasion they prepared a particularly beautiful brochure of twenty-seven pages, printed on heavy paper, illustrated with old woodcuts. Its title page was set in antique type, suggested, as the brochure explained, by the title page of the 1751 pamphlet by Henry Fielding reproduced above. The pamphlet opened with a foreword, which began: "William H. Taft, Chief Justice of the Supreme Court of the United States,

THE LAW

has said: 'The administration of criminal law in the United States is a disgrace to civilization'."

The Committee naturally invited William D. Guthrie, the distinguished president of the Association of the Bar, to say a word of welcome on behalf of that association to the guests assembled at the association's house to hear the principal addresses of Senator Root, President Lowell, and Dean Pound. Mr. Guthrie with eloquence and enthusiasm praised the objects of the endowment drive and the "exquisitely printed pamphlet which you all have before you." However, he went on:

Whilst I am inclined unqualifiedly to laud this learned and attractive pamphlet, I must challenge a quotation contained in the "Foreword", but not repeated or in any way referred to in the body of the essay. It is the aphorism which is said to have been uttered by the present Chief Justice of the United States, to the effect that "the administration of criminal law in the United States is a disgrace to civilization." I venture to assert that that is a quite intemperate term and that the administration of criminal law in the United States is not a disgrace to civilization, and emphatically not so in New York, New Jersey, Pennsylvania, Connecticut, Massachusetts, and other important States. When Judge Taft first expressed this idea it was, so far as I can ascertain after careful examination, at the Yale Law School in June, 1905, and therefore long before he was President or Chief Justice . . .

The phrase "a disgrace to our civilization" has now for a generation been avidly seized upon by the muckraker and the sensational press here and abroad; every radical has quoted it eagerly in support of attacks upon Government; it has been the inspiration for many dangerous or objectionable, if not preposterous, proposals; and I am inclined to think that it has really done more harm than any other single utterance made by a prominent public man during the past thirty years. It has made the circle of the globe and has brought us into worldwide and unmerited discredit.

But, however this may be, it seems to me that it ought not to have been quoted by Harvard in this pamphlet as a statement made by a Chief Justice of the United States, or given the imprimatur of Harvard University at home and abroad by being quoted in the "Foreword", which is properly and generally interpreted as epitomizing the spirit of what follows. It was, moreover, quite unfair to attribute to him as Chief Justice language that he had used many years before he went on the bench. Perhaps in a new edition of the pamphlet this sentence will be deleted, and its place will be supplied by some other quotation from among the very many admirable, eloquent, lofty and inspiring utterances of the Chief Justice, who deserves our highest esteem and profound gratitude for many great, patriotic and noble public services.

Chairman Powell, fearing that the committee had made some error in the Taft quotation, or that its implications were perhaps not well supported by the Chief Justice's later views, accepted on the spot Guthrie's proposal that he delete the passage from any future edition of the pamphlet. Dean Pound told Guthrie that he had never seen the Foreword before, and that it had gone into the pamphlet without his knowledge. On November 9, the day of the dinner, Chief Justice Taft, who had evidently seen or heard of an advance copy, had written to Assemblyman Cuvillier of New York: "I think that the alleged quotation from what I may have said, though I cannot identify it, is most unfair in that it gives the impression that since I have been Chief Justice

I have expressed such view." The New York *Sun* on November 11 reported Chief Justice Taft's letter. Other papers supported or attacked the substance of the Taft statement; the controversy began to excite public interest.

On November 13 Chairman Powell wrote Guthrie explaining that in 1905 Taft had originally made substantially the Foreword's statement; that he had repeated it in 1907, and again in 1909 when he had been President, and again in 1913; and that as late as August 1923 when Taft was Chief Justice he had been on the platform at a meeting of the American Bar Association when a report of the Committee on Law Enforcement was read to the association. The committee's report quoted Taft's statement as made "by Chief Justice Taft a few years ago"; in the Chief Justice's presence the association accepted the report without protest by Judge Taft. Powell therefore withdrew his offer to reprint the brochure omitting Taft's statement. On November 15, 1926, Guthrie wrote to Powell an answering letter, later printed as a pamphlet.

November 15, 1926

Dear Mr. Chairman:

I am in receipt this morning of your letter of Saturday, November 13th, with reference to my remarks last Tuesday evening at the dinner in support of the Harvard Law School Endowment Fund, in which letter you advise me of your present views and of the fact that you consider it necessary to print your letter for wider circulation. I am, therefore, telephoning you a request that you kindly print my reply at the same time. Of course, in all such matters the old Roman maxim, which they established and scrupulously followed long before the development of Anglo-Saxon jurisprudence, you will readily recall: *Audi alteram partem.*

I have also received a letter on the same subject from Henry L. Stimson, one of the distinguished members of your Committee, in which he states that the practice of criminal law in New York *is* a disgrace to civilization, and that he thinks that he could convince me in ten minutes by things that are going on in our Criminal Courts Building in this city every day. He writes, of course, in the friendliest spirit, and he says only in order "to challenge on a single point your (my) otherwise good reputation for veracity" . . .

As to Mr. Stimson's statement that he could convince me in ten minutes by things that are going on daily in the criminal courts of the City of New York, I can only reply that even if he could so convince me as to the criminal courts in New York City, and that justice is there being disgracefully conducted, I would reply that that would not be proof that all the criminal courts in this city are a disgrace to civilization, and would not prove that the same conditions existed everywhere or even generally throughout the United States so as to justify quoting as a saying of a Chief Justice of the United States, that "The administration of criminal law in the United States is a disgrace to civilization." Besides, I am inclined to suggest that if conditions are really so bad, it would be advisable for him to communicate at once with the Grievance Committee and our Committee on Criminal Courts, Law and Procedure

Probably the Guthrie controversy did not hurt the fund drive. It augmented newspaper discussion of the School's plans; undoubtedly many prospective donors agreed with the Foreword. In the retrospect of forty years the 1925–27 campaign seems to have been well planned, to have been carried out with energy, to have sought funds from all available sources, to have appealed to every reasonable impulse for contributions. The abundant published material was well written. Another brochure, for example, nine by eleven and a half inches, printed on heavy paper in distinguished type, bore the title *For the Safety of the Citizen and the Protection of Business.* Its subtitle proposed "A Plan to Eliminate from the Administration of Justice in this Country Many Elements of Delay, Waste, Friction, and Uncertainty which are threatening the General Security and hampering Commerce and Industry." Opposite the table of contents of this document was a quotation from Elbert H. Gary, chairman of the Board of the United States Steel Corporation: "Hand in hand with economic progress there must be enacted, observed and enforced law and order. Law is the only thing that separates the cave-dwelling past from the present civilization." The brochure told readers that "The administration of criminal justice — the safeguarding of the general security and of individual life against abuse of criminal procedure — must be a subject of first consideration in any practical program of legal research . . . Something must be done to substitute sound legislation — complete and well thought out — for the present flood of ill-considered statutes and administrative rulings." Besides these two proposals the pamphlet proposed research into improved judicial procedure, legal history, and comparative law.

In addition to persuasive literature, the committee undertook a nationwide personal appeal to every graduate by members of local committees, by individual letters written by members of the central committee, and by telegrams urging the laggards to action. A printed statement from the Law School Endowment Fund dated June 15, 1927, reporting progress to that date, gave the total "amount needed by commencement" as $3,450,000. Of this, $1,141,447 had been pledged by contributors from among the School's ten thousand graduate and nongraduate alumni; $192,000 had been pledged by nonalumni; the General Education Board had pledged $750,000; and Mr. Rockefeller, $100,000. The university had agreed to advance $1,250,000 to build Langdell Hall, which the School would have to repay with interest, out of tuition payments. On June 16, 1927, Chairman Powell was writing letters to influential alumni to announce that only about $19,000 remained to be raised by commencement "to clinch the $100,000 gift from Mr. Rockefeller and $750,000 from the General Education Board." By that time the original goal of $5,400,000 had been quietly and prudently shelved, and the committee was instead making a realistic effort to achieve whatever matching arrangement with the General Education Board would bring about its maximum contribution. The Treasurer's books show that the committee made it.

Aside from failure to achieve the overoptimistic goal originally set, the endowment fund effort carried on between 1925 and 1927 was a great success. It added a little over $2,080,000 to the funds available for faculty salaries. It added $236,000 to the endowment of the library. It added $30,000 for scholarship endowment. The campaign in all raised $2,346,000, almost twice as much as the total endowment of the Law School had been on June 30, 1925. This added endowment, at a yield of 5.25 percent, the rate calculated in 1931 by the university Treasurer, would bring the School over $130,000 of new annual income. With other additions to the School's funds not directly ascribable to the 1925–1927 campaign the School's endowment on June 30, 1931, stood at about $4,350,000. Six years earlier its funds had totalled $1,191,500. The increase, accomplished when the general economy was slowing down, was an extraordinary achievement. The response of alumni throughout the United States, their willingness to work and to give, the contributions of nonlawyers in money and effort, all testify eloquently to the stature the School had attained in its first century of life.

6

The "crime wave" has for generations been a feature of American journalism and political comment;[48] the 1920's were not excepted. Public prints reported that a tide of crime was sweeping over American society; that the crime rate was rising to unprecedented heights. Social critics reported many different causes for this phenomenon. There was much talk of the "postwar generation," of a general breakdown of morals ascribable to the violence of war, talk of Communism and other brands of socio-economic upheaval, of widespread disregard of Prohibition by the citizenry with a concomitant rise in rum-running and illegal distilling. Undoubtedly there was much crime in America, and good citizens rightly deplored it. Official corruption aroused well-justified indignation. The Teapot Dome oil-lease scandals involved members of President Harding's cabinet; in 1926 the Chief Justice of the United States gave an interview to *Collier's* which that magazine published under the title of "Stop Helping the Criminal."[49] Conditions in New York were to give rise to the Seabury Investigation of 1930–31. One result of outraged public opinion was a series of crime surveys which began shortly after the close of World War I,[50] and which at intervals, in one form or another, have continued ever since. To a number of these the members of the School's faculty have made significant contributions. The first was the Cleveland survey of 1920–1922.

On May 9, 1920, on a street corner in Cleveland, Ohio, gunmen shot to death a man named Harold Kagy. Some witnesses said that Chief Justice William H. McGannon of the Cleveland Municipal Court was present when Kagy was shot. Judge McGannon was indicted for second-degree murder; a trial jury was deadlocked; a second trial jury acquitted McGannon. However he was then prosecuted and convicted of perjury for falsely testi-

[48] See, for example, Kamisar, "When the Cops Were Not Handcuffed," New York *Times*, November 7, 1965, Magazine Section, p. 34.

[49] See Alpheus T. Mason, *William Howard Taft: Chief Justice* (New York, 1964), p. 279.

[50] I do not mean to suggest that nothing of the kind arose before World War I. Henry Fielding made a one-man crime survey in London in 1751. See above, page 230. For a more recent example, compare the public concern in New York over the racket murder in 1912 of a gambling-house keeper named Rosenthal, which gave rise to the trial and execution of Police Lieutenant Becker and others. See *People v. Becker*, 210 N.Y. 274 (1914); 215 N.Y. 126 (1915).

fying that he was not present at the shooting.[51] The McGannon-Kagy affair was a major scandal, and later in 1920 an institution called the Cleveland Foundation undertook a thoroughgoing survey of criminal justice in that city. The foundation persuaded Dean Pound and Professor Frankfurter to direct the survey; the resulting research and findings were published in a 1922 volume, 729 pages long, entitled *Criminal Justice in Cleveland*. In it appears with abundant documentation the perennial conflict between two necessities of criminal justice: some means of controlling evildoers, and some means of controlling the process of law enforcement itself. The Cleveland survey produced a mass of enlightening facts about the law-enforcement process; but a reconciliation of the necessity for power in government and the necessity of the limitation of power remains unachieved.

In 1926 Professor Frankfurter and a staff drawn in part from the Law School faculty, in part from outside its ranks, undertook a new enterprise in the field of criminal justice resembling in some ways that conducted in Cleveland. The 1926 project was called a "Survey of Crime and Criminal Justice in Greater Boston." The Harvard Corporation, through the Milton Fund, gave the survey financial support. The Rockefeller Foundation gave other grants. The Boston survey "proceeded primarily from a desire to trace the effect of legal control on the restraint of crime and the efficacy of the law's treatment of the criminal." Those in charge saw the necessity of "entire detachment on the part of the investigators from the local administration of justice," and recognized that the experts active in the enterprise had to "eschew publicity until the work is embodied in formal reports and be wholly unconcerned with the promotion of immediate programs for reform or with the effect of the findings of the Survey upon any institution, however cherished." [52]

In 1934 the first volume of the Boston survey appeared, Sheldon and Eleanor Glueck's *One Thousand Juvenile Delinquents*. Later in the same year appeared Professor Sam Bass Warner's *Crime and Criminal Statistics in Boston*, the second book of the survey. In 1934 also appeared a third volume, Leonard V. Har-

[51] See *Criminal Justice in Cleveland* (Pound and Frankfurter, eds., Cleveland, 1922), pp. 169, 217.
[52] These quotations and the description of the project are drawn from Professor Frankfurter's Introduction to Sheldon and Eleanor Glueck's *One Thousand Juvenile Delinquents* (Boston, 1934).

rison's *Police Administration in Boston*. A number of other studies, originally projected, never reached the stage of publication. Francis Bowes Sayre had been active in the Boston survey; Sayre's appointment as assistant secretary of state late in 1933 and his resignation as professor in March 1934, Professor Frankfurter's activity on behalf of Governor Franklin D. Roosevelt's candidacy for the presidency beginning early in 1932, and Frankfurter's increasing involvement in the New Deal after President Roosevelt's election in November 1932 may all have inhibited the completion of the survey. A mass of typewritten material prepared for it still remains in the Law School's possession, perhaps awaiting attention from experts of a later generation. And the money and effort expended was not wasted. The publications which did emerge from the survey were worth what they cost, and the methodology and detached spirit of the inquiry, if they are heeded, may well supply guidelines for future surveys. In January 1934 Professor Frankfurter wrote [53] from the perspective of the George Eastman professorship at Oxford:

The Harvard Crime Survey was planned on the conviction that, however important a critique of the functioning of the criminal machinery may be, and however systematically it ought to be pursued as self-analysis by state and national governments, the complexity of crime calls for a more penetrating attack than merely a study of the enforcement of the criminal law. Understanding of the problems subsumed by the term "crime" demands inquiry in three major directions: (1) what "crime" is there? (2) why is there crime? (3) what does society do about it? These were questions which the Boston Survey put to itself with the hope not of securing answers but of promoting the scientific process which would eventually yield answers. Each of the three simply-phrased questions must first be broken up into extremely complicated constituents. As in all attempts at scientific inquiry, the formulation of the true problems is of fundamental importance. That the subject-matter is overlaid with shibboleths and clichés, that it concerns everyone and is therefore assumed to be within the competence of everyone, makes all the more difficult, but all the more essential, the effort to separate the known from the unknown, to divorce fact from assumption, to strip all bias of authority. The truth is that in the present stage of our ignorance very few problems implied by "crime" are susceptible of even approximately quantitative answers; that as to most of them we are in virgin territory; that

[53] In the Introduction to Sheldon and Eleanor Glueck's *One Thousand Juvenile Delinquents*.

to a large degree scientific effort must aim at the formulation of means for future explorations.

Thus the Survey was conceived as a stage in a progression of inquiry. It was undertaken not as an agency for reform but as a contribution to knowledge, more particularly for the development of scientific standards and methods regarding concerns of society that heretofore had been left largely to improvisation, crude empiricism and propaganda. Above all, the undertaking registered the responsibility of universities for research into these problems of human conduct and social policy.

The Eighteenth Amendment to the federal Constitution, ratified in 1919, and the Volstead Act of the same year [54] which implemented it, brought prohibition of alcoholic liquor throughout the United States. With it came a mass of enforcement problems.[55] Whenever a law prohibits some act which large numbers of citizens wish to commit, and which they do not consider morally reprehensible, the law tends to provoke lawlessness by widespread breach and by official corruption. Many otherwise law-abiding men violated the Volstead Act; it brought in its train profitable smuggling, bootlegging, bribery, and gangsterism. The entire prohibition effort, which began as "a great social and economic experiment, noble in motive and far-reaching in purpose" [56] turned into a dreary and sinister failure.

By an Act of March 4, 1929, the Congress appropriated funds to conduct a thorough investigation into the enforcement of the Volstead Act and criminal law generally. To carry out this sweeping undertaking President Hoover appointed a commission of eleven highly able lawyers, judges, and citizens, under the chairmanship of former Attorney General George W. Wickersham. Among the members he appointed Dean Pound, to whom the university gave leave of absence for the full academic year 1929–30 in order that he might carry out this public duty. The reports of that commission appeared in a series of volumes during the two years of its life. They constitute a sort of Cleveland survey expanded to a national scale; they contain a vast amount

[54] Act of October 28, 1919, chap. 85, 41 Stat. 305.

[55] See, for example, for the glut of petty offenses clogging the United States District Court in Boston in the mid-1920's, A. E. Sutherland, "Federal Police Courts," *Massachusetts Law Quarterly*, 5:43–56 (1926).

[56] The words are those of President Hoover, written in a letter to Senator Borah on February 28, 1928. Hoover continued to the end of his term to oppose repeal of the amendment because he felt that Prohibition accomplished more good than evil. Fewer and fewer people agreed with him.

of information on the enforcement of criminal law in the United States, concerning not only Volstead Act violations but crimes generally. Though the commission, by a majority vote, opposed repeal of the Eighteenth Amendment, the separate statements of various commissioners, including Dean Pound's, expressed so much doubt about the wisdom of the policy of Prohibition that the net effect may well have contributed to the adoption of the Twenty-first Amendment in 1933, repealing the Eighteenth Amendment of 1919.

7

In 1927 began another sort of research under the auspices of the Harvard Law School, particularly stimulated and directed by Professor Manley Ottmer Hudson, LL.B. 1910, S.J.D. 1917. Harvard appointed Hudson a lecturer on law in September 1918, but he resigned in November to go to Europe with the international law division of the American Commission to Negotiate Peace. For the rest of his life he did double duty, devoting himself at Harvard to teaching, studying, and writing in the field of international law; [57] and working all over the world in various capacities in the undertaking of the League of Nations Secretariat and other international organizations. From 1933 to 1945 he was to be a member of the Permanent Court of Arbitration; from 1936 to 1946, to be a judge of the Permanent Court of International Justice. In 1948 he was to be the first Chairman of the International Law Commission of the United Nations.

In September 1921, after he had finished a tour of duty with the legal section of the League of Nations Secretariat, he returned to Harvard as a professor of law. Two years later he became the Bemis Professor of International Law. He was precisely what the donor of that chair had prescribed: "Not merely a professor of the science but a practical co-operator in the work of advancing knowledge and good-will among nations." [58]

In the mid-1920's, the Assembly of the League of Nations appointed a committee to take steps looking toward the progres-

---

[57] Like most teachers at the School, Manley Hudson could turn his hand to whatever teaching was needed. Students of the early 1920's remember his dramatic demonstration, in his course on torts, that sociological jurisprudence concerned live human beings, and was an old idea.

[58] See above, page 211.

sive codification of international law. To cooperate with that committee a group of the Harvard Law School faculty, under Hudson's leadership, organized a "Research in International Law" modeled on the American Law Institute. It had a membership of about fifty, scholars from various American universities and other experts in the field. International law people familiarly called it "the Harvard Research." The Research undertook to prepare a draft convention on each of the topics which the League of Nations committee considered ripe for codification, so that delegates from any country who might be sent to an international conference on that subject might have before them the collective views of a representative group of learned Americans, expressed after the fullest possible discussion. The Carnegie Endowment for International Peace gave the Harvard Research necessary financial support. With Hudson as director, it published, between 1929 and 1935, a series of draft conventions, with documentation and comment, on nationality; on responsibility of states for injuries to foreigners; on territorial waters; on diplomatic privileges and immunities; on the legal position and function of consuls; on the competence of courts regarding foreign states; on piracy; on extradition; on criminal jurisdiction; and on the law of treaties. In addition to these drafts, the Research published in 1930 a collection of the nationality laws of various countries, and in 1932 a similar collection of laws relating to piracy.[59]

But by 1935 the pacific adjustment of international disputes by orderly agreement had reached an unhappy moment. Germany was re-arming under Hitler; Italy dreamed of glory under Mussolini; Japan built ships and trained armies. Four years after the 1935 publication of the draft on treaties, World War II broke out. Yet to write off as useless the six years of work on the Harvard Research would be a sad mistake. The demonstration that the Law School of a great American university was intent on devising means of pacific coexistence among nations was itself impressive. Thoughtful men would remember it, even among the clatter of tank treads across grainfields and the deafening bombardment of great cities. Despite any discouragement and disillusion about the effectiveness of the United Nations during the two decades following World War II, its work, aided by such

[59] See the Special Supplements to volumes 23, 26, and 29 of the *American Journal of International Law.*

travaux préparatoires as the Harvard Research, may yet bring a time when reason rather than concourse of arms will govern the use of the world's resources, and determine the fate of the world's people.

8

Dean Pound's report for 1926–27 included a statement of admissions in September 1927. Six hundred and ninety-four students were first-year men. Of the 674 first-year men who had enrolled a year before, 426 survivors had returned in 1927; of the preceding year's 363 second-year students, 361 had come back. There were 64 graduate, special, and unclassified students, a total student population of 1545. The 1927–28 faculty consisted of twenty professors, six assistant professors, an instructor, two lecturers, and a teaching fellow — a total of thirty teachers. These men crowded into Austin and Langdell halls, structures no larger than they had been twenty years earlier when the School had less than half as many students and faculty.[60]

The Dean wrote in that year's report: "Hence until Langdell Hall is completed we shall be constrained to put a limit upon the number of those admitted to graduate courses . . . We must now await with patience the course of construction of a monumental building." Fortunately plans for the monumental building were under way. The firm of Shepley, Rutan and Coolidge, who had been the architects of the original Langdell Hall, had now become Coolidge Shepley Bulfinch and Abbott. In 1925 they had prepared drawings for additions to Langdell which would more than double the north-south main axis and add the west wing, thus including substantially all the exterior Langdell of today save for the International Legal Studies wing completed in 1959. At the close of the School year 1927–28 construction of the expanded Langdell began. In the fall of 1928, classes continued normally despite the building operations. The work on the new Langdell west wing went forward so vigorously that in January 1929 the final argument of the Ames Competition was held in the then new courtroom,[61] and the whole west wing was

[60] In 1907–08 the Law School had 719 students and a faculty of 12.
[61] The Langdell courtroom, then new, occupied the space in the west wing now constituting the catalogue room and the Pound Room.

occupied the next month. The entire reconstruction of Langdell was completed in time for the opening of the School in September 1929. All that remained was paying for it — an operation which took eighteen years more.

The added space had been badly needed, for students, for teachers, for the increasing staff of administrators, for secretaries and librarians, and for the library collection which was growing phenomenally. When Dean Pound took office in 1916 the library held over 290,000 books; when Pound left the deanship in 1936 it held 433,381 bound volumes and 63,000 unbound volumes and pamphlets, a category of acquisitions which had increased as fast as the books. The collection of portraits of judges, statesmen, lawyers, and professors, with prints, caricatures, and cartoons, was becoming a brilliant feature of the School. Foreign, international, and comparative law material had been part of the library from the beginning; it had notably increased with the Livermore gift in 1834; and had been magnificently augmented by the purchase in Spain of the Marquis de Olivart's collection of international law books in 1911. The Dunn collection of English works printed before 1601, acquired in 1913, is now displayed in the Treasure Room. These special collections, kept up to date, still did not and do not constitute the great bulk of the School's library. The American collection is its principal strength. The increasing output of American state and federal legislation, the administrative regulations, the mass of text material, the periodicals and "Services," [62] and, above all, American judicial records and opinions even in 1929 required all the space available in the expanded Langdell for their efficient and accessible storage.

On January 7, 1929, the Law School, using funds derived from its newly increased endowment, set up as part of the School a

[62] "Services" may require a word of explanation for nonlawyers. The increasing complexity and volume of important statutes, administrative regulations, and judicial decisions, pouring forth from the national and state governments, has made almost impossible the lawyer's task of keeping his information up-to-date. Great inclusive texts like *Williston on Contracts*, annually kept current by pocket supplements and revised in new editions every few years, are still essential for systematic study. But for immediate access to highly specialized professional fields, large publishing houses like Prentice-Hall and Commerce Clearing House have organized corps of editors who maintain for their subscribers, by weekly mailings of loose-leaf material, such elaborately indexed and literally up-to-date reference texts as the Prentice-Hall *Federal Taxes* and the Commerce Clearing House *Installment Credit Guide,* and numerous others. Subscription charges for these essential "services" make up an increasing and heavy part of the cost of a modern law library.

new enterprise in the field of criminal justice and criminology, an Institute of Criminal Law, thus implementing a leading theme in the appeals for contributions in 1926–27. The School proposed research into the crime problem which then, as earlier and later, was gravely troubling the American people. The Institute of Criminal Law was not a corporation. It was a group of the School's faculty who had demonstrated particular concern with criminal matters. Professor Francis Bowes Sayre [63] was director; Sam Bass Warner [64] was assistant professor of penal legislation and administration; Sheldon Glueck was assistant professor of criminology; and John Joseph Burns [65] was assistant professor of law. Dean Pound, Professor Beale, and Professor Frankfurter were a committee for the general guidance of the institute.

The difference between a professor not a member of the institute and one having this distinction was not at all clear; nor indeed was there a completely evident reason for the existence of the institute as a separate entity. For many years various professors at the School had studied the operation of law in their special fields and had written papers or books, or had drafted legislation, incorporating the results of their studies. Perhaps the faculty felt that members of the institute would derive added encouragement, perhaps even endowment contributions, from membership in a learned body with a separate personality.

For the year 1931–32 the Institute of Criminal Law announced a training curriculum for correctional administrators. The Announcement recited:

It is coming to be recognized that the administering of penal and correctional institutions, as well as the work of departments of probation, of parole boards, and other public and private agencies having to do with delinquency and criminality, are specialized careers calling

[63] LL.B. 1912, S.J.D. 1918. He became the Ezra Ripley Thayer Teaching Fellow on September 1, 1917, and became successively lecturer, assistant professor, and, in 1924, professor of law. He became commissioner of correction of Massachusetts in 1932. President Franklin D. Roosevelt appointed him assistant secretary of state in November 1933. He resigned his Harvard professorship on March 26, 1934.

[64] Sam Bass Warner, LL.B. 1915, S.J.D. 1923, had been Thayer Teaching Fellow, 1922–23; assistant professor of penal legislation and administration, 1929; professor, 1932. He resigned June 30, 1945.

[65] LL.B. 1925; S.J.D. 1926; assistant professor of law, 1928; professor, 1931; resigned to accept appointment to Massachusetts Superior Court, 1931. Judge Burns later had a brilliant career in the federal government and in private practice, ended by his death in 1957. The Burns Room in the International Legal Studies wing of Langdell Hall has been dedicated to his memory.

for a high degree of special training. To meet this need, the Institute of Criminal Law of the Harvard Law School is trying the experiment of a curriculum for correctional administrators, intended to prepare men of character and capacity for positions of leadership in correctional work and for research in criminalistics. Accordingly a two-year curriculum has been organized, consisting of pertinent courses at the Law School and in other departments of the University. It is designed to occupy the entire time of students during their two years at the University. The student body will be limited to college graduates whose records are especially promising of success in the correctional field, either as administrators or research workers.

Two years of successful study would earn a student a Certificate in Correctional Administration. The curriculum included work in law, government, sociology, criminal law, anthropology, psychology, social research, and statistical methods. The instructors were drawn from all relevant departments of the university, not from the Law School alone. Beginning in 1932, students who took prescribed courses might acquire the certificate by only one year of resident study after they had taken the Harvard LL.B., the Harvard A.M., or the Th.B. either from Harvard or from the Episcopal Theological School.

Unfortunately this admirably intelligent experiment in teaching correctional science failed for lack of sufficient students. Perhaps young men with two years of available time preferred to attempt the Doctorate of Philosophy. Perhaps correctional institutions did not welcome young intellectuals. In its first year, 1931–32, the institute enrolled one student in the Correctional Administrators' program; in 1932–33 it enrolled seven; in 1933–34, two; in 1934–35, one. Thereafter this category of students, and the institute itself, disappear from the School's records.

The appealing concept of a group of scholars devoting themselves to scientific study of criminal behavior and its social controls was then predicated on a somewhat doubtful assumption of likeness between the medical and the social sciences. From the literature of the 1925–27 endowment campaign had emerged a hopeful aspiration to cure social ills as we have conquered some organic diseases:

Few need to be reminded how many terrible scourges — hydrophobia, typhoid, diphteria, malaria, yellow fever, diabetes — have been brought under control through the patient searchings of men like Pasteur, Reed and Banting . . . Few diseases threaten civilization more persistently than the manifold forms of anti-social action which we call crimes. Few obstacles impede business and industry more seriously than the waste, delay and uncertainty involved in the present functioning of our legal institutions. And yet — strangely enough — only the most sporadic and incidental efforts have as yet been made to apply in the field of law the proved methods of Pasteur and Reed and Banting.[66]

Perhaps, after all, the Institute of Criminal Law faded away because the study of social misconduct and the study of bodily malfunctioning are more dissimilar than at first appeared. When the institute's scholars began to attempt fruitful research into criminal behavior and control, perhaps the problem seemed discouragingly obdurate. Of the institute group, only Professor and Mrs. Glueck have persisted during the succeeding quarter-century. Their patient and infinitely laborious study of thousands of criminal careers has yielded statistical bases for early prediction of subsequent social maladjustment, which have been valuable in sentencing procedures, and which may hold clues to legislative action looking to treatment of crime as a disorder of public health, rather than to persistence in treatment of criminals on the basis of a medieval concept of sin-by-choice. At Commencement in June 1958, Harvard evidenced its appreciation of the Gluecks' service when the university, by a single citation for husband and wife, awarded to both honorary degrees of Doctor of Science. Of all of us the Gluecks have come closest to Langdell's and Eliot's hope to treat the law as a science among other sciences.

9

This chronicle, at several points, has commented on the fact, obvious after all, that the times express themselves in the study, teaching, and public activity of a university's professors, and in the interests and attitudes of its students. So the economic disorganization which became evident sometime after the middle of the 1920's, which the nation sought to mitigate in the 1930's, inevitably and deeply affected the Harvard Law School. For one thing, the New Deal drew to Washington a number of

[66] *For the Safety of the Citizen and the Protection of Business*, Harvard Law School Endowment Fund (1927), p. 11.

faculty members, and so again demonstrated the function of university law schools in supplying government with trained experts, detached from the imperatives of party politics. Depression did not materially diminish the number of students seeking the school's education. But quite evidently a general change developed in the attitudes of the American people during the decade of the 1930's. They had tired of waiting for something to turn up. Expectations and attitudes of law students changed along with those of other people. The student of 1934 expected from his social system more than the student of 1924. He had seen it fail in important respects; perhaps he thought its failure even more drastic than it really was. The student of 1924 had been inclined to accept the School, perceiving and recognizing the shortcomings of some of its teachers, recognizing the human and therefore inevitable imperfection of some of their instruction, accepting its system with more wonder at its excellences than irritation at its shortcomings. But in the decade of the 1930's all things were put to the question. The American people, with such thoughtfulness as they could muster, challenged the whole civilization in which they lived, asking themselves whether there were not obvious ways in which that civilization could be made better, more humane, more uniform in the distribution of its benefits. Not only was an escape from this general movement impossible in the microcosm of the Harvard Law School, but for the School such an exemption from the restless questionings of the times would have been a sad thing. Any institution should continually scrutinize itself, examine its own functioning, challenge its own assumed traditional excellences.

Dean Pound began his report to the President for the academic year 1932–33 with a section headed "Some Considerations as to Legal Education." He referred at the outset to "The restless reaching-out for new things, at the moment characteristic of every type of activity, and no less of education," and spoke of the tendency in that moment to concentrate on one or another single objective rather than on many. He pointed out that in the 1930's, as always, university schools of law were subject to many competing and contradictory demands. Achievement of a balance between these claims required continuing consideration of the School's curriculum, of new studies pressing for recognition. He urged that the School give thought to all this under the aspect of a whole generation of men, not shortsightedly under the stresses of a single moment of national life.

During the years 1933–1935 the faculty, feeling the nation-wide impulse to self-criticism and appraisal, undertook under the guidance of its committee on the curriculum a systematic examination of all aspects of the School's life — the purposes of study of law at Harvard; selection of students from among the many applicants; techniques of instruction; examination, promotion, and dismissal; the life of students. Wisely the faculty sought and recorded student opinion. The records of all this, mimeographed and bound in six loose-leaf books preserved in the School's archives, demonstrate an intense and intelligent scrutiny of legal education.

In the spring of 1935 the faculty sounded student opinion through an advisory group of the third-year class. Professor Seavey, chairman of the faculty committee, wrote to nine representative members of that class, asking them as a group to obtain information on student opinion of the School and its problems. He suggested that among other matters the student committee might want to consider whether a fourth year of law study for the LL.B. would be desirable. Would abridgement of the college course by a year be a wise correlative move? Should the Law School introduce into its curriculum studies in the other social sciences such as politics, economics, business administration, and the like even without extension of the Law School course? Should methods of instruction be changed, particularly so as to allow the student greater opportunity for independent study and research? Should classroom teaching be revised? Did the School need a corps of first-year teaching fellows? Were the School's physical facilities adequate? Were dining facilities needed, a common room, more dormitories?

The student committee immediately devised a questionnaire and distributed it to all students. Responses came from 175 first-year men, 124 second-year, and 172 third-year men, a total of 471 answers, about a third of the School's population. Instead of merely tabulating these returns the student committee chose, in addition, to draw up a thirty-five page report expressing its own conclusions. Two members wrote separate opinions.

Like most men, students of law are, on the whole, quite conservative. The student committee approved of most of the procedures that had been carefully worked out over many years by the School's conscientious teachers. The three-year course should not be extended to four years; the college course should not be abridged. The students preferred existing course examinations to comprehensive examinations. Perhaps the most useful part of the student report was its discussion of the merits and demerits of classroom instruction by dialectic, the case method, particularly as then used in the second and third years of the School's curriculum. The committee repeated, undoubtedly without awareness, many of the objections raised against this form of instruction in the early days of Christopher Columbus Langdell. For the first year's work the student committee cordially recommended retention of the case method. It was "unexcelled as a means of presenting the issues of a question in concrete form, and of training the analytical and critical processes of the mind." But it lost its merit, they thought, after the first year. Students did not read cases; reading cases was not educationally remunerative. Furthermore "statement of the case" by students in the classroom was wastefully time consuming; the student made it badly; those who heard it paid little attention. The student committee recommended that the statement of the case be dropped during the second and the third years. They recommended that much more lecturing be introduced, and that while students be encouraged to introduce discussion during the classroom hour, discussion not degenerate into a dialogue between the professor and a few students, to which the remainder of the class paid little attention.

The student report on this subject was good-tempered, contained much wisdom, was very evidently written in an effort to be constructive and helpful. It curiously overlooked the value of training in the art of preparing and presenting a lucid statement setting forth the essence of a complex situation — a high art, a professional requisite of all lawyers, which is called into play not only in courtrooms but before legislative committees, boards of directors, civic groups, all assemblages of human beings for whom a complicated matter requires clear explanation. Underlying this portion of the student report is a somewhat disheartening but perhaps realistic appraisal of student effort. The committee's criticism rested on an implicit and unspoken assumption that the arduous process of self-education required for the preparation of such a lucid oral statement — valuable alike for the man called to present it in the classroom and for the listeners who make a tacit critique — will not occur. It is too much trouble for old hands, they thought; teachers make a mistake to expect it. The students of Langdell's day had said much the same thing though their words were a little different. They came to the School to have the professors give them wisdom, not to dig it up for themselves. *Plus ça change . . .*

The Student Committee made other criticisms. They deplored the decline of interest which students felt in the third year and recommended as a substitute for part of the existing curriculum an opportunity to engage in some independent study like that available to men working on the *Law Review*. Here, too, the students' critique arouses sympathy. Real satisfaction derives from composing a literary product representing much compiling of material by library study, careful documentation, effective marshalling of comment. Preparation of briefs for moot court arguments in the Ames Competition should of course accomplish this if the work is done with enough conscientiousness, under alert criticism from older students. And a student engages in an exercise of the highest value when, in effect, he writes his own textbooks by preparing a year-long summary of each of his courses, a continuous legal essay, documented by consultation of texts, decisions, and other material. This procedure was obviously accessible to any man in the school in 1934. Any student was free to do it and the best of them did so. Wise and energetic students have undertaken such tasks ever since Luther Stearns Cushing was preparing his beautifully written summary of lectures in the 1820's. But self-direction is a rare trait in human beings. The criticisms directed at the Parker-Parsons-Washburn school, which at least in part led to the Langdell revolution of 1870, were not that the School failed to offer opportunities for education to such students as cared to make use of them; the criticisms essentially turned on the lack of compulsory sanctions which would impel those not self-directed to follow a course profitable and useful to themselves. One is touched to find intelligent and thoughtful young men in 1935 asking their teachers please to require of them a procedure already open to them, already known to them to be wholesome.

The faculty committee on the curriculum took their words to heart, and the ultimate result, though delayed some years, was the requirement, as a prerequisite to the LL.B. degree, of a well-written documented paper, prepared in the third year under a professor's supervision. This program still presents difficulties which have not been solved. A law school curriculum, like the law itself, is a seamless web which cannot be altered at one point without readjusting much of the rest. The School has come to require what is essentially a thesis for its degree, but has only moot-court brief-writing and some volunteer second-year writing projects as a system for preparing the student to satisfy this requirement. And there is insufficient talented staff to give the personal attention to the student that a conscientious Oxford or Cambridge tutor gives to the British undergraduate. Sometimes faculty members console themselves about this situation by commenting that instruction in English composition is a proper matter for the undergraduate college, and are tempted so to dismiss the subject from their minds. But in a good many undergraduate colleges and universities the student of the 1960's gets no adequate instruction in the production of a carefully written document with authorities cited to support his statements. The program of guided writing or seminar work in the third year, in effect at the present-day School, stems at least in part from the curricular study of the early 1930's; involved in it are problems still under study a third of a century later.

The life of students outside the library and classrooms aroused somewhat poignant criticism from the student committee in 1935. For most, the committee said, life in rented rooms was much like living in a tenement district. They looked with some envy at the superior facilities available to undergraduates living in the then new Harvard Houses, and wished that in the Law School there might be a common room, and a place where law students might dine together in decent comfort, and dormitories where students might find university rooms at a low rental. They did not understand why graduate students of the law should be less considered than undergraduate college men. In these respects at least the amenities of student life at the School have much improved in the decades since 1935.

10

By the late 1920's the Dean, the School's secretary, and the librarian could no longer administer practically everything. Fifteen hundred students and a faculty of thirty-two teachers required a more complex organization. On January 10, 1928, the office of vice dean came into being with Professor Joseph Warren as the first incumbent. The faculty created an Administrative Board on which sat the vice dean, the chairman of graduate courses, and a chairman of the courses of each of the three LL.B. years, together with the secretary of that board. Dean Pound described some other faculty burdens in his report of 1929–30 under the heading "New Demands on Law Teachers." In that year, he pointed out, the faculty had been called on to furnish four reporters and five advisers for the American Law Institute; one member of the faculty, the Dean, had been absent for a whole year serving on the Wickersham Commission; two others had given a great deal of time to that commission; and the government had called away another professor to assist at an international conference. "Thus," wrote the Dean, "it is evident that in its desire to serve the public, the School is being driven back to the outgrown system of part-time teachers. No teacher can serve two masters." The professors on the augmented administrative staff attended to some of the management of the school, but thereby added to their own burdens.

With the coming of the New Deal governmental demands for the services of professors grew still heavier. On October 8, 1933, President Roosevelt appointed Professor Landis Federal trade commissioner. On the following July 1, 1934, the President appointed him to the newly created National Securities and Exchange Commission. Meantime the School had carried him on leave. Professor Sayre became assistant secretary of state on November 19, 1933, and although Harvard gave him leave of absence, he resigned the following March. On September 15, 1934, Vice Dean Calvert Magruder [67] became associate general counsel for the National Labor Relations Board, and later became gen-

[67] Joseph Warren because of illness had been obliged to resign as vice dean in 1929, less than a year after his appointment to that office. Professor Morgan became acting vice dean until Professor Magruder was appointed to that office in September 1930. Calvert Magruder was born in 1893, in Annapolis, Maryland. He was A.B. St. John's College; LL.B., *cum laude*, Harvard 1916. He was secretary to Mr. Justice Brandeis, 1916–1917; attorney, United States Shipping Board, Washington, 1919–1920; assistant professor of law at Harvard, 1920–1925; professor, 1925–1939; vice dean, 1930–1939. He went on leave from Harvard as general counsel of the wage and hour division, Department of Labor, 1938–1939, and was appointed U.S. Circuit Judge of the First Circuit, 1939. He was a lecturer from 1947 to 1959 at Harvard Law School. He retired in 1959.

eral counsel to that board. The university carried Vice Dean Magruder on leave status.

The flow was not all toward Washington. Erwin Nathaniel Griswold had taken his A.B. at Oberlin in 1925, his LL.B. *summa cum laude* at Harvard in 1928, and had been president of the *Law Review.* He returned for a year's graduate study and took the S.J.D. with unusual distinction in June of 1929. He practiced for a short time in Cleveland but later in 1929 was appointed to an attorneyship in the office of the Solicitor General, and in 1933 he became special assistant to the Attorney General of the United States. On September 1, 1934, the Corporation appointed Griswold an assistant professor for one year. Fortunately for the Law School his stay has continued to the present day.

The faculty was increasing. In September 1930 the School had twenty-five full professors, nine assistant professors, five lecturers, and one teaching fellow, a total of forty teachers. There were also fifteen research fellows. The intimacy of a small family which had obtained when Pound came to the deanship has disappeared. Professor Thomas Reed Powell's papers, preserved in the School's archives, contain memoranda which he wrote to himself mourning over the loss of the pleasantly close circle of companions whom he had known in his days on the Columbia faculty.

As the 1930's wore on, the Law School machine creaked a bit. Dean Pound had carried immense burdens for many years, and carried them well. In 1930 he passed his sixtieth year, and his ability under stress to tolerate differences with close associates, an ability which requires much strength, endurance, and wisdom, began bit by bit to slip away from him. Absence of colleagues, called away for duties with the Roosevelt administration, began to irritate Pound; and this irritation was aggravated by his disapproval of some of the New Deal's political and social programs. On the other hand, Felix Frankfurter, mercurial, quick, enthusiastic, also intolerant, was a close friend and adviser of President Franklin Roosevelt. He was frequently summoned to Washington somewhat unexpectedly, and so became a little unpredictable in his academic role. Pound, despite his own recent absence with the Wickersham Commission, allowed Frankfurter's absences to annoy him more than was wise or necessary. These differences, not grave, were still irritating. Some of the older professors tended to take sides, became to some degree Pound men or

Frankfurter men. The juniors, busy learning the details of their courses and the mysteries of instruction, were more apt to stand aside.

On November 4, 1931, the Harvard faculty gave a dinner for Professors Beale and Williston, to celebrate the seventieth birthdays which both had reached a few weeks before. In June of 1931 each had completed forty years of teaching at the Law School, and all but two of the faculty had been their students. At dinner, the faculty, wishing to honor these colleagues in a more permanent form, resolved to publish a book of essays, a festschrift, a celebratory volume, in their honor. Felix Frankfurter, always talented, always witty, undertook to be editor. But the New Deal interrupted his editorial work and Roscoe Pound served instead. Harvard University Press published the book in 1934. Selection of a title is an art: Roscoe Pound was a bit unimaginative in this one: he called the book: *Harvard Legal Essays, Written in Honor of and Presented to Joseph Henry Beale and Samuel Williston.*

In 1931 the faculty of law consisted of twenty-six Professors, four assistant professors, two lecturers, and the Ezra Ripley Thayer Teaching Fellow. Chronicles of the growing School come to a point in its evolution when a detailed biography of each teacher is no longer possible, yet the life of the School is teachers and students. Without an account of these, without the story of student life and sentiment, without some insight into the character and work of the faculty, the essence of the School is missing. The authors of the Williston-Beale festschrift essays were notable figures in the School's roster of teachers, and a brief review of their backgrounds and of their writings for this celebratory volume gives some idea of the sort of men then on the faculty, of the ideas which seemed to them worth discussing, and of their talents and styles.

The volume arranged the essays alphabetically under the names of the authors. Morton Carlisle Campbell, first of the essayists, was an LL.B. of 1900 who took his doctorate of juridical science fifteen years later. He came to the School as a lecturer on law in 1919, and became a professor in 1920. In 1931–32 he was teaching bills and notes, and suretyship and mortgages. Campbell wrote an essay for the festschrift called "Protection against Indirect Attack." During the war of 1917–1918 he had been an officer in the army, which here furnished him a picturesque but not entirely enlightening title for a somewhat technical essay. In his introduction he pointed out that an army is vulnerable to an attack on its communications and that similarly an individual, though not liable to a direct attack in litigation, may unless somehow comprehensively released by the law, be just as injuriously attacked by some circuitous route. A wastrel nephew persuades his elderly, affectionate, and gullible aunt to guarantee the young man's debt to a moneylender. If the moneylender releases the nephew but reserves his rights against the aunt, the aunt who has to pay can still recover against the nephew although the moneylender purported to release the young rascal.[68] Campbell's paper rings the changes on a number of such situations, designating the various parties only by letters of the alphabet then conventional in such literature, C for creditor, P for principal, S for surety; not telling stories of the predicament of human beings, but playing little games with movable counters. Campbell's professional mind was full of mathematical arrangements rather than vivid dramatics. Still he was a kind and understanding man. This somewhat dry essay on "Indirect Attack" hardly discloses his benign quality. One day a student, fatigued by a previous night's reveling, fell into a deep sleep during one of Campbell's classes and remained soundly slumbering as his fellow students left at the hour's end. Campbell went down to the youth, gently awakened him, and said, "Young man, perhaps you could help me in a personal difficulty. Recently I have been suffering from insomnia; can you perchance remember just what it was in my lecture that put you to sleep?"[69]

Zechariah Chafee wrote the second essay; it was quite different in tone. He called his paper "Professor Beale's Ancestor"; it told the story of a mid-seventeenth century legal squabble over some Boston real estate. Chafee had never been a real property specialist, but he relished the colorful past and could find adventure in a lawsuit over Benjamin Beale's claim to a share in Halsey's Wharf that Nathaniel Patten left when he died in January 1671/2. Chafee's paper is full of quotations from ancient documents with archaic spelling and strange, pleasing abbreviations.

---

[68] See, for example, the present-day Uniform Commercial Code, section 3–606 (2)(c).

[69] At a reunion of the 1925 class, held in 1950, Morton Campbell, though then old and unwell, came to the class dinner and told this story on himself. He was warmly cheered.

One reads at last, with a sense of satisfied partisanship, that Professor Beale's ancestor prevailed. Chafee obviously relished his own essay.

Edwin Merrick Dodd, LL.B. 1913, wrote on "The First Half Century of Statutory Regulation of Business Corporations in Massachusetts." From his appointment as professor of law in 1928 Dodd had been a historian of American corporations. Widespread use of the corporate form for business came in America earlier than one might suppose, but at first corporations were created by special legislative act, not by administrative order under a general statute. Still a lawyer's art developed for the drafting of each legislative act of incorporation. Their form became conventional, varying suitably between banking corporations, insurance companies, manufacturing enterprises, toll-bridge companies, turnpike and canal corporations, and, in the late 1820's, the first railroads. By 1830, Dodd concludes, the laws concerning Massachusetts corporations would not have appeared very strange to a 1916 lawyer.

Manley Hudson, as one would expect, wrote on international law. His paper, "The Law Applicable by the Permanent Court of International Justice," was part of a treatise on that court which professor Hudson published in 1934. Eldon Revare James, the scholarly librarian of the School, published "A List of Legal Treatises Printed in the British Colonies and the American States before 1801."

James McCauley Landis, professor of legislation since 1928, in 1931 was teaching labor law to third-year students and guiding graduate students in legislative research. He wrote "Statutes and the Sources of Law" — which Dean Griswold in 1964 called an article "that would surely be included in a collection of the great legal essays of all time." [70] Landis' paper was a scholarly plea for treating legislation less narrowly than had been conventional with Anglo-American lawyers and judges, trained to think of judicial decisions as the prime sources of legal policy. Conventional judges thought of a statute as a sporadic and abnormal intrusion into the decisional structure. Landis urged that the statute be treated not only as a specific prescription but as a declaration

---

[70] See Dean Griswold's memorial address on Dean Landis delivered in the Harvard Memorial Church on August 2, 1964. It is printed in the *Harvard Law Review*, 78:313 (1964).

of general policy, applicable by way of analogy where appropriate as well as within the precise limits of its verbal boundaries. His essay was prophetic; the principle he advocated has been gaining ground in the present day. The first clause of the second section of the Uniform Commercial Code, first enacted in Pennsylvania in 1954, reads "This Act shall be liberally construed and applied to promote its underlying purposes and policies." In June 1965 the Supreme Court of the United States, deciding *Griswold v. Connecticut*,[71] sought a principle for the decision of the case in a number of clauses of the federal Constitution not directly applicable to the facts of litigation; it sought in constitutional clauses general norms rather than specific governing words. The two dissenting justices based their disagreement with the majority on their divergence from the theory upheld by Dean Landis thirty-one years earlier.

Sayre MacNeil, LL.B. 1911, professor of law from 1926 to 1933, taught property to first-year men and municipal corporations in the third-year curriculum. He wrote "Some Pictures Come to Court," a playful account of celebrated lawsuits concerning paintings. MacNeill got centuries of fun out of his essay; he told the story of a letter written by Isabella d'Este (1474-1539) to Luca Liombeni, threatening to put him in prison if he did not hurry with some mural paintings. He told of Whistler's Parisian litigation with Eden; he described Holmes's 1903 opinion on circus posters as works of art.[72] John MacArthur Maguire, LL.B. 1911, who had become a professor of law in 1923, in 1931 was teaching evidence to second-year students and taxation to the third-year class. Emeritus forty-three years later, he is still a wise and discriminating writer on the law of evidence, busy in his office in Langdell Hall when he is not busy in his office in Boston. He combined the law of taxation and constitutional law in his essay "Taxing the Exercise of Natural Rights." In part Professor Maguire's essay deals with poll taxation, which in 1964 gave rise to the Twenty-fourth Amendment to the federal Constitution, and which, insofar as poll taxation affects the right to vote in state elections, the Supreme Court of the United States declared unconstitutional in 1966.[73]

[71] 381 U.S. 479 (1965).
[72] *Bleistein v. Donaldson Lithographing Co.*, 188 U.S. 239.
[73] *Harper v. Virginia Board of Elections*, 383 U.S. 663 (1966).

Edmund Morris Morgan, LL.B. 1905, like John Maguire, was an authority on the law of evidence. In 1931 he taught first-year civil procedure and second-year evidence. For the festschrift he wrote "Federal Constitutional Limitations upon Presumptions Created by State Legislation." He discussed the doubtful constitutional status of a statute which created a presumption having no rational basis — a ground on which the Supreme Court declared an Act of Congress unconstitutional in 1943.[74]

Roscoe Pound wrote "The Ideas of the End of Law Current in the 20th Century." He suggested that we think of jurisprudence as "a science of social engineering, [an] organized body of knowledge with respect to the means of satisfying human demands, securing interests, giving effect to claims or desires, with the least friction and the least waste, so far as these things can be brought about by the legal order, whereby the means of satisfaction may be made to go as far as possible." Here Pound restated the essence of his philosophy of law, which he had described in his 1911–12 paper "The Scope and Purpose of Sociological Jurisprudence."[75]

Pound was one of the two essayists who had not studied under Beale and Williston; they both joined the faculty in 1890 just after he left. Josef Redlich, Charles Stebbins Fairchild Professor of Comparative Public Law, was the other. Redlich was a civilian whose life had been spent in university teaching and service in government in Austria. The General Education Board had brought Redlich to Harvard; he stayed from 1926 to 1935. He was a member of the long line of distinguished visiting scholars at the School who have helped move the faculty out of whatever parochialism may impede its views. He had been professor of constitutional and administrative law at the university of Vienna since 1908, had been a long-time member of the Austrian Parliament, and in 1918 had been Austrian minister of finance. He was a noted author of books on the government of England. At Harvard in 1931–32 he was giving a seminar on comparative constitutional and administrative law. His festschrift paper was a comparative study of political theory, with the title "Sovereignty, Democracy, and the Rights of Minorities." Speculating on "the goal to which modern national feeling will finally

[74] *Tot v. United States*, 319 U.S. 463 (1943).
[75] *Harvard Law Review*, 24:591; 25:140, 489.

lead constitutional law and statecraft" he saw many signs that Europe would have to create new forms of cooperation of nations to function as an integrated whole. He saw in organically rooted racial and linguistic minorities causes of disintegration of the historic European state and the "waning theoretical authority of the notion of sovereignty in political science and jurisprudence." Perhaps there still may prove to be truth in what he predicted.

Professor Francis Bowes Sayre, then director of the Institute of Criminal Law, wrote on the mental element of crime under the title "The Present Signification of Mens Rea in the Criminal Law." Professor Austin Wakeman Scott in 1931–32 was teaching civil procedure to first-year men and trusts to the second-year class. He wrote for the Beale-Williston festschrift "Protective Trusts," an essay challenging the social desirability of protecting irresponsible inheritors of funds which they do not control. How far, he asked, is it desirable to permit the separation of the enjoyment of wealth from the responsibilities which normally accompany it? Characteristically he ended with a literary reference which he expected the reader to recognize: "How many Skimpoles will the traffic bear?" [76]

Warren Abner Seavey, LL.B. 1904, had come to Harvard as professor of law in 1927 when he was already an internationally known expert in the fields of agency and torts. He had practiced law in Boston; had taught law in Pei Yang University in China; had briefly taught pleading at Harvard; and then had been professor of law at Oklahoma, at Tulane, and at Indiana, before serving in France as a captain during World War I. He was proud of his work in France in 1919, after the armistice, as director of the American Expeditionary Force University College of Law. He returned to the United States as professor of law and dean at Nebraska; he went from there in 1926 to a professorship at the University of Pennsylvania, from which he came to Harvard for the balance of his long and useful life. Warren Seavey was a great "put-question," as Story had been a century before him. In the classroom he was a master of provocative thought. In 1931–32 he was teaching torts in the first-year curriculum and agency in the second. Appropriately, he entitled his festschrift paper "Speculations as to 'Respondeat Superior.'" His essay was

---

[76] Harold Skimpole was an idle, witty, extravagant gentleman in *Bleak House*. He lived by imposing on the generosity of his friends.

precisely that, a series of provocative inquiries on the curious fact that often in our law when Jones is at fault, Smith pays the loss Jones caused.

James Bradley Thayer's paper, "Unilateral Mistake and Unjust Enrichment as a Ground for the Avoidance of Legal Transactions," was filled with learning in comparative and Roman law. Grandson of a professor in the School, son of one of its deans, Thayer took his LL.B. in 1924 and went on to take the S.J.D. in 1925. His younger contemporaries in the School remember him with some awe as the only student wearing a beard — his was a sort of imperial, giving him vaguely the air of Napoleon III. The School has always been a breeding place for colorful legends, and Thayer figured heroically in one of the best of these. He had so the story went, been sailing with friends in the Aegean one summer when he developed appendicitis. His dismayed shipmates took him ashore on a small Greek island where the only medical man was a veterinarian. Thayer stoically submitted to the animal doctor's surgery, which proved to be so effective that his patient was able to go swimming again ten days after the operation. At Harvard he taught a course and a seminar in comparative law, using Roman law and modern civil law as frameworks. His festschrift essay exemplified his field of learning: it ranges from the restatement of contracts through various continental authors, the Swiss civil code, the German code of the day, to Holmes's *Common Law*, with footnote references to the law of ancient Rome.

Professor Edward Sampson Thurston wrote the last essay, "Trespass to Air Space." He was a Harvard LL.B. of 1901; after six years of practice in New York he taught law in several universities. His ideas about the right of a landowner to object to low-flying airplanes may have been stimulated by service in the judge advocate general's department during World War I. He was professor of law at Yale from 1919 to 1929, and then came to Harvard. Thurston was an adviser on torts and on trusts to the American Law Institute, and with Warren Seavey taught torts to first-year Harvard students. He also had a third-year class in quasi-contract and equitable relief against mistake. Professor Thurston's essay foreshadowed a Supreme Court decision [77] that was to come twelve years after the Beale-Williston

[77] *United States v. Causby*, 328 U.S. 256 (1946).

festschrift, holding that persistent intended low-level overflight by government aircraft across a man's land was a "taking" of some of his airspace, protected by the eminent-domain clause of the Fifth Amendment. But Thurston clearly saw that the doctrine of airspace ownership to an infinite distance above the owned surface could no longer hold in the day of the airplane; and that the proprietor's upward rights were limited by the reasonable altitude of the overflight.

The festschrift essays picture a school with an eager, imaginative and diverse faculty, learned in the law of past days and of other countries, but coping with problems of their own time, alert to change, diverse in style and in wit. They made the School vivid and interesting, in an interesting and vivid moment of its life.

In 1936 Harvard attained the three hundredth anniversary of her founding and appropriately celebrated this tercentenary with festival rites. During three August days of that year there gathered at Langdell Hall lawyers, judges, and teachers from every part of the United States, from Great Britain, Canada, and the Irish Free State, for a "Conference on the Future of the Common Law." Many of the visitors stayed in the Yard, as guests of the university. Each day they had luncheon together under the trees in front of Langdell. Each morning two distinguished scholars or judges read papers before the assemblage; and in the afternoon there followed a general discussion led by other noted men of the law. Appropriately Dean Pound opened the Conference with a paper called "What Is the Common Law?" [78] He touched on a theme which has run through legal thinking since before the beginning of the Harvard Law School — the nature of law as a science.

Although in political and juristic thought the nineteenth century is characteristically the century of history, the later eighteenth and the nineteenth centuries are marked by increasingly rapid development of the physical sciences. In the nineteenth century these sciences become more and more specialized and differentiated and are increasingly behind a growing industry which in turn stimulates research and invention and so furthers the growth of the sciences.

[78] *The Future of the Common Law*, Harvard Tercentenary Publications (1937), p. 4.

Toward the end of the last century the increased importance of the physical sciences for civilization has its influence upon political and juristic thought, and in the present century modes of thinking derived from or devised on the analogy of those sciences have been undermining what had been held to be the foundations of jurisprudence.

There is a clear gain for all thought in the habits of close observation of phenomena and subjection of theories to the test of such observation which the physical sciences have been teaching us. But the assumption that all our organized bodies of knowledge must be remade to the methods of the physical sciences, which the hegemony of those sciences in the present has made fashionable, is as ill-taken as the assumption that the physical sciences might be laid out *a priori,* which prevailed in the hegemony of metaphysics.

If in the era of faith in reason we took it for granted too lightly that human conduct might be subjected to rational principles, and adjustment of human relations might be carried on by rationally conceived formulas, yet the teachings of contemporary psychology, so far from undermining the work of ages of legal development, serve to show us how great has been the achievement of law and politics, by which the fundamentally unrational has been tamed to reason and law and order, and thus the research and experimentation and investigation which have given us the modern physical sciences have been made possible. It is not an accident that jurisprudence and ethics and politics grew up and reached what may prove their maximum before there was much development of the physical sciences. The latter, indeed, could not have arisen nor gone far had it not been for the stability and security brought about and maintained by the former. If not so striking to the eye at first glance, the subjection of human behavior to the exigencies of civilized life by ordered application of the force of politically organized society which has developed in the western world since the chaos of the earlier Middle Ages, is quite as significant as anything which has been done in the same time toward the harnessing of external nature to man's use.

This was Pound's declaration of faith as Dean. On the twenty-eighth of the next month, reaching the age prescribed by the university for retirement from administrative duties, he resigned his deanship, and went away for a half a year of rest. The Corporation wisely appointed him the first of its new University Professors. Released from the burdens and worries of the deanship, Roscoe Pound took a new lease on life. He studied, wrote, and lectured. From February to September 1946 he was in China as adviser to the Ministry of Justice of the Nationalist Government.

Pound returned to teach at Harvard during the academic

year 1946–47. He became emeritus in 1947, but his active life of writing and study continued as before. His first wife, Grace Gerrard, had died in 1928 and Pound was fortunate three years later in a second marriage with Mrs. Lucy Miller, who gave him companionship until her death in 1959. Then Pound, old and lonely, still walked early each morning from the Commander Hotel down Waterhouse Street to Langdell Hall. Friends from the Harvard faculty and from the Boston bar tried to give him some companionship. Honors came swiftly from all parts of the world. Visitors made pilgrimages to his office to talk with him. The Chinese Nationalist government never forgot its obligation to Roscoe Pound; on his ninety-second birthday the embassy sent a special representative to Langdell Hall to congratulate him. The reconstituted Pound Law Club, which had ceased to exist during World War II, came together again and the Dean would sometimes sit with its students and tell of old days at the Nebraska bar. At one such gathering in 1962 he sang "Ho, Azuram!" for them.

Late in the year 1962 he undertook to organize a festschrift in honor of Professor Scott who had been his colleague ever since Pound first joined the Harvard faculty.[79] Pound obtained the articles from distinguished contributors and himself wrote one of the pieces. He and Miss McCarthy [80] handled all the correspondence, during a year of arrangements. But by the early spring of 1964 time and strength were running out for him. His university found room for him in its infirmary, and for a while his nurse would occasionally bring him to Langdell Hall in a wheelchair so that he might answer a few letters. His friends Doctor Dana Farnsworth and Doctor Leo Cass of the University Health Services took endless pains to help in the last months. In June of 1964, a bronze plaque commemorating the Dean's 1906

---

[79] *Perspectives of Law: Essays for Austin Wakeman Scott.*

[80] Miss May McCarthy well earned a place in these annals. She had been Dean Thayer's secretary until his death, and then Pound's secretary ever since he became dean in 1916. She was a little, precise woman who in 1964 looked and behaved much as she had forty years earlier. She could on demand produce any paper from Pound's voluminous files; she could decipher his crabbed pencil manuscripts; she warned off overstaying visitors with meaningful glances. Under her dry severity was unlimited devotion. She never accepted the fact of Pound's increasing weakness in the tenth decade of his life, ascribing its symptoms to the incompetence of physicians. After his death she worked for a few months arranging his papers, but for her the purpose of living had gone, and one night she quietly and decorously died sitting in a chair in her solitary room.

speech on "The Causes of Popular Dissatisfaction with the Administration of Justice" was unveiled in the Minnesota Capitol. Pound could not go, and a faculty friend went to Saint Paul to accept the plaque on his behalf. A few days later, in the Harvard infirmary, Pound quietly died in his sleep.

The old Dean's paper for the Scott festschrift was in galley proof when he died. In it he dealt with the liability of government for seizure of a citizen's property; he rebelled fiercely against any survival of a concept in our society, from which we have cast off kingship, that some one among us whom we have clothed with our power can, as a "king," escape responsibility for his wrongs to those he serves. Reading Pound's piece, one thinks of pioneers in Nebraska.

IX

The School in Peace and War

The Landis Deanship
1937–1946

James McCauley Landis was a phenomenally brilliant man. Those of us who were his friends when he was a student at the School found him an appealing person, with a strange, wistful quality, evident all his life. His intellect was so encompassing, his understanding was so sensitive, he perceived so fully the infinite satisfactions of achievement that life might conceivably yield, that he never quite reconciled himself to the impossibility, even for him, of attaining that maximum.

Landis was born in Tokyo, Japan, in 1899, the son of missionary parents. He graduated from Princeton in 1921. He must have established a record for early law review publication: while he was still a Princeton undergraduate he wrote "The Commerce Clause as a Restriction on State Taxation," which the *Michigan Law Review* published in November 1921, when Landis was in his first year at the Harvard Law School. He took his LL.B. *cum laude* in 1924. He and his roommate, W. Barton Leach, had been respectively case editor and note editor of the *Review*. These were great men. Both were destined soon to be professors on the School's faculty, and Leach as this is written is the School's senior active professor. Even in those days Leach had the power of command which in World War II was to earn him high rank in the Air Force. In 1923 young men on the editorial staff of the *Review* brought to him drafts of their notes, and left his presence humbled by the weight of his learning, to sit up all the next night doing over again the work they had thought so brilliant.[1] Landis

[1] The printed page is a feeble medium. Perhaps some genius will one day

attained the same end by a quite different technique; his sway over younger men was exercised by a look from under his beetling brows; he held us with his glittering eye.

His memory was phenomenal. Once, early in the fall of 1924, a very junior *Review* editor heard Landis refer to a case he had come across in a little-known English report, about two young eighteenth century Englishmen "running their fathers against each other" — that is to say, agreeing that the one whose father died first would pay the other in consolation for his delayed hopes. Months later, well on in the spring, the young editor asked Landis whether by chance he could remember where there might be found the case about the two Georgian swells and their unfilial bet. Landis, deep in a survey of the Statutes at Large for Frankfurter, announced the citation from memory without hesitation, change of expression, or search for notes. Investigation proved that he was right. This sort of thing instills awe.

In 1924–25 Landis was a graduate student, sitting with a kind of somber mastery in Felix Frankfurter's seminar on federal jurisdiction and procedure. He was then working for his doctorate under Frankfurter, a distinction which lesser men understood only vaguely; they regarded him much as an Athenian slave must have regarded a free Hellene who was about to be initiated into the Eleusinian Mysteries. Although we stood in proper awe of this great man Landis, we were fond of him. He was helpful to the noninitiate. Those who went to him in bewilderment came away in mingled gratitude for his ready aid, and embarrassment that what had appeared so complex he could make so simple. He took the S.J.D. in June 1925. His doctoral thesis, "Constitutional Limitations on the Congressional Powers of Investigation," appeared in the December 1926 *Harvard Law Review*.[2]

After Landis had passed the year 1925–26 clerking for Justice Brandeis, he became an assistant professor on September 1, 1926.

---

invent a new device, as convenient as a book, which can show Leach in action, will make him magnificently audible, lecturing or playing his accordion and singing "Come to Uncle Erwin's School for Lawyers." If only such a machine had been available in 1923 it might now show Note Editor Leach sublimating the puny effort of a junior editor in "Actionable Interference with Commercial Relations: The Catch-Word Method," an essay which drew attention as far away as Egypt. See *Harvard Law Review*, 37:143, and Mohamed Abdullah El-Araby, *La Conscription des neutres dans les luttes de la concurrence economique* (Paris, 1924), p. 232.

[2] *Harvard Law Review*, 40:153. This paper expressed views akin to those in a

The Landis Deanship

In 1927 appeared *The Business of the Supreme Court*, by Frankfurter and Landis. Landis' appointment as professor of legislation came in 1928. He was one of the earliest academic recruits for the New Deal; President Roosevelt appointed him a federal trade commissioner on October 8, 1933, a duty for which Harvard gave him a year's leave. His appointment to the Securities Exchange Commission in the following July made necessary a second year's leave, for 1934–35; he became chairman of that commission in 1935, and Harvard gave him yet another leave.

At the age of 34 Landis thus rose to a place of great power in the national government. In the early days of the New Deal its dedicated initiates held few doubts. The forces of the national economy in those days were clearly divided between good and evil. The Business Establishment had by its own greed brought about the downfall of prosperity. The national presidency would now repair this wrong, and brave young disciples were the President's ministers in the good work. They felt the heady sense of power in a righteous cause. Young men who swiftly advance to posts of great power for righting wrong in the nation undergo a dangerous experience. Insidiously such a rise persuades them that all life continues in the same high trajectory, and unhappily this is rarely possible. Some say that Alexander wept because there were no more worlds to conquer; the story is a parable exemplifying a universal human trait. After Landis' three years of power in Washington, long duty as an academic was impossible for him. The role of the thinker, the teacher, is a part different from that of the governor. Few governors are content to teach; few are willing to be "committed to lives of proud dependence – the de-

---

New Republic editorial of April 23, 1924, unsigned but sometimes ascribed to Frankfurter. The editorial denounced "the preposterous assumption that an investigation into the conduct of public officials who are suspected of wrong doing should be conducted under all the limitations of a criminal trial." Landis in his final footnote writes of the Senate investigation of the Teapot Dome scandals: "What the 1924 investigations disclosed is not pertinent here; nor is it necessary to discuss the attitude that the press and the country look toward them. It is sufficient to remark that three out of ten Cabinet members were permitted or pressed to resign; that there were several indictments and two suicides." He cites Frankfurter, "Hands Off the Investigations," *New Republic*, May 21, 1924. These comments concerning congressional investigation into supposed official misconduct of cabinet officers possibly seemed less apt thirty years later when the House Un-American Activities Committee was investigating other officials, suspected of Communist tendencies.

pendence of men who command no factitious aids to success, but rely upon unadvertised knowledge and silent devotion; dependence upon finding an appreciation which they cannot seek, but dependence proud in the conviction that the knowledge to which their lives are consecrated is of things which it concerns the world to know." [3]

Professor E. M. Morgan became acting dean on September 28, 1936, the day of Dean Pound's resignation. President Conant and the rest of the Corporation meantime were engaging in a vigorous search for a man who could carry on all that Pound had so well accomplished, and who at the same time could repair some of the cleavages in faculty good feeling which for various reasons had begun to be apparent in the last years of Dean Pound's administration. At such a juncture in the life of a college or university someone usually brings forth the suggestion that what is really needed is a man of practical business experience, who can inject ideas gleaned from real life into the dreamy business of academic leadership. This suggestion came to President Conant, and was not lightly dismissed. He sent for many of the School's professors, some of the older men, some newer teachers, consulting with them on the future deanship, the future of the School, and the men in the world or the cloister who might lead it.

At length the Corporation decided that an academic person would make a better dean than would a lawyer for large business interests, or a judge. Every man to his own trade.[4] President Conant sent for Professor Landis' roommate, Leach, by that time a colleague on the faculty of several years' standing, to discuss Landis as a prospective dean. Conant said that, like all other human beings, Landis had more strengths in some respects than in others. On balance, he thought Landis a good gamble. At any rate, the Corporation felt so, and on January 4, 1937, appointed Landis Dean of the School.

He took over a faculty with thirty professors, two visiting lecturers, seven lecturers, and the Ezra Ripley Thayer Teaching

[3] Holmes, "The Use of Law Schools," *Collected Legal Papers*, p. 47.
[4] Here one remembers Langdell, who came to the School after many years of practice, and one hesitates. But Langdell had only Governor Washburn and Nathaniel Holmes as his original colleagues, and neither was a dyed-in-the-wool academic. Furthermore no one with Langdell's identical qualities turned up among the 1936 candidates.

Fellow, in all forty teachers. The School had 1498 students of all categories, about 215 less than it has at the present time. The new Dean had many problems. Despite the faculty's growth in numbers it was too small for the teaching it had to do. The School's resources were inadequate; the total income from all sources for 1937–38 was about $740,000, a fifth of the dollar income of the School three decades later. Though decline in value of the dollar can account for some of this difference, it by no means accounts for all; the School is financially better off in the late 1960's than it was in the late 1930's

Furthermore the School was in debt to Harvard for a million and a half dollars, the unpaid balance of the cost of reconstructing Langdell Hall in 1927–1929. The School is part of the university's corporate entity; we were all told early in our law study that one cannot be a debtor to one's self. However, when Langdell Hall was built, the university had advanced the money and required that the School pay it back, not as a debt in the usual sense but as a reallocation of university assets. In Dean Landis' first year he paid the university $42,472 for interest and amortization of the university's advance,[5] and still ended up with a surplus of nearly $26,000, a substantial triumph of prudence in academic house-keeping.

An academic administrator must be all things to all men — particularly to his governing boards. He must be a man of business, wise in the handling of funds, and in modern times experienced in the operations of government. At the same time in the eyes of his faculty he must be a teacher and a scholar, he must have met classes, supervised students, and have published wise things in hard-covered books. Landis had all this in his record. He had been a brilliant student at the Law School; he had achieved its doctorate; he had been clerk to Mr. Justice Brandeis, a sort of accolade; he had authored important published works; he had engaged actively in drafting national legislation; he had as chairman directed the business of an important administrative commission during its most creative period. He was young and energetic. He had the confidence of his faculty.

The result of all this was a pleasant and wholesome era of good

[5] Dean Griswold's report for 1947–48 records the final payment of this charge. "Over a period of twenty years, a total of $1,463,447 has been applied from the income of the School for this purpose, plus an aggregate of $431,064 for interest, or a total of $1,994,511. The final discharge of this obligation removes a heavy burden from the School" (p. 390).

feeling in the years between Landis' accession to the deanship and the outbreak of World War II. By his writing and his teaching Landis had become a leader in the School's scholarly activity. During those years, 1937–1941, Professors Casner, Freund, Fuller, and Katz joined the faculty. In 1938 Yale invited Landis to give its Storrs Lectures, probably the most distinguished lecture series in the United States, as distinguished a lectureship as has ever existed. Roscoe Pound's *Introduction to the Philosophy of Law*, Judge Cardozo's *Nature of the Judicial Process*, and Carl Lotus Becker's *Heavenly City of the Eighteenth Century Philosophers* all were Storrs Lectures, predecessors of Landis' 1938 lectures which the Yale University Press published in 1938 as *The Administrative Process*.

Landis' book is a tract for the times, a document of liberal orthodoxy in the late 1930's which looked to the administrative process as the solution for social ills, then thought mostly economic. Society's aches and pains were curable by federal agencies not hampered by Montesquieu's long-outdated postulates of governmental segmentation. Landis had been an active, dedicated missionary of the New Deal, and the New Deal was deeply elitist in theory. Indeed, a sensed but generally unspoken doubt of the traditional processes of majoritarian democracy was a profound trait of the intellectuals of the 1930's, just as it was among the intellectuals of the McCarthy era, just as it is among the intellectuals around faculty club tables in the 1960's. The only question is what elite group we choose. In the late 1930's we distrusted the Supreme Court, instead choosing to put our faith in administrative experts. In the McCarthy days of the late 1940's and 1950's we suddenly revived our faith in the Supreme Court to which we looked for protection against legislative and administrative tyranny. No word of this is said to undervalue Dean Landis. He was a man deeply imbued with the ideas particular to his own time, as almost all men are;[6] and this book is a history of men and ideas in the Law School. *The Administrative Process* is an eloquent declaration of faith in discretionary government carried on by an assumed enlightened and apolitical elite. The only serious shortcoming of the book is its author's neglect of the possibility that a governing elite might be neither enlightened,

---

[6] Perceptive and sympathetic essays on Landis' life and work, written at the time of his death by his faculty friends Erwin N. Griswold, Milton Katz, and Louis Jaffe, appear in the December 1964 *Harvard Law Review*, pp. 313f.

nor apolitical, nor wisely selected. Time was to disconcert many men, including Landis, by demonstrating this possibility.

Dean Landis' first report to the President covered the academic year 1936–37. Although the new Dean's appointment was made on January 4, 1937, orderly completion of his work with the Securities Exchange Commission required that he defer the start of his new duties at Harvard until the following September 1. The major substance of his report was curricular reform, recommended by the faculty studies during the preceding years, and now put in effect. The Dean wrote that the faculty's task was compression of the previous course material so as to permit the introduction of new matter presented by the rapidly developing law, without increasing the number of years devoted to legal study, or the number of teaching hours per year. He wrote:

An underlying principle of the new curriculum is the hope of having the fundamentals in legal training behind the student by the end of the second year, thereby permitting freedom in following bents or particular aptitudes in the third year. It will be seen that a distinct effort has been made to permit and encourage seminary work, ordinarily partaking of research characteristics, in the third year. Intimate contact with the Faculty is thus afforded in that period in the student's training when he is deemed best capable of benefiting from it.

As the law was rapidly changing, the School required some institution to watch its development — hence the faculty committee on instruction which was "to act as an agency both to appraise the working of the proposed curriculum and to develop the changes that may appear to be necessary. The adequate functioning of that Committee is as integral to the scheme as the scheme itself."

In a paragraph on admission policy in his 1936–37 report Dean Landis wrote that reduction in the number of students was desirable. He hoped that this might be achieved by excluding candidates who had not demonstrated sufficient excellence in their college academic work. This, he also correctly said, would cut down a large part of the first-year failures; but as his report for the following year pointed out, the number of men in the second- and third-year classes would increase, and no net decrease in the School's size would come about. It might even grow larger. In his 1937–38 report Dean Landis wrote a bit wistfully, "How far the School should now set as its definite aim reduction in numbers by say one-third, thereby leaving it with a total enrollment of 1,000 students is thus one of the major questions it now faces." In this report the Dean asked whether aptitude tests would point a way of escape from the School's population dilemma. Thirty years later aptitude tests have become deeply fixed in the School's criteria for admissions. But in 1937–38 the School had 1389 students; in 1966–67 it had 1716.

Henry L. Stimson in 1938 was one of the School's most distinguished alumni. A Yale A.B. of 1888 and a Harvard A.M. of 1889, he had studied at the School in 1888–90 but, like his contemporary Roscoe Pound, had left without taking a degree in laws. He had long practiced in New York, been secretary of war under Taft, secretary of state under Hoover, and was later to be secretary of war again under Roosevelt and Truman between 1940 and 1945. In 1938 Stimson contributed a fund which made possible at the south end of Langdell Hall reading room a junior common room, as it would be known at most universities. At Stimson's request the room was named for Elihu Root. Easy chairs and lounges are scattered through the Root Room; a table is covered with current magazines and books, and the bookshelves around the walls are filled with volumes of biography, the social sciences, history, and the like. Students are able to use the room for occasional relaxation, for widening horizons, in intervals of the somewhat fiercely concentrated study of law. To that end a sign on the center table notifies visitors that the room is not intended to be used for study. It was dedicated on April 1, 1939, with brief speeches by Dean Landis; by Zechariah Chafee, representing the class of 1913 which provided a gift for some of the books; by Elihu Root, Jr.; and by Stimson, the School's wise and generous friend.[7] The Root Room has become a symbol of the aspiration to maintain a scholarly tradition without assertion of self-conscious Spartanism.

2

Two years and a half after Landis was chosen Dean, World War II broke out in Europe. In the long run it was to affect

[7] In his autobiography, *On Active Service in Peace and War* (written with McGeorge Bundy in 1948), Stimson told of his sense of indebtedness to the School.

America and the Law School much more gravely and permanently than had World War I. For a year after the first guns
were fired on the borders of Germany and Poland, the people
of the United States hung uncertain, not quite decided on their
involvement, and Harvard's people reflected the national division
of opinion. "America First" was a national group with its deepest
roots in the Midwest, where the necessity or wisdom of America's
participation in war against Germany and Italy was least evident
to many men. America First had a Harvard student chapter. In
those early days men still doubted and debated.

To oppose America First, people holding the opposite views
organized The Committee to Save America by Aid to the Allies.
Mayo A. Shattuck, LL.B. 1921, a leader of the Boston bar, was
the Massachusetts chairman. Professor Seavey of the Law School
organized American Defense: Harvard Group, a subsidiary of
Save America. Professor Leach enthusiastically allied himself
with Seavey. American Defense wrote newspaper articles and
went on the radio. On December 7, 1941, Japan ended American
doubts on foreign policy by bombarding Pearl Harbor. Meantime the United States was mobilizing. The Acting Dean's report for 1941–42 stated: "In September 1941 there were about
1250 men in the School." An effect of the emergency was to
reduce the School to 828 in the autumn of 1941, and to 572 by
April 1942.

In January 1942 Dean Landis took leave from Harvard for
government duty in Washington and Professor Morgan became
Acting Dean. In the summer of 1942 a three-term year was established, with sessions in summer, fall, and spring. In June 1942,
171 students registered. By the summer of 1943 registration had
fallen to 72 men; by the summer of 1944 it fell to 48. The report
of Acting Dean Morgan for 1941–42 noted deaths of students
who had left the School to enlist. His reports on the faculty for
that year and the next should be quoted. Of 1941–42 he wrote:

During the year seven members of the Faculty and the Secretary
secured leave to enter the service of the United States Government,
and one already there had his leave extended. On January 12, 1942,
Dean Landis became Director of the Office of Civilian Defense at
Washington after having served as Regional Director in Boston since
June 1941. On February 7 Vice-Dean Hall joined the legal staff of
O.P.A. in Boston, and on March 1 Professor McLaughlin went to the

Washington office of the same bureau. He has since transferred to the War Relocation Authority in Washington. On March 6 Professor Warner was appointed Recruiting Specialist for duty in the First United States Civil Service District in Boston. In the latter part of May Professors Casner and Leach received Commissions as Majors in the United States Army. Professor Casner had been Director of the War Service Bureau since April 1942, and had previously acted as the head of the Defense Advisory Board. In June Professor Simpson was called to active duty as a Major of Artillery. Professor Katz continued in the legal department of the War Production Board in Washington. On May 1 Secretary Dimmitt took leave to become a Captain in the United States Army.

Professor Powell served from September 15 to November 15 as a member of the President's Fact Finding Board in connection with the threatened railway strike. He also gave one course in the Department of Government. Professor Fuller's teaching schedule was reduced as of April 1, 1942, to enable him to do important work with the firm of Ropes, Gray, Best, Coolidge & Rugg in Boston. Professor Baker, who was appointed Fessenden Professor as of September 1, 1941, took over in the Graduate School of Business Administration the duties formerly performed by the late Professor Isaacs, and continued to give one course in the Law School. Professor Morgan was appointed Acting Dean as of January 12, 1942. Mr. John Sherman Myers was appointed Thayer Teaching Fellow but resigned in August 1942 to enter the Army as a Captain.

On the year 1942–43 Dean Morgan reported:

The teaching staff has been further depleted during the past academic year. Ten regular members of the Faculty remain, and Professor Pound is carrying a full teaching load in the Law School. Professor Baker continues to give one course, devoting most of his time to his duties at the Graduate School of Business Administration. Professor Fuller, while in practice with Ropes, Gray, Best, Coolidge and Rugg, still conducts his course in Contracts.

The seven members in Government service at the time of the last report have been joined by several of their colleagues. Dean Landis was with the Office of Civilian Defense until September, when he was appointed American Director of Economic Operations in the Middle East, with the personal rank of Minister. Vice-Dean Hall has transferred from the Office of Price Administration in Boston to the Operations Analysis Section of the United States Air Force, and expects to go overseas shortly for the duration. Professors Casner and Leach have been advanced to the rank of Lieutenant Colonel; and the former has been in Ireland for some months. Professor McLaughlin has recently transferred to the Price Adjustment Board, Maritime

Commission; and Professor Warner is now with the Office of Strategic Services. Professor Simpson is now Lieutenant Colonel, IGD, Assistant Director Control Division, at the Headquarters of the 8th Service Command in Texas. Professor Katz, who has been on leave of absence since 1941, has gone over to the Office of Strategic Services. Professor Freund is with the Office of the Solicitor General; Professor Hart is Associate General Counsel with the Office of Price Administration in Washington.

Professor Hudson is on leave devoting his time to two important projects in the field of international law, (1) a fresh study of the problems connected with the international court of the future; (2) an attempt to accomplish a community of views among Americans and Canadians actively interested in international law, concerning a post-war program.

Professors Gardner and J. B. Thayer are on leave of absence for the year. Philip W. Thayer, Research Associate in Comparative Law, is with the American Embassy in Santiago, Chile. Secretary Dimmitt is now a Major, and during the year has been with the A.A.S. in Texas.

Of the full-time members of the Faculty several are giving time to Government services. Professor Glueck is a member of the Supreme Court Advisory Committee engaged in drafting Rules of Criminal Procedure for the Federal Courts. Professor Dodd is Compliance Commissioner for the New England Regional Office of the War Production Board. Professor Griswold is a member of the Alien Enemy Hearing Board for Massachusetts and is busy with various pieces of work for the Treasury Department. Professor McCurdy is chairman of one of the examining committees for the Federal Legal Register for the United States Civil Service. Professor Maguire is Tax Simplification Expert for the Treasury Department. Professor Powell is Consultant to the Board of Investigation and Research under the Transportation Act of 1940. Professor Seavey is a consultant for the Civilian Defense. Acting Dean Morgan is chairman of the War Shipping Panel of the National War Labor Board.

Dean Morgan's report on buildings for the same year gives an idea of the military occupation of Harvard.

A greater part of the space formerly occupied by the Law School has now been released to the use of the Armed Forces. At the end of last year they occupied Austin Hall, the north end of the Langdell reading room and Langdell North Middle classroom. At the end of this year, they are using also the Court Room, the south end of the Langdell reading room, Gannett House, the Chancery Club, and all the classrooms in Langdell. The Law School now occupies the center part of Langdell. The main entrance on the east, or Holmes Field, side of the building is the entrance for the offices and classrooms. Entrance to the reading room is still through the south entry.

The Landis Deanship

The offices of the Secretary, formerly housed on the first floor of Gannett House, are in the north wing of Langdell, directly opposite the Dean's offices. The offices of the Harvard Law Review, formerly housed on the second and third floors of Gannett House, have been moved to the first floor of Kendall House.

May 1945 saw the end of war in Europe, and September brought an armistice in the Pacific. Dean Landis returned to the School in January 1945; his Report for 1944–45 shows the start of the School's transition from war to peace. The student population at first continued low. In the summer term in 1945, only 58 men registered. But the armistice with Japan was the prelude to a rush of returning students. For the fall term 1945–46, 478 men registered. For the spring term of 1946, 1163 came, and for the summer term of 1946 the School enrolled 1445 men. Rebuilding of the faculty was necessary, since a number of professors had retired or resigned. President Conant appointed a committee drawn from the bench and bar to recommend needed appointments. Dean Landis designated a similar committee of the faculty. In the last months of the Landis deanship and the early days under Dean Griswold a series of men who had been in the armed forces or had otherwise served the government during the war joined the faculty, David F. Cavers, Robert R. Bowie, Mark DeWolfe Howe, Archibald Cox, Robert Braucher, Ernest Joseph Brown, Richard Hinckley Field, Benjamin Kaplan, and Robert Amory, Jr.

To meet postwar conditions, a further revision of the curriculum and of methods of instruction would require consideration; to cope with these needs Dean Landis appointed a new committee on legal education with Professor Lon Fuller as its chairman. The committee prepared a questionnaire distributed to a sampling of the School's graduates, asking about the actualities of practice and the defects in legal education which these observers saw. To James Landis the School owes much for men recruited as faculty in the last months of his deanship, and for the foresight which led him to arrange for re-examination of the School's curriculum. This self-scrutiny contributed much to significant revisions after Erwin Griswold became Dean.

But Landis had felt too much excitement in national service under the New Deal in Washington, and in overseas service during the war, to settle down contentedly to academic teaching and administration at Harvard. He was restless and discontented; his ability to confine himself to work in Langdell Hall declined. Finally, in May 1946, he resigned as dean and as a professor.

James Landis' later life never entirely satisfied him. President Truman appointed him chairman of the Civil Aeronautics Board in 1946 and he served until 1947. He went to New York City to practice law. He was elected Supervisor of the town of Harrison, New York, in 1955 and served until 1957. He became a member of the New York Public Service Commission in 1958. He returned to Washington as special assistant to President Kennedy in 1961, hoping, perhaps, for another glad confident morning like 1933. But instead the day was late for him. To his friends, it now seems apparent that he was ill, that his judgment had become distorted, that he no longer could think as a normal person. In 1963 he was back in New York again, practicing law, when the federal government instituted a prosecution against him in the Federal District Court for willful failure to file income tax returns for five years. He paid all the deficiencies and came to court from a hospital to plead guilty. He was sentenced to a month's imprisonment and spent most of that time in a hospital undergoing psychiatric treatment. The New York courts in 1963 suspended him for a year from the practice of law. He was well enough, after his month of imprisonment had ended, to return to his comfortable house in Rye, New York, where he tried to rest and rebuild his health. When the weather was warm he frequently went swimming in a pool in the garden behind his house. On July 30, 1964, a neighbor found him drowned there, dressed in his swimming trunks. No one had been with him at the end of his life, so full of early promise and achievement, and which had ended in such sorrow.

At the services held in his memory in Memorial Church in Harvard Yard, Dean Griswold spoke of the School's good fortune that so much of Dean Landis' intense talent had been devoted to the law at Harvard, and well said that surely one who had done so much should be judged by his best. Landis at his best was a great lawyer and legal scholar. Dean Griswold quoted Ben Jonson's words about Francis Bacon: "I have and do reverence him for the greatness that was only proper to himself . . . in his adversity I ever prayed that God would give him strength; for greatness he could not want."

After 1946: The Griswold Deanship

In the School's perspective of a century and a half, the end of the Second World War and the resignation of Dean Landis seem almost simultaneous. In May 1946, when Landis resigned, the School needed no change in policy as sudden and drastic as that which came with Eliot's inauguration in 1869. Neither the President of the university nor the faculty of law during that postwar moment conceived any one conspicuous change in the School's objectives or methods. It needed wise implementation of that which was already obvious. James Bryant Conant continued his administration of Harvard for eight years after the Japanese surrender had turned Harvard from problems of war to problems of peace, supporting the School steadily as he had from the beginning. Nathan Marsh Pusey, who succeeded Conant in 1953, had taught classical languages and literature at several colleges and had been President of Lawrence at Appleton, Wisconsin, for nine years before he became President of Harvard. As Eliot, Lowell, and Conant did before him, President Pusey has continued to uphold the School, giving its dean and faculty a free hand. He comes regularly to the Law School's faculty lunches and presides at its faculty meetings with perceptive quiet wit. He has left to the Law School the keeping of its own house.

This habitual delegation of control to the School's own people has been characteristic of the university's administration from the beginning. The President and Fellows have stepped in only at rare moments of crisis. Quincy and Story brought about the reorganization of the School in 1829. In 1847 President Everett and the Governing Boards tried to require the faculty of law to institute regular examinations; the effort failed and the General Regulation of that year, requiring examinations, was never put in force until Langdell became dean in 1870. President Eliot personally chose Langdell to reinvigorate the flagging School, the most important decision since the reorganization of 1829. Ever since Langdell's day the dean and faculty of the School have largely conducted their own affairs, except for the critical and rare business of appointing new deans, when the president has always taken an active part in the selection. Probably the Corporation took the initiative in the decisions to close out the Pound and Landis deanships, when time for wholesome change had become apparent. Choice of faculty has for generations been almost entirely by faculty co-option, the Governing Boards willingly ratifying faculty choice. Of course the direction of these choices and of faculty trends has not been ignored by the administration of the university. Gurney's almost agonized protest to Eliot at what he thought was the School's unwholesome drift toward unpractical scholasticism was an instance. Lowell gave sturdy support to Chafee, Frankfurter, and Pound when they came under criticism as unwholesome radicals in the early 1920's.

The dean of the Law School plays the single most important part in selecting new faculty members, but he can be and not infrequently is overruled by his colleagues. He and a faculty committee on appointments propose names to the faculty, which then discusses the proposals in faculty meetings. The dean then recommends to the Governing Boards of the university those men whom the faculty approves. The routine of recruitment is by three-year appointment as assistant professor, almost always followed at the end of that period by permanent appointment as full professor. But the faculty does not hesitate to propose invitations for direct appointment as full professors, either of distinguished men from other universities, or men from practice who have demonstrated the rather rare combination of experience in the use of professional skills, scholarly promise, and the almost indefinable traits of character and personality which make a teacher. It is worth remarking that invitations are not infrequently declined. There are many distinguished universities in the United States which compete vigorously with Harvard in the search for talent.

The School's overall financial management has always been a necessary concern of the President and Fellows, though here the dean is a sort of one-man bureau of the budget. It remains true that in general the university administration during the

An anteroom decorated with Constantino Nivola's avant-garde sculpture introduces the visitor to the library of International Legal Studies. Then through tall glass doors he enters a cheerfully lighted reading room where portraits of Judge Story and Judge Hudson benignly preside.

The Root Room has become a symbol of the aspiration to maintain a scholarly tradition without assertion of self-conscious Spartanism.

twentieth century has let the School run its own affairs. The result has been good.

2

The postwar School faced old problems in 1946, magnified and made more complex by the social and political developments it shared with the nation and the rest of the world. It needed steady and wise leadership to make required changes with all deliberate speed. The School had to adjust its study and its teaching to a United States in which three quarters of a century of urban growth and international rivalry had produced a congeries of governmental and legal difficulties, none new in kind, all aggravated in degree, which called for study and instruction on a new scale, vivified by fresh imagination.

Conduct of the postwar School required prudent overhaul of much student policy. It called for revision of the system of admission of students selected from among an increasing legion of applicants; for a new organization of study; for improved living conditions. Curricular developments made necessary a greatly increased faculty, equipped to deal with new matters, and an expanded and rearranged library. The School required more space, and more convenient facilities. Necessary to any of these developments was additional money. And no one of these requirements could be adequately met without continuous, well-planned, and farsighted management. A great part of the decade 1936–1946 had been scrambled by war and by administrative uncertainties. The time had now come for thoughtful, systematic rebuilding of the School's work.

The story of the twenty years from 1946 to 1966 is an account of this reconstruction for the future. Common justice must ascribe predominant influence in the enterprise to the dynamic and intelligent leadership of Dean Griswold; but the same common justice must acknowledge that the rest of the faculty, independent-minded men, often hard-pressed by exacting work, sometimes temperamental like most mortals, still in good heart made every effort to get on with what had to be done. It has been done more than well.

President Conant and the rest of the Corporation spent no long time choosing a sixth dean after James Landis resigned in May

1946. In June they picked a forty-one-year-old professor of law from the School's faculty who had first been appointed assistant professor in 1934. Erwin Nathaniel Griswold took over his new duties on July 1, 1946. To his task he brought twelve years' experience in teaching law, unlimited energy, and a high sense of organization. He had written a standard book on spendthrift trusts, and casebooks on federal taxation and on conflict of laws. When the Corporation announced his appointment his faculty colleagues felt new confidence in the School's future.

In July 1946 Harvard was besieged by former students returning from service in arms, and by others seeking original admission after years on active duty. By the end of 1945–46, "the School had become very much overcrowded, with the most unusual and probably the best student body it . . . ever had." [1] In February 1947, of the 1900 and more students in residence, 93 percent were veterans, of whom many had been off at the wars from three to five years. Their average age was 26 or 27. A large proportion had carried the responsibilities of command, sometimes in battle where their decisions involved life or death for their men. They were eager to take up their civilian lives again and earnestly sought a thorough education for peacetime work. Forty percent of them were married. No sensible man expected to treat these responsible and tested men as immature students; nor did the returned men willingly tolerate any such attitude. Pedagogical devices to persuade them to diligence were superfluous. They were adequately self-directed. No sane person would wish for the world a repetition of the years from 1939 to 1945; but no teacher in a graduate faculty during the immediate postwar period can help wishing that all teachers' lives might be lived with men like those who returned from the war to American universities.

The School was not designed for a student population nearly half of whom were married men, many of whom had young children. Harvard did all it could to ameliorate their living conditions. In the spring of 1946 Dean Landis had originated the idea of a lunchroom in Kendall House, run by volunteers from the "Law Wives," [2] to provide a place where men who brought

---

[1] See Dean Griswold's report for 1945–46 in the President's reports for that year, p. 345.

[2] "The Law Wives" organized themselves as early as the late 1920's. But the

their lunches to the School might eat them in some comfort. The School provided tables, chairs, and a little supplementary food. While the postwar emergency continued, an average of 300 men took lunches in Kendall House, five days a week. As months went on the burdens of service became such that it was desirable to pay the helpers, though the Law Wives continued general management and direction. A student could thus get lunch at an average cost of thirty cents, about half of the price the university was obliged to charge at its own dining halls, and about a third of the cost in a restaurant. Kendall House added humanity and sociability to convenience; midday meals at a low cost contributed substantially to the scholarship subsidies available to students. Success demonstrated the feasibility of future graduate commons.

The Law Wives organized and staffed a nursery school for which the Law School arranged quarters in the basement of Walter Hastings Hall. The staff of the Department of Buildings and Grounds cooperated by putting the rooms in shape. They equipped and fenced an outdoor pleasant-weather playground for the nursery school children in back of Kendall House.

On the whole it was a happy time at the Harvard Law School and in other graduate faculties throughout the country. Young families came together again after years of difficult separation, when wives had worried about their husbands, the fathers of their children, in the perils of war. With slender means, often aided by outside work, these women had managed to eke out a livelihood for themselves and their children until the war was over. Now most worries ended. Dwellings were poor and study was hard, but wartime comradeship between the returned men continued a little while, softened by shared family existence in a community where everyone was young, where no one was rich, where appearances were equal, and where young men and women were grateful for what life had to offer. Some of their teachers had come back to similar reassurance. Between such older and younger men in American universities, sharing the remembered experience of war, was a generous sense of unity in study. Sometimes the chances of academic choice brought service friends together. One teacher at another American law

great increase in married men after World War II has much increased the importance of the organization.

School remembers seeing, in his classroom in the autumn of 1945, a new student, still in an army captain's uniform, with one of his legs stiffly held in a cast. The wounded officer wore on his shoulder the Red I insignia of a division whose shoulderpatch the teacher, too, had recently worn. After the lecture, crutches delayed the younger man; the teacher went to him, spoke of his own pleasure at the sight of the familiar divisional patch, and asked if the captain had served in Tunisia. The young officer answered: "Sure; the last time I saw you was in Tunisia; it was in a hell of a rainstorm south of Maktar. You asked me the way to the command-post of C Company of the second Battalion of the 26th Infantry. Remember?"

For many of those men and women, teachers and students, wives and children, the first brief years of peace, spent in universities, were to prove the best of their lives. War had changed the ideas of many of these men about their objectives. For many of them, attainment of a reasonable livelihood was clearly not going to be very difficult, nor was the pursuit of conspicuous material success to be a satisfying object of existence. In the postwar students there was a strong strand of idealism, as there has been in their successors. They were not content to let the world stand as it was, either at home or abroad. Many of these young men were seeking outlets for this impulse in changed careers, in teaching at home and in other countries; in government work in the United States or overseas; in tasks such as some of their successors sought in the Peace Corps of the 1960's. This urge, in its fundamentals so much like that which had a century and a half earlier sent some of their great-grandparents out as missionaries, now found its springs in a different philosophy; but the impulse was much the same. It continued to be a notable feature of student life during the next two decades and is still powerful as the period of this history comes to a close.

When the World War II veterans graduated and went out in the world, the number of the School's students declined to normal, and except for the brief interval when servicemen returned from the Korean War, most young men again brought to the School only the preparation of college years. The proportion of married men also declined, but evidently a substantial number of students with wives and children were destined to be a permanent part of the School's family. In 1964–65 27 percent of the student body were married though only 9 percent had been in the armed forces. The continuing Law Wives organization of the present day is a symbol of this change in our habit of life.

After every war a great deal of ink is spent, much of it foolishly, in writing about traits of the "postwar generation." Postwar people are much like all others; but still there is something to the idea of a perceptible difference. Traditions of the depression of the 1930's and the war of 1941–45 affected men who had been too young for either. A spirit of skepticism persisted in them. The School generations which succeeded the World War II servicemen were, like the depression generation and the veterans, not content to accept whatever Harvard offered to them without questioning its merit. The Law School *Record*, a weekly student newspaper which began publication in July 1946, reflected some of this spirit, not alone about academic matters but about material conditions of life. Young men wrote frankly about their dislikes, and demanded betterment. For one thing, they saw no good reason why the university should provide so much pleasanter surroundings and living facilities for its undergraduates than for its older professional students. The School properly tried, within reason, to get them what they needed.

3

When the School opened in September 1950 women students appeared in the first-year law class. For nearly eighty years Harvard had stubbornly kept them out. In 1871 the Corporation had denied admission of one Helen M. Sawyer as a member of the Law School; in 1878 it barred another woman, not named in its minutes; in 1899 Frances A. Keay, a graduate of Bryn Mawr, was refused as a regular student of the Law School, but was cautiously told that if Radcliffe would admit her as a graduate student with a view to attending the Harvard Law School she could take the courses and examinations but not be eligible for the Harvard LL.B.

Harvard so put itself in a position which in time became untenable. For many years before 1950 Eleanor Glueck had been one of Harvard's two world-famous criminologists. Other great university schools of law accepted women. In 1948 Harvard invited a distinguished legal scholar then practicing law in New

York, Soia Mentschikoff, to come to the Law School for a year as a visiting professor to teach commercial law. Once the Law School had a woman professor it had no good excuse to continue barring the doors against women students.

The profound conservatism of academics had fostered many worries about the effect of such a radical innovation; when it happened there was no difficulty at all. Thirty to forty women now register each year in a class of 550 or so first-year students. Many of them live in Wyeth Hall, on Massachusetts Avenue at Everett Street, a university dormitory for women graduate students. Some are appointed senior residents of the smaller Radcliffe houses. About the same percentage of women as men make the *Law Review*. Now and then a woman student marries a classmate and outranks him in grades; from this disparity no domestic disaster has thus far ensued. Women find appropriate employment after graduation. One now wonders what caused all the worry between 1871 and 1950.

In one conspicuous academic aspect student existence since 1945 has become infinitely less rigorous than it was in 1935. The policy of keeping the School to a total student population of about 1700 now obliges the admissions committee to select from over 3000 applicants an entering class of about 550 on the basis of their undergraduate records and their performance in a "Law School Admission Test," used as a criterion of admission by a large number of leading American university law schools. Rigorous selection has eliminated almost all the hazard of subsequent academic failure from the study of law at Harvard. At the close of the academic year 1964–65, 528 first-year men took examinations. Only four failed, a rate of 0.8 percent, compared with 0.9 percent in the preceding year, and with 37 percent in June 1926. In June 1966 six men failed. The fluctuations in today's numbers are too small to be significant. The excellence of human material has eliminated waste in production – a waste in emotion that was even worse than the loss in time and energy.[3]

In April 1959 Louis A. Toepfer, Vice Dean and Director of

[3] In 1929–30 the School had 1641 students; in 1931–32 it had 1596. In 1966 the total reached 1716 — only 120 more than in 1931–32. But since that time the teaching staff has more than doubled — from 33 to 77. In 1932 Harvard gave degrees in law to 464 men; in 1965 it gave 557 such degrees. On the average not only are more capable men selected as students, but the faculty does far more teaching of the men selected.

Admissions, wrote for the *Law School Bulletin* an article on "Admissions: Procedure, Policies, Views."

Ours is not the fairly easy task of separating sheep from goats, but the more difficult responsibility of sorting out the best from among the good.

From each applicant we receive a collection of information, which, when judged in the light of our experience and instincts, lets us decide whether to accept him. Each applicant must tell us about all the colleges and graduate schools he has attended, and he must ask these schools to send us a complete transcript of his record. He must also give us a complete account of his undergraduate honors, his extra-curricular activities and responsibilities, employment record, the nature and extent of any physical disabilities, a report of any disciplinary action or suspensions while at college, or convictions of crimes. From the Dean of Students at each of his colleges we receive a report about each applicant's qualities of character, and in many cases, other helpful news of his virtues or shortcomings. The applicant's college health service completes a questionnaire for the information of our Health Service, which may, in appropriate cases, advise us whether health problems make admission unwise. Every applicant must take an Admission Test which has been developed as a measure of capacity for law study. Interviews and letters of recommendation are not required but each year many prospective students visit the School in order to see and be seen, and, quite naturally, letters in support of applicants come in by the hundreds.

All of this information is brought together for each applicant in the Admissions Office where it is carefully summarized and sent to the Admissions Committee. The Committee must then evaluate and appraise the candidate, and compare his accomplishments and prospects with those of other applicants. Clear cases can be processed quickly, but between those who are clearly in or clearly out, there is a wide borderline area. This is where the Committee works and worries all Spring, until finally the class is full and the waiting list formed.

There is no mystery or magic to our admission work. There are no mathematical formulae, or quotas, or premiums for distance, or fixed course requirements, or absolute minimums of any kind. It is a sorting job, and in our attempt to do it well we use our experience, judgment and speculative instincts in much the same way any sensible person would. It is not easy; sorting people never is, and our efforts are far from perfect.

Dean Griswold's report for 1963–64 showed that an embarrassment of riches in candidates for admission could present new and puzzling problems. He wrote:

Although the increased volume of applications has changed the whole character of the admissions situation, our methods of selection have remained essentially the same. These methods were developed when we were trying to separate those whom we thought could do our work from those who were not really qualified . . . I believe that our methods of selection have become inadequate and unrealistic. Too many able and interesting students fail to survive the first cut, which is now made in terms of college records and admission test scores. The final choice now is made essentially on the basis of the most refined discrimination in terms of marks and scores. It may well be that in the zone in which we are operating, reliance on marks and scores, though having the appearance of objectivity, is in fact quite arbitrary . . .

Our new students are a very fine group, with a high level of academic ability. It is possible, though, that this ability is more limited in range and type than it should be. We may be overlooking qualities and virtues which are not adequately reflected in the college records and test scores which we receive. Indeed, it seems to me that, in view of the high academic caliber of so many of our applicants, we might well get a better class, more representative of the range of abilities which are useful and important in the practice of law and other legal work, if we simply took all the persons whom we regard as qualified — which would be close to 2,000 in terms of the current year's applicants — and drew by lot from this group for places in the class.

The survival rate associated with the present-day highly selective admission policy, a rate which approaches totality, has long since eliminated the appropriateness of "Bull" Warren's legendary prediction to new first-year men that one in three would fail. Instead the present phrase should run, "Look to your left and look to your right; a quarter-century hence very likely one among the three of you will be a distinguished public man, or one may be a noted legal scholar, or all three may be talented and useful practicing lawyers. At any rate the chances are overwhelming that all three of you will be back in Cambridge next September."

Has this reassuring change weakened the fiber of students? One questions fear as an inducement to diligent study. Probably its effect is minimal. The impulse for success at the School is ambition, not terror. A policy of occasional dismissal of tolerably successful but unfortunately low-ranking men, intended to spur on a supposed column of laggards, would affect only the least able, the minimally motivated, who perform passably, who maintain themselves afloat above the small percent who perceivably sink. A conceivable policy would be rigorously to dismiss as failures the lowest, say, 5 percent of the class; but as grading is an inexact art that plan would be cruelly impersonal and would have an unpredictable effect — like decimating a regiment. Surely it would be intolerable to establish the procedure Voltaire ascribed to the British when they shot Admiral Byng for his retreat from Minorca.[4] Surely we should not fire a few students at random in order to put heart in the others.

Beginning in the autumn of 1949 the School launched an innovation in first-year teaching which might have shocked the faculty of 1909. The philosophy of Edward H. Warren's *Spartan Education* called for a beginning law student to be tossed into a confusion of case-method studies, encouraged, but largely left to find his own way through months of initial bewilderment. We elders as students had come to take pride in this ordeal; it showed how tough we were. We teachers had all survived it; we intended to pass it to our successors, undiluted, unweakened. By this process we had learned to guide our own studies. But the student questionnaires of the early 1930's had begun to challenge the value of unrelieved confusion. Three years are short enough, and if the student's introduction to law could be expedited without softening his intellectual muscles, so much the better.

In the fall term of 1949 six teaching fellows, recent graduates of law schools, most with a little experience in practice, began a process intended to diminish the classic first-year bewilderment. They dealt with the first-year class in groups of twenty men, each group having a weekly tutorial session with a teaching fellow lasting an hour and a half. The teaching fellows eased the transition from college to professional school, helped the new students gain a competence in handling legal materials, and gave them some instruction in the drafting of simple legal documents. Professor Cavers guided the teaching fellows during their first years. As all teachers do, the teaching fellows gained from their teaching as much as their students learned. The process is now a familiar part of the first-year instruction.[5]

[4] "Dans ce pays-ci il est bon de tuer de temps en temps un amiral pour encourager les autres." *Candide*, chap. 23.

[5] I have described the work of teaching fellows as though individual instruction of law students were an innovation. In Stearns's day the whole School was

In the twenty-first year of Griswold's deanship, 1966–67, the Law School Catalogue listed seventy-seven active teachers. The teaching staff had more than doubled since 1930, while the size of the student body had increased very little. On February 26, 1966, the Dean, at a meeting of the faculty with the Overseers' Committee to Visit the Law School, was discussing the causes of faculty growth and some of the administrative problems it presented. He pointed out that four additional teachers were joining the School's faculty in September 1966, for whom office space would have to be found in already overcrowded quarters. He gave a simple and correct explanation of the increase: "There's a lot more going on around here than there used to be!" The students and faculty were doing not only far more, but far different things. Some general analysis of the two most recent decades of curricular development is here appropriate.

4

During the ten years which followed World War II the School had adapted itself to changing social and governmental objectives, to new emphases in old developments in public policy and law, which deeply affected the United States internally and in foreign relations. Most of these changes were associated, in one way or another, with the accelerating technological evolution which for a century had been increasing production and speeding transport and communications. The degree of change in society and government had almost produced a change in kind. Social and economic interdependence of all parts of the United States was turning the country more and more rapidly toward unitary national government, toward Washington rather than the states as the primary source of statutory and judicial rules. The School's teaching increasingly had to stress federal sources of law.

The same technological developments made more conclusively evident the impossibility that the United States could go her way unconcerned with what went on in Europe, in South Amer-

---

smaller than a present-day section of first-year students. In his 1826 report Stearns told of the great amount of his time spent in solving students' difficulties and doubts "which they are encouraged and desired to suggest with freedom when they occur."

ica, in Africa or Asia. The United States found itself involved in large cold wars, smaller but deadly hot wars, multiplying international organizations, a national economy more and more tied to the economies of other nations throughout the world. Events in any part of the world became critically important in all others. Electronics brought foreign happenings to television screens in hundreds of thousands of American homes. This close-knit world became uncomfortable. International cooperation had become far more than a subject for attractive cultural discussion: economic interdependence between nations and the menace of unbelievably destructive weapons had made international studies, legal, economic, and diplomatic, a peremptory concern of universities.

The intricate technology of transport and communication brought more and more of the world's people to live in immense cities. The cities, so growing, in turn made necessary still more complex technical and human organizations in order that people might feed themselves and do their work. Technology augmented the city which brought more technology. This accelerating urbanization brought in its wake increasingly aggravated problems of administration of justice, of government controlling people and people controlling government, of trouble caused by technological imperfection. Interdependence has its drawbacks. Failure of an electrical relay in a Canadian power station darkened northeastern United States on a memorable night in the autumn of 1965. A little machine broke in Ontario and Harvard went dark. In a multitude of ways the city became an increasing concern of American government and law and so of the Harvard Law School.

Perhaps instant communication of pictorial news, the dramatic presentation before everyone's eyes of the widespread misery of existence, has contributed to a phenomenon whose existence is indisputable even though its causes may be obscure — a wide increase in sympathetic sensibility among much of civilized mankind. In the United States this has been most conspicuous in the change in race relations during the decades since 1945. Through the century that has passed since the Civil War most of the American people, at first slowly, more recently at an accelerated rate, have come to see the moral imperative of racial equality which that war made inevitable. Since World War II this imperative was dramatized in law and in government first by a series of Supreme Court decisions [6] and more recently by a procession of new federal civil rights acts beginning in 1957, and by corresponding state legislation. It appears in such human impulses as that which led Dean Griswold to accept membership on the federal Civil Rights Commission in addition to his heavy load of duties at Harvard. It has prompted the School, during the summers of 1965 and 1966, to bring undergraduates from Negro colleges in the South to Harvard for instruction, both in the Yard and at the Law School, looking toward their possible inclination to a career in law after their college graduation. It has sent teachers from the School's faculty to teach for awhile in southern universities. The postwar university generation is prompted to generous concern for all sorts of social and governmental misfortune, at home and overseas.

The brute fact of war continually intrudes into today's university life. The draft is a continuing reality in student existence, growing sometimes more, sometimes less evident with the varying intensity of hostilities overseas. War in Korea took students from the School in the early 1950's; a Berlin crisis called out some university students in 1961–62; the draft or call-up of reservists for service in Vietnam is taking young graduates of the School as these words are written. The hopeful among us still wistfully wait for the promised time when war shall reign no more, but signs of that day's coming are not numerous, and the wait for the promised time seems long.

All these developments are properly evident in the substance of today's study and teaching. One conspicuous change in method during the last four decades is the shift from judicial opinions to sweeping, inclusive statutes as the basis of our law and so of instruction at the School. This change was foreshadowed in 1928 by the appointment of James Landis as professor of legislation, and by his 1934 essay "Statutes and the Sources of Law." [7] Study of law in modern America is coming more and more to be the study of what are essentially codes, long, intricate, and carefully drafted statutes covering large areas of law. A half-century ago the single most important element of

[6] See, for example, *Brown v. Board of Education*, 347 U.S. 438 (1954). The list increases at every term of the Supreme Court.

[7] *Harvard Legal Essays in Honor of Joseph Henry Beale and Samuel Williston*, p. 213.

the Law School's instruction was the judicial decision. We studied opinions of courts with scrupulous care; we learned to distinguish one case from another according to minute differences in their facts; thus we concentrated on the individual controversy as the essential core of a lawyer's learning. Today the student must still master this mystery. But in recent years we have come to see with increasing clarity that "the hit and miss method of deciding single local controversies upon evidence and information limited by the narrow rules of litigation" is not a sufficient means to solve comprehensively such vast and intricate problems as present themselves to the nation and the states in the late twentieth century. "Spasmodic and unrelated instances of litigation cannot afford an adequate basis for the creation of integrated national rules." [8]

Thus, for example, instruction at the School in what during the 1920's were separate traditional "casebook courses" in negotiable instruments, sales, and security devices, is now given in the several sections of a single course, the core of which is the Uniform Commercial Code. At the time these words are written, the code has been adopted in forty-nine states, in the District of Columbia, and in the Virgin Islands. It is very nearly a Commercial Code for the entire United States. In a class in commercial transactions the facts of a case are often discussed to exemplify the purpose and the application of a section of the code.

Labor relations offer another example. Matter which, in the days of Dean Ames, would have been treated, if at all, under the rubric Master and Servant is today changed out of all recognition to accord with modern industrial processes, taught as labor law with the National Labor Relations Act as its governing theme. The law of taxation is centered around the federal Internal Revenue Code. Congressional enactment of a series of inclusive statutes regulating race relations during the past decade is furnishing another instance.[9] Quite possibly much of the substance of what in recent years has been taught as constitutional law — the constitutionality *vel non* of state regulation of race relations — is becoming a study of the construction and application of

[8] The quoted words occur in the dissenting opinion of Justices Black, Frankfurter, and Douglas in *McCarroll v. Dixie Greyhound Lines*, 309 U.S. 170 (1940) at p. 188 and p. 189.
[9] A recent example is the Voting Rights Act of August 6, 1965, Public Law 89–110, 79 Stat. at L. 437.

federal statutes, whose constitutionality has been well established.[10]

An analogous movement from specific adjudication to something like inclusive legislation appears in international law. The subject, at one time largely a study in adjustment of individual controversies, now becomes the law of great multilateral treaties, notably in our day the Charter of the United Nations, the sort of international agreement for which Professor Hudson appropriately used the term "international legislation." [11]

The faculty of the Harvard Law School during the two decades which followed World War II have undertaken to adapt their teaching materials and teaching methods to this changing face of American law. Professor Louis Loss in the 1951 introduction to his *Securities Regulation* noted: "it should no longer require demonstration that the case-method of instruction rapidly approaches the point of diminishing returns as applied to advanced law students."

The essence of Dean Langdell's case method appears, in the perspective of nearly a century, to have been the requirement that the student, in advance of each classroom meeting, discern by his own effort some principle of law as judicially applied to specific human situations. The student who came to the classroom thus prepared could profitably to himself and his classmates discuss with a professor one of those specific instances, or several similar instances synthesized, reconciled, adjusted each to the other, in such a way as to perceive and formulate a legal doctrine susceptible of judicial application to new situations which might arise thereafter.

The essential elements of this process — previous study by the student of appropriate material, and application of this material to individual human controversies — provide a system as wholesome for the study of statutes as Langdell's system was for study of judicial opinions. Indeed, as Story demonstrated a century and a third ago, the same method can be used where the student's material is a doctrinal text. The essence of the case method is not necessarily the study of judicial opinions, nor the student's "statement of the case," though that process requires high art,

[10] See, for example, *Katzenbach v. McClung*, 379 U.S. 294 (1964).

[11] He edited a series of volumes under that title published by the Carnegie Endowment for International Peace. In 1965 the School's library carried forward that work by bringing out a new and essential aid to research — the *Index to Multilateral Treaties*.

greatly useful in the university and in professional life. The essence of Langdell's system was the student's own previous active intellectual effort to devise a rational adjustment of a conflict of interest, later tested by lecture-room debate before an eager class. To put the same point negatively, the case method avoids using the classroom hour for oral transmission of abstract doctrine, with the students as passive recipients of the teacher's wisdom. A passive spectator is less concerned with the game than is the player or his backers and his adversaries; the teacher's art is to change mere spectators to eager partisans. A book can transmit doctrine, but no book can replace a free dialogue between intelligent living men in the presence of others deeply concerned.

The modern casebook necessarily differs greatly from the casebook of Langdell's day which was, as its title indicates, a collection of judicial opinions. The economic transactions which occupy much of the attention of lawyers and courts are more complex than they used to be. Dean Ames's monumental 1881 *Cases on Bills and Notes*, except for its index and summary and a few explanatory pages, was entirely a compilation of opinions, many of them quite old, largely English. Although some of the opinions were difficult to read because of certain archaisms, they presented rather simple business situations. On the other hand the student of today, seeking to understand Article Nine of the Uniform Commercial Code which treats of chattel security, trying to understand its application to the distribution and financing of the nation's output of motor vehicles, will be unable to unravel its intricacies solely by studying judicial opinions. The successive sales and the repeated financing involved in the progress of automobiles from manufacturer to distributor, from distributor to dealer, and from the dealer to the individual purchaser, with a new loan and security transaction at each stage,[12] make up a series of economic processes much more difficult to understand than the comparatively simple legal principles which govern those transactions. The business arrangements are more mysterious than the applicable sections of the Commercial Code. Hence a large part of two volumes used in much modern instruction in commercial transactions at the Harvard Law School consists not of judicial opinions but of textual explanation of business com-

---

[12] There were outstanding in the United States at the close of 1965 over twenty-seven billions of dollars of such loans on automobiles.

plexities.[13] Authorship of such volumes consumes more of a professor's time than editing old-style casebooks.

Mechanical production of material for the study of law has changed. Statutory and judicial pronouncements pour out of legislatures and courts. When a significant new statute is enacted, or when a court hands down a new and important decision which the student should study immediately, production of several hundred copies by the conventional letterpress method is often too slow and expensive. Some rapid process must be used to multiply the text and perhaps to reproduce an explanatory comment. The case method in its broadest sense — that is, the presentation to students of situations in contemporary life in which principles of law are applied to people — is often effective in proportion to its freshness. A case is most striking when it has lately arisen in the daily existence with which the student is familiar. Thus a modern law school does well to install mechanical devices which will photograph, on plates from which prints can be made, the pages of a statute or opinion or a typewritten legal essay, and to acquire printing machines from which several hundred copies can be immediately run off for student use. To an increasing extent today's School thus prepares its "books" from week to week as it goes along.[14]

The School's greatly enlarged faculty is busy in these diverse ways with many types of research and scholarship — activities difficult to separate from teaching. The products of a teacher's studies appear at once in his seminar, his lecture hall and, as soon as may be, in his printed publications. And the law professor's enterprises often have an objective far beyond classroom horizons, in the improvement of law or government in action. Amid a multitude of examples of the work of active professors, of emeriti, and of visiting professors one selects illustrative instances at random. Professor Braucher as a Massachusetts Commissioner on Uniform Laws took part in the final stages of drafting the Uniform Commercial Code and has had much to do with drafting other significant uniform legislation. Professor Haar in the 1960's has been engaged in an American Law Institute project concerning control

[13] See Braucher and Sutherland, *Commercial Transactions* (Brooklyn, 1964). By March 1967 every state but Louisiana had enacted the Uniform Commercial Code.

[14] In the fiscal year ending June 30, 1965, the School used more than five million sheets of mimeograph paper.

of land use in the modern city. In the spring of 1966 Harvard granted him leave of absence to become assistant secretary for metropolitan planning and development in the new United States Department of Housing and Urban Development. Professor Keeton has been studying, writing, and teaching about the substitution of some procedure resembling Workmen's Compensation for traditional litigation as a means of distributing among all motorists the inevitable risk of loss from traffic accidents. The Gluecks and Professors Maguire, Hall, Vorenberg, Kamisar, Bator, Fried, Dershowitz, and Weinreb all have been active in various aspects of criminal justice. Professor Donald Turner, a trained economist as well as a lawyer, has long given particular attention to anti-trust matters, and in 1965 resigned to become assistant attorney general of the United States in charge of anti-trust matters. The faculty, that is to say, is busy in the study, development, and practical application of American law. This list of activities is a sampling, not an inclusive account. It could be much extended.

Dean Landis in his report of 1937–38 mentioned efforts of the faculty to associate the work of the Law School with the work of the university as a whole. He mentioned the fact that cautious beginnings were already under way through which the School of Public Administration, the School of Business Administration, the Graduate School of Arts and Sciences, and the Medical School were together with the Law School considering some possibilities for joint attack upon problems common to all these faculties. He wrote:

Law is such an integral part of public administration as a whole, and the obligations of our universities further to professionalize the public service are such, that emphasis upon the public aspects of law must continue. The record of the School in this respect serves to give some index to the quality and character of the legal training that it affords. But for the School adequately to continue to perform this function, broadening of its approach to legal issues and of the content of its curriculum is essential.

Dean Landis returned to this theme in his report for the following year, 1938–39. He told of a joint appointment between the Law School and the School of Public Administration (a procedure continuing in 1966 for a number of faculty members), and said that a committee of the Law School and the faculty of Arts and

Sciences had been exploring the possibility of better relating the collegiate and professional programs of students.

Dean Griswold reopened the same subject in his 1964–65 report with a section headed "The Law School as a Part of the University." Harvard's first professor of law, he reminded the reader, lectured to undergraduates in Harvard College, and if there had been times when the School's outlook had differed from that of the rest of the university, that state of affairs had ended. Joint appointments of professors of history and economics by the Law School and the departments of history and economics, masterships and other appointments in Radcliffe and Harvard houses held by members of the Law School faculty, all demonstrated increasing participation by the School's professors in the work of other Harvard departments. "The Law School has no sense of isolation . . . it is reaching out, in many ways, on many levels, and through many individuals, for contacts with other disciplines and with the wide realm of knowledge which is so well represented in the University . . . We hope that the contacts will continue to grow so that legal education may be as broadly based as possible, and so that the fruits of thought and experience in legal work may be more widely known in other areas which are concerned with closely related problems."

These developments have mainly concerned the law internal to the United States and the work of the faculty in studying and teaching it; but perhaps the most striking evolution in the School's intellectual commitment since 1945 has occurred in the field of international legal studies, a term which now connotes far more than the "international law" of Professor Strobel's day. Dean Griswold wrote in his report for 1954–55:

The term "international legal studies" is new as a formal designation of an area of law teaching and scholarship. It includes international law and international organization, but is wider and more varied. It comprehends comparative law, but the comparison of legal systems is only a part of it. It includes "private international law" in the sense of conflict of laws problems which arise in international transactions, as distinguished from such problems arising out of transactions within more than one of the states of the United States. Beyond these, it extends to legal problems of doing business abroad, international problems of taxation. In sum, it deals with the legal aspects of international transactions involving American business, individual American citizens or the United States government.

When the faculty reassembled in the autumn of 1945 and confronted a world seeming quite different from that of 1936, a great part of the School's task had evidently changed accordingly. The role of the United States in postwar readjustments among nations; the economic involvement of Americans in the lives of millions of people overseas; the presence in every part of the world of hundreds of thousands of Americans, military men, civilian government officers, and private citizens; the creation in New York of what amounts to an international enclave in which sits a Parliament of Man — all this imposed new responsibilities on the School and offered it new opportunities.

The School had a long head start of course. Story and Beale and Griswold had done notable work in conflict of laws including the international aspects which have brought to the subject the alternate name of "private international law." Dean Pound was a scholar of world renown in comparative law; in his old age he well deserved the salute of a congress of comparatists who met in Spain and, to Pound's diffidently dissembled delight, sent him a greeting as "el patriarco mundial del derecho comparado." The Bemis professors and others on the faculty had accomplished memorable achievements in public international law, beginning with Strobel's pioneer service in the part of Southeast Asia then called Siam, and during the pre-1941 period when Manley Hudson was guiding the Harvard Research. The School's library collection was unrivaled in this field. What was needed for the postwar era was comprehensive planning which would put all the pieces together in a related scholarly and administrative structure.

In November 1946 Professor Fuller proposed an Institute of International Legal Studies directed primarily to comparative law, to the training of American lawyers in foreign legal systems and of foreign lawyers in American law. Professor Cavers submitted a complementary memorandum on research opportunities, suggesting the possibility of directing studies toward international law and organization, international trade and finance, and social legislation.

In concert with other members of the faculty who were specially interested in international legal studies, Professor Cavers undertook to plan a pilot program. Everybody cooperated. From seven courses and seminars with international aspects which had been offered in 1950–51, the School moved to an array of four-teen in 1951–52, and twenty-one in 1955–56. The faculty decided not to emphasize differences in subject matter by designation of a separate academic degree. More important, instead, seemed the preservation of the closest practicable relationship between these growing new fields of international study and the basic curric-ulum. Symbolic of this was the breadth of faculty interests. Of eleven members teaching some part of the international program in 1955–56, all but three were also teaching conventional courses outside the international area. Student participation, too, has grown; both underscore the School's attitude toward interna-tional studies as a normal, integral part of American legal education.

The catalogues, beginning with that of 1951–52, carry a sep-arate section headed "International Legal Studies." Previously the School's publications had categorized instruction related to international affairs as "Comparative Law," "Public International Law," and "Private International Law (Conflict of Laws)." A large body of learning concerning more nations than one did not fit readily into any of these three academic categories. The 1951–52 catalogue attempted more descriptive terms for the taxonomy of international matters. They were described as "Prob-lems of World Order," "Problems of the World Economy," and "The Comparison of Legal Systems."

Exploration of research opportunities began with renewed vigor. Professor Cavers, appointed associate dean in 1951, was aided by William Sprague Barnes, who had taken his LL.B. at the School in 1947 "as of" 1943, after combat service in the Army Air Force. Barnes had then proceeded to a Doctorate at the University of Geneva, Switzerland, had for a short time held an appointment at the University of Michigan, and had then come to serve the School as director of foreign law research study. He discovered that the fiscal division of the United Nations felt a need for aid in research in tax laws of nations with outmoded fiscal systems and in the training of tax officers from their finance ministries. Working with United Nations officials, Professor Cavers, Dr. Barnes, and Professor Stanley Surrey,[15] who had

[15] Stanley Sterling Surrey was born in 1910 in New York City. He took his B.S. at the College of the City of New York in 1929 and his LL.B. at Columbia in 1932. After serving in the National Recovery Administration, the National Labor Relations Board, the Treasury, and, during World War I, the Navy, he became

recently come to the faculty from Berkeley, developed a plan for an international program in taxation, dedicated to tax training and research. In 1952 they began activities with a substantial grant from the Ford Foundation. A conspicuously useful product of this enterprise has been the World Tax Series, a set of basic reference works on the tax systems of other countries prepared by a research staff at Harvard with the assistance of scholars and officials of the nations in question and by the fiscal and financial branch of the United Nations. Since 1957 volumes have appeared covering the tax systems of the United Kingdom, Brazil, Mexico, Australia, Sweden, India, the Federal Republic of Germany, the United States, Colombia, Italy, and France. Cumulative supplements on the United Kingdom and the United States have appeared. Each year scholars and officials from all over the world come to the school to study, consult, and write in this field. The School's faculty studies and advises in other countries. The present director, Professor Oliver S. Oldman, has carried forward the work, spacing his teaching in Cambridge with scholarly journeyings to far places.

Since 1945 the School has added to its faculty a number of other specialists in comparative and international law. In 1946 Louis Bruno Sohn became a research fellow in international law; in 1951, assistant professor and John Harvey Gregory Lecturer on World Organization. In 1953 he became professor of law, and in 1961 Bemis Professor of International Law, as well as Gregory lecturer. Richard Reeve Baxter, who had been a member of the international law branch of the Regular Army Judge Advocate General's Corps, became a research associate in law in 1954 and moved up through the grades to become professor of law in 1959. Roger Dummer Fisher, also an international law specialist, came from the Solicitor General's office to the faculty as a lecturer in 1958 and became a professor in 1960. Abram Joseph Chayes became an assistant professor in 1954 and a professor in 1958. He resigned in 1961 to become legal adviser to the Department of State; on his resignation from that post in 1965 Harvard brought him back to the School as professor of law. A series of distinguished visiting professors from other

---

professor of law at the University of California at Berkeley. In 1950 he came as a professor to the Harvard Law School. In 1958 he was named Jeremiah Smith, Jr., Professor. He resigned in 1961 to become Assistant Secretary of the Treasury for tax policy.

countries and from other universities in the United States have enriched Harvard's insights into international studies. Clearly the School has carried out in the spirit as well as the letter the testamentary injunction of George Bemis in 1878.

The School has searched for comparatists as actively as for internationalists. An unusual and promising procedure was followed with Arthur Taylor von Mehren, who became assistant professor of law on September 1, 1946. A graduate of the law school of 1945, and a Ph.D. in government from Harvard in 1946, Professor von Mehren has always been a specialist in comparative law. During the first period of his appointment as an assistant professor, he went to the University of Zurich to study the Swiss and German legal systems and then went to Geneva, Switzerland, perfecting his French to prepare for intensive study of comparative law at the University of Paris.[16] In 1953 he became professor of law. His work as a comparatist has taken him to every part of Europe, to India, and to Japan. At Harvard, besides his teaching and writing on comparative law he has taught and written on conflict of laws. The School has other comparatists. Professor Harold Berman is a specialist on Russian law, though like most of the School's faculty he also teaches in the American field — in this instance a section of torts. In 1964–65 Jerome Alan Cohen, a specialist in Chinese law, came to Harvard as a visiting professor, and in 1965 he became a permanent professor on the Law School's faculty. Professor Charles Fried in 1965 reintroduced Roman law at the School after a lapse of twenty years. In 1966–67 Professor J. N. D. Anderson of the University of London came to Harvard as visiting professor to teach Islamic law.

On January 10, 1955, the Ford Foundation announced a grant to the School of $2,050,000 to develop and expand international legal studies. The grant consisted of three elements: $800,000 to endow two professorships, including secretarial and related costs; $750,000 to be spent, principal and income, on research fellowships for American and foreign lawyers, and for cooperation with the bar and other law schools in the United States and abroad. The remaining $500,000 was to cover half the cost of a new wing

[16] Here the School followed an ancient precedent. In 1815 Harvard appointed Edward Everett to its chair of Greek literature and arranged for his first four years of service to be spent in Europe preparing for his new duties. Gottingen awarded Professor Everett his Ph.D. in 1817; he was the first American recipient of that degree. He began teaching at Harvard in 1819.

of Langdell Hall to house the international legal studies, on condition that the School raise an equal amount from other sources in two years. One of the two chairs endowed by the Ford Foundation grant the School named for Henry L. Stimson, and invited as its first professor Milton Katz, who had resigned his previous professorship at the School in 1950 to direct the Marshall Plan in Europe, with the rank of ambassador. Professor Katz, besides his Stimson Professorship, is director of international legal studies at the School.

How should the school organize its American and international legal studies so that in a student's span of three years, by a combination of required and elective courses, progressively arranged, the wisest education will be available to him? For the one man in sixteen who engages in further study, what graduate program should be devised? What part of the curriculum should teachers prescribe; what should they leave to the free choice of their students? How should they divide their students' time between the analysis of concepts and the acquisition of skills? Before professional teaching of law begins, a modern university law faculty must not only analyze its corpus of learning, but arrange it in an orderly, progressive curriculum in which each of the two first years of work provides a foundation for the succeeding year.

In 1966–67 the first-year courses at the Harvard Law School are all prescribed as they have been for generations. The names of most of them are the same as those of courses with which men began to study law at Harvard when Pound came here in the fall of 1889. Like Pound, today's student must begin on contracts, torts, property, and criminal law. A fifth course which Pound studied as "common law pleading" has been replaced by "civil procedure." To these traditional five the School has now added "development of law and legal institutions," an introduction to legal history. Much teaching in all courses in 1889 was historical; one might suppose that the first-year material had therefore changed little during the last eight decades. This would be a serious misunderstanding, induced by continuity of nomenclature. Today's criminal law course is vastly different from that of eight decades ago, and that of four. The procedure in civil litigation in American courts and the instruction on that subject at any modern American law school, including Harvard, is far different from that prescribed by the Hilary Rules which Pound studied under Ames. The economy in America in 1966 is obviously far different from that of the 1880's; and today's course in contracts takes full account of this change. The apartment house in a modern city presents a multitude of property relations quite different from those important to the 1890 lawyer. The automobile has deeply affected the American law of torts. Contracts, property, and torts have a content quite different from the contracts, property, and torts of 1890.

The work of the teaching fellows, whose primary objective is to help the beginning student gain an understanding of basic legal processes as quickly as possible, is an enterprise in 1966 quite properly denominated a "course" in problems in legal practice and method, though the student is not graded on his performance. Asahel Stearns must have undertaken a very similar general objective in his conferences with students a century and a half ago. The social conflicts he discussed were of course not those of today, but his primary purpose must have been quite like that of today's programs.

Indeed the beginner in legal study in all western civilizations must start with a few established concepts — the retributive sanctions against unreasonable conduct we call the law of tort; the enforcement of promises we call the law of contract; the extent of legal domination, by some man of some thing, which we call the institution of property; the punitive application of public force to those who engage in criminal behavior; and the system of judicial functioning we confusingly call "procedure." No matter what the nomenclature, a man who seeks to understand the legal structure of our society must understand these concepts, and have an idea as to how civilized government adjusts conflicting human aspirations concerning them. Along with these beginnings of substantive wisdom, he should as he starts his life in the law, acquire the habit of closely scrutinizing words, and so understanding the ideas they represent. He should know the difference between the memorization of terminology and the comprehension of ideas. If he acquires a reasonable share of these things in his first year's law study, he has spent his time well. *Non multa sed multum*, Samuel Williston used to say.

In the second-year curriculum come more obvious departures from older subject matter. The student must turn to new fields in order to accord satisfactorily with this generation's changes in society and in government. And as one might expect from these changes, in his second year the student meets sweeping, comprehensive statutes, characteristic of modern American legal development, which necessarily form the core of an increasing number of law-school courses. The Internal Revenue Code, the Uniform Commercial Code, the National Labor Relations Act — he will certainly spend much time with the first of these, and he may well find himself with one or both of the others. Here the student begins the election of subject matter, a process which in the third year becomes inclusive. The second-year man is required to study American constitutional law, the law of corporations, the law of federal taxation, and is required to learn the fundamentals of financial accounting in its legal context. He must elect two additional half-year courses and two additional courses running throughout the year; he may choose the half-year offerings from a tempting abundance, which ranges from the hard practicalities of administrative law through various studies in jurisprudence; comparative law of the Roman system, the modern civil law, Soviet law, and Chinese law; legal history; or study of criminal justice more advanced than that of his first year. He must choose his two full-year elective courses among four fields: trusts; commercial transactions (with the Uniform Commercial Code as its core); economic regulation, including anti-trust and labor relations; and the field of international legal studies.

The second year at Harvard is a hard one. The student at the end of his first year has learned how to study law hard; now he is given a great deal of hard law to study. The elective opportunities are so arranged as to require a man who most inclines to reflective generalities, nevertheless to cope with some of the sharp edges of a legal system regulating a technological civilization. Conversely electives are so arranged as to induce a man who suspects that contemplation of general theory is a self-delusive pastime, serving mainly to avoid practical thought, instead to be persuaded with Holmes that we "have too little theory in the law rather than too much."

Student epigrams, like most such generalizations, have as their charm an adroit mixture of distortion and truth. This goes for the old saying "At Harvard in the first year they scare 'em to death; in the second year they work 'em to death; in the third year they bore 'em to death." What the School actually does in these three years — indeed, what it intends to do — on these points there can, among the fourscore men who teach law at Harvard, be only a rather vague consensus. One who sits through a year-long faculty debate on curricular reform, and thinks about what he there hears, can scarcely avoid this impression of intellectual diversity. So, too, among students, there are all sorts and conditions. Some may well be bored. Many, one hopes, reach the opening of their third year eager to use their techniques and substantive learning, acquired in the two strenuous previous years, to explore new territory. The third-year curriculum is now entirely elective. The student's most significant single undertaking of the year is a piece of original writing, produced by work in a small group organized as a seminar, or else written under the individual instruction of a professor as any other graduate thesis is written.

The program of written work is probably the most valuable part of the third year at the Harvard Law School. For the imaginative man its challenge is unequaled. And this academic exercise has realistic usefulness for the man going into the practice of law. A large proportion of a lawyer's professional activity is not alone the analysis of complex questions of fact and law, nor is it advocacy, but it is essentially creative, prescribing a course of action or declaring rights in a written document. Much of his effectiveness consists in the excellence of his written exposition, its clarity, simplicity, and precision. An able man can learn to write this well, but it requires much practice under skilled criticism. The instruction is most effective when one man gives it to one other. Like the best of all education, it is not available in wholesale lots.

The seminar system had beginnings long before World War II. In the early 1920's Felix Frankfurter conducted a brilliant seminar on federal jurisdiction and procedure. Professor Hudson and Dean Pound conducted seminars on international law and jurisprudence. The Register for 1938–39 announced that groups of not more than 12 third-year students would be given "opportunities for research and practice in writing on legal subjects, under the direction of a member of the Faculty." The Register for 1939–40, after stating the required hours of instruction for the second and third years, added a mandatory requirement that every third-year student do "satisfactory written work in some selected field of study," either in a seminar or individually under guidance of an instructor. This program, after interruptions during the war and the years immediately thereafter, again went into effect for all men graduating in June 1950 and for subsequent classes. The Register for 1950–51 announced that the standard for written work would be "that of a satisfactory law review article." The standard remains the same today. Papers of distinguished excellence are deposited in the library and indexed; they are sometimes sent for by other libraries, on loan for the benefit of some researcher far away. Every year some of them are published in law reviews, affording joint pride to the authors and to their teachers.[17]

The seminars provide an opportunity for teachers and students alike to explore new areas of legal learning. The Associate Dean readily assents to any experiment which one professor or several professors jointly may want to try; the announcement of the new seminar goes in the annual catalogue; and students can elect it if they see fit. Seminars differ in size, from a very few

[17] There are many other opportunities for an energetic student to gain voluntary practice in writing. The top-ranking 5 percent of each second-year and third-year class is selected for the *Law Review*. Since 1887 this has been the best-known scholarly distinction available at the School. The rigorous training which third-year editors give their juniors has for some of them been one of the most valuable educational experiences at the School. Brief-writing for moot courts is coached and criticized by older students in the law clubs. The Williston Competition in drafting legal documents, open to second-year and third-year students, gives intensive experience to fifty or sixty students each year. The Legislative Research Bureau, manned by second-year and third-year students, undertakes selected legislative research and drafting at the request of national or state legislators, state attorneys-general, law revision commissions, law school faculty members, and civic groups. Each piece of its work goes through exhaustive editorial criticism and review by senior students and a faculty member. Founded in 1963, the *Harvard Journal of Legislation* now appears thrice yearly; it contains drafts of legislation, and articles and comment. The Legislative Research Bureau has provided for its members an experience much like that of the *Law Review*, and this training has been available regardless of academic ranking.

The International Law Club, founded in 1958, has about 350 members, roughly one student in every five at the School. The membership includes candidates for the S.J.D. and the LL.M. as well as candidates for the first degree in laws; all are interested in the practice and problems of international law. The club's members write and edit the *Harvard Journal of International Law*, which has appeared twice a year. The *Journal* tends to emphasize work of graduate students; a counterpoise is the Second-Year Writing Program, conducted under the auspices of a faculty committee consisting of Professors Herwitz, Sander, and Vorenberg. The committee and other members of the faculty and alumni give oversight and training to about thirty second-year students in writing and editing material like that in the *Law Review*. Offset publication has been launched under the title *Harvard Legal Commentary*. A group concentrating on civil rights and liberties issues an offset *Review* concerning those subjects.

men who may be interested in some esoteric subject, to twenty-odd. With more than twenty students the effectiveness of intimate instruction declines, and most teachers limit registration in seminars to groups of such a size as permits individual supervision. In 1966–67 the School offered fifty seminars for third-year and graduate students, which would, if all seminars were equally subscribed, provide an average attendance of about twelve students in each. The subjects listed in the catalogue are worth surveying as a demonstration of the range of interests in a modern law school. The gamut runs from conventional corporate matters and federal taxation to such novel explorations as Chinese attitudes toward international law, and legal protection of environmental quality

A student rarely elects more than one seminar in his entire third year, and then only by permission of the third-year faculty chairman. The burden of research, the time consumed in writing and rewriting one paper aspiring to the standard of a satisfactory law review article, make almost impossible the adequate production of two. The third-year student must complete at least ten hours of classroom and seminar work in each semester and must complete twenty-four semester hours in his third year. He must thus elect a substantial number of classroom courses, either from the second-year offerings which he has not previously elected, or from the courses specially designated for the third year.

In the academic year 1965–66 the School registered 537 first-year students, 519 for the second year, and 517 for the third — a total of 1573 candidates for the LL.B. In addition 90 students enrolled as candidates for graduate degrees, mainly the LL.M., and much less frequently the Doctorate of Juridical Science. Twenty men came as special students, not candidates for degrees; most of these were participants in the international taxation program.

To earn a master's degree a candidate must already hold the LL.B. from an American law school, or have undergone equivalent training abroad. He must spend a year in residence, complete eight class hours a week, and satisfactorily write a legal essay under the direction of an instructor. He may, if he contemplates changing his candidacy from the LL.M. to the S.J.D., present a more ambitious piece of work amounting to a thesis; if the committee on graduate studies, which supervises the work of all graduate students, gives the LL.M. candidate permission to present a thesis, his class work requirement is reduced to five hours a week. To earn the LL.M. he must obtain an average grade of 65 for all his work, and a minimum of 60 in every course.

The doctoral degree is difficult to earn at the Harvard Law School and few complete the rigorous requirements. In June 1966, for example 515 candidates became bachelors of laws, 71 became masters of laws, but only 4 became doctors of juridical science. Admission to doctoral candidacy is available only to those who have demonstrated unusual scholarly promise in previous graduate study, or in teaching or practice combined with published writings of high merit. The degree requires a year's study in residence with high performance in courses. There is no set of courses specially designated for graduate students. Each candidate's course is individually chosen to meet his needs and interests from among the courses offered to LL.B. candidates. Candidates write their theses or dissertations under the guidance of some specially qualified professor. The candidate must within five years after his year of residence submit a dissertation in publishable form, in English, which constitutes a significant contribution to legal scholarship. He is then examined orally on his dissertation area by a committee of the faculty, and if he is successful, receives his doctoral degree.

These graduate programs serve both foreign and American students. Candidates for the master's degree are often Americans contemplating practice in the United States who already have an LL.B. from another university and who wish to perfect themselves in some specialty, such as taxation or international legal studies. A number of candidates from other countries come for additional training for practice at home, or to add to their qualifications for public service in their own countries. Doctoral candidates almost always contemplate careers of teaching.

Today, as in the days of Parker and Stearns and during all the years since their time, an important part of the ordinary student's work is briefing and arguing questions of law arising on imaginary appeals. For nonlawyer readers I should explain that in this stage of litigation no question arises concerning disputed facts; there are no witnesses contradicting one another; all the facts have, by hypothesis, been decided at a trial in a lower court. The students investigate only questions of law; they examine statutes and previous dicisions, organize this material in carefully documented written arguments called briefs, and then submit these briefs and present oral arguments to moot courts. The court usually consists, for a student's first argument, of three older students, or two older students and a member of the faculty. Each first-year man normally briefs and argues two such cases, in the first of which he is pitted against a single adversary; in the second he is one of two co-counsel opposing another two.

In a first-year class of more than five hundred, this plan contemplates well over a thousand first-year arguments. The administrative work of preparing so many cases, organizing the arguments, procuring the judges, teaching student counsel the rudiments of brief writing and oral argumentation, all would be impossible without two long-standing student institutions: the system of law clubs, and the Board of Student Advisers.

The law clubs originated in the School's earliest years and once had some elements of exclusiveness. Now every first-year student is invited to join a club, which is made up of eight first-year, eight second-year, and eight third-year men. The clubs are encouraged, advised, aided, and furnished with cases to argue by the Board of Student Advisers, sixteen high-ranking members of the second- and third-year classes, for whom the School provides secretarial help and office space in Austin Hall. To suppose that this elaborate procedure is no more than a complicated extracurricular law game or the teaching of a practical trade technique, is to miss the point by a wide margin. This "disputation" is an academic process as old as universities. When any man, lawyer or not, has learned to perceive the precise point of cleavage between two contentions, has learned to distinguish the relevant from the irrelevant considerations bearing on these contentions, has schooled himself to accept reasoned opposition in good grace, he has gone far on the road to becoming a rational being and a useful adjuster of other men's controversies.

Students who complete two first-year arguments are eligible for the Ames Competition which begins in the second year, an inter-club elimination tournament of moot-court arguments. Second-year cases are prepared under the direction of a young graduate "faculty assistant in charge of the Ames Competition."

They are substantially more demanding than first-year cases. The briefs are more elaborate; the judges include members of the bar and of the faculty. The eight clubs which rank highest in a qualifying round compete in the quarter-finals arguments later in the second year. Eight second-year men from each club prepare the briefs which the School prints, and two of the men from each club represent it in one of four oral arguments before courts composed of eminent state and federal judges. The semi-finals and the finals occur in the third year. For many of the final arguments, one of the justices of the Supreme Court of the United States comes to Cambridge to sit on the moot court. Participation in these later rounds of the Ames Competition is one of the higher honors obtainable in the School. The arguments draw large audiences; the students watch and listen with critical interest whether they have participated in preparing their club's briefs, or are only spectators who have read the printed record and briefs and who then observe the conduct of the argument with the discriminating sophistication of drama critics at an opening night. The names of winning finalists and their clubs appear on a bronze plaque in the Langdell Reading Room. The whole operation is one of the most effective educational devices which students find at the School.

This preparation and argument of questions of law, that is, disputations as to whether the rule is one way or another, are admirable exercises. But taken by themselves these may oversimplify the legal process. In man's affairs the rule of conduct is often quite clear: the driver must not exceed fifty miles per hour on a given road; a man must not forge another's name on checks; one who libels a public officer concerning his official duties may do so with impunity unless the misstatement is made with malevolence. Thus a law student, or indeed a student of political science, who habitually overlooks the omnipresent contingencies of life which depend on determinations of fact may end with a wholly unrealistic concept of the governmental process. Rules of law are immensely important to mankind in general, but to individual man, proper decision of disputed fact is at least equally crucial. Was the motorist indeed exceeding the speed limit? Was the signature on the check false or genuine? Was the critic of the public officer prompted by malice or not?

To give novice lawyers some introduction to established methods of deciding disputed questions of fact, to emphasize the lesson that past events are now only conflicting impressions in human memories, Professors Cavers, Morgan, and Field in the autumn of 1949 revived a teaching device which from time to time had been used in the school, beginning at least as early as the 1830's: a model jury trial for the instruction of the entire first-year class, in which witnesses would testify to their conflicting recollection of events they had observed. The 1949 trial involved a tort question: false imprisonment of an employee in an atomic research plant whom his employer detained after a report that fissionable materials had been missing. The teaching fellows discussed the pleadings with their groups of first year men; the students worked on trial memoranda exploring evidence that might be available. During these preparatory weeks, student interest rose to a peak. On the appointed evening the entire first-year class assembled in the School courtroom to hear the trial.

Professors Field and Morgan acted as counsel for the plaintiff and defendant, and United States District Judge Charles E. Wyzanski, Jr., LL.B. 1930, presided. The court impaneled a jury made up of students and students' wives, some of them from other parts of the university. Plaintiff and defendant called witnesses, also drawn from the university community; the witnesses had learned the general outlines of their testimony, but had not memorized the words. Opposing counsel subjected them to adroit cross-examination. An experienced court stenographer reported the entire trial, including Judge Wyzanski's charge. The jury retired and in due course came in with a verdict for the plaintiff for $500, a verdict not required by the scenario but found by the jury in its best judgment of the evidence. The court reporter then transcribed his stenographic notes of the proceedings, copies of this record were furnished to all the first-year students, and the teaching fellows went over the entire trial with them, discussing the tactics of counsel, the law, and the procedure.

The disappointed defendant appealed. Appellate counsel that first year were students, members of the Board of Student Advisers. They prepared briefs which were distributed to all first-year students; and they argued the appeal before a three-judge court, made up of professors Scott, Hart and Kaplan. The argument of the model appeal, like the conduct of the trial, aroused a high

The James Barr Ames Courtroom in Austin Hall. The School's archives have student records of moots argued as early as February 1820. Today's student-counsel, who read of those long-decided arguments, find them strangely familiar.

Austin Wakeman Scott, Dane Professor Emeritus, and Erwin Griswold, Dean and Langdell Professor, in the Dean's office, November 1966. The Dean sits at the desk which Harvard presented to Joseph Story in 1829 when Story became the first Dane Professor.

pitch of student interest. I unhappily report that neither research in back numbers of the *Harvard Law School Record*, nor inquiry of the appellate judges, nor correspondence with counsel, has turned up the outcome of that model appeal. Professor Field asserts a firm opinion that the appellant won; but this view is based only on his undocumented generalization that his successes as counsel on the model trial are foredoomed to reversal by benches of overtechnical appellate judges. The actual outcome of the 1949 model appeal must forever remain a mystery.

The annual model trial and appeal have been continued successfully to the present time. The teaching fellows now divide the first-year students into plaintiff's and defendant's groups, thus adding the realism of partisanship. During the trial participating counsel feel the familiar sensations of trying an actual case. Arguments over questions of evidence arise unexpectedly; counsel and trial judge cope with them on the spur of the moment as in any other courtroom. Rulings of the trial judge produce surprising situations which counsel have to meet as best they may. Sometimes after the case has gone to the jury the puzzled jurors argue in secret until the small hours of the morning and finally hand down a "sealed verdict," a note in an envelope to be opened when the next School day starts.

Cases arranged for the model trial are now so designed that however the jury may decide the facts, an arguable question of law remains. Judges of appellate state or federal courts generally hear the argument of the appeal which is presented by professors experienced in appellate work. Ordinarily the student audience listens to the proceedings with great seriousness, though occasionally, five hundred students being what they are, something happens at the trial or on the appeal which produces a roar of injudicious laughter. On one model appeal a member of the three-judge court was a distinguished visiting legal scholar from England. Dean Griswold was counsel for the appellant; as he was making one of his points, the English judge admonished him: "Mr. Griswold, you talk like a professor." The court took some time to restore order.

The popularity of the model trial suggested that the School's system of instruction had underemphasized the importance of disputed fact in the legal process, and had not afforded to the students an adequately thorough regimen of procedure for trials in courts of first instance. Old-fashioned lawyers would say that the School had neglected *nisi prius*. Of course this phase of legal procedure appeared in many parts of the curriculum, most conspicuously in the course on evidence. Professor Maguire's book *Evidence of Guilt* expounded some of the knotty difficulties arising in proof of fact in criminal trials. But surprisingly often one heard a student wave away a puzzling question by remarking airily "Oh that's just a question of fact," as if somehow the matter under discussion involved a minor order of dispute, not worthy of much scholarly thought. To the extent that this impression arose in young minds it required some unlearning later in life. In 1955 Professors Field and Keeton, both of whom before their professorial days had had thorough experience in the trial of cases, introduced a course in trial practice. In it students receive systematic instruction, by demonstration and participation, in the presentation and counterproof of matters of fact. The course has been extremely popular, and in many years the School has had to call on distinguished trial lawyers from the Boston bar to take over extra sections of students.

The model trial and the trial practice course were much facilitated when the Austin Hall interior was largely reconstructed in the summer of 1954. The old library reading room on the second floor, then largely out of use, became a handsome new courtroom, named for James Barr Ames, with seats for more than five hundred spectators. The little classroom on the third floor of Austin, which had become battered and largely neglected, was built over for trial practice sessions and was appropriately named the Morgan Room for Royall Professor Emeritus Edmund M. Morgan, whose work in the field of evidence had been so conspicuously useful.

5

The School has become a better intellectual enterprise since 1946; it has also become a more comfortable, more companionable place for student living. Two major efforts undertaken in 1948–49 went far to provide for students of law some of the amenities of life which the house system and the Union have afforded for Harvard undergraduates. One was the construction north of Langdell of five new Law School dormitories, Dane, Ames,

Holmes, Shaw, and Story,[18] and the Harkness Graduate Commons where students of the Law School and of other graduate faculties might dine together. The other undertaking was the successful effort to raise money for this construction.

The Corporation required that to the cost of these buildings the School contribute $1,650,000. John B. Marsh, LL.B. 1910, of New York City as chairman and Wilkie Bushby, LL.B. 1921, as vice-chairman generously and effectively organized the Harvard Law School Fund to produce this large sum. The President and the Dean invited an alumnus in each state to serve as a local chairman. By the close of the fiscal year 1948–49, three thousand two hundred and four contributors in forty-four states and the District of Columbia had subscribed a little over $925,000. By the end of 1950 the total subscribed to the Law School Fund reached $1,532,169.05, very nearly the entire Law School portion of the cost of the new construction.

The committee in charge originally thought of the Law School Fund as a single effort to produce the capital sum necessary for the building improvements of 1948–49; but its success demonstrated its continuing value. As a result, after the capital sum for dormitories and commons was raised, the fund was reorganized in 1950 as a continuing arrangement for annual giving. Now, under the leadership of Assistant Dean Wesley Bevins, LL.B. 1948 it is a permanent feature of the School's financing. Its success has been almost incredible. During the first year of annual giving the School somewhat timidly aspired to raise fifty thousand dollars; that sum proved to be a great underestimate of the possibilities. In each of the three fiscal years which ended June 30, 1963, 1964, and 1965, the fund produced nearly nine hundred thousand dollars. These recurring annual gifts by graduates are an essential means of keeping the School going, and permitting it to carry on its evolving programs of instruction, research, and financial aid to students.

Meantime the dormitory and graduate commons construction, which began in 1948–49, was finished in time for the opening of the School in the autumn of 1950. Some students moved into parts of dormitories on which the final work was still underway. On September 17, 1950, the contractor finished the last details

[18] With these dormitories for aspiring jurists are two for graduate students of other disciplines: Richards and Child halls.

and next day students took full possession. The new dormitories and Harkness Commons now stand where older graduates remember the wind-swept tennis courts. To those of us who were traditional-minded, the new buildings were a little startling at first; they were built of steel, concrete, brick of different colors, and glass. The new structures surround a grass courtyard in which Walter Gropius, architect of the whole complex, erected a branching framework of stainless steel tubing, compared by the irreverent to an apparatus for drying laundry. This is The World Tree. When the weather is cold enough, the courtyard is flooded for skating; young men and women and boys and girls cling to the World Tree for support while they rest tired ankles. Sometimes as the winter holiday season approaches, wags decorate the Tree with faintly satirical Christmas ornaments. In the autumn, touch football games swirl around it; on spring afternoons, "frisbies" [19] sail through its aspiring branches. Arbor Day ceremonies have included the planting of ball-bearings in the hope of more world trees in years to come.

Harkness Commons has proved a great blessing. On the ground floor there is a pleasant student lounge with a record player, and leather chairs where students of law or those from other graduate faculties may find a moment or two of leisure, to look through large plate-glass windows at the vistas outside, to read newspapers, or talk with friends. An even larger adjoining room, faced with glass on the side toward the World Tree and its courtyard, equipped with a piano for gay occasions, serves for student parties, for faculty luncheons, for dinners of state, and like pleasant episodes.

The second floor of the Commons is given over to a dining hall and cafeteria counter. Here, too, the arts are not neglected. On the north wall is a large ceramic mural by Miro. The colors are mild and pleasing; the figures suggest mysterious creatures, largely marine. At the upper right one discerns a cephalopod, tentacles extended for prey. Underneath it is a sea scorpion, perhaps. Amid these monsters, lower left, is a humanoid face, staring at the observer through expressionless eyes, one orange, one green. Other parts of the dining hall have quite dif-

---

[19] Am I the only citizen of the United States who has had to have somebody explain to him that a plastic flying saucer about a foot across, with which it is possible to play a rather graceful game of catch, is called a frisbie?

ferent decorations. The southwest wall bears a painting which appears to picture feathered wings of bright-green bodiless angels. To break up the dining space, the architect has pleasantly provided partial partitions ornamented by odd-shaped panels of wood. Most of the exterior walls are of glass. In these rooms too the traditionalist, after a little original shock, can be quite happy. All is light and space. From breakfast through dinner at night scores of young men and not a few young women sit at small tables, learnedly distinguishing one case from another, eagerly discussing perennial problems of mankind, righting the political wrongs which beset the sorry world.

The School and its sister graduate faculties are much the better for these facilities. Vice Dean Livingston Hall wrote of the first year's experience with the Graduate Center: [20]

A new and stronger sense of social cohesion has developed among our own students as a result of the existence of the Graduate Center. The presence in the dormitories of men from all three law school classes has facilitated the introduction of first year men into the social fabric of the School, and to the traditions of work and study methods of its upperclassmen. The actual assignments of men of any one class into the dormitories is by lot. But the system of class priorities used insures some 250 first year men places in the dormitories. The careful work of Assistant Dean Bevins in making the assignments has been effective to keep a proper balance between first, second and third year men. A number of places are also reserved for graduate law students.

The common use of the new Center by students in the Law School and in the Graduate School of Arts and Sciences has justified our hopes that it would lead to social and intellectual interchange among all these students. The Law School has lost none of its distinctive flavor in the process.

On the day before Commencement every June the Law School and other graduate faculties have an Alumni Spread in the court-yard. The green around the World Tree is dotted with tents and great umbrellas. Tables bear signs identifying the schools and classes whose members are returning to greet old friends. To left and right of the Tree the Commons staff serve tray lunches to the lines of graduates and their guests, and to those aspirants who will get their diplomas next day. The crimson flag, bearing

[20] Dean Hall's comments on the Harkness Center appear in Dean Griswold's annual report for 1950–51.

the three open books which contain the Truth, flies from the Harkness flagstaff. All of us sense that no matter what our diverse undergraduate ties may be, here we have another scholarly home. The Harvard Glee Club sings. There are two addresses, usually one by a distinguished alumnus of the Law School, one by an alumnus of another graduate faculty. Few of us who heard Kingman Brewster, Jr., LL.B. 1948, speak at the Alumni Spread on June 10, 1964, will forget his witty and deeply perceptive discourse on the danger that scholarly endeavor may unprofitably expend itself in routine refinement of the elaborately documented obvious, instead of pursuing fundamental understanding. He introduced his talk by remarking that he had slipped into a low state, long the object of professional scorn. He had, he said, become "*a layman,* a lapsed lawyer; a refugee from law teaching; a defector from this very place." True! He had left our faculty to become the President of Yale.

6

Undoubtedly the most conspicuous change in library arrangements since World War II is the new International Legal Studies wing, built north of Langdell's westerly extension. Faithful alumni of the School and business organizations from virtually the entire range of the American economy matched the Ford grant of half a million dollars and contributed three hundred thousand dollars additional to meet the unexpectedly large construction costs. The international collection, of which the Olivart acquisition was the core, used to be shelved in the north basement of Langdell Hall. A resolute scholar, not afraid of the dark, could find his way there, could fumble to a light switch, could even discover the card catalogue. If sufficiently determined he could find his book and perhaps a carrel where he could read it. Nothing demonstrates the dedication of the pre-1958 internationalists and comparatists so convincingly as the hardships they underwent for the sake of their callings. Some of them became quite fond of their cavern, as Bonnivard may, now and then, have come to feel at home in the dank dungeon of Chillon.

Now everything is different. The visitor to the new International Legal Studies library passes through an anteroom decorated with avant-garde sculptures, through tall glass doors, and finds himself in a cheerfully lighted, comfortable reading room, with the stacks readily accessible, where portraits of Judges Story and Hudson preside benignly over the pleasant scene. The catalogue and delivery desk are conveniently at hand; periodicals in esoteric tongues fill the reading racks; easy chairs invite the weary scholar. Seminar rooms and much needed offices in the International Legal Studies wing get hard use; and the motherly and kindly purveyors in a staff lunchroom do what can be done to minimize the American noonday habit of eating and running back to work. Surely the Ford Foundation and the generous matching-givers deserve psalms of praise for delivering us out of our dungeon.

During the two decades which followed the Armistice of 1945, the School had of course to provide for continuous development of its huge domestic library resources as well. The School properly concerns itself with international matters but its predominant daily concern must be the law in the United States. The library approaches the ideal of accumulating a complete record of the law of the entire world — materials constitutional, statutory, decisional; doctrinal treatises; learned journals, other current publications — but the great bulk of this is American. Explosive increase in publications, including publications relevant to the law, requires not only great additional space for storage of conventional printed books and pamphlets, but also new and improved means to make their contents easily available to the seeker. It will soon require a convenient system to reproduce many publications in compact form so that sheer bulk will not crowd the School out of house and home.

An example is not far to seek. The New York *Times* is an essential resource in a modern law school. Its pages contain an account of proceedings in the courts from day to day, and give much valuable commentary on those proceedings, particularly cases in the Supreme Court of the United States. Statutory development can be followed in some respects better in the *Times* than in most other places. Its pages tell the story of political and social events which underlie the law, which produce the controversies which make the law necessary. For many years the School maintained a series of bound volumes of the *Times*, great heavy books bound in canvas, day-by-day accounts of the world as it moved, immensely useful and immense in bulk.

Gradually the fact became obvious that if this accumulation continued the library would sooner or later need a building for the New York *Times* alone. The solution was microfilm reproduction of all but the latest few months' issues of the *Times*. A microfilm reading room has been set up in the School; its apparatus includes a photocopying device. A professor or other member of the School can, on short notice, find and read any part of any issue of the *Times*, and if he needs it can get a photographic copy for study, for inclusion in his lecture notes, or for use as a part of an article or book. In some ways this is less convenient than the old set of canvas-bound volumes. Most human arrangements involve submission to the disadvantages of compromise.

No thoughtful man who compares a first-rank law library with a collection of material in some of the other social sciences can help marveling at the ready accessibility of legal materials, made possible by a wonderfully detailed doctrinal indexing system, by careful digests filling scores of volumes. In the purchase of such law-finding devices, in the preparation of others by our own library staff, there appears a sort of race, like the old-time naval race between gun and armor. The volume of library material increases at an explosive rate; acquisition and invention of more efficient law-finding methods race to keep up with it. One recurs to the increasing need for able people. No matter how ingenious any cataloguing apparatus, library material can never be classified and indexed so as to accord with the analytical processes of the future searcher's mind, without the work of intelligent, imaginative, and industrious human beings. Neither in the law nor anywhere else is there a substitute for man's brain. The School's library requires not only the latest mechanical devices but also requires, as the bulk of its recorded information inevitably increases, an increasing staff of energetic and thoughtful men and women.

And if the library is to serve its purpose, it must be ready to give out the information stored in its unique treasury of human records not only to members of the university, but to other members of the American learned community. Harvard University, its Law School, and the School's library, remain "private" institutions only in a narrow and technical sense. They have become in fact great public resources, held in trust for the people of the

United States. During the postwar decades an increasing task of the School has been to make these records available to anyone who needs them, not only here but abroad. Again an example is ready at hand. In South Africa in 1957, a large number of people were on trial for treason. These were state trials in the classic sense, involving charges of seditious activity against the government, resembling some of the notable trials in the United States against persons charged with various forms of Communist activity during the late 1940's and early 1950's. Counsel for the several score defendants asked the Harvard Law School for the testimony, documentary exhibits, and legal rulings in the American trials. The School already had these records available on microfilm reels, and readily lent them to the defense counsel in the South African trials. The School's library resources are known and sought far beyond our national boundaries.

In 1948–49 the School for the first time in its history acquired an adequate place to preserve, display, and use its great collection of rare historical books. At the north end of the Langdell Hall Reading Room a Treasure Room was fitted-up with display cases and air-conditioning arrangements to keep constant its temperature and humidity. Connected with the Treasure room proper is a stack area three floors high, similarly air-conditioned. With these facilities the School's rare books and manuscripts are now easily available for use by scholars. Fifteen hundred alumni and friends of the School and the Harvard Law School Association made a gift of $55,000 in all, which made possible the creation of the Treasure Room. Besides a resource for study and preservation of the library's most valuable items, it serves as a war memorial for the members of the school who lost their lives in the two world wars. Their names are inscribed on marble panels at the entrance to the room. Teachers, students, and visitors going in can stop a moment, read the names, and think of the men.

7

In 1796 when Harvard sold Isaac Royall's Granby lands for $2000, it set up the first endowment available to support the study of law at our university. The Treasurer's Report for 1964–65 shows that the School at the close of that year had a total endowment capital of $18,669,866 yielding about $850,000 of income during the year. The School's endowment has more than quadrupled since 1931. Gifts to the School's permanent funds through its history fill twelve pages of the Treasurer's 1964–65 Report. Of these gifts, twenty-one exceeded $100,000. The largest single accrual was a new Ford Foundation endowment for professorships in 1965, amounting to two million dollars. But the bulk of the School's endowment has come from large numbers of much smaller gifts.

To Parker and Stearns in 1817, a funded income of more than $850,000 every year would have seemed incredible riches, even allowing many times over for the depreciation of the dollar since their day. But the School's undertakings in our time would also have seemed incredible to its earliest professors. For the year 1965–66 the Dean, in his budget submitted to the faculty in May 1965, projected total expenses of a little over $4,290,000. The cost of instruction was the largest element in this estimate. For salaries of men with teaching appointments, and for their secretarial expenses, retirement contributions, and other incidental costs, the Dean budgeted a little over $1,280,000. The next most costly feature of the School was $655,000 for scholarships and the cost of administering them. The library expenses came to a little more than $600,000. Building maintenance was estimated just under $453,000. The program of International Legal Studies, including that in International Taxation, was estimated at $443,000. The administrative expenses of the School came to $260,000; the Fund Office and Fund Development cost was $190,000. The remainder of the budget, $669,000, was projected for a number of items, each sum less than a hundred thousand dollars. Faculty research, faculty allowance for supplies, teaching materials, a summer session in Cambridge for Negroes from disadvantaged undergraduate colleges, the admissions office, a study of auto accident litigation, research in delinquency, the Board of Student Advisers, the Legal Aid Bureau, the Alumni Office, and other select miscellany, make up this balance.

Where does the School find annual resources for carrying on such a program costing more than four and a quarter million dollars? Now, as always, far and away the largest resource of the School is income from tuition payments. Sixteen hundred students each paying $1500 would bring in $2,400,000. Endowment income in the year 1966–67 yielded $850,000. During each of the three years ending June 30, 1965, alumni annual giving was approximately $870,000. The $170,000 balance of the 1965–66 budget of $4,120,000 came from various specific grants made by foundations or similar groups for support of this or that activity. On September 19, 1966, the President and Fellows approved an annual tuition charge of $1750 for each student for the years beginning in September 1967, which would add a litle more than $240,000 to the annual income of a school of 1600. The variables make the net income uncertain.

There is little room for maneuver. A substantial decline in the return from tuition, or in the yield from investments, or in annual giving would leave the School no option save a curtailment of some of its program. There is no margin for an expanded faculty, for new construction. On February 26, 1966, Dean Griswold announced a proposed fund-raising enterprise which, the School hopes, will produce $15,000,000 of additional capital endowment. The new funds would support the existing and expected larger faculty needed to accomplish the study, teaching, research, writing, and public service which make up the School's program. The new funds would also provide an augmented material establishment for the School, particularly additional classrooms, professors' offices, and space for the administrative personnel needed to carry on the whole enterprise.

This is a moment to pause, look back over the road, and see where it has led. The Harvard Law School has made a long and useful journey since 1817. On its way, through a century and a half, there have been many days of success and pride, some days of discouragement, no days without labor. About forty thousand young men, and latterly some young women, have here studied the recorded efforts of mankind to apply reason in adjusting human conflicts. They have learned, in much hard detail, how man has governed himself in the United States, and among many of her neighbors.

A history of this School properly considered, should be more than a summa of enrollments, courses, teachers, books, and buildings — though without any one of these the School could not exist, and their story well deserves the telling. But, in the end, the School's significance is its usefulness. Here the objectives and the achievements have much changed since the first student enrolled in the autumn of 1817. Early instruction was too circumscribed. The School has always thought of itself as serving the nation as well as training individuals for a private calling, but conscious concentration on the first of these missions has much increased, and rightly so, during the last third of the School's existence. This development has been inevitable. Our grandfathers carried on many things in our national existence by nongovernmental means which we have come to undertake through the politically directed public process; the School has given increasing attention to the legal and governmental structures which make this possible.

Thus the Harvard Law School, like the other great university law schools of the nation, and like the other departments of American universities, has ceased to be primarily an organ of private concern, and has become a national resource. As each spring comes, as another five hundred of the School's students approach the day when they will go out into the world, the teachers occupy themselves, every year a little more, in filling out questionnaires from departments of the national government concerning prospective graduates who seek or are sought for public service. Few weeks go by without a visit from some representative of a branch of the government asking about the qualifications of some students for governmental duty.

And, more and more during the last fifty years, there has been a continual going and coming of professors to and from different branches of the national and the state governments for short or long periods of service. With all the problems that this presents for the School, with all these interruptions of a calm and untroubled academic existence which most professors have once fondly imagined but few have ever found, still increasing involvement in public service is rightly welcome. Fair return for benefits given is no more than just; Harvard survives because neither state nor nation taxes her. Great foundations and generous graduates of the School have aided it without stint, and the School returns some of this support by the careful and ready services of professors, services performed not alone when they go from the School to occupy themselves in the departments or bureaus of national and state governments — even more by their study and their published writing, professors continually contribute to the wisdom with which we govern ourselves. The study of man's self-government is no less useful to the nation than the study of the material world which surrounds us. American universities properly and usefully occupy themselves with both.

And no one can overlook the public contribution that the Harvard Law School and its great sister schools make in supplying the nation and the states with those who privately practice the profession of the law. Over the years, and in great volume, this is the School's principal contribution to national well-being. Americans are, after all, that rather wonderful thing, a law abiding people. We abide in our law because we could not live without it. Every day and at every turn our incredibly complex, interdependent society continues to exist only because of the willingness of the great majority of people to go by the rules. But even for the great majority, for law abiding men of good will, some of the rules are still complex. Mankind requires teaching, needs the corps of which Holmes wrote: "I know of no teachers so powerful and persuasive as the little army of specialists. They carry no banners, they beat no drums; but where they are, men learn that bustle and push are not the equals of quiet genius and serene mastery . . . In the army of which I speak lawyers are not the least important corps." [21] Men who have spent a youth of study and a lifetime of professional effort accustoming themselves not only to the details of rule, but to the spirit and the momentum of a society ruling itself according to law, are invaluable assets of that society. With its fellow institutions the School contributes greatly to this corps. As it does so, it justifies its existence.

[21] The "Use of Law Schools," Holmes's speech at the meeting of the Harvard Law School Association held November 5, 1886, as part of Harvard's two hundred and fiftieth anniversary celebration. *Collected Legal Papers*, p. 35.

XI

Tomorrow: The Familiar and the Necessary

This book, which has traced a century and a half of the School's past, may well end with a glance at its future. Prediction is a safe sort of speculation. At least for the moment no one can prove the prophet wrong. Yesterday, fixed forever, is principally useful for lessons respecting time to come. To be sure, what has happened is often diverting; one can watch the experiments, eccentricities, hopes, and failures of predecessors, just as a man goes to the play. But the utility of experience, personal or vicarious, concerns tomorrow. One remembers, again, that an oarsman steers by his boat's wake.

These chronicles have occupied themselves with four matters: with the students at the School, their aspirations, their character, their lives; with its teachers and their work, their doctrines, their writings, their standing as men; with the recorded rational adjustment of past controversy collected in the library; and finally with the material fabric, the various structures which constitute the School's house. What will happen to these four in the years to come?

Probably the most acute problem will concern numbers. One hopes that the School will not grow larger, but the pressure is upward. In 1955–56 1513 students enrolled; in 1966–67 there were 1716. During the past decade in effect another school has been added half-again larger than the one Langdell joined in 1870. The Harvard Law School has seen two irregular plateaus of enrollment. From 1845 to 1870 the student population ranged between 100 and 150, tending to recur to a level around 140.[1] This 1845–1870 average continued without planning; all who

[1] The general trends of the School's population from 1817 to 1917 appear most clearly in the graph at page 345 of the Centennial History.

360

came were accepted; demand regulated the numbers. During the late 1920's enrollment came close to the present student population and except during the war of 1941–45 the total has remained fairly constant between about 1450 and 1700. This second plateau has been the result of an effort, through a third of a century, to resist unwieldy increase. The faculty imposed increasingly strict tests on admission to cut down the first-year class. Immediately the two upper classes grew larger as more first-year men survived; the School thereupon rejected more and more applicants, and has managed to hold the line fairly well. But Dean Landis' annual report of 1938, with his wistful thought of a reduction to a school of a thousand members, seems beyond the imaginable possibilities. Any change will probably be an increase.

A school of 1700 and more students has disadvantages. One who talks with college undergraduates who aspire to law school hears a good deal about Yale, less than half this size. There is a widespread feeling that the smaller school permits more intimate and easy association between teachers and students. The 1966–67 register of the Harvard Law School shows about twenty-two students per teacher, which should permit a good deal of tutorial contact, though many of the classes meet with well over one hundred students in the classroom. The School long since exceeded the size where any student could know all the others; indeed no man can even know everybody in his own class, more than casually.

Despite continuous and conscientious efforts by professors to know students well, once in a while a man gets a little lost in the shuffle. Each year brings to professors in the School a flood of requests for recommendations — recommendations for employment, for graduate study, for fellowships, for commissions in the armed forces, for all manner of things. Some students come to professors a bit apologetically saying that they really do not know any of the faculty well; that they hesitate to ask for recommendations from comparative strangers, but are obliged to do so. Such moments sadden the teacher. In the autumn of 1966 the faculty began to experiment with some first-year sections of about thirty-five men. The objective is excellent; it also obviously increases the total number of classroom hours for professors and suggests continued increase in the faculty.

One can predict valiant faculty resistance against any proposals to increase the present total student enrollment, and also predict failure. Perhaps increase may first come in the number of LL.M. and S.J.D. candidates, in special students like those in the International Tax Program, perhaps in other new categories. These men will come highly motivated, capable of much self-direction; but the more advanced the student the more individualized his instruction. Proper teaching will require for each such candidate much more faculty time and time of the library staff than for most students working toward the LL.B.

If the School increases in size much more the faculty will have to give consideration to some system of breaking it down into smaller units to escape the anonymity of sheer numbers. The means of accomplishing this are not entirely clear, nor is it certain that subdivision would help more than it would hurt. Physically the School's population could be grouped in clusters of dormitories, each with its sub-dean, its junior faculty, and whatnot. But such a segmentation would not increase the number of Willistons or Beales or Scotts. To cut up the School into small parts would not increase the access of individuals to great men unless the number of great men were increased, a difficult undertaking. Subdivision of the Harvard Law School would merely produce a cluster of several small closely federated schools where one had been before.

Dean Griswold wrote of the possibility of growth in his 1963–1964 Report.

There is another solution which I think has great merit. This is that a considerable number of other law schools should increase their size. We have many schools with 200 students, 300 students, or 400 students. This has been a cozy, fine, friendly, and comfortable number, and many schools have liked this small size. Nevertheless, it may be a luxury which cannot and ought not to be afforded in our present situation. A few schools, like the University of Texas Law School, have increased substantially in size, and others, like the University of Michigan Law School, have slowly become considerably larger. I am not thinking about these schools, which are already carrying a substantial part of the load. But there are many other law schools in the country, still of substantially small size, which might well be bigger, and might be actually benefited in the process. If 40 schools increased by 250 students each, there would be an overall increase of 10,000 places in law schools. There might, too, be some reduction in the pressure to get into some law schools. And overall, legal education might be considerably benefited.

Such changes would involve capital costs, for buildings, for libraries, for additions to faculty and staff. But these, spread through many schools, could be handled. In some cases, the increases could come at state universities, and legislative appropriations might be obtained to cover the necessary costs. There is no sound reason why so much of the pressure, and so much of the need for capital costs, should be focused on a few law schools. This is a heavy burden, and it should be shared much more widely by the many excellent law schools in the country.

Growth in the student bodies of excellent but smaller schools of law such as Cornell and Duke and a number of others could, of course, absorb some of the increasing numbers of first-rate candidates for the bar and aspirants to public service in the United States. But the national population continues to increase; the cities grow; there is more government and more law. The Harvard Law School will not grow smaller, and the demand for more direct instruction, for closer contact between student and teacher, will continue. Increasing the number of teachers can increase contact with students, but here there are limits to what is practical. Professors of law able "to teach law in the grand manner, and to make great lawyers" [2] are hard to come by. Not many are developed; growth in other schools will draw down the supply. There are problems of cost; the fewer students each one teaches, the more expensive the instruction. Tuition in the mid-1960's provides more than half the cost of operating the Harvard Law School, and every increase in the costs makes more difficult the undertaking to see that no talented man is denied access to the School. This hope would have been impossible without the generosity of donors of scholarship funds. Already the School spends on financial aid to students a sum equaling a quarter of the charges for tuition; accounting is complex, but the net effect of the scholarship policy and resources is to rebate on the average about $460 of every $1750 present-day tuition payment.

Probably the School's faculty must increase in size for a reason quite unconnected with the demand for more personal attention to students. The growth of government and the increase of its variety of functions, with accompanying increase of intricacy and technical character, demand a degree of specialized expertness in public affairs which draws increasingly on many different

[2] Again Holmes, in "The Use of Law Schools" (1886), in *Collected Legal Papers*, p. 37.

university faculties; among others it draws heavily on faculties of law. Ever since 1917 the United States government has had continual and apparently increasing recourse to university law schools for governmental services. In the future we must be prepared not only to have one seventh of our professors continuously absent on sabbatical leaves for research and study, but to see another absent delegation usefully serving the United States and, one hopes, State and local governments as well.

This is not to say that every instance of such service will require continuous absence and so remove the professor from teaching for a period of a year or two or more. Much of the demand will require comparatively short episodes of consultation, or the sort of service which takes a professor away for a day or two a week. Still the aggregate of diverted effort and time will be substantial, and the schools will be obliged, more and more, to increase the staff of teachers to compensate for these episodic withdrawals from teaching duties. The alternative of threatening able men with permanent severance if they go to serve the public awhile is impracticable; and even if it were possible it would be a poor policy.

A common remark of teachers who are thinking about the future of American education is the impossibility of foreseeing the demands to which graduates must respond when most of them reach their greatest responsibility, thirty years after they leave the School. Hence, we continually remind ourselves, our duty is to teach men to educate themselves in a corpus of professional learning not yet in existence. Is it not possible that in introducing students to the process of higher learning we have not made adequate use of the admirably developed intellects and energies of our highly selected young men and women? Are we perhaps giving too many courses, requiring the young to spend too many hours in lecture halls, when they are well able to educate themselves from books which we are well able to write for them? Are we preparing them for the lifelong task of self-education? Here perhaps will be one wholesome means of serving our students better, without endless increase in the numbers of our teachers.

In the vast enterprise of learning which is Harvard there are many types of instruction and many types of students. One student is the advanced doctoral candidate who has to a large extent finished his days of classroom thralldom. He is busy in the preparation of his dissertation, getting a little guidance now and then in some seminar, or from occasional conferences with his principal instructor. To a large extent he is guiding himself. Perhaps under modern conditions the system devised for LL.B. candidates by Christopher Columbus Langdell and James Barr Ames ninety-odd years ago may not be the ultimate for today's university graduate who studies law. Quite possibly we have much to learn from the techniques of our brethren in other departments of graduate study. Some of the *Law Review* editors and some other top-ranking law students are efficiently educating themselves as lawyers by their editorial and other apprenticeships; they succeed excellently in examinations despite somewhat desultory attention to the formalities of course study. Possibly we may be well advised to learn from their experience.

Here may be a clue to possible change in the instructional pattern of tomorrow. If, as is obvious, there are practical limits to the expansion of the faculty, and yet the professors are to be called on for more and more governmental functions from time to time, and for more time-consuming small-group and individual teaching, perhaps educational materials should be prepared so talented and highly motivated young college graduates can accomplish substantially more of their legal education with fewer large classroom meetings. Perhaps students should be examined less often but more effectively, in order that examination may better serve as a means of instruction. The merit of today's examining process may have been left unexamined, as Parker, Parsons, and Washburn left theirs. The teacher should continually remind himself that the accustomed is not the inevitable. Perhaps the written general examination for the Ph.D. is a pattern for our future, more promising than today's course examinations.

Scanning the School's history one is continually reminded that changes in American social and governmental objectives must and do appear, after a little time, in corresponding changes in the School's study and teaching. In the future law schools will be concerned more and more with governmental assumptions of social burdens; "Medicare" and "Medicaid" and various forms of public housing are recent and familiar examples. There will be numerous others. Some expressions are apt to be irritating, and a conspicuous one is the term "welfare state." It calls up images of unworthy idlers ignobly cadging luxuries from the yield of taxes, taxes imposed on an industrious and self-denying citizenry by an undeserving multitude voting for bread and games. This is an ancient image. In 1821 Chancellor Kent, protesting against a proposed extension of the suffrage to the propertyless, told the New York Constitutional Convention:

> The apprehended danger from the experiment of universal suffrage applied to the whole legislative department, is no dream of the imagination. It is too mighty an excitement for the moral constitution of men to endure. The tendency of universal suffrage, is to jeopardize the rights of property, and the principles of liberty. There is a constant tendency in human society, and the history of every age proves it; there is a tendency in the poor to covet and to share the plunder of the rich; in the debtor to relax or avoid the obligation of contracts; in the majority to tyrannize over the minority, and trample down their rights; in the indolent and the profligate, to cast the whole burthens of society upon the industrious and the virtuous; and there is a tendency in ambitious and wicked men, to inflame these combustible materials. It requires a vigilant government, and a firm administration of justice, to counteract that tendency.
>
> Thou shalt not covet; thou shalt not steal; are divine injunctions induced by this miserable depravity of our nature.[3]

Kent had no success in restricting New York's suffrage to those he called "the free and independent lords of the soil, worth at least $250 in freehold estate, over and above all debts charged thereon," and in 1966 the Supreme Court of the United States has held that a state could not constitutionally condition the right to vote even on the voter's ability to pay a trifling poll tax.[4] A perceptive man will see in the future much more, not less, concern of government for the welfare of the individual than has been true in the past; and this concern will particularly make provision for the individual least able to provide for himself. The Harvard Law School will have to keep this social and political movement in mind in planning its curriculum. Even if we wanted to, we could not make the welfare state go away by turning our backs on it.

Here somebody will remind me (as though I had forgotten it) that traditionally the School has trained leaders of the bar and

---

[3] *Reports of the Proceedings and Debates of the Convention of 1821 Assembled for the Purpose of Amending the Constitution of the State of New York* (Nathaniel Carter and William L. Strong, Reporters, Albany, 1821), p. 221.

[4] *Harper v. Virginia,* 383 U.S. 663 (1966).

that these leaders have been the experts in human organization for great enterprises; that America has constructed her greatness by the use of the corporate form; that the School has for a century and more provided the leaders in this sort of economic endeavor. Granted, of course. The lawyer's task will not grow simpler any more than society will grow simpler. We must continue to train corporate experts; the corporate device will have more use, not less; we must train our corporate experts to have a full realization of the part that urban renewal and medical service and pollution control and civil rights legislation will play in the society and government of A.D. 2000. We must train students to apply to the legislative and other complications of this trend the same clear hard-eyed expertness that has been our pride in earlier and simpler days. Otherwise they will perhaps be lawyers, but they will be less expert, less wise, than the interests of their private and governmental clients require. In many ways the School's task tomorrow will be more complex, not simpler, than its task has been in the past half century. Somehow we must develop men who can train themselves in all the now unforeseen aspects of this governmental movement as it develops during the coming two and more generations.

So the faculty must grow, one guesses, and there will be no decline in the rate of library increase, and with it growth of library staff. The law today is coming to rely far more than formerly on books once thought alien to the lawyer's calling, books on the fringes of the legal process. The School cannot send students to the central university library for all of this, though one perceives the increasing use of that collection. But distance is some discouragement to library use; the Law School's own working library in history, economics, government, sociology, international relations, and the like will necessarily increase along with the continually accelerating growth in judicial, legislative, and administrative materials, and in treatises and periodicals specifically produced for practicing lawyers.

Here, too, unyielding space sets limits to shelving. But perhaps in library matters, as in other things, we are all too conventional. Books are consulted in direct proportion to their newness. Occasions for consulting the first hundred volumes of the New York Reports, or the first two hundred of the Federal Reporter, grow less frequent day by day. The collections of such material much be complete, of course; perhaps the older parts of sets can be stored in less accessible and so cheaper quarters, while in the School proper, micro-records of these older volumes can be ready at hand for consultation. The expense of acquiring an adequate number of reading devices will be considerable; one may question whether that expense will even approach the astronomical cost of land and structures for the storage of old letterpress books in central Cambridge.[5]

Increased space to house the School will be imperative, no matter how the library materials are compressed. There are no micro-professors. Faculty offices cannot be conveniently interchanged so that when Smith is away in New York or New Delhi for ten days Jones takes over Smith's study and desk. The room where a professor works is his own; it is arranged to suit his needs; his books are there; spread out where he can turn to them; his increasing accumulations of files are there; his half-finished manuscript is arranged ready to hand. A scholar's study is not like a lodging for the night at an inn, good for one man today, another tomorrow. When Jones goes to Berkeley on Thursday, or Smith flies to The Hague for a three-day conference, or Brown goes to Washington for a half-year of governmental service in his field of special competence, each within reason must expect to find his work-in-progress as it was when he left, and Jones's or Smith's or Brown's stand-by man must have other room of his own. Space is expensive, but teachers' time is the most costly purchase the School makes, and there is a relation between teacher-space and teacher-time. And as the trend to more seminars and other small-group instruction continues, these will require more rooms and more men to teach in them.

Future needs for space present technical and economic difficulties. Land in central Cambridge is largely occupied and what is available comes in small bits. Harvard is now growing tall instead of wide, and probably the future Law School will follow this pattern. Man is a creature of habit and tends to like what he has. We are used to the existing fabric of the School

---

[5] One foresees, in the future, much more use of wired television for libraries. If infrequently needed books can be stored in cheap space away off yonder, we can telephone a reference service there and summon the image of a page to our desks. And if this now seems expensive, pause with paper and a yellow pad to compute the cost of old-fashioned facilities in mid-Cambridge. Of course the television reference service postulates intelligent, willing, and highly trained people at the far end, working far more than thirty-odd hours a week.

and, for a while, some of us would be startled to see rising in the vicinity of Langdell a structure like the Leverett Towers or William James Hall. But much of wise living consists in acceptance of whatever is an inevitable though disadvantageous concomitant of the attainment of a greater good. There is a lot more going on around here; the things going on are good things; more people are necessary to do them. We can fill up our courtyards and other remaining spaces, but soon still more space will be necessary for more people. The School cannot expand laterally much more. Excavation has disadvantages. The Harvard Law School has nowhere to go but up.

Review of the past century and a half is heartening for the years ahead. The future will hold its difficulties, but none now predictable can be as perilous as the School's state in 1829. No prospect now in sight seems as novel and experimental as that of 1870 when Eliot brought Langdell to Harvard, when the other two professors of law, Emory Washburn and Nathaniel Holmes, were seventy and fifty-five years old respectively, and Langdell at the age of forty-four was obviously going to rebuild the School according to his own radical ideas. Student requirements during the coming half-century will be heavy, but these will stem from the sheer numbers of young men and women of demanding intellect who will seek the law at Harvard. Faculty problems will present themselves, but these will not arise from lack of intelligence or aspiration. Granted human resources, material problems will disappear as material problems did when Story came to the School a century and a third ago.

One imperative lesson is written in these annals. The familiar is not the necessary. What has been habitual in the law and in education for it may be deadening if it fails to accord with new demands of society. The Harvard Law School of 1869, resting on formulas devised when America was far different, only began to prepare itself for the next half-century when the shock of Langdell's innovations awoke it to change. So for tomorrow; the School must be ready to put away former things even when these in their own time have demonstrated great value, if change all around calls for new selection of students, new fields of study and new means of studying them, new literature, new ways of testing the training given to candidates. Our universe is changing. We had better accept it changes and all.

Appendix

Pièce Justificative

Why any Appendix? Surely no book needs an unvisited attic for discarded footnotes. If the stuff of the Appendix is worth its ink and paper, why not print it with the rest of the book? If not, why not resolutely send it on its way toward that undiscovered bourn from which no waste paper returns? For this Appendix I claim justification more respectable than a tender weakness for material otherwise thrown away. I hope some readers may really like to look at it. This history should not close without a picture of the School as it is today, and of course the tenth chapter is largely such a tableau. But that chapter (like all parts of all books) had to be selective. I still miss some overall description — no matter how scant in detail — of today's teachers, research scholars, and administrators. Adequate biographical essays would at least double the book's size, and this book is already long enough. So in compromise I here list the names of all the teachers, research people, and administrators and I add little vitas of professors and assistant professors not earlier described. In Chapter X I tried to sketch the essence of the rich curriculum described, course by course, in the annual catalogues. In these places, in faint outline, is a picture of the School's ideas and men today.

A picture, that is, of the School's men except the most important ones. Our Play (one luxuriates in variety of metaphor) would then have no Hamlet. Without students we would have no reason, and no means to exist. Yet thumbnail vitas of seventeen hundred and more people would be out of the question. Another compromise: I only add in this appendix a list of the 362 colleges and universities, all over the world, from which in 1965–66 came the Law School's 1683 students. I include a note of the number of students coming from each. From this diversity of provenance one can infer something of their diverse thought. Most of these young men and women are, of course, Americans training themselves for private practice. But beside these are

371

people of many other cultures, nations, and schools of thought; students coming from all categories of political organizations, all concepts of law. Have all these any dominant trait in common? Perhaps they share an anxious seriousness, inseparable from thoughtful existence in a world of much trouble. Wishing for them every good thing, one hopes that some of this intensity and the causes of it may grow less with passing years.

Vitas of professors and assistant professors on the faculty in 1966–67, and of a few others, whose biographies are not sketched in the text. Faculty members are here described in the order of their names in the catalogue.

Ralph Jackson Baker was born in Octoraro, Pennsylvania, in 1888. He received his A.B. from Swarthmore in 1907, and his LL.B. from the University of Pennsylvania in 1911. During that same year he was made Assistant Professor of Law at the University of Pennsylvania. From 1914 to 1932 he practiced law in Harrisburg, Pennsylvania, and in 1932 he became professor of law at Harvard. He was made Fessenden Professor of Law in 1941 and Weld Professor of Law in 1946. In 1958 he became professor of law, emeritus. Professor Baker taught and wrote in the fields of corporations and trusts. He died November 5, 1966.

George Knowles Gardner was born in Worcester, Massachusetts, in 1891. He took his A.B. in 1912 and his LL.B. in 1914 from Harvard University. He practiced law in Boston from 1914 to 1928. From 1921 to 1928 he was an instructor at Northeastern University, and he became professor of law at Harvard in 1928. In 1958 he was made professor of law emeritus. Professor Gardner taught and wrote in the fields of contract and insurance. He was active in civil liberties questions.

James Angell MacLachlan was born in 1891 in Ann Arbor, Michigan. He took his A.B. in 1912 from the University of Michigan and his LL.B. from Harvard in 1916. From 1916 to 1924 he practiced law in Chicago, except for service as a captain of field artillery from 1917 to 1918. MacLachlan was made assistant professor of law at Harvard in 1924 and full professor in 1927. In 1960 he became professor emeritus. In World War II he served with the Office of Price Administration and later with the Price Adjustment Board and United States Maritime Commission. After his retirement at Harvard, Professor MacLachlan taught several years at the Hastings Law School of the University of California. He has written and taught extensively in the field of bankruptcy.

William Edward McCurdy was born in Augusta, Georgia, in 1893.

He took his A.B. in 1916, his LL.B. in 1921, and his S.J.D. in 1922 from Harvard University. From 1921 to 1923 he was legal secretary to Mr. Justice Brandeis. He was appointed to the Harvard Law School faculty in 1923 as instructor of law and was made assistant professor of law in 1924. He became full professor in 1928 and in 1960 he was made professor emeritus. Mr. McCurdy has written and taught in the fields of contracts and domestic relations.

Charles Fairman was born in Alton, Illinois, in 1897. He took his A.B. at the University of Illinois in 1918. In 1920 he received an A.M.; he did graduate study at the University of Paris from 1925 to 1926; and in 1926 he received a Ph.D. from Harvard. He continued his studies at the University of London in 1934 and in 1938 received an S.J.D. from Harvard. Mr. Fairman has taught in the field of political science and government at Pomona, Williams, Harvard, and Stanford, and Washington University where he was made Nagel Professor of Constitutional Law and Political Science. From 1955 to 1962 he was a professor of law at Harvard and was made professor emeritus in 1962. From 1942 to 1946 he served in the U.S. Army rising to the rank of colonel. Professor Fairman has taught and written in the fields of political science, military law, legal history, and judicial biography.

Sheldon and Eleanor Glueck should be described in a single vita — as Harvard recognized in 1958 when it simultaneously made both Gluecks honorary Doctors of Science and the President read a single citation for the two. Sheldon Glueck, born in Warsaw in 1896, came with his parents to the United States in 1903. He studied law at Georgetown in 1914–15 but changed to the A.B. program at George Washington University and a program in laws at the National University Law School. In 1920 he took his A.B. at George Washington and a LL.B. and LL.M. at the National University, and in the same year became an American citizen. In 1921 he entered the Harvard Graduate School; in 1922 he became a Harvard M.A., and married Eleanor Touroff of New York, a Barnard A.B. then engaged in graduate study at Harvard. The Gluecks have been Harvard criminologists ever since. Sheldon Glueck became a Harvard Ph.D. in 1924, an instructor in Harvard College in 1925, an assistant professor in the Law School in 1929, a professor in 1931, and Roscoe Pound Professor in 1950. He became emeritus in 1963. Eleanor Glueck took master's and doctor's degrees in education at Harvard in 1923 and 1925. She has been engaged in criminological research ever since; her most recent appointment is that of research associate in criminology in 1953.

Andrew James Casner was born in Chicago in 1907. He took his A.B. and LL.B. at the University of Illinois and joined its faculty of law in 1929. He was a professor of law at the University of Maryland from 1930 to 1935 and at Illinois, from 1935 to 1938. He has been at Harvard from 1938 until the present. He took his S.J.D. at Columbia in 1941. Casner was an officer in the United States Army Air Force from 1942 to 1945. He is now Weld Professor of Law and Associate Dean of the Law School.

David Farquhar Cavers was born in Buffalo, New York, in 1902. He took his first degree at Pennsylvania in 1923 and his LL.B. at Harvard in 1926. He practiced law in New York City for three years, and then was an instructor at Harvard in 1929–30, an assistant professor at the University of West Virginia Law School in 1930–31, and assistant professor and professor at Duke from 1931 to 1945. During the war he was with the Office of Price Administration in Washington. He joined the Harvard faculty as a professor of law in 1945 and became Fessenden Professor in 1952. He was associate dean from 1951 to 1958, and is currently chairman of the Division of Graduate Studies.

Louis Adelbert Toepfer took his A.B. at Beloit College in 1940 and his LL.B. in 1947 at Harvard, delayed four years by wartime service. He became assistant dean and director of admissions in 1947, was secretary of the School from 1956 to 1959, and in the latter year became vice dean and member of the faculty of law. He continued as director of admissions from 1947 to 1966; he also, in more recent years, taught admiralty. In 1966 he resigned to become dean of Western Reserve Law School in Cleveland.

Joseph Edgar Leininger was born in Ashland, Ohio, in 1923. In 1951 he received his A.B. from the University of California. He took his LL.B. from Harvard in 1959. During World War II he was a member of the Office of Strategic Services in China; from 1946 to 1955 he served with the United States Foreign Service and the Central Intelligence Agency. From 1960 to 1962 he practiced law in Denver, Colorado. In 1962 Mr. Leininger became Secretary of International Legal Studies, Harvard, and on July 1, 1966, he became vice dean, replacing Mr. Toepfer.

W. Barton Leach was born in 1900 in Boston, Massachusetts. He took his Harvard A.B. in Government in 1921, and his LL.B. at the Law School in 1924. From 1924 to 1925 he was legal secretary to Justice Holmes. Before coming to the School as an instructor in 1929, Leach practiced law in Boston. He became professor of law in 1931 and a member of the faculty of the Graduate School of Public Administration in 1954. In 1942 Leach was commissioned major in the Army and rose to the rank of brigadier general in 1949 in the United States Air Force Reserve. He is interested in the fields of property and estate planning. He holds the Story professorship.

John Philip Dawson was born in Detroit, Michigan, in 1902. He took his A.B. at the University of Michigan in 1922, and his J.D. in 1924. He became a Doctor of Philosophy at Oxford in 1930. In 1927 Dawson became professor of law at the University of Michigan. He was visiting professor at the University of Chicago in 1955. From 1942 to 1943 he was chief counsel in the rent section of the Office of Price Administration; from 1943 to 1945 he was chief of the Middle East division, Foreign Economic Administration, and acting regional economic counselor for the Middle East. From 1947 to 1948 he was Director of the Foreign Trade Administration. He became a professor of law at Harvard in 1956. Particularly interested in contracts, restitution, and legal history, he is Fairchild Professor.

Arthur Eugene Sutherland was born in Rochester, New York, in 1902. After schooling in the United States and Switzerland he spent 1919 in the Near East with American Relief. He took his A.B. at Wesleyan in 1922, and his LL.B. from Harvard in 1925. From 1926 to 1941 he practiced law in Rochester, except for 1927 to 1928 when he was legal secretary to Justice Holmes. Sutherland was a member of the New York Constitutional Convention of 1938. From 1941 to 1945 he served in the Army in the grades major to colonel in the United States and in the European, African, and Mediterranean theaters. From 1945 to 1950 he was a professor of law at Cornell. He became professor of law and member of the faculty of Public Administration at Harvard in 1950, and Bussey Professor of Law in 1955. He was a Fulbright lecturer in 1956 at Brasenose College, Oxford. During 1965–66 he was Acting Master of Lowell House. Sutherland has taught and written in the fields of constitutional and commercial law, and of government.

Livingston Hall was born in Chicago in 1903. He took his first degree at Chicago in 1923 and his LL.B. at Harvard in 1927. He was in private practice in New York City for four years and then became assistant United States attorney for the Southern District of New York. In 1932 he came to the Law School as an assistant professor of law, became a full professor in 1937, and was vice dean from 1938 to 1958. He is now Roscoe Pound Professor of Law. During World War II he served in the Office of Price Administration and then was commissioned a lieutenant colonel in the Army Air Forces. He has given particular study to the criminal law.

Lon Luvois Fuller was born in Hereford, Texas, in 1902. He took his A.B. and J.D. at Stanford; taught at Oregon, Illinois, and Duke from 1926 to 1940; became a professor of law at Harvard in 1940. In 1948 he became Carter Professor of General Jurisprudence. Contract and jurisprudence have been his special concerns. His Storrs Lectures at Yale became his 1964 book *The Morality of Law.*

Louis Leventhal Jaffe was born in Seattle in 1905. He took his A.B. from Johns Hopkins in 1925, his LL.B. from Harvard in 1928, and his S.J.D. in 1932. He was legal secretary to Justice Brandeis in 1933–34. He was with the legal staff of the Agricultural Adjustment Administration and the National Labor Relations Board from 1935 to 1936. From 1936 to 1948 he was professor of law at the University of Buffalo, and became dean of the Law School in 1948. In 1950 he was made Byrne Professor of Administrative Law at Harvard, and a member of the faculty of Public Administration. From 1944 to 1945 he was a public member of the Ship-Building Commission of the United States War Labor Board. Jaffe has written and taught in the fields of foreign relations and administrative law.

James Harmon Chadbourn was born in Spartanburg, South Carolina, in 1905. He took his A.B. at The Citadel in 1926 and his J.D. at the University of North Carolina in 1931. Between 1931 and 1950 he was a member of the law faculties of North Carolina, Duke, and Pennsylvania. From 1950 to 1963 he was Connell Professor of Law at the University of California. During the year 1961–1962 Chadbourn was a visiting professor at Harvard. He became professor at Harvard in 1963. In 1931–32 he was a member of the Southern Commission on Interracial Cooperation. Professor Chadbourn teaches civil procedure and evidence.

Richard Hinckley Field was born in Maine in 1903, took his A.B. in 1926 and his LL.B. in 1929, both at Harvard. He practiced law in Boston from 1929 to 1942. He spent 1942 to 1946 with the Office of Price Administration, ending that period of service as its general counsel. He joined the Harvard faculty as visiting professor of law in 1946 and became professor the next year. He has specialized in civil procedure, most recently in developing, with Professor Robert Keeton, the course in trial practice.

Henry Melvin Hart, Jr., was born in Butte, Montana, in 1904. He received his A.B. from Harvard in 1926, his LL.B. in 1930, and his S.J.D. in 1931. From 1931 to 1932 he was legal secretary to Justice Brandeis. He became assistant professor of law at Harvard in 1932, and professor of law in 1937. In 1960 he was made Dane Professor. Mr. Hart was Julius Stone Visiting Professor at Ohio State University from 1954 to 1955. He served in the solicitor general's office from 1937 to 1938, and the United States attorney general's office from 1940 to 1941. From 1942 to 1945 he was with the Office of Price Administration and from 1945 to 1946 he was general counsel, office of Economic Stabilization. Professor Hart has taught and written books on the federal system and on jurisprudence.

Ernest Joseph Brown was born in Louisiana in 1906. He took an A.B. at Princeton in 1927 and his LL.B. at Harvard in 1931. He practiced law in Buffalo from 1934 to 1941; and served as a captain in the United States Army in the China theater during the war. He was professor of law at the University of Buffalo between 1937 and 1942 and became a professor of law at Harvard in 1946. He is a specialist in constitutional law and the law of taxation.

Milton Katz was born in New York in 1907. He took his A.B. and LL.B. at Harvard. He served the federal government in various capacities from 1932 to 1939, and became a professor of law in 1940. From 1941 to 1944 he had a leave of absence from Harvard to serve in administrative posts in Washington and, from 1944 to January 1946, to serve in Africa and Europe as a naval officer. He was again granted leave from Harvard in 1950–51 to serve as the United States special representative in Europe in connection with the Marshall Plan with the rank of ambassador. He was Associate Director of the Ford Foundation, 1951–54. He is now Henry L. Stimson Professor of Law and Director of International Legal Studies at Harvard.

Samuel Edmund Thorne was born in New York City in 1907. He took his B.A. at the City College of New York in 1921; his LL.B. from Harvard in 1930; and his M.A. from Yale in 1948. From 1930 to 1932 he was assistant librarian at Columbia Law School, and was professor of law at Northwestern University from 1933 to 1942. He was librarian at Yale Law School from 1945 to 1948, and professor of law at Yale from 1948 to 1956. He was appointed jointly in the Law School and the department of history at Harvard in 1956. From 1942 to 1945 he served in the United States Navy. Professor Thorne teaches English legal history, and is master of South House, Radcliffe.

Paul Abraham Freund was born in St. Louis in 1908. He took his A.B. at Washington University in 1928, and his LL.B. and S.J.D. at Harvard in 1931 and 1932 respectively. He served as law clerk to Mr. Justice Brandeis, 1932–1933; was on the legal staff of the Treasury and the Reconstruction Finance Corporation, 1933–1935; and was in the office of the solicitor general from 1935 to 1939. He became a lecturer in law at Harvard in 1939, professor in 1940, Fairchild Professor in 1950, and Royall Professor in 1957. In 1957–58 he was Pitt Professor of American History and Institutions and a Fellow of Trinity College, Cambridge University. He is President of the American Academy of Arts and Sciences. In 1958 he became Carl M. Loeb University Professor at Harvard. His writing and teaching have especially concerned constitutional law and the history of the Supreme Court.

Mark DeWolfe Howe was born in Boston in 1906. He took his A.B. at Harvard in 1929 and his LL.B. in 1933. He was secretary to Justice Oliver Wendell Holmes in 1933–34; practiced law in Boston from 1933 to 1937; was professor of law at the University of Buffalo from 1937 to 1945, where he was dean from 1941 to 1945. He served as major, lieutenant colonel, and colonel in the United States Army, 1943 to 1945, and earned the Distinguished Service Medal, the highest military decoration awarded to any member of the faculty during the Second World War. He has written a number of books on legal history, particularly volumes dealing with the life and works of Mr. Justice Holmes. In 1966 he became Warren Professor of Legal History. He died suddenly on February 28, 1967.

Benjamin Kaplan was born in New York City in 1911. He took his first degree at the College of the City of New York in 1929 and his LL.B. at Columbia in 1933. He practiced law in New York City from 1933 to 1942. From 1942 to 1946 he served as an army officer rising to the rank of lieutenant colonel. In 1947 he became visiting professor of law at Harvard for one year, and he became a professor of law in 1948. In 1961 he was appointed to the Royall professorship. Among many areas of learning, he is a specialist in the law of copyright.

James Norman Dalrymple Anderson was born in 1908 in Aldeburgh, England. He took his B.A. in 1930, LL.B. in 1931, M.A. in 1934, and LL.D. in 1954, all from Cambridge University. Mr. Anderson became a lecturer in Islamic law in the London University School of Oriental and African Studies in 1947; he was a reader in Oriental laws in the University of London, 1951 to 1953. Since 1953 he has been professor of Oriental laws in the University of London and head of the department of law, School of Oriental and African Studies. Since 1959 he has been Director of the Institute of Advanced Legal Studies, University of London, and since 1964 Dean of the Faculty of Laws. Mr. Anderson served in the British Army in World War II in the Civil Affairs Branch, General Headquarters, Middle East Command. He was political secretary in 1942, and chief secretary with rank of colonel in 1944. As Visiting Professor in 1966, he taught Islamic Law at Harvard.

Robert Richardson Bowie was born in 1909 in Baltimore. He is an A.B. of 1931 at Princeton, and an LL.B. of Harvard in 1934. He practiced law in Maryland, became an assistant attorney general of that state, and then served in the army from 1942 to 1945. He was a professor of law at Harvard from 1945 to 1955. During his membership on the Law School's faculty he spent two years, 1950 to 1951, as general counsel and special adviser to the United States High Commissioner for Germany and from 1953 to 1955 was director of the policy planning staff of the Department of State. Professor Bowie resigned his professorship of law in 1955. He served as assistant secretary of state for policy planning from 1955 to 1957, when Harvard appointed him professor of international relations and director of the Center for International Affairs. He is on leave from Harvard for the year 1966–67 as counselor to the Department of State.

Appendix

Milton Howard Cohen was born in Milwaukee, Wisconsin, in 1911. He took his A.B. at Harvard in 1932 and his LL.B. in 1935. He was with the Securities Exchange Commission from 1935 to 1946. From 1947 to 1961 he was engaged in practice of law in Chicago. Since 1961 he has again been with the Securities Exchange Commission, as director of special study of securities markets. He is a visiting professor at Harvard, 1966–67; he is particularly concerned with securities regulation and corporate finance.

Richard Abel Musgrave was born in Konigstein, Germany, in 1910. He received a diploma from the University of Heidelberg in 1933, an M.A. from Harvard in 1936, and a Ph.D. in economics in 1937. From 1936 to 1941 he was an instructor of economics at Harvard. From 1941 to 1947 he was a research economist for the Board of Governors of the Federal Reserve Board. He became a professor of economics at the University of Michigan in 1948, at Johns Hopkins University in 1959, and at Princeton in 1962. He came to Harvard as professor at the Law School and a member of the faculty of economics in 1965. Professor Musgrave teaches public finance, money, and macro-theory.

Archibald Cox was born in Plainfield, New Jersey, in 1912. He is a Harvard A.B. of 1934 and LL.B. of 1937. He served as law secretary to Judge Learned Hand, and then practiced in Boston between 1938 and 1941. He was an attorney in the office of the solicitor general of the United States between 1941 and 1943 and assistant solicitor in the Department of Labor from 1943 to 1945. He became a lecturer on law at Harvard in 1945–46 and was professor of law from 1946 to 1961. President Kennedy appointed him solicitor general of the United States in 1961; on his resignation in 1965 he was reappointed at the School. He is now Samuel Williston Professor of Law. He has written and taught in labor law and constitutional law.

Louis Loss took his B.S. degree at the University of Pennsylvania in 1934 and LL.B. at Yale in 1937. He was an attorney with the Securities Exchange Commission from 1936 to 1944, was chief counsel of the Division of Trade and Exchange from 1944 to 1948, associate general counsel from 1948 to 1952. He was a lecturer on law at Catholic University of America, 1941 to 1942; visiting lecturer at Yale from 1947 to 1952; professorial lecturer at George Washington University from 1949 to 1952; and professor of law at Harvard from 1952 to 1962. In 1962 he became William Nelson Cromwell Professor of Law. Professor Loss has lectured widely at foreign universities, is draftsman of the Uniform Securities Act, and is author of *Securities Regulation* (1951; a second edition in preparation) and co-author of *Blue Sky Law* (1958). Professor Loss teaches courses in corporations and securities regulation.

Robert Amory, Jr., was born in Boston in 1915. He took his A.B. at

Harvard in 1936, his LL.B. in 1938. He practiced in New York City from 1938 to 1940, entered the army in 1941 as a private, and after combat duty in the Southwest Pacific was discharged as a colonel in 1946. He became professor of law and accounting at the Law School in 1946 and remained in that post until 1952 when he became deputy director of the Central Intelligence Agency in which he continued for ten years. He became chief of the international division of the Bureau of the Budget in 1962 and remained in that post until 1966 when he resigned to practice law in Washington. As this book goes to press Mr. Amory is Chairman of the Harvard Law School Sesquicentennial Fund.

Clark Byse was born in Oshkosh, Wisconsin, in 1912. He took a B.Ed. from Wisconsin State Teachers College in 1935 and an LL.B. in 1938 from the University of Wisconsin. Columbia made him an LL.M. in 1939 and an S.J.D. in 1952. From 1938 to 1940 Byse was a member of the faculty of law at the University of Iowa. Between 1940 and 1946 he held a number of legal positions in the federal government. He was assistant professor at the University of Pennsylvania Law School from 1946 to 1947; associate professor, 1947–48; professor, 1948–1957. He became a professor of law at Harvard in 1958. He teaches administrative law and contracts.

Louis Bruno Sohn was born in Lwow, Poland, in 1914. He took his first degrees at the John Casimir University; he came to the United States in 1939, and took an LL.M. at Harvard in 1940 and an S.J.D. in 1958. He became a research fellow at the School in 1946, a lecturer in 1947, an assistant professor and the John Harvey Gregory Lecturer in World Organization in 1951, professor of law in 1953, and Bemis Professor in 1961. He has served the federal government and the United Nations in many consultantships.

Robert Braucher was born in New York City in 1916. He graduated A.B. at Haverford in 1936 and LL.B. at Harvard in 1939. He practiced law in New York City from 1939 to 1941, when he entered the United States Army Air Force as a flying cadet and advanced through the grades to major in 1945. He served in India and Burma; and served in the War Department in the closing months of the war. He became visiting professor of law at Harvard in 1946 and professor in 1949. He was a Fulbright lecturer at Chuo and Tokyo universities in Japan in 1959. His principal work has been in the fields of contract and commercial law. He is a Commissioner on Uniform State Laws.

Harold Joseph Berman was born in Hartford, Connecticut, in 1918. He is a Dartmouth A.B., studied at the London School of Economics, and became a Yale M.A. in 1942. After war service he took a Yale LL.B. He spent a year as assistant professor at Stanford and came to Harvard in 1948, becoming professor of law in 1952. He has lectured in a number of foreign universities including the Moscow State University. Berman teaches torts, comparison of Soviet and American law, and law of international trade. His particular interest in Soviet law has led to his connection with Harvard's Russian Research Center.

Vern Countryman was born in Roundup, Montana, in 1917. He received an A.B. from the University of Washington in 1939 and an LL.B. in 1942. He was legal secretary to Justice William O. Douglas from 1942 to 1943. He served in the Army Air Force from 1943 to 1946, and in 1946–47 he was an instructor in law at the University of Washington. From 1947 to 1948 he was Sterling Law Fellow at Yale, and was made assistant and then associate professor at Yale Law School where he taught until 1955. After four years of practice in the District of Columbia, in 1959 he became dean of the University of New Mexico Law School. In 1963–64 he was visiting professor at Harvard, and he became professor in 1964. He is particularly interested in commercial transactions, corporate finance, and creditors' rights.

Harold Marsh was born in Tyler, Texas, in 1918. He took his B.S. at Rice Institute in 1939; LL.B. at the University of Texas in 1942; LL.M. from Columbia in 1947; and Jur. Sc.D. in 1951, also from Columbia. In 1947 he was an assistant professor of law at the University of Washington. He was again assistant professor of law at the University of Illinois from 1949 to 1950. From 1954 to 1955 he was visiting professor at the University of California where he became professor in 1958. He is a visiting professor of law at Harvard in 1966–67. Mr. Marsh practiced law for eight years in California and New York. He teaches in the fields of corporations and creditor's rights.

Charles Monroe Haar was born in Antwerp, Belgium, in 1920. He took his A.B. at New York University in 1940, M.A. at Wisconsin in 1941, and LL.B. at Harvard in 1948. From 1941 to 1945 he served in the Navy. After study of English control of land use as a Sheldon Fellow from 1948 to 1949, Haar became assistant professor at Harvard Law School in 1952. He became professor in 1954. Professor Haar has taught property and land use planning. Among his books is *Land Planning in a Free Society*. He has served the federal government in many consulting capacities, and is on leave in 1966–67 to be Assistant Secretary of the U.S. Department of Housing and Urban Development.

Robert Ernest Keeton was born in Texas in 1916. He took his undergraduate and LL.B. degrees at the University of Texas, was an officer in the Navy from 1942 to 1945, and practiced law in Houston until 1951 when he became an associate professor of law in Southern Methodist University. Keeton came to Harvard as Thayer Teaching Fellow in 1953, became an assistant professor in 1954, took his S.J.D. here in 1956, and in the same year became professor of law. He has specialized in torts and in procedure. With Jeffrey O'Connell he wrote "Basic Protection: A Proposal for Improving Automobile Claims Systems," *Harvard Law Review*, 78: 329 (1964), and *Basic Protection for the Traffic Victim* (1965).

Albert Martin Sacks was born in New York in 1920. He took his B.A. from the College of the City of New York in 1940, served in the Army during the war and then took his LL.B. from Harvard in 1948. He was legal secretary to Judge A. N. Hand in 1948–49 and to Justice Felix Frankfurter in 1949–50. He practiced law from 1950 to 1952. From 1952 to 1955 he was assistant professor of law at Harvard and became professor in 1955. Professor Sacks teaches in the fields of jurisprudence and civil rights.

Richard Reeve Baxter was born in New York City in 1921. He took an A.B. in philosophy at Brown in 1942 and then entered the Army. He was demobilized in 1946 and took his LL.B. at Harvard in 1948. Meantime he had been commissioned in the Army Judge Advocate General's Corps where he remained as a specialist in international law until 1954. He joined the Harvard faculty in 1956, becoming Professor of Law in 1959. While in the Army he had taken a diploma in international law at Cambridge and an LL.M. in international law at Georgetown. Besides international law, he teaches criminal law and contracts. He was acting master of South House, Radcliffe, in 1965.

Donald Frank Turner was born in Wisconsin in 1921, took his A.B. at Northwestern, became M.A. at Harvard in 1942, Ph.D. at Harvard in 1947, and LL.B. at Yale in 1950, where he also taught economics during his law study. He was legal secretary to Justice Tom C. Clark from 1950 to 1951. After four years of practice in Washington he became an assistant professor at the Harvard Law School in 1954, and a professor in 1958. In 1964–65 he was visiting professor at Stanford. He has taught courses and seminars in economic regulation. Turner has been the United States attorney general in charge of the Anti-Trust Division of the Department of Justice since 1965.

Arthur Taylor von Mehren was born in Albert Lea, Minnesota, in 1922. In 1942 he received his B.S., in 1945 his LL.B., and in 1946 his Ph.D. from Harvard University. From 1946 to 1947 he studied at the Faculty of Law of the University of Zurich, and from 1948 to 1949 he studied at the Faculté de Droit of the University of Paris. From 1945 to 1946 he was legal secretary to Chief Judge Calvert Magruder of the United States Court of Appeals, First Circuit. Von Mehren was an assistant professor at the Harvard Law School from 1946 to 1953 and has been professor of law since 1953. From 1947 to 1948 he was acting chief of the legislation branch, legal division, in the United States Military government in Germany.

Oliver Oldman was born in New York city in 1920, took his bachelor's degree at Harvard in 1942, and subsequently became an economist with the Office of Price Administration. During the war he was an officer in the Army. He was in the construction business in Buffalo, New York, from 1946 to 1950, and an instructor in economics at the University of Buffalo during the same four years. He returned to Harvard in 1950, taking his LL.B. in 1953. After two years of practice in Buffalo he joined the staff of the Harvard Law School international program of taxation. He has been a consultant on taxation of the Venezuelan government and is one of the authors of *The Fiscal System of Venezuela* (1959). He became professor of law in 1961, and is director of the international tax program.

Abram Joseph Chayes was born in Chicago in 1922. He took his A.B. at Harvard in 1943, and after Army combat service returned to Harvard to take his LL.B. in 1949. He was legal secretary to Justice Frankfurter from 1951 to 1952 and practiced law in Washington from 1952 to 1955 when he joined the Harvard faculty, becoming Professor of Law in 1958. From 1961 through 1964 he was Legal Adviser to the Department of State. He again became Professor of Law at Harvard in 1965. He is a Faculty Associate of the Institute of Politics of the John F. Kennedy School of Government.

Roger Dummer Fisher was born in Winnetka, Illinois, in 1922. He took his A.B. in 1943 and his LL.B. in 1948 from Harvard. From 1958 to 1960 he was a lecturer at Harvard Law School and became a professor of law in 1960. Before joining the Law School faculty he served as assistant general counsel and then assistant to the deputy United States special representative to the Economic Cooperation Administration in Paris, all in 1948 and 1949. Between 1950 and 1956 he practiced law in Washington, D.C., and from 1956 to 1958 was assistant to the solicitor general. He is a faculty associate of the Institute of Politics of the John F. Kennedy School of Government.

Adam Yarmolinsky was born in New York City in 1922. He took his A.B. from Harvard in 1943; and LL.B. from Yale in 1948. He served with the United States Air Force from 1943 to 1946. From 1948 to 1949 he was legal secretary for Chief Judge C. E. Clark, Second Circuit; he practiced law for one year in New York City; and became legal secretary to Justice Stanley Reed, of the United States Supreme Court, from 1950 to 1951. From 1951 to 1955 he practiced law in Washington. He was director of the Washington office of the Fund for the Republic from 1956 to 1957; public affairs editor for Doubleday and Company from 1957 to 1959; consultant to private foundations from 1959 to 1961; and special assistant to the secretary of defense from 1961 to 1966. He has been a lecturer at Yale Law School and became professor of law at Harvard in 1966. He is particularly interested in criminal law and urban studies, and is a member of the

Appendix

Institute of Politics of the John F. Kennedy School of Government.

David Richard Herwitz was born in Lynn, Massachusetts, in 1925. He served in the Navy, 1944–46, took his B.S. at Massachusetts Institute of Technology in 1946, and his LL.B. at Harvard in 1949. He was a legal secretary with the United States Tax Court in 1949 and 1950; in 1950–51 he was a teaching fellow at Harvard. While practicing law in Boston, Herwitz was a lecturer at Northeastern Law School from 1951 to 1954. In 1954 he joined the faculty at Harvard and became a full professor in 1957. His subjects include accounting and business planning and taxation.

Donald Theodore Trautman was born in Cleveland, Ohio, in 1924. He took his A.B. and LL.B. at Harvard in 1951. After a year and a half at Harvard he joined the Army and served until 1946. He then completed his undergraduate and law study in the "Seven Year Plan," which called for three years of college study followed by two years of Law School, followed by a final two years of coordinated law and final undergraduate study. Following this plan, Trautman took both degrees with high distinction. The program was admirably conceived but there are few Trautmans; it has regrettably been discontinued. Trautman was legal secretary to Mr. Justice Felix Frankfurter in 1952–53. From 1953 to 1956 he was assistant professor of law at Harvard and became professor in 1956. He is interested in conflicts of laws and many aspects of public law.

David Westfall was born in Columbia, Missouri, in 1927. He took his A.B. from the University of Missouri, in 1947 and his LL.B. from Harvard in 1950. From 1950 to 1955 Westfall was engaged in the practice of law in Chicago. From 1955 to 1958 he was an assistant professor at Harvard Law School and became a professor in 1958. He teaches estate planning, economic regulation, and real estate planning.

Frank Ernest Arnold Sander was born in 1927 in Stuttgart, Germany. He took his A.B. and LL.B. degrees at Harvard. From 1946 to 1947 he was in the United States Army. He was legal secretary to Chief Judge Magruder, of the United States Court of Appeals, First Circuit, from 1952 to 1953, and legal secretary to Mr. Justice Frankfurter from 1953 to 1954. From 1954 to 1956 he was with the United States Department of Justice, and from 1956 to 1959 he practiced law in Boston. In 1957 he became a lecturer at Boston University Law School and taught there until 1959 when he became an assistant professor at Harvard Law School. He became a full professor in 1962, Professor Sander teaches accounting, family, law, taxation, and a tax policy seminar.

Detlev Frederick Vagts was born in Washington, D.C., in 1929. He received from Harvard his A.B. in 1948 and his LL.B. in 1951. Vagts practiced law from 1951 to 1953 and from 1956 to 1959 in New York, in the interval serving three years in the Air Force. From 1959 to 1962 he was assistant professor at Harvard Law School, he became professor in 1962. He teaches in the fields of corporations, international transactions and relations, and accounting.

James Vorenberg was born in Boston in 1928. He took his A.B. at Harvard in 1948 and his LL.B. at Harvard in 1951. He served in the Air Force from 1951 to 1953. After eight years of practice in Boston he came to the Law School as a professor in 1962. He is reporter of the American Law Institute Prearraignment Project, and is, in 1966, on leave to handle the important duties of executive director of the President's Commission on Law Enforcement and the Administration of Justice.

Phillip Elias Areeda was born in Detroit, Michigan, in 1930. He took his A.B. in 1951 and his LL.B. in 1954 from Harvard. He was a Sheldon Traveling Fellow from 1954 to 1955. In 1961 he became an assistant professor at Harvard and full professor in 1963. Areeda was assistant special counsel to the President from 1955 to 1960. He teaches anti-trust law, legal process, and administrative law. He is a member of the Institute of Politics of the John F. Kennedy School of Government.

Yale Kamisar was born in New York City in 1929. He took his A.B. at New York University in 1950 and his LL.B. at Columbia in 1954. He served in the United States Army from 1951 to 1952. He practiced law in Washington, D.C., from 1955 to 1957. He became associate professor at Minnesota Law School in 1958 and professor there in 1960. He was a Social Science Research Council Fellow in 1960–61. In 1964–65 Mr. Kamisar came to Harvard as a visiting professor and taught criminal law and evidence, and in 1965 became professor of law at Michigan. He has in his writing and elsewhere been a vigorous exponent of the rights of persons accused of crime.

Paul Bator was born in Hungary in 1929. He took his A.B. at Princeton in 1951 and his M.A. and LL.B. degrees at Harvard in 1953 and 1956 respectively. He practiced law in New York until he joined the Harvard Faculty as assistant professor of law in 1959, and became a professor in 1962. In 1966 he was a visiting professor at the University of California at Berkeley. He is associate reporter of the American Law Institute Prearraignment Project.

Derek Curtis Bok was born in Bryn Mawr, Pennsylvania, in 1930. He took his A.B. at Stanford in 1951, and his LL.B. at Harvard in 1954. In 1958 he received an M.A. from George Washington University, and in 1954–55 he was a Fulbright Fellow in Paris. Bok became an assistant professor of law at Harvard in 1958 and became full professor in 1961. His subjects include economic regulation and labor law.

Jerome Alan Cohen was born in Elizabeth, New Jersey, in 1930. He took both his A.B. and his LL.B. degrees at Yale in 1951 and 1955 respectively. He was clerk to Chief Justice Warren in 1955 and clerk to Mr. Justice Frankfurter in 1956. He practiced law in Washington, before joining the faculty at the University of California Law School, Berkeley, in 1959. He became professor there in 1962. In 1965–66 he was a visiting professor at Harvard Law School and joined the faculty permanently in 1966. His subjects include Chinese law and Chinese attitudes toward international law.

Gareth Hywel Jones was born in Tylorstown, Glamorganshire; Wales, in 1930. He received his LL.B. in 1951 at the University of London. In 1953 he received a B.A. and an LL.B. and in 1958 an M.A. from Cambridge. He was a Choate Fellow at Harvard in 1953–54, taking Harvard's LL.M. in 1954. In 1961 he received a Ph.D. from the University of London. He became a barrister of Lincoln's Inn in 1955. He has been a lecturer at Oriel and Exeter colleges, Oxford, and at King's College, London. He is presently University Lecturer at Cambridge, where he also is a fellow and lecturer at Trinity College. During 1966–67 he is a visiting professor at Harvard where he is teaching trusts, contracts and restitution, and law and equity in England.

Andrew Lee Kaufman was born in Newark, New Jersey, in 1931. He took his A.B. at Harvard in 1951, and his LL.B. in 1954. From 1955 to 1957 he was legal secretary to Mr. Justice Felix Frankfurter. From 1954 to 1955, and 1957 to 1965 Kaufman was engaged in law practice in New Jersey. He became a lecturer in law at Harvard in 1965 and professor in 1966. He teaches commercial transactions and constitutional law.

John Howard Mansfield was born in Morristown, New Jersey, in 1925. He took his A.B. from Harvard in 1952 and his LL.B. in 1956. In 1956–57 he was law secretary to Mr. Justice Traynor of the Supreme Court of California; in 1957–58 he was legal secretary to Mr. Justice Frankfurter. He became an assistant professor at Harvard in 1958 and professor in 1961. He is interested in the fields of evidence and torts.

Henry Jacob Steiner was born in Mount Vernon, New York, in 1930. He received from Harvard his B.A. in 1951, his M.A. and LL.B. in 1955. From 1955 to 1956 he was a Sheldon Traveling Fellow. He was secretary to Mr. Justice Harlan from 1957 to 1959. Steiner was assistant professor of law at Harvard from 1962 to 1965, and became professor in 1965. He practiced law in New York City from 1958 to 1961, and in 1962 was consultant to the Agency for International Development. His subjects include conflict of laws, international transactions and relations, and torts.

William Dorey Andrews was born in New York City in 1931. He

received his A.B. from Amherst in 1952 and his LL.B. from Harvard in 1955. From 1958 to 1963 he practiced law in Boston. From 1961 to 1963 he was a lecturer at Harvard Law School; he was assistant professor from 1963 to 1965, and has been a full professor since 1965. Andrews is interested in accounting, taxation, and problems of federal tax reform.

Robert Harris Cole was born in Park Falls, Wisconsin, in 1931. He took his A.B. from Harvard in 1952, and his LL.B. in 1955. From 1955 to 1956 he was secretary to Mr. Justice Sherman Minton of the United States Supreme Court. He was acting associate professor of the University of California School of Law from 1961 to 1964 and became a professor in 1964. During 1966-67 he is a visiting professor of law at Harvard. He is active in the fields of evidence and torts.

David Louis Shapiro was born in New York City in 1932. He took at Harvard his A.B. in 1954, and his LL.B. in 1957. Between 1957 and 1962 Mr. Shapiro was engaged in law practice in Washington, D.C. From 1962 to 1963 he was secretary to Mr. Justice Harlan. In 1963 he became an assistant professor at Harvard Law School and professor in 1966. He is interested in civil procedure, and labor law.

Morgan Shipman was born in Memphis, Texas, in 1933. He received from the University of Texas his B.B.A. in 1955, and his LL.B. in 1958, interrupting his Law School career by army service. From 1958 to 1963 he was engaged in law practice in Washington, D.C., and was with the Securities Exchange Commission from 1963 to 1965. In 1965 he became an assistant professor of law at Harvard. He is particularly interested in corporate securities and taxation.

Charles Fried was born in Czechoslovakia in 1935. He took an A.B. at Princeton in 1956, a B.A. at Oxford in 1958, and his LL.B. at Columbia in 1960. After a year's clerkship for Mr. Justice Harlan, he became assistant professor of law at Harvard in 1961 and professor in 1965. Mr. Fried is a consultant on the American Law Institute Prearraignment Project. His interests include criminal law, commercial transactions, jurisprudence, and Roman law.

Frank Isaac Michelman was born in New Rochelle, New York, in 1936. He took his A.B. at Yale in 1957 and his LL.B. at Harvard in 1960. From 1960 to 1961 he practiced law in New York, and from 1961 to 1962 he was secretary to Mr. Justice Brennan. He became assistant professor of law at Harvard Law School in 1963 and professor in 1966. He is concerned with the law of property and of local government.

Lloyd Lobell Weinreb was born in New York City in 1936. He took his A.B. at Dartmouth in 1957, A.B. at Oxford University in 1959 (A.M. 1963), and LL.B. at Harvard in 1962. From 1962 to 1963 he was legal secretary to Judge Lumbard, United States Court of Appeals;

Appendix

from 1963 to 1964 he was legal secretary to Mr. Justice Harlan of the United States Supreme Court. Weinreb was with the Criminal Division of the Department of Justice from 1964 to 1965. He was made assistant professor of law at Harvard in 1965. He is particularly interested in criminal law.

Clifford Leslie Pannam was born in Melbourne, Australia, in 1937. He received his LL.B. at the University of Melbourne in 1958, and was tutor and senior tutor there from 1958 to 1959. He took an LL.M. at the University of Illinois in 1960. From 1960 to 1961 he was an International Legal Fellow at Columbia University working toward an S.J.D., which he took in 1967. From 1963 to 1966 he was senior lecturer at the University of Melbourne Faculty of Law. He is the Ezra Ripley Thayer Teaching Fellow at Harvard Law School in 1966–67. Mr. Pannam is interested in restitution and constitutional law.

Alan Morton Dershowitz was born in New York in 1938. He took his A.B. at Brooklyn College in 1959, and his LL.B. at Yale in 1962. In 1963 he was clerk to Judge Bazelon of the Court of Appeals of the District of Columbia, and in 1964 he was clerk to Mr. Justice Goldberg of the Supreme Court of the United States. He joined the Harvard faculty in 1964–65 as assistant professor. He has done much work in criminal law and in the relation to it of psychiatry.

Charles Rothwell Nesson was born in Boston, Massachusetts, in 1939. He took his A.B. from Harvard in 1960 and his LL.B. in 1963. During 1963–64 he was a Sheldon Traveling Fellow. In 1964–65 he was legal secretary to Mr. Justice Harlan, and in 1965–66 he was with the civil rights division of the Department of Justice. He was appointed assistant professor of law at Harvard in 1966. He is interested in the fields of property and civil rights.

Colleges and Universities Represented by Students at the Harvard Law School, 1965–66

Ahmadu Bello University (Nigeria)	1	Antioch College	2
Alabama, University of	1	Aquinas College (Michigan)	1
Albion College	3	Arizona, The University of	2
Algiers, University of (Algeria)	1	Arkansas, University of	1
Allegheny College	1	Arlington State College	1
American University. The	4	Auburn Community College	1
Amherst College	32	Auckland, University of (New Zealand)	2
Amsterdam, University of	1		
Amsterdam, Free University of (The Netherlands)	1	Barnard College	6
Anderson College	1	Basle, University of (Switzerland)	1

Appendix

389

Grinnell College	4	Linfield College	1
Grove City College	1	London, University of (England)	18
		Long Island University	2
Hamilton College	6	Los Angeles City College	1
Hamline University	1	Los Angeles State College	1
Hampden-Sydney College	2	Louisiana Polytechnic Institute	1
Harpur College, State University		Louisiana State University and	
of New York	3	A & M College	2
Harvard University	269	Louisville, University of	1
Hastings College	1	Loyola University (Illinois)	2
Havana University (Cuba)	1	Loyola University (Louisiana)	1
Haverford College	4	Lyons, University of (France)	1
Hawaii, University of	3		
Hebrew University of Jerusalem		Madrid, University of (Spain)	1
(Israel)	6	Manchester, University of (Eng-	
Heidelberg, University of (Ger-		land)	2
many)	2	Manhattan College	3
Hendrix College	1	Marquette University	5
Hobart College	1	Maryville College	1
Holy Cross, College of the	11	Marywood College	1
Houston, University of	2	Massachusetts, University of	6
Howard University	1	Massachusetts Institute of Tech-	
Hunter College of the City of		nology	18
New York	2	Mercer University	1
		Miami, University of (Florida)	3
Idaho, University of	2	Miami University (Ohio)	5
Illinois, University of	13	Michigan, The University of	43
Indiana University	9	Michigan College of Mining &	
Institute of European Studies		Technology	1
(France)	1	Michigan State University	8
Iowa, State College of	2	Middlebury College	1
Iowa, State University of	6	Milan, University of (Italy)	1
		Minnesota, University of	7
John Carroll University	1	Mississippi, University of	1
Johns Hopkins University	14	Mississippi State College	1
Joliet Junior College	1	Missouri, University of	5
Juniata College	1	Monmouth College	1
		Montana State College	1
Kansas, University of	6	Montana State University	3
Kansas State University	2	Montreal, University of (Canada)	1
Kentucky, University of	1	Moravian College	1
Kenyon College	5	Morehouse College	5
Knox College	3	Morgan State College	1
		Morris Brown College	1
Lafayette College	6	Moscow State University	
Lake Forest College	1	(U.S.S.R.)	1
La Salle College	1	Mount Holyoke College	1
La Sierra College	1	Multnomah School of the Bible	1
Lausanne, University of		Munich, University of (Germany)	2
(Switzerland)	1	Muskingum College	1
Laval University (Quebec)	1	Mysore, University of (India)	1
Lawrence College	1		
Lehigh University	9	Nagoya University (Japan)	1
Le Moyne College	1	Naples, University of (Italy)	1
Liberia, University of	1	National University of Ireland	1
Lille, University of (France)	1	Nebraska, University of	4
Lincoln University	1	New Mexico, University of	2

Appendix

New York, The City College of   10
New York, State University of   1
New York City Community
   College   1
New York University   13
Niagara University   1
Nigeria, University of   1
North Carolina, University of   9
North Park College   1
North Texas State University   1
Northeastern University   1
Northwest Nazarene College   1
Northwestern College (Iowa)   1
Northwestern University   23
Notre Dame, University of   20

Oakland City College (California)   1
Oberlin College   10
Occidental College   6
Ohio State University, The   9
Ohio Wesleyan University   1
Oklahoma, University of   7
Oklahoma State University   1
Oregon, University of   2
Oregon State University   1
Oslo, University of (Norway)   1
Osmania University (India)   1
Oxford, University of (England)   34

Pacific, University of the   1
Panjab, University of the (Pakis-
   tan)   1
Paris, University of (France)   16
Pembroke College   1
Pennsylvania, University of   46
Pennsylvania State University,
   The   3
Pittsburgh, University of   2
Pomona College   6
Pontificia Universidad Javeriana,
   Bogota (Colombia)   1
Poona, University of (India)   1
Portland State College   1
Pratt Institute   1
Princeton University   93
Principia College, The   3
Providence College   3
Puerto Rico, University of   3
Purdue University   3

Queens College (City University
   of New York)   6
Queens University (Canada)   1

Radcliffe College   14
Reed College   3
Regis College (Colorado)   1

Rensselaer Polytechnic Institute
   (New York)   1
Rice University   6
Richmond, University of   1
Rio Grande do Sol, University
   of (Brazil)   1
Rochester, University of   4
Rockford College   1
Rockhurst College   1
Rutgers, The State University   4

St. Bernardine of Siena College   1
St. Bonaventure University   1
St. Francis College (Pennsylvania)   1
St. John's University (Minnesota)   3
St. John's University (New York)   2
St. Joseph's College (Pennsyl-
   vania)   1
St. Joseph's Junior College
   (Missouri)   1
St. Joseph's Seminary (Michigan)   1
St. Mary's University
   (Halifax, Nova Scotia)   1
St. Michael's College   1
St. Norbert College   1
St. Paul's College (D.C.)   1
St. Peter's College (Maryland)   1
St. Thomas, College of (Min-
   nesota)   1
St. Vincent College (Pennsylvania)   1
San Diego State College   2
San Fernando Valley State
   College   1
San Francisco, University of   1
San Jose State College   1
Santa Clara, University of   4
Santa Monica City College   1
Scranton, University of   1
Simpson College   1
Smith College   7
Soochow University (China)   3
South Carolina, University of   1
South Dakota, University of   1
South Dakota School of Mines
   and Technology   1
South Dakota State University   1
Southern California, University
   of   11
Southern Methodist University   6
Southern Missionary College   1
Spelman College   1
Spring Hill College   1
Stanford University   45
Stockholm, University of
   (Sweden)   3
Strasbourg, University of
   (France)   1

Swarthmore College 5
Sydney, University of (Australia) 2
Syracuse University 3

Talladega College 1
Tamkang College of Arts and
  Sciences (Taiwan) 1
Tehran University (Iran) 1
Texas, University of 8
Texas Technological College 1
Tohoku University (Japan) 1
Tokyo, The University of
  (Japan) 2
Toledo, University of 1
Toronto, University of (Canada) 2
Toulouse, University of (France) 1
Transylvania College 2
Trinity College (Connecticut) 10
Tübingen, University of (Ger-
  many) 1
Tufts University 10
Tulane University 4
Tuskegee Institute 1

Union College (New York) 4
Union Theological Seminary
  (New York) 1
United States Air Force Academy 1
United States Coast Guard Acad-
  emy 1
United States Military Academy 5
United States Naval Academy 8
Ursinus College 2
Utah, University of 2
Utah State University 3

Valparaiso University 1
Vanderbilt University 8
Vassar College 2
Vermont, University of 1
Victoria University of Welling-
  ton (New Zealand) 1
Virginia, University of 5

Virginia State College 1
Virginia Union University 1

Wabash College 3
Waseda University (Japan) 1
Washburn University of Topeka 1
Washington, University of 12
Washington and Lee University 1
Washington State University 1
Washington University
  (Missouri) 3
Wayne State University 1
Wellesley College 9
Wesleyan University 14
West Virginia University 1
Western College (Ohio) 1
Western Michigan University 2
Western Reserve University 2
Westphalian Wilhelms Univer-
  sity of Münster (Germany) 1
Wheaton College (Illinois) 2
Wheeling College 1
Whitman College 3
Willamette University 1
William and Mary, The College
  of 1
Williams College 30
Wilmington College (Ohio) 1
Wisconsin, University of 24
Wisconsin State College 1
Witwatersrand, University of the
  (Union of South Africa) 1
Wooster, The College of 3
Worcester Polytechnic Institute 1

Xavier University (Ohio) 2

Yale University 137
Yeshiva University 4

Zurich, University of (Switzerland) 1

Grand Total   2045

Names counted more than once   325
Number of college graduates   1683
Number of colleges represented during the school year   362

Appendix

Faculty and Administration of the Law School of Harvard University, 1966–67

FACULTY

Nathan Marsh Pusey, PH.D., LL.D., L.H.D., President.

Austin Wakeman Scott, A.M., LL.B., LL.D., D.C.L., Dane Professor of Law, Emeritus

Ralph Jackson Baker, A.M., LL.B., LL.D., Weld Professor of Law, Emeritus (died November 5, 1966)

John MacArthur Maguire, A.B., LL.B., LL.D., Royall Professor of Law, Emeritus

George Knowles Gardner, A.B., LL.B., Professor of Law, Emeritus

James Angell MacLachlan, A.B., LL.B., Professor of Law, Emeritus

William Edward McCurdy, A.B., LL.B., S.J.D., Professor of Law, Emeritus

Charles Fairman, PH.D., LL.B., S.J.D., Professor of Law, Emeritus

Sheldon Glueck, PH.D., LL.M., LL.D., S.D. (hon.), S.S.D. (hon.) Roscoe Pound Professor of Law, Emeritus

Erwin Nathaniel Griswold, A.M., LL.B., S.J.D., L.H.D., LL.D., D.C.L., Dean and Langdell Professor of Law

Andrew James Casner, A.M., LL.B., J.S.D., Associate Dean and Weld Professor of Law

David Farquhar Cavers, S.B., LL.B., S.J.D. (hon.), Chairman of the Division of Graduate Studies and Fessenden Professor of Law

Louis Adelbert Toepfer, A.B., LL.B., Vice Dean, Member of the Faculty and Director of Admissions (until June 30, 1966)

Joseph Edgar Leininger, A.B., LL.B., Vice Dean (from July 1, 1966)

Walter Barton Leach, A.B., LL.B., S.J.D. (hon.), Story Professor of Law

John Philip Dawson, A.B., J.D., DR.PHIL., Charles Stebbins Fairchild Professor of Law

Arthur Eugene Sutherland, A.B., LL.B., S.J.D. (hon.), Bussey Professor of Law

Livingston Hall, PH.B., LL.B., S.J.D. (hon.), Roscoe Pound Professor of Law

Lon Luvois Fuller, A.M., J.D., Carter Professor of General Jurisprudence

Louis Leventhal Jaffe, A.B., LL.B., S.J.D., Byrne Professor of Administrative Law [On leave for the second semester 1966–67]

James Harmon Chadbourn, A.B., J.D., Professor of Law

Richard Hinckley Field, A.B., LL.B., Professor of Law

Henry Melvin Hart, Jr., A.B., LL.B., S.J.D., LL.D., Dane Professor of Law

393

Appendix

Ernest Joseph Brown, A.B., LL.B., Professor of Law [On leave for the second semester 1965–66]

Milton Katz, A.B., LL.B., Henry L. Stimson Professor of Law and Director of International Legal Studies [On leave for the year 1965–66]

Samuel Edmund Thorne, A.M., LL.B., LITT.D., Professor of Legal History

Paul Abraham Freund, A.B., LL.B., S.J.D., LL.D., L.H.D., Carl M. Loeb University Professor

Mark DeWolfe Howe, A.B., LL.B., Charles Warren Professor of American Legal History

Benjamin Kaplan, A.B., LL.B., Royall Professor of Law

James Norman Dalrymple Anderson, A.M., LL.B., Visiting Professor of Law [First semester 1966–67]

Milton Howard Cohen, A.B., LL.B., Visiting Professor of Law

Richard Abel Musgrave, DIPL., A.M., PH.D., Professor of Economics in the Faculty of Arts and Sciences and in the Law School.

Archibald Cox, A.B., LL.B., LL.D., Samuel Williston Professor of Law

Louis Loss, B.S., A.M., LL.B., William Nelson Cromwell Professor of Law

Clark Byse, B.E., LL.B., LL.M., S.J.D., Professor of Law.

Louis Bruno Sohn, LL.B., M.DIPL.SC., LL.M., S.J.D., Bemis Professor of International Law and John Harvey Gregory Lecturer on World Organization

Robert Braucher, A.B., LL.B., J.D. (hon.), Professor of Law

Harold Joseph Berman, M.A., LL.B., Professor of Law

Vern Countryman, A.B., LL.B., Professor of Law

Harold Marsh, Jr., A.B., LL.B., LL.M., J.S.D., Visiting Professor of Law

Charles Monroe Haar, A.M., LL.B., Professor of Law [On leave for the year 1966–67]

Robert Ernest Keeton, B.B.A., LL.B., S.J.D., Professor of Law

Elisabeth Ann Owens, A.B., LL.B., Lecturer on Law and Research Associate in Law

Albert Martin Sacks, B.B.A., LL.B., Professor of Law

Richard Reeve Baxter, A.B., LL.B., LL.M., Professor of Law [On leave for the year 1966–67]

Arthur Taylor von Mehren, S.B., LL.B., PH.D., Professor of Law

Oliver Oldman, S.B., LL.B., Professor of Law and Director of the International Tax Program [On leave for the second semester 1966–67]

Abram Joseph Chayes, A.B., LL.B., Professor of Law [On leave for the year 1965–66]

Roger Dummer Fisher, A.B., LL.B., Professor of Law [On leave for the year 1965–66]

Adam Yarmolinsky, A.B., LL.B., Professor of Law

David Richard Herwitz, S.B., LL.B., Professor of Law

Appendix

Donald Theodore Trautman, A.B., LL.B., Professor of Law

David Westfall, A.B., LL.B., Professor of Law

Frank Ernest Arnold Sander, A.B., LL.B., Professor of Law

Detlev Frederick Vagts, A.B., LL.B., Professor of Law

James Vorenberg, A.B., LL.B., Professor of Law [On leave for the first semester 1966–67]

Phillip Elias Areeda, A.B., LL.B., Professor of Law

Paul Michael Bator, A.M., LL.B., Professor of Law [On leave for the second semester 1965–66]

Derek Curtis Bok, A.B., LL.B., A.M., Professor of Law

Jerome Alan Cohen, A.B., LL.B., Professor of Law

Gareth Hywel Jones, LL.B., LL.M., PH.D., Visiting Professor of Law

Andrew Lee Kaufman, A.B., LL.B., Professor of Law

John Howard Mansfield, A.B., LL.B., Professor of Law

Henry Jacob Steiner, A.M., LL.B., Professor of Law

William Dorey Andrews, A.B., LL.B., Professor of Law

Robert Harris Cole, A.B., LL.B., Visiting Professor of Law

David Louis Shapiro, A.B., LL.B., Professor of Law

Morgan Shipman, B.B.A., LL.B., Assistant Professor of Law

Charles Fried, A.M., LL.B., Professor of Law

Frank Isaac Michelman, A.B., LL.B., Professor of Law

Lloyd Lobell Weinreb, A.M., LL.B., Assistant Professor of Law

Clifford Leslie Pannam, LL.B., LL.M., S.J.D., Ezra Ripley Thayer Teaching Fellow

Alan Morton Dershowitz, A.B., LL.B., Assistant Professor of Law

Charles Rothwell Nesson, A.B., LL.B., Assistant Professor of Law

John Howard Beckstrom, A.B., J.D., Teaching Fellow [1964–66]

Arthur Jan Lombard, S.B., LL.B., Teaching Fellow [1965–66]

Spencer Neth, A.B., LL.B., Teaching Fellow [1964–66]

Gary Lee Anderson, S.B., J.D., Teaching Fellow

Donald Howard Berman, A.B., LL.B., Teaching Fellow

Peter Barry Bloch, S.B., LL.B., Teaching Fellow

Walter Allen Reiser, Jr., B.S. IN MECH.ENG., LL.B., Teaching Fellow

Aaron David Twerski, A.B., LL.B., Teaching Fellow

Richard Wallace Ziebarth, A.B., LL.B., Teaching Fellow

Kurt Hans Nadelmann, J.U.D., LIC. EN DROIT, Research Scholar and Member of the Faculty

Lewis Hyman Weinstein, A.B., LL.B., Lecturer on Law

Peter Francis Coogan, LL.B., A.M., LL.M., Lecturer on Law

Ernest James Sargeant, A.B., LL.B., Lecturer on Law [Second semester 1965–66 and 1966–67]

395

Appendix

James Draper St. Clair, A.B., LL.B., Lecturer on Law

James Patrick Lynch, Jr., A.B., LL.B., Lecturer on Law

Jerome Paul Facher, A.B., LL.B., Lecturer on Law

William John Curran, LL.B., LL.M., S.M.HYG., Lecturer on Legal Medicine

Alan Abraham Stone, A.B., M.D., Lecturer in Psychiatry

John Rhodes Quarles, Jr., A.B., LL.B., Lecturer on Law [Second semester 1965–66]

Evan Yervant Semerjian, A.B., LL.B., Faculty Assistant in Charge of the Ames Competition

RESEARCH STAFF

Yung-fang Chiang, LL.B., LL.M., J.D., Research Associate in Law

Hungdah Chiu, LL.B., S.J.D., Research Associate in Law

David Finkelstein, A.B., LL.B., Research Associate in Law

John Richard Garson, A.B., M.LITT., B.C.L., LL.M., Research Associate in Law

INTERNATIONAL TAX PROGRAM

Charles Kane Cobb, Jr., A.B., LL.B., Research Associate in Law

Rex Lee Coleman, A.B., LL.B., M.JUR., Research Associate in Law

Martin Norr, B.S., LL.B., Research Associate in Law

Arie Kopelman, A.B., M.B.A., LL.B., Research Assistant to the International Tax Program

William David Popkin, A.B., LL.B., Teaching Fellow and Research Associate to the International Tax Program

ADMINISTRATIVE STAFF

Wesley Everett Bevins, Jr., S.B., LL.B., Assistant Dean and Director of the Harvard Law School Fund

William Lane Bruce, A.B., LL.B., Secretary of the Law School

John Pasley Wilson, A.B., LL.B., Assistant Dean

Russell Avington Simpson, B.S., LL.B., Assistant Dean and (from July 1, 1966) Director of Admissions

David Nathan Smith, A.B., LL.B., Secretary, International Legal Studies, and Adviser to Foreign Students

Wilson Hunt Pile, B.S., Assistant Director of the Harvard Law School Fund

John Herman Muller, Jr., A.B., LL.B., Assistant Director of the Harvard Law School Fund

Appendix

Gardner Edward Campbell, Jr., Assistant Director of the Harvard Law School Fund

Leo Joseph Cass, A.B., M.D., Director of the Law School Health Service and Physician to the University Health Services

Mary Conlan, A.B., Administrative Assistant to the Dean

Janet Ann Murphy, A.B., Secretary to the Dean

Margaret Evelyn Quinn, Assistant Secretary and Registrar

Julie Grenier, PH.B., A.M., Associate Editor of the *Harvard Law School Bulletin*

Jean Ryan, A.M., Secretary to the Division of Graduate Studies

Mrs. Edith Duehay Oliver, Assistant Director of Admissions

Eleanor Roberts Appel, A.B., Placement Director

Mrs. Marjorie Moody Traverse, Director of the Reunion Office

Mrs. Cora Libby Woodaman, Fund Recorder

Mrs. Hannah Crutchfield Kilmer, Secretary to the Vice Dean

Mary Veronica McDonald, Assistant for Alumni Records

Virginia Eva Klisiewicz, Financial Aids and Dormitory Secretary

Margaret Theresa Smith, Secretary to the Director of International Legal Studies

Mrs. Elizabeth Peach Allebach, Jr., A.B., Secretary to the Legal Aid Bureau

Norma June Thompson, Administrative Assistant to the Fund Director

Nancy Murray Mahoney, A.B., Assistant to the Secretary

LIBRARY

Earl Charles Borgeson, B.S.L., LL.B., B.A. in Law Librarianship, Librarian, and Member of the Faculty

Philip Austin Putnam, LL.B., Assistant Librarian

Margaret Mae Moody, B.A., B.S. in Library Science, Assistant Librarian for Cataloguing

Myrtle Annette Moody, B.S. in Library Science, Assistant Librarian for Acquisitions

Vaclav Mostecky, J.U.D., M.A., M.S. in Library Science, Assistant Librarian for Foreign Law Reference

George Alfred Strait, LL.B., Assistant Librarian for Reference

Dénes Dezsö Boronkay, DR.JUR., B.A. in Library Science, Cataloguer

Kenneth Coe, LL.B., M.A., LL.M., PH.D., Bibliographer

Mara Efferts, B.M., M.S. in Library Science, Cataloguer

Edith Guild Henderson, A.M., LL.B., S.J.D., Curator, Treasure Room

Finn Henriksen, A.B., CAND.JUR., M. OF LIBRARIANSHIP, J.D., Reference Librarian

Appendix

Olga Matta Kay, LL.B., M.S. in Library Science, Cataloguer
June Mary Ann Rossier, DIPLÔME DE BIBLIOTHÉCAIRE-SECRETAIRE, Acquisitions Librarian
Thomas Joseph Callahan, Senior Supervisor
James Thomas Coward, Senior Supervisor
Thomas Hay, Senior Supervisor

Index

Index

Index

reads Frankfurter-Wigmore counter-battery, 261; early career sketched, 288; joins faculty as assistant professor in *1934*, 288; dean in *1946*, 316; on admissions policy, 321–322; appointed to U.S. Civil Rights Commission, 326

Haar, Charles Monroe, professor, 330, 381

Harkness Commons, 349–354; World Tree, 350; Miro mural, 350; alumni commencement spread in courtyard, 351–352

Hart, Henry Melvin, professor, 346, 376

Harvard: Thomas Pownall gives land to, for either "Hollisian" or law professorship, 27; Isaac Royall leaves land to, for professorship of "physick" or law, 39; Massachusetts constitution of 1780 names as a university, 42; sells Royall lands, 42; Corporation sets up Royall professorship, 45; Law School founded, 56–57; in 1820's, 64. *See also* University

Harvard Law Review, founded *1887*, 197–198; membership a coveted honor, 248–250; an excellent educational experience, 341

Harvard Law School Association, genesis (1886), 197

Harvard Research in International Law, 275–277

Hayes, Rutherford Birchard: enters School (1843), 129; describes School career, 129–134; only graduate to become President of United States, 129

Henderson, Edith, Dr., 92n, 398

Henry II, 9

Henry VIII, 9

Hoar, George Frisbie, U.S. Senator, writes of School of 1840's, 141–142

Hoffman, David, publishes his *Course of Legal Study* (1816), 55; suggests sociological jurisprudence, 55; Story reviews his work, 56

Holmes, Nathaniel, appointed Royall Professor (1868) to succeed Parker, 156

Holmes, Oliver Wendell: enrolled in Law School (1829), 101; dislikes it and leaves (1830), 101; saves Old Ironsides, 102

Holmes, Oliver Wendell, Jr.: on resting on a formula, 134; with Arthur

G. Sedgwick takes over editorship of *American Law Review* (1870), 140; *Review* strongly criticizes Law School (October 1870), 140; praises school of his student days in 1886 address, 147, 197; on valet without imagination, 158; first Weld Professor (1882), 186; on lawyers as part of "the little army of specialists," 359

Howe, Mark DeWolfe, professor, 311, 377

Hudson Manley Ottmer, lecturer and professor (1918–1919), career outlined, 275; directs Harvard Research in International Law, 276–277; contribution to Beale-Williston festschrift, 291

Inns of Court: by 1400's a sort of university of common law, 1; Sir John Fortescue writes of, 1; in fifteenth century gave some general education, 1; never a *studium generale*, 2; in eighteenth century became ancient clubs with apprenticeship to law, 2

Institute of Criminal Law, 278–281. *See also* Criminal justice; Glueck, Sheldon and Eleanor

Institutional treatises: English, 3; Scots, 3n

International legal studies, 332–337; new building to house, 352–353

Iredell, James, orders Blackstone's *Commentaries*, 24

Jaffe, Louis Leventhal, professor, 305n, 376

Jefferson, Thomas, thought Coke a sound Whig, 13

Judges, pay of, around *1800*, 44

Justices of Supreme Court, high ranking students hold secretaryships, 231, 249

Justinian's *Institutes*, 2; students of on continent, 2; lack of English "Institutes," 10

Kamisar, Yale, professor, 331, 385

Kaplan, Benjamin, professor, 311, 346, 378

Katz, Milton, professor, 305, 337, 377

Keener, William Albert: considered for appointment, 186; appointed assistant professor (1883), 187; his teaching, 201, 203

Index

lecturer (1852), 151; Overseers refuse to confirm as professor because Loring as U.S. Commissioner returned Burns, a fugitive slave, to Virginia, 151

Lowell, Abbott Lawrence: became President of Harvard (1909), 226; his support of School, 226–227

Lowell, James Russell: describes Cambridge of 1820's, 64; enrolls in School (1838), 128; wavers in intentions of continuing, 128–129; LL.B. (1840), 129; later career, 129

Lowell, John: career at bar, 44; Fellow of Harvard (1810), 45; declines Royall chair, 47; with Gore drafts statutes for chair, 47–48

Loyalists, in Massachusetts, 33f; Absentee Act, 40; Conspirators Act, 40; 1805 legislation aided Royall's devisees, 41

McCarthy, John, ruled stacks and delivery desk, 1910, 163

McCarthy, May, secretary for Deans Thayer and Pound, 243–244, 298

MacNeil, Sayre, professor (1926–1933), 292

Magruder, Calvert, vice-dean (1930–1939), 287

Maguire, John MacArthur: career outlined, 163; contribution to Beale-Williston festschrift, 292; work on evidence in criminal law, 331

Married students, 316–319

Marsh, John Bigelow, chairman of Law School Fund, 349

Massachusetts, character of population in 1770's, 32; loyalists, 33f

Master of Laws degree, 233–234; 342–343

Medieval scholars, 2

Mentschikoff, Soia, visiting professor (1948–1950), 319

Miro mural, 350

Model jury trial, 127; demonstrates questions of fact, 345–348

Moot courts hear questions of law, 73–76, 343–345

Morgan, Edmund Morris, professor (1925): contribution to Beale-Williston festschrift, 293; acting dean during World War II, 308–311; work on model trial, 346; Morgan Room, 348

New Deal, carried away faculty members for government service in 1930's, 287–288

Oldman, Oliver S., professor, 335–383

Olivart collection of works on international law, see Library

Oxford: Blackstone lectures at (1753), 1; with Cambridge, ignored English common law until 1753, 2. See also Blackstone; Civil law; Common law; Henry VIII; Viner

Parker, Isaac: John Lowell recommends for Royall chair, 47; elected, 49; estimates of character, 49–50; installation with pomp, 50; inaugural address suggests founding Law School, 51; his 1816 lectures, 52; renews suggestion for Law School early in 1817, 53–54; Peabody's estimate of his lectures, 53; judicial duties consumed much time, 65; resigns chair (1827), 81

Parker-Parsons-Washburn School: criticized by Holmes and Sedgwick, 140; left students free to study, assuming intelligent maturity, 152–153; resisted change, 153–154; resistance to examinations required by university statutes, 154–156; President Eliot's appointment (1869) shook School up, 157; evaluation of, 158–161; library ran down, 159–160

Parker, Joel: with professors Parsons and Washburn conducted School most of quarter-century 1845–1870, 141; elected Royall Professor (1847), 149

Parsons, Theophilus: with professors Parker and Washburn conducted School most of quarter-century 1845–1870, 141; elected Dane Professor (1848), 150; his Contracts and other books, 152

Peabody, Andrew Preston: his estimate of Parker's course, 53; as Acting President (1869) decries cramming and sees value in low-ranking students, 156

Petrarch, Francesco, 2

Photocopy reproduction of current teaching material, 330

Plimpton, Francis T. P.: wrote In Personam: A Lyrical Libel, 248n; on Jimmie's Lunch and Dean Pound, 248; on Chafee's "Trial at the Harvard Club," 258–259

Index

Political change, *see* Change

"Postwar generation" at School, 319

Pound, Roscoe: took no LL.B. but became eminent in law, 63; his student recollections (1889–1890), 199–204; his "Liberty of Contract" (1909), 208; career (1890–1910), 236–238; Story Professor, 238–239; his sociological jurisprudence, 239; Carter Professor of General Jurisprudence (1913), 239–240; dean (1916), 243; character and undertaking as dean, 243–244; and Cleveland Survey, 271–272; and Wickersham Commission, 274–275; burdens and irritations in early 1930's, 288; contributor to Beale-Williston festschrift, 293; "What is the Common Law," 296; retires as dean and becomes University Professor, 297; later career and death, 297–299

Pownall, Thomas, gives land to Harvard for "Hollisian" or law professorship, 27

Practice of Law: Stearns combined with teaching, 59; Stearns counsel to university, 69–70; Greenleaf opposed Harvard in *Charles River Bridge Case*, 124, 125; experience in, as desirable qualification for teacher, 184, 191

Presidents of Harvard, 139. *See also* Conant; Kirkland; Abbott Lawrence Lowell; Peabody; Pusey; Quincy

Professorships of law in America: proposed at Yale (1777), 25; established William and Mary (1779), 26; George Wythe first professor at William and Mary, 26–27; Blackstone, basis of teaching, 27; St. George Tucker succeeds Wythe, 27; Tapping Reeve establishes Litchfield School (1784), 27; James Wilson, associate justice, professor at Pennsylvania (1790), 29; James Kent professor at Columbia (1793), 30; Royall endows chair at Harvard, 32–42; early proposals at Harvard, 56–57

Public service, by graduates and professors, 330–331, 358–359, 363–364

Pusey, Nathan Marsh, President of Harvard (1953), allows autonomy to School, 313

Quincy, Josiah: recruited for presidency, *1829*, 85; resigns in *1845*, 138–139

Race relations, change in American attitude toward, *see* Change

Record, Law School weekly newspaper, founded (1946), 319

Redlich, Josef, professor, 293

Reeve, Judge Tapping, establishes Litchfield Law School, 27

Roman law: respectable at continental universities, 2; Oxford and Cambridge take pride in, 2; relation to "civil law," 2; in Medieval England, 3; affected Glanvill and Bracton, 4, 6; continues in English universities, 8, 10; reinstituted at School (1964), 10n; taught at School in 1920's and 1930's, 295

Ropes, John Codman, with J. C. Gray, launched *American Law Review* (1866), 140

Royall, Isaac: endowed chair of law at Harvard, 32, 42; Royall family, 33; Feke portrait of, 34; Medford estate, 34; Antigua sugar plantations, 35; goes to Halifax, 1775, then England, 36; will, 37; dies, 38; Harvard sells Royall lands, 39–42; establishes Royall professorship, 45, 47. *See also* Loyalists

Sacco and Vanzetti Case, 259–262. *See also* Frankfurter

Sayre, Francis Bowes, member of faculty (1917–1934), 279; contributes to Beale-Williston festschrift, 294

Scholarships, 363

Science, law as, 20–21; develops in seventeenth and eighteenth centuries, 21–23; Addison's spacious firmament, 22; Blackstone's cosmic clock, 22; Judge Reeve at Litchfield taught law "as a science," 28; Langdell attempted, 174–176; evaluation of Langdell's concept, 177–178

Scots law, 7

Scott, Austin Wakeman: early career, 219; describes School in *1906–1907*, 219–221; joins faculty in December 1909, 234–235; acting dean (1915), 243; aids model trial, 346

Sedgwick, Arthur G., *see* Holmes, O. W., Jr.

Seminars, 340–342

Smith, Jeremiah, professor (1890–1910), 217–218

Social change, *see* Change

Statutes, comprehensive, instruction on, 326–327; modern stress on foreshadowed by Landis' work, 326

Index

Stearns, Asahel: chosen University Professor of Law, 58; Peabody's estimate of, 66; Stearns's teaching, 66–68, 71–73, 78; collects library, 68–71; urges new building for School in 1825, 71; establishes moot courts, 73–76; "dissertations," 76; his system better than office study, 77; Harvard awards LL.D. (1825), 79; resigns (1829), 86; his letter giving reasons for decline of School, 86–87; portrait in Langdell, 91

Stiles, Ezra, President of Yale: plan for instruction in law, 1779, 25

Stimson, Henry Lewis, distinguished alumnus, 241; aided Frankfurter's early career, 241–242; in 1939 gave School a "junior common room" named for Elihu Root, 307

Story, Joseph: aspired to be poet, 2; education in law, 12; professional beginnings, 43; toasts Kent at Harvard (1823), 79; Harvard seeks him for professor (1820, 1825, 1827), 81–82; Nathan Dane writes to him about endowing School (1828), 92; co-counsel with Dane in a case about cows, 93; edits English law books, 95; Justice, U.S. Supreme Court (1811), 95; much in Harvard affairs, 95; discusses reorganization of School with Dane, Quincy, and Corporation (1828–1829), 96–97; appointed Dane Professor, 99; inaugurated, 99–100; moves to Cambridge, 100; enrollment in School rises, 100; his familiar classroom dialogue, 105–107; publishes his series of *Commentaries*, 107–117; *Bailment* (1832), 109; *Constitution* (1833), 110–113; *Conflict of Laws* (1834), 113–115; *Equity Jurisprudence* (1835), 115; *Equity Pleadings* (1838), 115; *Agency* (1839), 116; *Partnership* (1841), 116; *Bills of Exchange* (1843), 116; *Notes, Guaranties and Checks* (1845), 116; his collection of books, 117–118; last days and death (1845), 134–135; Justice Holmes's estimate, 135; Roscoe Pound's estimate, 135–136; Story's philosophy of law, 136–137; Story Hall (1950), 348

Strobel, Edward Henry: first Bemis Professor of International Law (1898), 186, 211; adviser to Siamese government, 211–212

Student life: in 1820's, 63–65, 70; in 1920's, 246–248; students in 1934–1935 criticize living conditions, 286; Root Room mitigates self-conscious Spartanism, 307; veterans after World War II, 316–318; improved facilities (1950–1967), 348–351. *See also* Brandeis; Dana; Fiske; Hayes; Hoar; Holmes, O. W.; Holmes, O. W., Jr.; James R. Lowell; Pound; Scott; Sumner

Students: Dustin School's earliest, 62; in early days, 62–63; came and left at odd times during year until 1833–34, 63, 123; law degrees not essential to Washburn, Pound, or Stimson, 63, 307; early moot courts, 73–76; records (1817–1840), 100–101; eminent men studied under Parker, Parsons, and Washburn, 141; less than half in School had previous degrees (1868–1869), 148; demand re-examination of School, curriculum and services (1934), 282; advisory committee and its report, 283–285; faculty undertakes to adjust instruction, 285–286; criticism of living conditions, 286

Study of law, *see* Adams; Inns of Court; Story

Sullivan, William, estimate of Isaac Parker, 49–50

Summa and *Magna* degrees after 1926, 249

Sumner, Charles: LL.B. 1834, 102; student letters, 102–103; instructor, 124; in 1845 lacked professional eminence and had irritated Boston establishment by speeches, so not given a professorship, 148–149

Surrey, Stanley Sterling, professor, 334n

Sweetnam, John, janitor of Dane Hall who acted as librarian, 160

Teaching Fellows: instituted (1949) to guide first-year men, 323; Professor Cavers first director, 323; work in 1966–67 denominated a "course," 338

Technological change, *see* Change

Thayer, Ezra Ripley: becomes Dean (1910), 231; estimate, 231–232; death (1915), 232

Thayer, James Bradley, Royall Professor (1873), 183; influence of his 1893 paper on constitutional law, 207; "Our New Possessions" (1899), 209–210; death (1902), 210

Thayer, James Bradley, member of faculty (1925–1945), 295